Constance Loeb

College for Women

ELIZABETHAN
AND
SEVENTEENTH-CENTURY
LYRICS

Elizabethan
and
Seventeenth-Century
Lyrics

Selected and Edited by
MATTHEW W. BLACK
UNIVERSITY OF PENNSYLVANIA

1938
J. B. LIPPINCOTT COMPANY
CHICAGO · PHILADELPHIA · NEW YORK

COPYRIGHT, 1938, BY J. B. LIPPINCOTT COMPANY

PRINTED IN THE UNITED STATES OF AMERICA

PR1205
B55

PREFACE

For nearly four decades lovers of English lyric poetry have been
familiar with two admirable collections edited by Professor Felix
E. Schelling of the University of Pennsylvania, entitled *Elizabethan
Lyrics* and *Seventeenth Century Lyrics*. Some years ago these were
regrettably allowed to go out of print and their editor devoted
some thought and effort to the project of combining them into
a single volume with the material re-arranged so as to bring together poems of similar type and period. The inception of this
scheme, however, happened to coincide with his retirement from
active teaching and his consequent preoccupation with other work,
and since I was already giving a course in which the material was
organized along the proposed lines, Professor Schelling, with characteristic generosity, turned over the entire design to me, to carry
out in whatever way was best suited to the needs of my students.

At first glance it seemed entirely feasible to follow the original
plan of condensation and re-arrangement. But the attempt to
re-group the original selections chronologically and by type revealed that the lyrics chosen as most illuminating in a strictly
chronological order could not be satisfactorily re-grouped as to
type. Some of the resulting sections were too long, others too
short; some contained lyrics which, despite their poetic excellence,
had to be dispensed with because they illustrated a development
of the type already sufficiently shown; others required the inclusion of new material illustrating ramifications of the type. Since
it appeared desirable to keep the sections of approximately equal
length, there was room for such inclusion. In the end it seemed
best to reconsider the whole matter of selection from the new
point of view. The result is a volume containing 580 lyrics, about
100 more than the total of the two original collections, and including 225 pieces not there given. To keep the size of the book
within reasonable limits, some space has been saved by the omission of the headings indicating the source and date of each poem
in the original volumes, and by limiting the scope of the notes

v

554737

and transferring them to the bottom of the page. In view of these and other departures, a statement as to the purpose and method of the present volume seems desirable.

The book is designed to illustrate the development of the English lyric from *Tottel's Miscellany* (1557), in which its affiliation with the Italian Renaissance is first fully apparent, to the close of the seventeenth century, in terms of the successive fashions which dominated public taste in this form: courtly making (I), pastoral writing (II), sonneteering (III), the metaphysical vein (VI), the classical taste of Jonson (VII), seventeenth-century Spenserianism (VIII), devotion (IX), and cynical wit (X). Special sections (in which the influence of the fashions already named is interestingly apparent) are devoted to lyrics in plays (IV), and to songs (V).

The happy conjunction of the beginning of Elizabeth's reign, in 1558, with the publication of *Tottel's Miscellany* renders the term 'Elizabethan' sufficiently accurate to describe the bulk of the sixteenth-century pieces included. But seven lyrics dating in the reign of Elizabeth's father, Henry the Eighth, two of them by the King himself, are prefaced to the earliest group, to emphasize the link with the English tradition and to show the degree to which that tradition anticipated the spirit of what was to come. Skelton, on the other hand, is excluded, despite his intrinsic interest, because his strongest links are with the past.

Each section is designed to include those lyrics of its *genre* which a modern reader—and especially one who is approaching for the first time the systematic reading of the lyric poetry of this period— will find best worth knowing for one of several reasons. Artistic excellence has been the first, but not the only criterion. After including the pieces which by long tradition cannot be ignored, and unabashedly adding my own prime favorites and bidding avaunt the nightmare voices of those who inevitably quarrel with the anthologist's sins of inclusion and omission, I have made room for poems representative of the development of each vogue and of the variety of mood and subject within it; for poems especially popular in their own day; for poems in which some personage glamorous in history essays the poetic fashion of the moment.

I have taken special pains to illustrate the diversity of theme in Elizabethan poetry by including as many poems as possible on subjects other than love, and I have admitted a few poems which experience has shown to be especially understandable and enlightening to the kind of reader I have in mind. But the only conscious sacrifice of poetic quality for the sake of historical representativeness alone is made in the first section, where some of the sonnets illustrate the difficulty of transplanting this form, and in the final section, where it seemed desirable to emphasize the growing preference for mere wit. As mentioned, the sections have been kept of approximately equal length for the convenience of teachers. To maintain the length decided upon, curtailment of desirable material in some sections has obviously been necessary, but no padding. Opinions will differ as to the intrinsic merit of the poetry in different sections, but there is interesting and memorable poetry in all.

The dates under the section-headings indicate the period of the ascendancy of each fashion, the time during which it appears to have been foremost in the favor of lyric poets and their audience. But wherever possible I have added a few pieces which date before and after the period of ascendancy, to illustrate the earlier development of the vein, and its later persistence in favor with older authors or with a substantial body of readers. A few famous poems excluded because of their length are discussed and partially quoted in the introductions to the sections in which they belong.

Within each section the arrangement is chronological. Each poem or group of poems by a known author is headed with his name and dates. If the poem is anonymous, or if the author's dates are not known, one date is given, that of the selection. The date of the first selection given for each author determines his place in the chronology. The poems of each author are in the order of first appearance in print, unless known to have been extensively circulated in manuscript, in which case they are inserted according to the probable date of composition. Occasional departures from strict chronology are made for the better understanding of some custom or development. The 'answer' to a poem, for example, is placed immediately after it; the gulling sonnet of Sir John Davies is put at the end of the group to symbolize the wane of the serious popularity of sonneteering. In the section, Lyrics in Plays, the order is that of the first performance of the play, where this date is known; and in the section, Lyrics in Song-Books, the order (and text) is that of first appearance in a songbook and not in print.

The selections are either separate wholes or units within a play or longer poem, designated to be sung or said as a whole. With a few exceptions carefully described in the notes, each selection is given entire.

The method of preparing the text, like the selection of the poems themselves, aims at the presentation of a body of poetry intelligible and aesthetically pleasurable even to an inexperienced reader. The text of all but a few of the poems is that of the first appearance in manuscript or print. In a few cases where the first edition is unsatisfactory, or where the author has indulged in revision, I have presented what I consider to be the best early text. A surprising number of the originals are now available in libraries in Washington, Philadelphia, and New York City. Where the originals were inaccessible to me I have used facsimile editions, scholarly reprints, or photostats. For the text of three poems I am indebted to Mr. Norman Ault, who discovered them in manuscript or in rare editions and printed them for the first time in his *Elizabethan Lyrics* or *Seventeenth Century Lyrics*. Separate acknowledgment of these will be found in the notes. Each text has been collated with the authoritative modern edition or editions. Where serious textual difficulty occurs, of a kind recognizably due to the carelessness or fallibility of the early printer,[1] I have adopted whatever emendation is most in favor among modern authorities. The source of such emendations, well known to the expert, is immaterial to the undergraduate or general reader, and is not indicated.

The spelling and punctuation are modernized. A grave accent (`) indicates the Elizabethan pronunciation of a separate syllable not now so pronounced, and also rhythmically important differ-

---

[1] A description of these will be found in *Shakespeare's Seventeenth-Century Editors, 1632–1685*, by Matthew W. Black and Matthias A. Shaaber, published by the Modern Language Association, New York, 1937.

ences in accentuation of words. An apostrophe marks elision
('d, 'n, 'wat'ry' for 'watery,' etc.) where failure to observe it would
seriously impair the rhythm, and also decapitation in such words
as ' 'gan' for 'began,' ' 'scape' for 'escape.' To save notes I have
indicated by hyphenation the more literal meaning of such words
as 'care-full,' full of care, 'dis-ease,' unrest, 'hard-ly,' with difficulty.
Elizabethan and seventeenth-century capitals are retained only
where personification is emphasized in the poem or where, as occasionally, their omission might lead to ambiguity.

Titles in which the important words are capitalized are original
titles or are derived from the context of the original poem. Otherwise the first line or a portion of it stands as title. For the lyrics
from plays no titles have been given. Instead, the dramatic setting
of each lyric is described with sufficient fullness to suggest what
it contributed to the play.

The notes are placed at the bottom of the page for convenience
of reference. Should they seem unduly copious, it may be explained that I have attempted, possibly for the first time, to clarify
all the difficulties of vocabulary and syntax which readers actually
do find in these poems.[2] Considerations of space have made some
excisions necessary: I have refrained from literary comment and
from interpretation of the imagery; allusions and unfamiliar meanings to be found in any desk dictionary are not annotated, nor
has it seemed necessary to gloss archaic spellings such as 'seely,'
'desart,' retained for the sake of the rime, or to point out that
'clerks' and 'larks,' 'souls' and 'bowels,' 'enter' and 'venture,' 'heart'
and 'desert,' 'bait' and 'deceit' were in all probability good rimes
at the time they were written. Except in special instances, an archaic
word is glossed the first time it occurs and not thereafter. Most
of the common ones occur in the first section only. On the other
hand, particular care has been taken to gloss words such as 'wanton,'
'still,' 'prevent' from which the modern reader may get a meaning
which is not the Elizabethan meaning.

The introductory essay 'On Reading Lyric Poetry' is an attempt
to bring together: (1) the fundamentals of aesthetic theory which,

---

[2] My thanks are due to three of my students who volunteered their assistance in
this phase of the enterprise and who read the text, indicating the words and passages which gave them pause.

as applied to poetry, will enable the beginner to know what to look for in his reading; (2) an analysis of technique which will increase his appreciation of lyric art; (3) certain cautionary advice based upon the writer's experience of the misunderstandings which are likely to arise; (4) suggestions for studying the lyric and (5) a brief bibliography of the general subject. A brief account of 'Elizabethan Meters and Metrists' is appended for the more advanced student. The introductions to the separate sections are designed primarily to point out the relation of each fashion to that which precedes, follows, or overlaps it, and so to preserve a sense of the chronological development of the lyric during the period. Other topics in each are the social and literary background of the fashion itself, the qualities and relationships of the authors, the variety of themes, and individual poems of special interest or difficulty.

One concludes the preparation of such an anthology with a deep sense of many obligations: to those older editors, such as Bullen and Arber, whose sound taste established the 'indispensability' of certain poems in all the anthologies which have followed theirs; and to the later researches of Ault, Chambers, Grierson, Hebel and Hudson, of whom the first mentioned has, by a rare combination of sensitive taste and tireless scholarship, made especially notable additions to the range and accuracy of our knowledge of the field. More personal thanks are due from me to Professors Baugh, Kitchen, Shaaber, Viteles, and other of my colleagues and friends, who have read my manuscript in whole or in part and made valuable suggestions. Librarians here and abroad have been courteously and promptly helpful. Miss Elizabeth M. Barton's patient and accurate assistance in typing, proof-reading, and index-making has been indispensable. My debt to Professor Schelling for my initiation into the project and for the use of his material I have already indicated. He has also given generously of his time to settle knotty problems in my notes. To thank him for the awakening in his classroom of my interest in these lyrics and all the pleasure I have had in them, and for twenty years of encouragement and friendship, mere prose will not suffice.

M. W. B.

CONTENTS

Section	Page
On Reading Lyric Poetry	3
Suggestions for Study	30
Bibliography	36
Elizabethan Meters and Metrists	37
The Courtly Makers	49
The Pastoralists	107
The Sonneteers	161
Lyrics in Plays	213
Lyrics in Song-books	267
Donne and the Metaphysicals	321
The Tribe of Ben	379
The Spenserians and Milton	429
The Devotional Lyrists	479
The Cavaliers and Dryden	533
Index I	591
Index II	597

INTRODUCTION

ON READING LYRIC POETRY

Poetry is an art which transcends definition. It arises in the obscure yet powerful impulses of a complex human type, the poet; it has for its subject the entire outer world of things and events and the inner world of feeling; and it has a different appeal for each of the great multiplicity of listeners. Small wonder, then, that it can be but fragmentarily apprehended by any one mind.

A poet may, to be sure, tell us what moves him to write, and give us a glimpse almost poetic in itself of the process of creation as it goes on in him. But, on the surface, at least, the poets' accounts of these mysteries are almost ludicrously unlike. To the quizzical Duke in Shakespeare's *Midsummer Night's Dream,* poetry is the art which gives to airy nothing a local habitation and a name. Milton, on the other hand, compares it to philosophy, though it is 'more simple, sensuous, and passionate.' To Wordsworth it is the spontaneous overflow of powerful feeling: it takes its origin from emotion recollected in tranquillity. But to Byron it is the lava of the imagination whose eruption prevents an earthquake. Edwin Arlington Robinson and Carl Sandburg concern themselves with its suggestive power when they say, 'Poetry is a language that tells us through a more or less emotional reaction something that cannot be said,' and 'Poetry is an echo asking a shadow dancer to be its partner.' But to Robert Frost a complete poem is one where an emotion has found its thought and the thought has found the word. When we consider these, together with a hundred other statements of poets about poetry, it becomes apparent that each is but a different fragment of the truth.

It is the same when readers begin to tell what they get out of poetry, how it makes them feel, what it is for them. And the critics who, discounting the subjectivity of the poet and of his listeners, attempt to define or limit poetry with respect to its only remaining aspect—its subject matter—have been confounded one after another by new poets who have arisen to make poetry out of the very subject matter which the critics had pronounced unpoetical. Wiser than his own definition of poetry is Dr. Johnson's

3

aphorism, 'To circumscribe poetry by a definition can only show the narrowness of the definer.'

Yet the fact that poetry in its largest sense is a thing too great and various for definition does not place it beyond the reach of description or, at least, of implication. About the physiological tests suggested—not altogether in jest, perhaps—by certain enthusiastic readers of poetry there is a fine air of certitude. 'If I read a book and it makes my whole body so cold no fire can warm me, I know that is poetry. If I feel physically as if the top of my head were taken off, I know that is poetry.' So Emily Dickinson. Mr. William Lyon Phelps relies upon a certain dorsal prickling, a sensation felt along the spine, which warns him that he has encountered something authentic and first-rate. Mr. A. E. Housman, in *The Name and Nature of Poetry,* is even more humorously specific when he says that poetry seems to him 'more physical than intellectual,' that it is recognized because it draws tears to the eyes, takes the breath away, betrays the voice with trembling, stabs the heart—and the pit of the stomach! Robert Frost sums it up more seriously: 'The right reader of a good poem can tell the moment it strikes him that he has taken an immortal wound, that he will never get over it.'

Moreover, the persistent reader of definitions arrives at an awareness that, however confusing and incomplete, they have three things in common. And although these common elements when they are analysed prove to be as complex and various as poetry itself, it will be well to set them down as the basis of a working description. Poetry has something to do with emotion, something to do with imagination, something to do with beauty and with truth. Let us call it the language of intense emotion made beautiful and significant by the creative imagination.[1]

All racial literatures begin with poetry, but poetry of two types, song and story, or, to give them the names we employ when, centuries later, they come to be cultivated artistically—lyric and narrative poetry. A narrative poem is a story beautifully, imaginatively, and emotionally told. Since it deals with characters and events

---

[1] The form and substance of art are inseparable. Hence 'language' must be taken as symbolizing the whole conception and design of a poem.

it is apt to be of considerable length. A lyric poem is the direct expression of a single, personal emotion, employing, as we shall see, only so much story, if any, as will serve to make clear the nature and source of that emotion. Since it expresses a single feeling at the moment of greatest intensity, the lyric is necessarily brief.

Whether the song or the story came first it would be futile to inquire, but there is no doubt which is the higher literary form; for although the best lyrics contain little story or none at all, the best stories are those in which there is the freest use of lyric inter-breathing. This is true even of novels and prose plays. The parts we respond to most and remember best are those in which the characters or the authors burst out into lyric words. Some of the finest lyrics of our time have been written so. It is one of the ways in which the lyric impulse maintains its supremacy in an age which has ceased to acknowledge that supremacy and 'does not care for poetry.' An example is the lament of Marty South at the end of Thomas Hardy's novel *The Woodlanders*. Another is the ending of Galsworthy's story *Indian Summer of a Forsyte*.[2]

In the latter, old Jolyon Forsyte, neglected and lonely, gets word that his favorite daughter-in-law is coming down to the country to see him at last. Before she comes he dies. This is how Galsworthy tells of his last hour:

Coming down! *After all!* Then she did exist—and he was not deserted. *Coming down!* A glow ran through his limbs; his cheeks and forehead felt hot. He drank his soup, and pushed the tray-table away, lying very quiet until they had removed lunch and left him alone; but every now and then his eyes twinkled. *Coming down!* His heart beat fast and then did not seem to beat at all. At three o'clock he got up and dressed, deliberately, noiselessly. The grandchildren would be in the schoolroom, and the servants asleep after their dinner . . . He opened the door cautiously, and went downstairs.

[Followed by his dog Balthasar, he steals out to sit in the shade under a great old tree.]

[2] From *Five Tales*, New York, 1925. Reprinted by permission of the publishers, Charles Scribner's Sons.

He smelled the scent of limes and lavender. Ah! that was why there was such a racket of bees. They were excited—busy, as his heart was busy and excited. Drowsy, too, drowsy and drugged on honey and happiness; as his heart was drugged and drowsy. *Summer— summer*—they seemed to be saying.

The stable clock struck four; in just half an hour she would be here. He would have just one tiny nap, because he had had so little sleep of late; and then he would be fresh for her, fresh for youth and beauty coming towards him across the sunlit lawn. And settling back in his chair he closed his eyes. Some thistledown came on what little air there was and pitched on his mustache more white than itself. He did not know; but his breathing stirred it, caught there. A ray of sunlight struck through and lodged on his boot. A bee alighted and strolled on the crown of his Panama hat. And the delicious surge of slumber reached the brain beneath the hat, and the head swayed forward and rested on his breast. *Summer— summer! So went the hum.*

The stable clock struck the quarter past. The dog Balthasar stretched and looked up at his master. The thistledown no longer moved. The dog placed his chin over the sunlit foot. It did not stir. The dog withdrew his chin quickly, rose, and leaped on old Jolyon's lap, looked in his face, whined; then leaping down, sat on his haunches, gazing up. And suddenly he uttered a long, long howl.

But the thistledown was still as death, and the face of his old master. *Summer—summer—summer! The soundless footsteps on the grass!*

The twenty-five words italicized, over half of them simple repetitions,[3] transform this from a merely adequate scene of the death of an old man accompanied by his faithful dog into something moving and memorable. One has but to try the effect of the passage without them to feel the power of lyric interbreathing.

Lyric poetry is the quintessence of literature, its rarest and highest manifestation. To understand and appreciate it is to admit oneself to the finest pleasure that reading can give. Yet it is a pleasure within the reach of any reader of ordinary feeling and experience. The only prerequisite is that he shall put aside those prejudices commonly felt against poetry in an age predominantly

---

[3] It is interesting to note in them also alliteration and a marked rhythm, both of which, like repetition, are elements of poetry in verse.

scientific and utilitarian—such as that poets, and people who like poetry, are abnormal, impractical, effeminate; [4] that poetry is 'highbrow,' difficult to understand, or alternatively, that it is mere words —'sound and fury signifying nothing'—and give himself wholeheartedly to reading it.

The reader who is so minded will find it profitable to think about each of the elements in the definition given above and determine what meaning, and how much meaning, each has for him. It has been said that lyric poetry, like all art, has for its end the creation of beauty. But beauty is no more objectively definable than poetry itself. We may say that it is 'the combination of qualities which delights the senses and the mind'; but that leaves the apprehension of it to each man's senses and each man's mind. Beauty is in the eye—and ear—of the beholder. Of one thing we are sure, on Emerson's high authority: that beauty is its own excuse for being. The beautiful object delights us for its own sake. The pleasure which it gives is unmixed with any selfish impulse, such as the acquisitive; it is selfless, universal. And being universal, it is imperishable, a joy forever, in the phrase of Keats, who adds yet another certain attribute when he says, 'Beauty is truth.' Beauty in its highest form is but another aspect of the age-long goal of the scientist and the philosopher. The poet's concern with life is to reveal the ideal essences of things, the higher realities that are obscured from common view.

'Beauty is truth, *truth beauty.*' Unless we dismiss Keats' line as mere word-juggling, it must follow that beauty, in its larger sense, can be found by the right beholder in anything. It admits of no restriction as to subject. Falstaff, Cyrano, Criseyde, Lear— all their stories have moments of the beauty that is truth. Beauty is not a matter of externals. Its name is too great to be wasted on mere prettiness, as those would seem to do who dismiss poetry as 'music and moonlight,' concerned chiefly with the picturesque,

[4] As Professor Schelling remarks, Elizabethan poetry is the best possible refutation of that theory which makes literature the pursuit of dreamers or of abnormal departures from typical manhood instead of a divine realization, by those who can see more deeply than the crowd, of the ideal image of man and nature toward which the world is striving. The men who wrote the lyrics which follow were the men that bore arms, or sat in the councils of their sovereign; men who courted the good opinion of their neighbors and valued the shows of the world.

romantic past or the sights and sounds of a spring morning. So the emotions evoked by lyric poetry are not only the ones usually thought of as pleasurable, but all the emotions, the deepest and most tragic as well. There is lyric beauty in Nashe's *Adieu, farewell, earth's bliss,* no less than in Spenser's marriage song, *Prothalamion;* in the anger and contempt of Raleigh's magnificent *The Lie,* no less than in the old courtier's loyal vow, *His golden locks time hath to silver turned;* no less in the sharp bitterness of Meredith's *Modern Love* than in his idyllic *Love in the Valley.* The warning which Meredith pens over the threshold of the former volume is true of all lyric poetry: 'This is not meat for little people or for fools.'

The precise nature of the 'pleasure' which we derive from the tragic in art need not detain us here. Aristotle believed that it proceeded from the purging, the *catharsis,* of our own feelings of pity and terror. Certain modern aestheticians conceive the pleasure as arising from 'redemption by beauty'; that is, from the spectacle of the artist making beautiful that which in life is pitiable and terrible. Whatever the reason, men do 'enjoy' tragedy in novels and in drama; and the lyric, with its more direct and immediate appeal, can move us to pity and terror as well as to light-hearted laughter and deep joy. Whether or not a given poem dealing with the tragic or the sordid achieves beauty for any considerable number of readers—whether, for example, Sandburg's *Nocturne in a Deserted Brickyard* or his *Chicago, hog-butcher for the world* is a great poem or no—there is lyric writing which can transfigure every human experience and mood. Since the end of poetry is beauty and truth, its range is the range of life itself, and of all the cries life wrings from the hearts of men.

Emotion, the second element in our description, is—so far as it concerns poetry—the effect of beauty. The artist, of whatever sort, is first of all inspired by some emotion which in turn finds its response in those who hear or see what he creates, if what he creates is beautiful and true. All creative literature aims to arouse, quicken, and refine the reader's emotions, 'to arrest, for the space of a breath,' as Conrad says, 'the hands busy about the work of the earth, and compel men entranced by the sight of distant goals to glance for a moment at the surrounding vision of form and colour, of sunshine and shadows; to make them pause for a look, for a sigh, for a smile.' But whereas the novelist and the play-wright do this slowly, gradually, intermittently, by telling a story, the lyric poet does it suddenly, impetuously, by crying out, by singing what he feels. Emotion is more than his inspiration and his aim; it is his chief material. It is at this point that the reader, however unpoetic, should begin to feel himself on solid ground and unhesitatingly declare his kinship with the poet, for the poet is a man, and his emotions are the emotions of all mankind: love, pity, gratitude, wonder, exhilaration, anger, fear, disgust, despond-ency. Out of these and allied feelings, which color our everyday lives and determine our actions and our states of mind, are lyric poems made. These are our fundamental equipment for under-standing and responding to what the poet says.

A little reflection on one's own emotional states will raise a doubt about the phrase 'a single emotion,' used above in the defi-nition of lyric poetry, especially when the word 'single' is coupled with the word 'intense.' Emotions are complex things. They rarely come singly, and the more intense they are the more likely they are to merge with allied feelings. Love, for example—how often is it pure or single? Even at its best, unmixed with the al-loy of avarice or social ambition, does it not familiarly involve self-abasement, exhilaration, despondency, jealousy, and joy? Its powerful opposite, the feeling we call hate, is a mixture of anger, fear, disgust, envy sometimes, and even a little love. But here again the poet is as other men. It is rarely that a lyric arises from a single emotion. Rather it will cry out a brief series of distin-guishable though closely related feelings, a core of commingled emotions which includes a dominant one and others aroused by it, frequently including its opposite. This emotional core of a lyric poem is what is called its *mood*.

A little further self-analysis will bring to light another quality of emotion: not only is it seldom or never pure in the sense of being unmixed with other emotions; it is never pure in the sense of being unattached to some object, idea, or experience. We do not simply love or hate; we love or hate someone or something.

We are not simply angry or afraid; we are angry or afraid because of what has happened or is going to happen. Romantic
idealists, it is true, talk of divine dissatisfaction, of tears from the
depths of some divine despair. They long for they know not
what. But such longings usually turn out to have some source or
end in actuality, as yet undiscovered or unadmitted, rather than
non-existent.

In this, once more, the lyric poet is as other men. It is true that,
being more readily emotional, more imaginative, and more idealistic than the average of mankind, poets are sometimes inspired by
abstract ideas and adventures of the spirit that are difficult to
share or even understand. Shelley in his *Hymn to Intellectual
Beauty*, Swinburne in *Hertha*, and Walter de la Mare in his fantasy
The Listeners, are cases in point. It has been argued indeed by one
critic [5] that the reason modern poetry has lost its hold upon a large
audience is that so much of it is not about anything. However this
may be, it is not true of the Elizabethans. Theirs is the concreteness
of young minds, of Renaissance minds. Romantic they are and
idealistic as well, but rarely over-intellectual or other-worldly; and
their characteristic power is that of communicating an ideal emotion in concrete, familiar, and even homely images and setting.
They frequently are betrayed by their enthusiasm for letters into
another sort of artificiality, inevitable in an age so crammed with
lyric utterance that a poetic convention established by some great
leader was promptly overworked by a swarm of imitators. But
great or small, they are seldom abstract. When they are happy
it is because the day is fine, a mistress is beautiful, or England has
defeated her enemy. When they are sad it is because they are
growing old or have been contemplating the tombs in Westminster
Abbey or have found a mistress obdurate or fickle. This is one
secret of their greatness. Other things being equal, the best lyrics
are the most concrete.

The mood of a lyric poem, then, is attached to some idea or
circumstance represented as evoking that mood. This is called
the *theme*. Obviously it is the first, indeed the chief, thing the
reader must 'get' if he is to make the poem his own. He must

[5] C. B. Tinker, *The Good Estate of Poetry*. Little, Brown and Co., 1929.

read and re-read it until he knows and feels what it is about. Once
is seldom enough, nor are a dozen readings too many. The first
reading may give no more than the vaguest impression of mood
and idea; the final lines may contain a climax in the light of which
the whole must be re-perceived. Moreover, first impressions are
here even less trustworthy than usual: truly great poems mean
more every time one goes back to them; second-rate ones may
sweep one away with their novelty and brilliance but, re-read with
maturer judgment or merely in another mood, yield nothing save
a kind of puzzled disappointment.

Peace and quiet are indispensable to the reader of poetry, for
he will need all the wit, all the imagination he has. Ideally, perhaps, he should read poetry, and hear it read, aloud in a group
of sympathetic listeners who are in the right mood. That, at least,
seems to be Herrick's assumption in his epigram *When he would
have his verses read:*

> In sober mornings do not thou rehearse
> The holy incantation of a verse;
> But when that men have both well drunk and fed,
> Let my enchantments then be sung, or read.
> When laurel spirts i' th' fire, and when the hearth
> Smiles to itself and gilds the roof with mirth;
> When up the thyrse is raised, and when the sound
> Of sacred orgies flies—'A round, a round!'
> When the rose reigns, and locks with ointments shine,
> Let rigid Cato read these lines of mine.

The beginner, whether in company or alone, will find it as in-
advisable to read a great many lyrics for the first time at one sitting
as to 'see' one of the world's great picture-galleries in an afternoon.
Lyrics are infinitely varied in form and method, and their language
is condensed and full of artifice. He who goes too fast may suc-
cumb in natural bewilderment to the evasion of enjoying the expression—the images, the sound, the rhythm—without penetrating
to the themes themselves. Beautiful though he may find poetic
expression, it will be the more beautiful when he sees what inspires
it. Let him make haste slowly, satisfying himself as to the theme

of one poem before going to another, or passing on and then returning to a piece which he finds difficult. Encouragement will come with the clarifying discovery that certain themes are so universal, so basic, that they are repeated again and again.

The oldest and most enduring theme of lyric poetry, as old as the Bible or the oldest Latin hymns and as recent as A. E. Housman or the latest volume of Miss Edna St. Vincent Millay, is life itself, so good to live—and so short.

> Then I commended mirth, because a man
> Hath no better thing under the sun,
> Than to eat, and to drink, and to be merry:
> For that shall abide with him of his labor
> The days of his life.
>
> Let us be glad then while we are young.
>
> Where are those who before us were in the world?
>
> Where are the snows of yesteryear?
>
> Golden lads and girls all must
> Like chimney sweepers come to dust.
>
> Crimson and black on the sky, a waggon of clover
>   Slowly goes rumbling, over the white chalk road;
> And I lie in the golden grass there, wondering why
>   So little a thing
>   As the jingle and ring of the harness,
>   The hot creak of leather,
>   The peace of the plodding,
>   Should suddenly, stabbingly, make it
>   Strange that men die.[6]

These lines span some twenty centuries in which poets have sung our human longing to live, our joy at being alive in a world of beauty and our regret that it cannot go on forever for us.

Love of nature and of God, love of family and of friends, and love of country are other themes which make their appearance in the earliest poetry we know, and are renewed in every age.

---

[6] From *The Poems of Alfred Noyes,* New York, 1919. Reprinted by permission of the publishers, the Frederick A. Stokes Co.

Romantic love of man and maid is surely as old, though the pre-eminence which it now has dates only from the age of chivalry. J͡i͡S.
To perceive how these basic themes are repeated, in every variety of setting, every degree of intensity of mood, is the first step in ap-prehending the unity which underlies the multiplicity of lyric poetry.

Two elements of our original definition remain to be discussed: the rôle played by imagination in the making of a poem, and the somewhat paradoxical meaning of 'personal' as applied to the lyric. These are best discussed together. It would, indeed, be impossible to explain them separately, for the part played by the creative imagination in determining the theme of a lyric is precisely what makes the adjective 'personal' misleading.

The lyric is personal yet impersonal. Compared with a narra-tive poem, it is personal because its material is feeling and not event, because it is subjective in origin. Moreover, it is cunningly devised to seem personal even though it is not entirely so, and from this appearance arises the common and very natural mistake of treating lyric poetry as though it were a sort of naive autobiog-raphy. But the spiritual process which results in poetry is not so simple as that. It begins with some actual experience which stirs in the poet a feeling—of reverence, of yearning, of deep joy, of regret, perhaps, or the pangs of despised love. But—and here enters the paradox—the more violently personal his feeling is, the less he is able to transmute it into a fine lyric *at that time*. Illustra-tions of this fact are so numerous and so striking that, to the reader who interprets a poet's lyrics as the product of immediate experience, they sometimes convey an impression of the poet as a perverse romantic who, at any given moment, deliberately chooses to express in immortal lines the exact opposite of what he ought to be feeling. Kipling, penning *The Recessional,* with its warning refrain

> Lord God of Hosts, be with us yet,
> Lest we forget—

while England's shouts of rejoicing over the Queen's Diamond Jubilee echoed in his ears, is a classic example. Equally in point is the gray melancholy of Yeats' *Wild Swans at Coole,* which he published after a period of non-productiveness during which some of the happiest experiences in life had come to him. Readers who become interested in this paradox, or who find that it hinders their understanding of lyric poetry, will derive profit as well as amusement from a short story by John Erskine,[7] in which a literal-minded young business man falls in love with a girl who writes lyric poetry. Her lyrics describe in outspoken and passionate terms the abandon with which she could leave all for love if only the right man were to appear. Not unnaturally convinced that he is the right man, her lover wins and marries her. After an intensely happy honeymoon unclouded by literary activity on the part of the bride, they settle down, he to business and she to housekeeping, whereupon her typewriter re-appears and she proceeds to compose new lyrics which describe in passionate terms how happily she could leave all for love if only the right man came along. The ending devised by Mr. Erskine is interesting for other reasons. But the young husband's consternation puts our paradox vividly, and the wife's defense of her lyrics, 'Of course I mean what I write—but not literally!' answers it as well as it can be answered. It is worth noticing also that while they were intensely happy together, she wrote nothing at all. Poetry written out of immediate experience is either simply bad, like Robert Burns' stilted addresses to Mistress M'Lehose of Edinburgh (his best-loved poems appear to have been written to girls he had met for but a moment or never seen), or, like so much of Byron, striking when read for the first time, disappointing to go back to.

In the creation of a lyric of enduring fineness, then, expression does not follow immediately upon experience. Instead, the experience, together with the emotion which it arouses, sinks into what Mr. Lowes would call the deep well of the poet's subconscious.[8] There the irrelevancies, the pettinesses, the crudities of immediate experience are leached out of it until what remains is of universal texture and validity, until, in other words, that which had been

---

[7] 'Variation XII,' in his volume called *Young Love,* copyright 1936. Used by special permission of the publishers, the Bobbs-Merrill Co., Indianapolis. 1936.

[8] J. L. Lowes, *The Road to Xanadu,* chapter III. Houghton Mifflin Co., Boston, 1927.

personal and immediate becomes impersonal and timeless. When the feeling emerges once more into conscious thought it may be entirely dissociated from the experience which gave it rise.

In time there follows what Wordsworth describes as 'the spontaneous overflow of powerful emotion recollected in tranquillity.' And here imagination takes command, to shape for the feeling a mold—wholly dissimilar, perhaps, to the original experience—which will express it clearly, powerfully, and beautifully. The lyric is born when the emotion in its ideal guise finds words.

The rôle of imagination in this ultimate step, the finding of the words, is more generally appreciated than what it does in shaping the theme. It is especially apparent to those readers who enjoy words for their own sake. To fall under the spell of the word-magic of poetry is so easy, to analyse it, so difficult—and unprofitable—that little need be said of it. Suffice it to repeat here that the verbal felicities of the lyric, like its theme, are the product of imagination stirred by feeling.

A few basic devices and patterns may be briefly described, for no discussion of the substance of poetry and of the process by which it comes to birth can prepare us for the complex beauty of its form and technique. To approach the actual reading with only the assurance that its moods are few, powerful, deeply human, that its themes, however various, are all within the scope of universal experience, could but increase the impression it gives of bewildering novelty and intricacy.

Let us therefore beg the aesthetic questions whether substance is separable from form, and whether the poet is addressing an audience, or only unburdening his heart,[9] and imagine him, conscious of feeling within himself, and consciously or unconsciously impelled to express it, seeking a medium of utterance. How shall he tell what he feels? In what pattern of thought and circumstance, of words and sounds, may his emotion be seized at its moment of greatest intensity and held, imperishably beautiful? In the infinite variety of poets' solutions to this problem, conditioned by all the individual qualities of mind and manner that we class as 'style,'

[9] On this point Mr. Housman quotes, and apparently concurs in, the confession of Robert Burns: 'I have two or three times in my life composed from the wish rather than the impulse, but I never succeeded to any purpose.'

and by all the variations of individual human experience, lies the source of our bewilderment.

Perhaps the initial difficulty is with the imaginative heightening and condensity of the language itself. As previously remarked, this difficulty will yield only to devoted reading, but certain of the properties of poetic diction are so distinctive as to fall within the scope of profitable analysis. The first of these is imagery—the naming or describing of one thing in terms of another. It includes *simile,* the assertion of the likeness, and *metaphor,* the assumption of the identity of two objects:

> My heart *is like* a ship on Neptune's back.
>
> My Daphne's hair *is* twisted gold.

Imagery of a less obvious sort is involved in the poet's choice of words to name and describe the objects and actions with which he deals. Without rehearsing the array of formidable terms used by rhetoricians in analysing the devices of imagery, we may instance those picturesque and suggestive figures of speech in which an object is referred to in terms of some characteristic, as when Masefield calls the sea 'the gull's way and the whale's way'; or a general or abstract idea is symbolized by some concrete attribute, as in

> Scepter and crown
> Must tumble down,
> And in the dust be equal made
> With the poor crooked scythe and spade.

where 'scepter and crown' symbolizes the power and wealth of kings, and 'scythe and spade,' the laboring masses; or a whole is recognized by its characteristic part, as when a ship is referred to as a sail, or a part by the whole, as in 'England, be glad.' Though the two latter figures were given separate names by the old grammarians, it is easy to see how difficult they might be to distinguish. The other devices of poetic diction are still less distinguishable, shading off into such matters as deliberate overstatement, deliberate understatement, and all the delicacies of surprise and innuendo. The finding—sometimes, indeed, the coining—

of the inevitable adjective and the inevitable verb involves figures of speech beyond the reach of any analysis, and, in fact, beyond the need of any. It is only necessary to give oneself to the reading of them with the eye, the ear, and all the senses of the mind, remembering that imagery is best when it is most concrete, when it evokes pictures, sounds, sensations. Another quality of the best imagery is unexpectedness. The poet's mind perceives similarities in objects which to the literal mind may seem quite dissimilar, identities which most of us have never thought of but which, as he states them, seem utterly convincing. Our surprised acceptance of these is a source of constant delight.

Once the poetic use of imagery has come through familiarity to yield both understanding and pleasure, it becomes easier to master the larger problem of what the poem as a whole is about—in what pattern or medium the poet has chosen to tell his love, his anger, or his grief. As before, the undismayed and thoughtful reader will find that certain recurrent types of lyric medium emerge.

First of all, perhaps, he will notice that in some lyrics the poet appears as speaker, while in others he prefers to speak through the mouth of an invented character. The first type, the lyric proper, needs no distinguishing name; the second, the lyric of projected emotion, is commonly—though at the risk of some confusion with the lyric in drama—called 'dramatic,' especially by admirers of Robert Browning's volume *Dramatic Lyrics*. It is important to recognize dramatic lyrics as such, in order to understand aright not only the poems themselves, but also the poets back of them. In the work of Browning, for example, so many of the invented characters are villains or rascals of some sort that confusion of them with him would lead to endless misunderstanding. His *Confessions* is a case in point. In it an unregenerate old man on his death-bed scandalizes the anxious priest who has come to perform the last rites by rhapsodizing over an unhallowed love-affair of his youth instead of viewing the world he is so soon to leave as a vale of tears. A reader who, in the absence of any stage-directions, was misled into identifying the speaker with the poet, would be so puzzled by the piece that he could hardly enjoy it, and he would do a grave injustice to Browning's character. Many

Elizabethan lyrics are dramatic. Sometimes the fact is rather clearly indicated, sometimes not. In the latter case one's first question after reading a lyric and beginning to organize one's impressions of it, might well be, Who is speaking? Related questions are, Where? Under what circumstances? Is the piece a soliloquy, or are others present? If others are present, does the poem, or any part of it, suggest that they say or do anything? Is there an assumed situation, real, as in *Go and catch a falling star,* where Donne seems to address with his mockery some luckless champion of the constancy of womankind; or fantastic, as in his sonnet *Death, be not proud,* in which he speaks as though some personification of Death were actually before him?

But the poet's central problem is still unsolved: how shall he— or his invented character—tell us what he feels? Through which of our faculties shall he move us? There seem to be five chief mediums which, singly or in endless natural combinations, serve for the transmission of lyric feeling. The first, obviously, is simple outcry, an appeal direct from the singer's heart to ours. 'Feel with me,' he seems to say. 'I love! I hate! I fear! I suffer!'

> Amid my bale I bathe in bliss,
> I swim in heaven, I sink in hell.

This way of doing it, though it might appear to be the simplest and most natural, is employed less frequently than one would expect, perhaps because lyric poets are not such complete egoists as they sometimes appear, and are well aware that the recital of emotional symptoms may embarrass the listener or weary him very soon. Quite as frequently, at any rate, they *picture* the object of their joy or their desire, relate (necessarily with the utmost brevity) an *incident,* or share an *idea,* and trust to these to make us feel as they do.

Lyrics of pure picture, without hint of the underlying feeling or idea, are not common. The modern revolutionaries called Imagists have made something of a fetish of these, and Mr. George Moore includes a considerable number in his *Anthology of Pure Poetry.* In older writers, they are more likely to occur as parts of longer poems, as when in Browning's *Pippa Passes,*

> Faster and more fast,
> O'er night's brim, day boils at last:
> Boils pure gold, o'er the cloud-cup's brim.

or when Edmund Bolton in his *Canzon Pastoral in Honor of her Majesty* describes the winter of nature in contrast to the warmth in English hearts:

> Lo, matron-like the earth herself attires
>   In habit grave;
> Naked the fields are, bloomless are the briars,
>   Yet we a summer have.

But many fine lyrics have a picture as their principal element: 'I must down to the seas again,' Masefield cries out in the first line of his *Sea Fever,* and then paints for us 'the lonely sea and the sky,' 'a tall ship and a star to steer her by,' a 'gray mist on the sea's face and a gray dawn breaking.' In *Cargoes* he relies on two sharply contrasted pictures of ships. Alfred Noyes' *The Waggon,* quoted on page 12, begins with a picture, as do also, to choose at random, Miss Millay's *From a Train Window* and Philip Ayres' *On a Fair Beggar* (p. 584). Many of the best Elizabethan lyrics, especially those in the pastoral and sonnet groups, are pictorial in this way.

Within the limits of his brief space the lyric poet may also relate an incident. It may have the appearance of reality, as in Rupert Brooke's sonnet *The Hill,* or be fanciful and fantastic, as in Thomas Hardy's *Ah, are you digging on my grave?* or Alfred Noyes' *A Victory Dance.* The Elizabethans were very fond of the incident as medium, especially in a pastoral or mythological setting. The lyrics beginning

> As it fell upon a day
> In the merry month of May,

and

> Cupid abroad was lated in the night;
> His wings were wet with ranging in the rain.

are typical examples.

The lyric of idea is frequently considered a further step away from pure lyricism because to most of us thought and emotion are mutually destructive, and the broken rhythm of thinking is not the beat of feeling. When Edwin Arlington Robinson writes,

> I don't say what God is, but it's a name
> That somehow answers us when we are driven
> To feel and think how little we have to do
> With what we are.[10]

the reader is more likely to remember the subtle suggestion of the thought than to find the lines echoing in his ear. Yet Rose Fyleman in *The Fairies* employs paradox musically and with charm when she tells us, 'You can never be poor as the fairies are, and never as rich; . . . never as young and never as old.' Surely the chief appeal of this popular piece lies in the idea. It sets forth a definition of fairies that is as mentally satisfying as one will find in many a treatise on folklore. It tells us that they are creatures of our fancy, happily free from the two greatest hardships we know—poverty and old age, or, more colloquially, death and taxes.

Perhaps the oft-heard critical caveat against too much of thinking in the lyric really applies only to speculative thought, for certainly long-pondered, familiar universal ideas have a feeling and a music of their own:

> They are not long, the weeping and the laughter,
> Love and desire and hate:
> I think they have no portion in us after
> We pass the gate.
>
> They are not long, the days of wine and roses:
> Out of a misty dream
> Our path emerges for a while, then closes
> Within a dream.[11]

The Elizabethan lyrists are frequently both musical and thoughtful. The transiency of earth's loveliness and of the glories of this world is ever in their minds, and in Donne and the seventeenth-century men the stirrings of the new scientific speculative thought

---

[10] From *King Jasper*. New York, The Macmillan Company, 1935. Quoted by permission of the publishers.
[11] From *The poems of Ernest Dowson*, New York, 1929. Used by permission of the publishers, Dodd, Mead and Co.

are increasingly heard. The Elizabethans, moreover, in their young enthusiasm for the lyric, have the droll habit of treating their poems as though they were arguments and answering them, as Raleigh, for example, answers Marlowe's *Come live with me, and be my love.* They are especially fond of gay, light-hearted songs which have for medium a toying with a figure of speech, as in the following madrigal of Thomas Weelkes:

> Like two proud armies marching in the field,
> Joining in thundering fight, each scorns to yield;
> So in my heart, your beauty and my reason,
> One claims the crown, the other says 'tis treason.
> But O! your beauty shineth as the sun;
> And dazzled reason yields as quite undone.

Altogether, the lyric must be conceded to be intimately concerned with ideas, although it cannot be too strongly emphasized that the ideas are but a medium for the release of the creative impulse.

Finally, as to medium: the true lyrist, whether he is painting a picture, relating an experience, or thinking aloud, has always at his command the *music* of words. All poetry, but especially the lyric, should be listened to while it is read, to hear how the cadence, the lilt or dying fall, the lingering or acceleration of movement, the subtle repetition and modulation of vowel sounds and onomato-poetic consonants blend with and enhance the meaning. Word-music is no accident nor is it explicable as a matter of deliberate intention, but it is the very essence of the poet's craft. The eerie rustling of the *s*-sounds in

> Keen, fitful *gusts* are whispering here and there
> Among the bu*shes* half leafle*ss*, and dry;

the streaming and volleying, with alternate lulls, of Shelley's *Ode to the West Wind,* the subtle modulations of cadence in his *When the Lamp is Shattered,* the drag of the last line of each stanza in Masefield's *Sea-Fever,* and the vowel-music of Tennyson's *Sweet and Low* are famous examples.

So native and proper is word-music to the poet's art that it is small wonder if some lyrists indulge in it to excess. Effective *tours de force* which set themselves the technical problem of imitating actual music or sound, such as Tennyson's *Bugle Song,* Poe's *The Bells,* and *The Barrel Organ* of Noyes are widely popular among people who 'do not care for poetry.' And aside from these special exceptions, popular song in every age is characterized by excesses of feeling which can only be expressed by combinations of sounds, often sung as refrains, which are almost or entirely meaningless. The familiar *hey nonny no, falero lero loo,* and *jug jug, tu whit tu whoo* of Elizabethan song are at least no sillier than their modern counterparts. One ventures to doubt that anything could be.

But among the finest of all lyrics are those in which some familiar reflection on man's life and fate finds utterance in music which by sheer loveliness of phrasing and richness of overtones gives it new depth and urgency. The best of Shakespeare's sonnets have this quality in almost unequaled degree.

> Like as the waves make towards the pebbled shore,
> So do our minutes hasten to their end;
> Each changing place with that which goes before,
> In sequent toil all forwards do contend.
> Nativity, once in the main of light,
> Crawls to maturity, wherewith being crowned,
> Crooked eclipses 'gainst his glory fight,
> And time that gave doth now his gift confound.
> Time doth transfix the flourish set on youth,
> And delves the parallels in beauty's brow;
> Feeds on the rarities of nature's truth,
> And nothing stands but for his scythe to mow:
>   And yet to times in hope my verse shall stand,
>   Praising thy worth, despite his cruel hand.

Here is no picture, save for the momentary flashes involved in the figures of speech, and no reflection that has not come a thousand times to every reader who has outlived the feeling of immortality in youth. The poet's vaunt in the last two lines that his verse will outlive time is but a conventional afterthought. How then can the sonnet bring tears to our eyes? Surely, in large part, at least, by its music; by the deep organ roll of dignified resignation

in the first two lines, by the piercing *f*-sounds in 'Time doth transfix the flourish set on youth,' by the interlacing vowels of the rimes.

But music is a property not only of the words but of the whole
pattern, the metrical form, of a lyric. This is a consideration which
we have deliberately postponed in dwelling on the nature of the
lyric impulse and the possibility of its expression in prose or in
verse. The study of lyric meters involves technical and historical
considerations of the greatest intricacy and difficulty; considerations,
moreover, which change radically in each new period of lyric expression. The study of meter should follow long after, never
precede, the reading of lyric poetry for understanding and appreciation.

For this reason the later section on the subject may be lightly
passed over by the inexperienced reader. It will be sufficient for
him to remember that lyric poetry is traditionally associated with
the music of the *lyra* or lyre, which gives it its name, and that
many of the lyrics in the pages which follow were actually set to
music, while each of them has a metrical pattern, either conventional or to some degree peculiar to itself. He can appreciate without special study the symmetry of the whole pattern in Sidney's
First Song from *Astrophel and Stella* (p. 172), where the continuing
refrain

> To you, to you, all song of praise is due,
> Only in you my song begins and endeth.

with the repetition of the first stanza at the end:

> Doubt you to whom my muse these notes intendeth,
> Which now my breast o'ercharged to music lendeth!
> To you, to you, all song of praise is due,
> Only in you my song begins and endeth.

creates an effect of cumulative fervor that marks the piece as a
model of the harmony of feeling and metrical design.

On the other hand, the Elizabethans were enthusiastic even about
the meters and forms of their new lyric art, and refer to them
continually, so that even the most casual reader of this book may
well be haunted by the thought that he needs an understanding
of certain terms as the Elizabethans used them, as well as of certain

fundamental concepts and facts. These are given in the section on 'Meters and Metrists' (pp. 37–46).

Our discussion so far has been concerned with the individual reader, and has had for its end the cultivation of his personal enjoyment of lyric poetry. Rightly or wrongly, however, few readers are content with this. A natural desire arises to match one's taste with that of the majority, and especially with that of acknowledged connoisseurs or critics; to know, in other words, what is a great lyric poem and what makes it great. The only safe answer is one against which the devotee instinctively rebels. It is that a great poem is one which has stood the test of time, one which has in it some quality which makes it precious not to one, but to many readers and not to its own generation only, but to centuries. One is conscious of a deep-seated inclination to agree with Robert Frost when he objects that 'It is absurd to think that the only way to tell if a poem is lasting is to wait and see if it lasts. The right reader of a good poem can tell the moment it strikes him that he has taken an immortal wound—that he will never get over it. That is to say, permanence in poetry, as in love, is perceived instantly. It hasn't to await the test of time.' Perhaps the wisest reader is he who cultivates his taste by reading first those poems which have stood the test of time—the great things of the Renaissance and the nineteenth century—before attempting to exercise the gift of prophecy on contemporary work whose test lies still ahead. On this assumption let us inquire of the great lyrics of the past, what makes them great? What has made them endure?

The answer can only be, a subject or substance of universal appeal and workmanship at least approaching perfection. As to substance, the greatest lyrics are those which are based upon the most universal feelings, those arising out of experiences common to all. So true is this that if the reader will think back over our discussion he will see that we have been betrayed into speaking as though no other than universal emotions could be made into lyric poetry. This is, of course, not true. There are degrees of excellence in this as in every product of the human race. A great idea may fall short of perfection in utterance, as every writer knows; and a perfectly wrought lyric may enshrine an emotion too transient or too individual to be universally true. An interesting case in point is Thomas Hardy's *Ah, are you digging on my grave?*, a piece which is well known to readers of anthologies, but which few would call great. It takes the form of a dialogue between a little dog and its dead mistress. Its theme is the woman's bitter realization that to die is to be forgotten by friends and enemies alike, even by the supposedly ever-faithful dog. But most people do not believe this, and find it difficult to believe that Hardy did. It is thus interesting to ask oneself whether a great poem could be written on this theme, and if so, why Hardy's poem is not great. Most people would say that it falls short because of the transiency and singularity of its emotion, that in fact it was not meant seriously in a literal sense. But a reader who did not understand Hardy's irony might say that the ballad-meter and the talking dog destroy its seriousness, that, for him, it lacks *sincerity*.

This latter objection, if just, is fundamental. A great lyric is one which sweeps the reader gladly into its mood, untroubled by doubt of the genuineness of the poet's feeling or of the ultimate truth of his idea. If, at first reading or afterwards, the reader suspects that the poet is pretending to a feeling which he has not, or exaggerating the feeling which he has, then—for that reader at least—the poem is not great because it is not sincere.

At this point, however, it may be well to repeat that artistic sincerity and not fidelity to some actual experience of the poet's life at the moment, is what is meant. In fact, as well be clear to one who has followed carefully our account of the poetic process, the more actuality, the less poetry. The romantic reader of Sir Thomas Wyatt or Sir Philip Sidney is naturally thrilled when he is told that this or that set of verses was 'actually written to' Anne Boleyn or the Lady Penelope Devereux, 'with whom the poet was actually in love.' But the statement should, if anything, make him suspicious of the quality of the verses themselves, should make him ask himself whether his pleasure in them is due to their artistic merit or to his vicarious participation in an old love story. It is, however, equally dangerous to carry our logic to the other extreme and to suppose that any poem written for a particular occasion is therefore something less than great. It has been said of Tennyson's *Break, break, break* that it was actually written while the poet was at the bedside of a dying friend within hearing of the sea, and that Nashe's *Adieu, farewell earth's bliss* was written during one of the sixteenth-century epidemics of the plague. But in what sense is this really true? Are such poems exceptions to Wordsworth's rule that art takes its origin from emotion recollected in tranquillity? Were they in all their perfection miraculously produced at a day's, an hour's, a moment's notice? Or had they in the larger sense been composed long before and were they attached to a contemporary event only in the sense that it spurred them to utterance? Whichever explanation we accept, there is little doubt that a poet is likely to do his greatest work when he has met as an individual with some universal experience. But it is the poem that matters in the end and not the experience, and the wise reader will therefore read the poem, forgetting even what the poet himself says about how it came to be written and to whom it was written, since circumstances can neither make it great nor lessen its greatness. He will probably find that many a so-called 'occasional' poem has an artistic sincerity which argues that its connection with the occasion was the result of accident or of courtesy.

Perfection of workmanship is the mark of artistic sincerity and a certain requisite of greatness. The phrase means that everything about a poem, from the shaping of the whole for the creation of a single effect, to the rhythmical pattern and the choice of every word, shall have a kind of inevitability, a natural rightness, like the shape of a flower, so that we accept it with a delight unmixed with thought of criticism or of emulation. The slightest change, we feel, could not but be for the worse. Of course, perfection is a large word and it would be strange if the expectation of a novice or, worse, the ingenuity of a critic, could not conjure up a dream of perfection such as not even a poet could fulfil. There are, for instance, finicking ears which carry the test of singleness of effect to extreme, as when one critic objected to what he supposed must be an ejaculation—'Dear God!'—in Wordsworth's perfect sonnet *On Westminster Bridge.* Happily, however, such criticism is little heard in our time. A practical corrective for the over-expectation of the novice is readily found: let him read a little in the great mass of *im*perfect poetry, beginning with the second-rate and descending through magazine and newspaper verse to the efforts of any serious but untalented amateurs whom he may know. The sentimentality, the strained emotionalism of really bad verse; above all, the phrasing, sometimes banal, frequently inverted and padded at the mercy of the meter and rime, should effect a cure; but if not, the speaker should attempt to write some perfect poetry for himself. This remedy, one suspects, will prove infallible, and he will turn back to the great things with a truer notion of what is meant by perfection of workmanship.

It need scarcely be added that a great style—using the word in its true sense, as meaning the whole impress of a personality and character upon what is said and the way it is said—can emanate only from a great man. Nothing can come out of the artist that was not first, sometime, in the man. Style *is* the man. And style in this sense is more important than technique. Technical standards, themselves derived from Homer at his best, are pointless when applied to Homer nodding. It is conceivable, for example, that a musician might find Haydn technically as interesting as Beethoven. But even if he were superior technically, his unaffected cheerfulness, pleasant though it is to certain moods, could never take rank in the estimation of mankind with the dignity and tragic import of Beethoven's feeling. It is the same with Shakespeare: in his sonnets we see life through a great soul. Yet they have been called 'sonnets of magnificent beginnings' and, by implication, of feeble endings—a serious technical fault. Perhaps they are; it does not matter. The beginnings are there, and of a quality so absolute that 'wholeness of good tissue' becomes an empty phrase. The adequate expression of a great soul, whatever its technical defects, is a great style.

It is to be hoped that the reader who has persevered thus far will wish to read and re-read lyric poems, and will know what to look for in them and what he may hope to gain from them. The aesthetic pleasure that great poetry can give is reward enough for any man's seeking. But the habit of reading it results also in a kind of spiritual growth, an awakening and refining of his own emotional nature. Poetry cannot give a man responses that it is not in him to feel. But it can 'educate the heart' in the sense that it can reveal to him a range of feeling in himself of which he was unaware. If he is conscious of such expansion, it is a source of constantly increasing pleasure; but often the growth is observable only to others who know him intimately. In any case, only the completest honesty can promote it.

Thus if a reader finds that he strongly prefers some great lyrics to others, he should take this rather as a sign of grace than otherwise. (Let him put the rejected ones aside, however, with the thought that, later, life may teach him what they mean.) Such preferences are entirely natural. Like stories, plays, and essays, different lyrics have different human values. The lyrics of the Elizabethan pastoralists, like those of Keats in later time, have the power to transport us out of the here and now, into a lovely dream world of their own. Those of Wyatt and Surrey, of Jonson, Carew, and the Cavaliers, on the other hand, are emphatically of our world: they penetrate and clarify certain social situations and attitudes. Still others record, in outbursts of sheer joy that lift the heart, the happy moments and the good things—love, friendship, patriotism, fortitude in disillusion and disaster, in old age and in the contemplation of death, loyalty, religious devotion—which have made great lives worth the living. He would be a rare soul whose ideal of love found no enrichment in Shakespeare's sonnet

> Let me not to the marriage of true minds
> Admit impediments.

or whose determination to live life to the full was unquickened by the words of the old king in Tennyson's *Ulysses*. And dull were he who reading Shakespeare's sonnet *When to the sessions of sweet, silent thought,* or Arnold's *Dover Beach,* or better still the two of them together, was not convinced—insensibly, perhaps, but irresistibly—that friendship or love is sometimes the only brightness in a darkling world. Even though he had thought this for himself a thousand times, his perception of it would still be strengthened.

To be sure, the inherence of such values in the lyric is a secondary consideration. Least of all the forms of literature does lyric poetry exist for the purpose of informing our minds, guiding our conduct, or inculcating moral lessons. Art does not do our thinking for us; it shows the thing that breeds the thought. Yet because they are sincere and beautiful, great lyrics are 'true to life' in the highest sense. They are the concentrated record of how great men have felt about life, and it is almost impossible that our own philosophy should be unaffected by them as we read. Escape, understanding, ideals, then—lyric poetry offers all of these, and the wise reader is he who takes, at any given moment of his life, that which he needs the most.

If he has not already anticipated it for himself, the beginner may follow to his lasting advantage a final word of advice. It is this: let him lay by in some fashion—in a notebook if necessary, but better still in a retentive mind if he is so happy as to have one—the passages that move him most, against the time when he shall encounter the experiences therein distilled; preserving so the memory of great lines:

> Sweet are the thoughts that savor of content,
> The quiet mind is richer than a crown,
>
> Were I as base as is the lowly plain,
> And you, my love, as high as heaven above,
> Yet should the thoughts of me, your humble swain,
> Ascend to heaven in honor of my love.
>
> Love's not Time's fool, though rosy lips and cheeks
> Within his bending sickle's compass come;
>
> Shall I compare thee to a summer's day?
> Thou art more lovely and more temperate.
>
> Sweetest love, I do not go
> In weariness of thee,
>
> The glories of our blood and state
> Are shadows, not substantial things.
>
> Death, be not proud, though some have callèd thee
> Mighty and dreadful, for thou art not so.

in which to make articulate the high moments of life.

SUGGESTIONS FOR STUDY

A word may be added to those for whom reading is not enough, who by choice or necessity are studying the lyric. In the first place, it is strongly recommended that until he has gained a fair degree of experience the beginner should concentrate upon single lyrics or on small groups related by their theme. The formulation of historical and critical generalities may follow the development of an appreciation of the individual poems but it cannot well precede it.

Having read a lyric, then, and enjoyed it, what more may one profitably do? Probably the best answer is, re-read it several times so as to make it forever one's own; and think about it so as to clarify the source of the pleasure it gives. The following suggestions may be of use:

What is the mood of the poem? That is, what emotion dominates the poet's outcry? What other feelings, related or even contrasted with the dominant one, are also involved?

What is the theme? That is, about what, or whom, or in what circumstances, is the emotion felt?

Particularly valuable is the attempt to summarize a lyric in a sentence so as to bring out its mood and theme, as in the following examples:

Herrick, in *To Daffodils,* regrets the brevity of the daffodils' flowering; but the reflection that the growth, bloom, and decay of the flowers really parallel man's life dulls the keen edge of his pain.

In *To Lucasta Going to the Wars* Lovelace sings with an exaltation that shows through his Cavalier polish and formality, of a love so fine and deep that it does not blind one to duty and honor.

In Greene's *Sephestia's Song* a woman broods lovingly over her little son, keeping at bay the thought that he must grow up and, like his father, meet with misfortune and grief, by her joy in his innocent happiness.

Michael Drayton's *Since there's no help* is in the mood of a typical lovers' quarrel: anger and renunciation are succeeded by a pleading for the renewal of the love which underlay the anger and, perhaps, caused it.

Note that the purpose of this exercise is very different from that of a paraphrase. The point here is not what the poem says, but how it makes you feel, what it does to you; in Housman's words, the peculiar function of poetry is to transmit emotion, to set up in the reader a vibration corresponding to what the poet felt, and it is this emotional vibration that you should record.

What is the medium? That is, is the poet speaking, or some invented character? Is the speaker soliloquizing or addressing someone else? Is the mood created by the music of the words alone, or does the poem make a picture, relate an incident, or express an idea? Is the poem laid in a world resembling that of every day, or in a world of myth or fantasy?

What is to you the best line in the poem? Can you say why you think so? Is it a famous and familiar line or does it strike you with a sudden, new beauty? Is it the meaning you like, or the way it is said, or both? Is there a daring and original figure of speech? Is there one particular word which has sheer perfection, which is *the* word, inevitable, irreplaceable?

As intimated above, the lines of even the greatest poems are of unequal brilliance. Some poems are seemingly remembered for a single line, in relation to which the other lines are like the setting to a jewel, adequate in that they display the jewel without obscuring or dulling its beauty. An often-quoted example is Matthew Arnold's sonnet, *East London*. It has been said that anyone might have written twelve lines of it, but that only a great poet could have written the other two. It is quoted here so that the reader may decide for himself whether or not he agrees.

> 'Twas August, and the fierce sun overhead
> Smote on the squalid streets of Bethnal Green,
> And the pale weaver, through his windows seen
> In Spitalfields, look'd thrice dispirited.

I met a preacher there I knew, and said:
'Ill and o'erwork'd, how fare you in this scene?'—
'Bravely!' said he; 'for I of late have been
Much cheer'd with thoughts of Christ, *the living bread.*'
O human soul! as long as thou canst so
Set up a mark of everlasting light,
Above the howling senses' ebb and flow,
To cheer thee, and to right thee if thou roam—
Not with lost toil thou laborest through the night!
Thou mak'st the heaven thou hop'st indeed thy home.

A similar experiment may be made with the dirge from Webster's *White Devil* (p. 259), of which it has been said that its power over our imagination is attributable to the haunting suggestiveness of a single word.

This point of view is one which can easily be exaggerated, with a consequent impairment of one's appreciation of the beauty and nobility of the whole design. Nor would all critics agree that the parts so much admired—the tenth and eleventh lines of Arnold's sonnet and the word 'friendless' in Webster's dirge—were the only, or even the chief, claim of these poems to greatness. But however inconclusive, the experiment provides an interesting test of one's own taste.

Does the lyric suggest to you a story of which it might be the high moment? If so, can you reconstruct imaginatively the persons and the events? Is the lyric the end of the story, the beginning, or the climax? What happened before or afterward?

A particularly valuable exercise is to study lyrics in small groups related by their themes, since by this means individual qualities of style and workmanship are thrown into contrast and are thus more readily appreciated. Since, as we have seen, great poetry is written on but a few central themes, groups of every size and degree of similarity will form themselves in your mind as you read. The example quoted here is chosen because in it a contemporary poet has found the very theme of Tennyson's *Ulysses* in a character as unlike as possible to a king of Greek legend—that of a Southern mountaineer of today. Re-read *Ulysses* and then read the lyric on page 33 and see for yourself how their differences of style and setting emphasize their essential sameness in theme.

Little More West [1]

Hate to be dependin,
Hate to be beholdin,
Gals all pitchin
Because I live alone;
Little more west,
Somewheres in the Ozarks
Fore I turn to dirt and
Settle like a stone.

Give me a rifle, a cow
And some biddies—
Boy, I'd shake the timbers
Way I'd aim to sing;
Boy, I'd harry under;
Boy, I'd ride the thunder
For one more go to
Wrastle with the spring.

Hain't beat yet, though
I'm broke and creaky:
Little more west when
I sink in the loam:
One more chance to
Heave against the winter
And a little more west 'fore
I have to go home.

Takin out a lease on the
Stars behind the sunset;
Takin out a patent on a
Scope of windy sky:
Give me a rifle, a froe
And a broad axe,
And a little more west, 'fore
I settle down to die.

Perhaps the most enviable of all responses to a great poem is to be so moved by it that one writes an imitation of it, in which

[1] From *Lonesome Water,* by Roy Helton. New York, 1930. Reprinted by permission of Harper and Brothers.

the subject, style, and structure characteristic of the poet are faithfully copied. The subjoined lyrics are student imitations of Sidney and Swinburne respectively.

Sonnet

The year begins in April; the best things
Of all the seasons in it are contained:
No sickly heat of summer, none of spring's
Late gaudiness; no lushness, autumn-stained,
But into winter's bitter emptiness
Have flown a pleasant warmth, a melody,
A few pastels, a perfect loveliness,
The sweet rain sobbing softly from the sky.
It is the time of Easter, time of pain,
But apotheosis, not requiem,
When winter's dead ones wake and live again
Like mankind's soul in old Jerusalem.
Yet over all my love to it is due
Because it was that month gave birth to you.

The End of Love

When the chains of the world are broken
And the earth is flooded with fire,
And the ultimate word unspoken
Dies on the lips of desire,
Then love that was lighted with wonder
And toil that was troubled with tears
Will be carelessly trampled under
With the dust of the blowing years;
And whatever the sum of your sorrow
And no matter how heavy your grief,
They will be as the wind tomorrow
Or the sigh of a falling leaf.
They will be as the wind tomorrow
Or the flame at the candle's end,
And love will be none to borrow,
And grief will be none to spend.

Reading them, it is interesting to try to decide which is better, and whether its superiority is due to the circumstance that one of the poets is easier to imitate than the other. In any case, one feels that it would be difficult to convey in equal space by any other means an equal understanding and appreciation of the poets' art.

BIBLIOGRAPHY

As a basis for further reading about the lyric, the following books will be found useful in their various fashions.

Untermeyer, Louis, and Davidson, Carter, *Poetry: Its Appreciation and Enjoyment*. Harcourt, Brace and Co., New York, 1934. [Valuable; comprehensive, and contains a useful book list.]

Eliot, T. S., *The Sacred Wood: Essays on Poetry and Criticism*. Methuen and Co., London, 1920.

Housman, A. E., *The Name and Nature of Poetry*. The Macmillan Co., New York, 1933.

Masefield, John, *Poetry*. The Macmillan Co., New York, 1932.

Russell, George ('A. E.'), *Song and Its Fountains*. The Macmillan Co., New York, 1932.

[Four writers who speak primarily as poets.]

Arnold, Matthew, 'The Study of Poetry,' *Essays in Criticism: Second Series*. The Macmillan Co., New York, 1924.

Coleridge, S. T., *Biographia Literaria,* in 'Everyman's Library.' E. P. Dutton and Co., New York, 1908. (Read especially chapters 14, 16, and 18.)

Eastman, Max, *Enjoyment of Poetry,* rev. ed. Charles Scribner's Sons, New York, 1921.

Lowes, J. L., *Convention and Revolt in Poetry*. Houghton Mifflin Co., Boston, 1919.

————, *The Road to Xanadu: A Study in the Ways of the Imagination*. Houghton Mifflin Co., Boston, 1927.

Rylands, G. H. W., *Words and Poetry*. Payson and Clarke, New York, 1928.

[Critical studies.]

Schelling, F. E., *The English Lyric*. Houghton Mifflin Co., Boston, 1913.

[A history of the lyric.]

ELIZABETHAN METERS AND METRISTS

I

An understanding of the mechanism which underlies the rhythm and music of poetry can add to the pleasure of reading it. The first step must necessarily be that of definition; the student should learn the meaning of the following terms:

Meter is measured rhythm. In English poetry it is marked by the regular recurrence of accented and unaccented syllables.

The *foot* is the smallest metrical unit; it is a repeated group of accented and unaccented syllables. The common English feet are those of two and three syllables: the *iambus* (‿́), the *trochee* (́‿), the *anapest* (‿‿́), and the *dactyl* (́‿‿).

The *verse,* or line, is a group of feet, commonly in English of three, four, or five, though longer and shorter lines also occur. It is normally marked by a strong pause, or *caesura,* at the end.

A *stanza* is a group of verses, usually arranged according to a rime-scheme or other pattern, and forming a section of a poem.

Rime is the exact correspondence in sound of the final accented vowels and all succeeding letters in two or more lines. When but one syllable is involved the rime is called *masculine;* rimes on two syllables are *feminine.*

Most readers of verse have from the outset an instinctive enjoyment of simple, regular rhythm; but as the ear becomes more perceptive, an added pleasure is found in the freedom with which great poets use meter. Certain departures from the basic rhythm for the sake of variety, emphasis, suggestion of physical movement, and the like, are so common that one soon learns to look for them. For example, the iambus and the anapest are freely interchanged, as are the trochee and the dactyl. When the interchange results in extra syllables, these are partially suppressed (*elided*) in reading; omitted syllables are compensated for by a slight lengthening of the remaining ones. Unaccented syllables are sometimes omitted at the beginning (*truncation*) or at the end (*catalexis*) of a verse. (The tendency of editors when an accent is missing, as in

$$\text{Únder} \mid \text{wĭde héav} \mid \text{ĕns,} \wedge \mid \text{bŭt yét} \mid \text{nŏt súch.} \mid \quad \text{(p. 181)}$$

is to consider the line defective.)   Again, the order of accented and unaccented syllables is frequently reversed in one or even two feet of a line, for variety, or to emphasize a certain word, or for any of a number of reasons.   This device is called a *resolution*. It is especially likely to occur in the first foot of a line, or after an internal caesura.   Thus Tennyson writes

$$\text{Múch   hăve} \mid \text{Ĭ   séen} \mid \text{and   knówn,} \mid - \text{cítĭes} \mid \text{ŏf   mén} \mid$$

in a poem of which the prevailing rhythm is

$$\cup \; \diagup \mid \cup \; \diagup \mid \cup \; \diagup \mid \cup \; \diagup \mid \cup \; \diagup \mid.$$

In this way the important word *Much,* and the word *cities,* the first of a long series of memorable things that the speaker has seen, are made more impressive to the ear.   Another type of variation in rhythm is *enjambement,* or run-on line, in which the final caesura of a verse is disregarded by the phrasing, which 'runs on' into the succeeding line.   A light extra syllable at the end of a line, producing what is called a *feminine ending* is another common effect.   There are many others.   The recognition of such technical devices, both for themselves, and as characteristic of the art of particular poets, is a pleasure which can be cultivated by attention to the meter of verse.

II

In the meters of the Elizabethan lyric, three chief influences are observable, the native English, the classical, and the contemporary Italian, which was exerted both directly and through the French followers of Italian practice.   In Anglo-Saxon poetry, a verse consisted of four accented syllables, some or all of them alliterative, with considerable freedom as to the number and distribution of unaccented syllables between.   The popular meter called the 'four-teener,' usually broken into alternate lines of four and three beats (ballad meter), is the medieval development of the Anglo-Saxon line. Fourteeners are used by the Elizabethan lyrists, at times with something of the Anglo-Saxon syllabic freedom. Thus in *A Proper Song* (p. 274) the line

Thŭs faín | woŭld Ĭ hăve hád | ă prét | tў thíng |

is to be uttered in the same time interval as

Ŏ lá | dў, whăt | ă lúck | ĭs thís! |

In Spenser's *Roundelay,* on the other hand, while most of the four-beat lines have the customary eight syllables, some have only five:

∧ Heý | ∧ hó | ∧ hól | ĭdáy |. . .

∧ Heý | ∧ hó | thĕ hígh | ∧ híll. |

Here the syllables *Hey, ho, hol, hill* must each be read in the time interval normally occupied by two syllables. In other words, the poetic license to modulate the rhythm by the inclusion of extra syllables or by the omission of unaccented ones, had in English verse a strong traditional background. Alliteration also, though it had long since fallen under critical ridicule, is frequently indulged in by the Elizabethans for the sake of the jingle. Thus while they made notable advances in meter, they did not forsake entirely the native tradition.

Their debt to classical meters is less demonstrable, though far from unimportant. In Latin and Greek poetry, meter was the regular recurrence of quantitatively long and short syllables. The adaptation of this principle to English verse, which as we have seen, was basically accentual, was the purpose of a long series of experiments by Sidney and others—experiments which, though doomed to artistic failure, considerably improved English technique, and left recognizable traces in the English work of Sidney, Campion, and Jonson.

The most important influence is that of contemporary Italian and French meters, which were, like the English, accentual, but which had advanced far beyond the English in the smooth ordering of syllables, in the designing of stanzaic forms, in variety of line-length, and in technical perfection in general. So great was this superiority that in feeble hands the English lyric was but an imitation of the Italian. The better men, as always, took what they needed of foreign form and employed it in a new and vital native utterance. The acceptance of the sonnet, the madrigal, and other foreign forms as models, the adaptation of these to the demands of the English language and habit of thought, and the resultant training of English poets to utterance more truly English are the typical developments of the age.

The sonnet is the commonest foreign form in English. The Italian sonnet was an integral stanza of fourteen five-stress iambic verses, devoted to the expression of a single thought or passion, ordinarily that of love. Its lines had feminine endings, unless for comic effect, and the whole was composed of two metrical systems, the octave, consisting of two quatrains, and the sestet, consisting of two tercets. Each system had its own rimes: the octave two, either enclosed (*abba abba*) or alternate (*abab abab*); the sestet two or three, commonly alternate, though various arrangements were allowable, exclusive, however, of a concluding couplet.

This highly specialized form was followed in full detail by but one Elizabethan, Constable, who had lived much abroad. In general it was the subject of immediate and continuous experimentation, the chief tendency of which was to increase the number of different rimes from four or five to seven, and thus decrease the number of rimes on one sound, since in a prevailingly monosyllabic tongue like English, rimes are far less frequent than in Italian. Lacking, moreover, the delicate Italian ear that sought the avoidance of a closing couplet lest the unity of the whole be destroyed by undue prominence of any part, English poets preferred this arrangement for its effect of climax and epigrammatic vigor. The result was a series of three quatrains riming independently, followed and closed by a couplet (*abab cdcd efef gg*). This is the English sonnet practiced by Surrey, Shakespeare, and the majority of the sonneteers. Experiment produced an almost endless variety of other arrangements, however, most notable of which is Spenser's link sonnet of five rimes (*abab bcbc cdcd ee*), suggested by the stanza of his *Faery Queen*, and used by him almost to the exclusion of all others. The Italian division into octave and sestet was observed in England only when the movement of the thought made it desirable. The English fondness for masculine rimes reduced the number of syllables in the line from eleven to ten, and at times the ten-syllable lines were replaced by octosyllabics or Alexandrines (twelve-syllable iambic lines). In fact, the term sonnet was extended in common use, in England as in Italy, to denote a short lyric of almost any form or length, and in its significance as *sonetto,* 'a little song,' it was used also as a generic term including the madrigal, canzon, ode, and other forms.

Next to the sonnet in Elizabethan popularity was the madrigal. Its name is said by some scholars to be derived from Italian *mandria,* 'herd'; others derive it from *madre,* 'mother,' as implying a song in the mother tongue. A third explanation, easier from the point of view of phonology, is that its source was *carmen * metricale,* 'a metrical song'; the change of *e* to *a, t* to *d,* and *c* to *g* necessary to transform * *metricale* into *madrigale* are familiar enough in Italian philology. The madrigal originally consisted of a combination of two or three tercets variously arranged as to rime, followed by one or by two couplets or occasionally even by a quatrain, the measure being usually hendecasyllabic. English madrigals seldom preserve the actual Italian arrangement of rime, or the hendecasyllabic meter. In length they range from six to sixteen verses, sometimes more, and employ a variety of rhythms, with verses of differing lengths, preferably of five and three accents. The chief Italian characteristic which they retain is a preference for feminine rime. An example of an early madrigal which follows the usual Italian form, except for the variation of meter, is the following, from Thomas Morley's *Canzonets* (1593):

> Say, gentle nymphs, that tread these mountains
>> Whilst sweetly you sit playing,
>> Saw you my Daphne straying

> Along your crystal fountains?
>> If that you chance to meet her,
>> Kiss her and kindly greet her;

>> Then these sweet garlands take her,
> And say from me, I never will forsake her.

Eventually the freer form superseded those more closely imitating the Italian, until the madrigal became indistinguishable from any other short form. It was, of course, commonly set to music and its musical technique is perhaps its true distinguishing mark in English.[1]

Forms of less frequent occurrence are the *canzon* and *canzonet,* from the Italian *canzone,* 'a song unaccompanied.' Like madrigal and sonnet, the term canzon originally had a precise significance. It was a highly organized lyrical form extending to from five to ten stanzas of from nine to twenty verses, each with an added *commiato* or *envoi.* Barnabe Barnes affords the best example of the strict application of the term in his *Canzon III,* the rimes of which exactly reproduce the arrangement of those of the second *Canzone* of Petrarch, *O aspettata in ciel, beata e bella.* Later canzons are freer in construction, shading off into irregular odes, epithalamia, and the like, and losing entirely any sense of an original, Italian, classical, or English. The canzonet is simply any short lyric, generally not exceeding a single stanza, though Drayton uses the term for a poem of three stanzas, and once for a sonnet.

The *pastoral* is a literary mode and not a special metrical form. Certain terms which have metrical, or at least formal, significance are familiarly associated with the pastoral, however, such as the *eclogue,* the *barginet,* more correctly *bergeret,* a shepherd's song, made up of a series of tercets and, rarely among Elizabethan authors, the *idyl.* The eclogue is really a dialogue between shepherds rather than a metrical form. The only meter which can be said to have become identified with the pastoral mode in English is the octosyllabic iambic measure, riming either in couplets or alternately, with its derivative, the heptasyllabic trochaic common in the works of Breton. But in *England's Helicon,* the miscellany most typical of the pastoral mode, a variety of titles are lavished indiscriminately upon poems little distinguished as to form. Thus sonnet is applied to anything, whether a quatorzain or of other lengths, while long stanzaic poems, equally with shorter ones, are called madrigals, ditties, idylia, songs, or simply pastorals. The latter word, too, is affixed to any term, as pastoral ode, pastoral

[1] See p. 269.

song, pastoral sonnet, or canzon pastoral. Many titles of pastoral songs and their corresponding words are derived from popular terms for dances, as the *jig,* a merry, irregular song in short measure, more or less comic and often sung and danced by the clown to the accompaniment of pipe and tabor; the *branle,* Englished *brawl,* confused with a very different significance of the same word; the *roundelay,* a light poem, originally a shepherd's dance, in which an idea or phrase is repeated, often as a verse or stanzaic refrain. Terms which have no exact Italian or French counterpart are *passion,* used especially by Watson, *contention, complaint,* and *lament,* all in their meanings sufficiently obvious.

Thus the Elizabethans are seen to have imported from Italy and France a variety of formal stanzaic patterns, together with the terms by which they are known. But the terms like the forms themselves prove upon examination to have been employed with the utmost looseness, and often describe the mood and setting rather than the form. A few, such as *terzine* and *sestine,* rarely used because the forms were rarely practiced, retained something of their precise significance.

To the richness of the sources outlined above, on which the Elizabethans drew for inspiration, may be attributed in part the remarkable variety of their metrical effects in the lyric. But all praise must be accorded the genius of the poets who carried pastoral and sonnet to heights of sheer perfection, as well as to the energy and enthusiasm of the scores of lesser lyrists whose occasional successes add glory to the outburst. At all events, in the total output of lyric during this remarkable age is to be found the greatest possible diversity of metrical effect. Every kind of basic rhythm is found in the variety of feet employed. The commonest English foot, the iambus, is everywhere, of course; but the trochee is found in Greene, Breton, Barnfield, Shakespeare, Jonson, Fletcher, Browne, and Wither, frequently mingled with the iambus, as in Greene's *Sitting by a river's side.* The anapest is admirably used by Raleigh in *As you came from the holy land;* less successfully by Jonson in *The Triumph of Charis;* and the dactyl appears in Shakespeare's *Come away, come away, death.*

Equal diversity is found in the length of the verses. They range from a verse of two accents, like 'Sing we and chant it' to the long iambic fourteener, or *septenary,* of *The Burning Babe.* The popular verse of six iambic feet (Alexandrine) generally occurs, in the lyric, divided into two verses of three accents each, as in

> The gods that saw the good
> That mortals did approve,
> With kind and holy mood
> Began to talk of love.

but is also found undivided as in the first sonnet of *Astrophel and Stella.* The Alexandrine and the fourteener in combination make what was called 'Poulter's measure,' which, though considered by serious poets in the Elizabethan age to be homely or old-fashioned, is still found occasionally, as in Vaux' *The Aged Lover* (p. 75). The commonest line lengths are ten syllables and eight syllables. The ten-syllable iambic verse is that of the sonnet. Outside the sonnet, octosyllabics are the favorite lyrical measure, whether iambic as in

> At last he set her both his eyes;
> She won and Cupid blind did rise.

or trochaic, often with a silent last syllable (*catalectic*) as in

> On a day—alack the day!
> Love, whose month is ever May . . .

Variety of feet entering into the organism of the stanza is found in a number of Shakespeare's best-known songs, and in Campion; variety of line length within the stanza in Greene, Lodge, and Jonson. The distribution of rime to emphasize these effects, and the use of *enjambement* to vary the variations still further, will repay endless study.

In the number and arrangement of the rimes a similar fertility of invention is displayed. Men like Lodge, Nashe, and Shakespeare did not hesitate to play upon a rime for emphasis, serious or otherwise, to the extent of four, six, or even eight successive lines. Notice the effect of this—here increased by the strong caesura in the middle and at the end of each line—in

> Accurst be love and those that trust his trains!
> He tastes the fruit whilst others toil;
> He brings the lamp, we lend the oil;
> He sows distress, we yield him soil;
> He wageth war, we bide the foil.

The Elizabethan lyric, like all English verse, displays an overwhelming preference for masculine rimes as compared with feminine ones. Occasionally, not often, rime is dispensed with, as in Jonson's *Æglamour's Lament.*

An additional source of metrical variety and beauty is found in the close alliance of the Elizabethan lyric with music (see pp. 267–74). The most obvious evidence of this is the frequent use of the refrain, a phrase or verse(s) repeated at intervals, especially at the end of each stanza in a poem or song.

III

Historically, the three most important sixteenth-century English metrists are Sidney, Spenser, and Marlowe. Of these, Marlowe's achievements in dramatic blank verse do not concern us here. As to Spenser, the stanza of *The Faery Queen* is only the most striking instance of the perfect taste and unerring metrical tact which enabled him, more successfully than any other English poet, to choose or invent precisely that medium which was best fitted to his thought. Nothing could be finer than the liquid flow of the long stanzas of the *Prothalamion,* or the diversified musical vigor of the *Roundelay.* In form as well as in matter, Spenser stands at the head of the pastoral lyrists. But his muse is idyllic rather than lyrical: he is less successful in the sonnet than in the eclogue. Thus Sidney remains as the chief representative of Italian influence in the sonnet, as well as the most ingenious experimenter in classical meters.

So far as the lyric is concerned, Italian influence was completely assimilated by the close of Elizabeth's reign, and a demand arose for something more than imitation, a demand satisfied by various literary leaders, each in his own way. In Shakespeare, for example, we find an increasing and masterly freedom, both in the blank verse of his dramas, and in the incidental lyrics. John Donne, the

most independent lyrical metrist of the age, departs from the smooth
and somewhat nerveless iambic flow of Spenser and the Petrachans.
Obedient to rhetoric rather than to verse-rhythm, Donne breaks up
his line into quick and slow beats, with frequent elision, which he
marks not by the conventional apostrophe and the omission of a
letter, but by an apostrophe standing after the word affected.[2]

But the metrist of greatest historical importance in the seventeenth century—and later—is Ben Jonson, who, despite his unusual versatility in the invention and practice of new and successful
lyrical forms, displays a conservative temper throughout in avoid-
ing mixed meters and stanzas of irregular structure or of differing
lengths, and in such small matters as his careful indication of
elision where the syllable exceeds the strict number demanded by
the verse-scheme. Many of Jonson's critical utterances, too, attest
his dislike of license (for example, 'that Donne, for not keeping
of accent, deserved hanging'); his esteem of the formal element
in literature (for example, 'that Shakespeare wanted art'); and his
dislike of innovation. Towards the close of his life, Jonson grew
increasingly fond of the decasyllabic rimed couplet, the meter which
was to become the maid-of-all-work in the next generation. This
meter it was that he defended in theory against the heresies of
Campion and Daniel, and in this meter he wrote at times with a
regularity of accent and an antithetical form that remind us of
Dryden in the next age. Jonson's tightening of the reins of regularity in the couplet and in lyric forms is greatly in contrast with
the course of dramatic blank verse, which, beginning in the legiti-
mate freedom of Shakespeare, descended, through the looseness of
Fletcher and Massinger, to the license of Davenant and Crowne.
It was thus the 'assimilated classicism' of Jonson—as far as possible
removed from the imitative classicism of Harvey and Spenser in
the days of the Areopagus[3]—that finally came to prevail. It was
his example in conservative nicety of style and regularity of versification that led on through Herrick, Carew, and Waller to the
classicism of Dryden and Pope.

---

[2] These elisions are not marked in the text of Donne which follows, but the student must be continually on the watch for them if he would convince his own ear
that 'Donne at his best is not less melodious than Milton.'   [3] See p. 108.

I

THE COURTLY MAKERS

Chiefly
Before 1580

THE COURTLY MAKERS

The term 'courtly makers'[1] is a happy one to describe the group of poets in whose hands the English lyric first assumed those qualities which we call Elizabethan. It was coined by the author of *The Art of English Poesy* (1589), George Puttenham or another, in the following passage:

In the latter end of the same king's [Henry VIII's] reign sprung up a new company of courtly makers, of whom Sir Thomas Wyatt the elder and Henry, Earl of Surrey, were the two chieftains; who, having traveled into Italy, and there tasted the sweet and stately measures and style of the Italian poesy, as novices newly crept out of the schools of Dante, Ariosto, and Petrarch they greatly polished our rude and homely manner of vulgar poesy from that it had been before, and for that cause may justly be said the first reformers of our English meter and style.

A courtly maker is by implication one who is a member of the court and whose attitudes and interests both social and poetical are those of the court. He would naturally be a soldier and a statesman, a devotee of art and of sport, and a squire of dames. All this describes admirably the 'company' which the old writer had in mind as well as, indeed, a great number, if not the majority, of Elizabethan and seventeenth-century lyric poets. The present section includes with those in 'the latter end of the same king's reign' a number of other 'makers' to the end of the century and even later, who were not entirely diverted by the pastoral and sonnet fashions from the more serious concerns of the courtier, such as patriotism, contemplation, and satire. The foremost poet among these, Michael Drayton, if not exactly a courtier, was known

---

[1] *I.e.,* courtly poets; from the literal meaning of Latin *poeta*.

at court, and his odes must have pleased King James. Three of the others are named by Puttenham in a later passage:

And in her Majesty's time that now is [1589] are sprung up another crew of courtly makers, noblemen and gentlemen of her Majesty's own servants, who have written excellently well . . . Edward, Earl of Oxford, Sir Walter Raleigh, Master Edward Dyer.

The Elizabethan lyric, then, had its origin among the cultivated classes in the generation which first felt the full tide of the Italian Renaissance. Through their enthusiasm for the newly rediscovered literatures of Greece and Rome the English lyric was subjected to a long series of experiments in classical meter and eventually benefited by classical discipline as to form. In particular, through their mania for everything Italian came the Petrarchanism of the early lyric: its form, the sonnet; its subject, love; its attitude in love poetry, the plaintive and despairing adoration of a mistress supremely beautiful and obdurate; and even some mannerisms of style such as the hyperbole and the 'conceit.' It was Petrarch's Laura, half real, half an abstract ideal, who inspired the long line of fancifully named ladies—the Geraldines, Stellas, Zepherias, Auroras—to whom Italianate sonnets were written.

On the other hand, the success of the lyric at its height was due to the adaptation of foreign form to the expression of what was natively English in subject and feeling. Moreover, England had its own tradition in popular poetry, deriving through the minstrels from Anglo-Saxon verse, and this tradition, though at a temporary stalemate in the languor of Hawes, and the eccentricity of Skelton, was by no means abrogated by the importation from Italy and France of a new lyric of art. Part of the charm of the early sonnets and rondeaux is to find them juxtaposed with such quaint and delightful examples of the native tradition as *England, be glad* and *Ah, Robin, gentle Robin,* the latter by a musician of Henry's Chapel, and with the equally old-fashioned verses which the royal patron of the arts himself made and set to music. The first seven of the selections which follow, together with the ballad *If ever I marry, I'll marry a maid* (p. 78), and several of the pieces by minor authors illustrate the sturdy persistence of 'our rude and homely manner of vulgar poesy.' Elizabeth herself had gone to school to old Roger Ascham and had laughed at the rude cleverness of Heywood, the epigrammatist. Her verses *When I was fair and young* (p. 79) express the vixenish archness of young womanhood in somewhat irregular Poulter's measure.[2]

It may well have been within the lifetime of Elizabeth—she was born in 1533—that the first and most important of the new company of courtly makers began to write. Sir Thomas Wyatt (1503-1542) began as a boy his life-long acquaintance with the court. The Anna of one of his poems is supposed to have been Anne Boleyn, with whom an old tradition states he was in love. After taking the degree of M.A. at Cambridge he was sent by Henry, in 1527, on a mission to Italy, where he learned from the love sonnets of Petrarch the form which was to mold so much of his own and of later English poetry. He actually translated some fifteen sonnets of Petrarch and adapted a number of others. But some of his most effective sonnets, like *A Renouncing of Love,* are original in substance and in tone, the lover offering his mistress hard truths, instead of Petrarchan flattery—a fact which suggests that the revolution in the mood of amorous verse effected by Donne[3] may have been simply a return to the English manner after half a century of Italianism. Wyatt was skilled in French as in Italian and, perhaps under the influence of poets whose work he had come to know on a diplomatic mission to Paris, he practiced with considerable success the rondeau and other French forms.

Wyatt's difficulties with the careful ordering of syllables, necessary to the harmonious smoothness of the sonnet but not to the earlier accentual system of English verse, as well as with the task of finding four rimes upon a single sound in a language where rimes are few compared with the Italian, are apparent in the wrenched accents, the artificial rimes, and the effect of padding and strain in such a sonnet as *The Lover Compareth his State to a Ship;* but he rapidly acquired greater ease in the form. Yet neither the difficulties of the new technique nor the fact that poetry was

[2] See p. 44.   [3] See p. 322 ff.

after all but one recreation of a busy and adventurous life could prevent him from writing himself down a genuine poet. He has energy and passion, and in such a piece as that which begins 'They flee from me,' a half-playful animus which seems to proceed from actual experience and is altogether delightful. Through his own verse and through his influence on his young friend, Surrey, he set the fashion for the early courtly makers.

Henry Howard, Earl of Surrey (1517?–1547), like Wyatt, knew the English court from boyhood, being an intimate of the Duke of Richmond, Henry's illegitimate son. Like Wyatt, too, he traveled in France (though Puttenham is at fault in implying that he went to Italy) and led a busy and adventurous life in the King's service, taking part in several military expeditions. Haughty and quarrelsome, he was in and out of prison several times and earned the name of 'the most foolish proud boy in England.' He was executed, a fortnight before the King's own death, on a charge of treason fabricated out of Surrey's alleged intention to lay claim to the throne as Henry's successor. Despite the difference in their ages, he seems to have had a whole-hearted admiration for Wyatt's work, and it was this, rather than the French verse with which he must have become acquainted during his sojourn in France, that inspired him to write. Though sensitive to nature and to physical beauty, he does not transcend Wyatt in theme or manner of treatment to any important extent. He is a more finished metrist, having learned by Wyatt's experiments, as well as displaying the competence and refinement of the highly educated courtier. Being both shallower than Wyatt and a better technician, he was more readily admired and imitated in his own time, and his significance in the history of English meter is scarcely less, since in his translation of two books of the *Æneid* into unrimed iambic pentameter he was responsible for the only metrical innovation which can compare in importance with that of the sonnet, namely, blank verse.

For our knowledge of the courtly makers we are indebted chiefly to a great anthology, *Songs and Sonnets,* published by Richard Tottel in 1557 and usually called *Tottel's Miscellany.* Tottel found the opportunity for assembling his material in two customs common in the Elizabethan age and later. The first was the practice of circulating poems in manuscript among the poet's friends, publication being considered undignified for a gentleman. The other was the allied habit of keeping 'commonplace books,' which were in effect manuscript miscellanies containing bits of the owner's or his friends' verse, translations, and the like which he wished to have by him. From such sources, with or without the consent of the authors—the 'two chieftains,' of course, were dead—Tottel procured and printed in his volume forty poems by Surrey, ninety-seven by Wyatt, forty by Nicholas Grimald, two by Vaux, two by J. Canand, one by John Heywood, one by Anthony St. Leger, and one hundred twenty-six by 'uncertain authors,' among them Sir Francis Bryan and Thomas Churchyard. Doubtless to the surprise of all concerned, English readers proved to be so eager for this first taste of the new lyric poetry, till then the private recreation of a few gentlemen of culture, that the collection went through eight editions by 1587; and as late as 1601 Shakespeare made Cousin Abraham Slender say—though with what precise inflection we cannot, of course, be sure—'I had rather than forty shillings I had my Book of Songs and Sonnets here,' when invited to dine out.[4]

Before 1580, the publication of four, possibly six, other miscellanies was inspired by the success of Tottel. They are of varying poetic quality but are at one in selecting the most alluring titles their editors could devise. An early edition of Clement Robinson's *Handful of Pleasant Delights* (1584) was licensed in 1566 with a title suggesting imitation of *Songs and Sonnets*. It is chiefly a collection of broadside ballads but contains several charming songs. Richard Edwards' *Paradise of Dainty Devices* (1576) is graver and more moral in tone than *Tottel's Miscellany* and contains a smaller proportion of love-songs, but seems to have been equally popular. Timothy Kendall's *Flowers of Epigram* (1577) reprints short pieces by Surrey, Grimald, Turberville, and others. *A Gorgeous Gallery of Gallant Inventions,* whose printer chose this title after rejecting *A Handful of Hidden Secrets* and *Delicate*

[4] *Merry Wives of Windsor* I. i. 205–6.

Dainties to Sweeten Lovers' Lips Withal, was apparently collected by Thomas Procter. It was less popular, probably because many of its poems had already been printed by Tottel and Edwards. *A Hundreth Sundry Flowers* (1572) and *The Forest of Fancy* (1579) are of doubtful status and may be the work of individual authors, respectively of George Gascoigne and one H. C., who has been tentatively identified as Henry Cheke. As has been intimated, the poetry of these miscellanies after Tottel was not strictly limited to the courtly vein, but they are more, rather than less, interesting on that account since they represent the taste of the time and show the lyric reaching out toward a wider audience.

George Gascoigne (1542?–1577) was the most important literary figure between Surrey and Spenser. His popularity, which was considerable, was based in part upon a happy lyrical vein and a ready if mechanical skill in meter. Though an important innovator in the fields of drama, satire, the novel, and verse criticism, he was and is best known for his songs and sonnets in the manner of Surrey, *A Hundreth Sundry Flowers Bound Up in One Small Posy,* published in 1572, probably with Gascoigne's entire consent but with an elaborate prefatory apparatus designed to preserve his anonymity, describing the contents as verses by sundry gentlemen, printed from a manuscript book delivered to A. B. by H. W., who had it of his friend G. T. for private recreation only and not for publication. Three years later a second edition appeared as *The Posies of George Gascoigne.* The whole parade of reluctance masking a real eagerness to get poetry before the public is typical of the time. *The Posies* themselves further the lyric tradition of Wyatt and Surrey but are more thoroughly English in spirit and vocabulary. At their best they are direct and forceful and convey an impression of sincerity, this last being due to the pervasiveness in them of Gascoigne's own somewhat egotistical personality and, no doubt, to the presence of autobiographical facts. For his versatility and energy, and for smoothness such as neither Wyatt nor Surrey had attained, which Gascoigne learned from his Italian models, especially Ariosto, and succeeded in maintaining in his love poetry and his verses of compliment to the Queen, he well deserved his contemporary reputation. He was, however, soon overshadowed by the rising brilliance of Spenser and Sidney, and by 1593 when, as Gabriel Harvey remarked, there was a busier pageant upon the stage, 'old Gascoigne's rimes' were 'hopelessly out of date.' A similar and better deserved obscurity shrouds the names of Gascoigne's friends and poetical associates, George Turberville, Thomas Howell, George Whetstone, Humphrey Gifford, and others, minor followers of Surrey. Thus in the period up to 1579 all the forms and influences which were to mold Elizabethan poetry had appeared, but none of the great artists. These were to follow immediately.

Of the poems selected to represent the continuance of the courtly vein during the decades of the pastoral and the sonnet, Oxford's epigram *Were I a king* (p. 88), which was pointed enough to draw several 'answers,' one of them from Sidney, reminds us how genuine must have been the taste for letters at court when even a dissolute fop could share it. *My prime of youth is but a frost of cares* (p. 88), which was reprinted in several song-books and other collections, was believed to be the work of Chidiock Tichborne, executed at the age of eighteen for participation in the Babington conspiracy against Queen Elizabeth. Dyer's *My mind to me a kingdom is* (p. 89) and Sir Henry Wotton's *How happy is he born or taught* (p. 102) are two of the finest of the many poems in which men of high position paid tribute to the old classical ideal of the golden mean. Bacon, of course, was so great and busy a man that we are surprised to find that he wrote any poetry, and in point of fact he was a translator, not a creative artist. Yet his pessimistic epigram *The world's a bubble* (p. 95), however close to a Greek original, has a dignity and power of its own, appropriately foreshadowing its author's tragic fall.

The two chieftains of the later courtly makers were Raleigh and Drayton. Pastoralist, sonneteer, master of compliment yet arrogant satirist of the very court which he adorned, royal favorite and gentleman adventurer yet visited at times by a strain of genuine piety, Raleigh typifies to a degree only less than Sidney himself the ideal man of Renaissance England. Owing to his indifference as to the fate of most of his writings save one ambitious piece of courtly compliment to Elizabeth as Cynthia, we cannot be certain that all the poems commonly attributed to him are his and, on the other hand, we can be certain that unsigned work of his is extant. Any good poem, clear, intelligent, and full of vigorous and somewhat old-fashioned music, with little Italianate embroidery, was apt to be attributed to him, especially if from its tone it might have been written in the Tower the night before he was executed. Not many have been found, however, worthy to stand with the high and insolent vein of *The Lie* (p. 90) and *Give me my scallop-shell of quiet* (p. 93).

Drayton, neither a courtier nor a man of action, as was Raleigh, was even more versatile as a poet, writing in addition to lyrics in every fashion, legends, historical narratives, plays, and a huge 'topographical' poem, the *Polyolbion*. He was brought up as a page in the household of Sir Henry Goodere at Polesworth, in a circle so cultivated that membership in it has been offered as an explanation of the culture of one William Shakespeare, a boy from nearby Stratford about a year younger than Drayton. But patronage did not impair the soundness of Drayton's character, which seems to have made an unusual impression upon his time. Meres says that 'among scholars, soldiers, poets, and all sorts of people [he] is held for a man of virtue and well-governed carriage, which is almost miraculous among good wits of this declining and corrupt time.' He has a kind of honesty of heart which, with his zeal, eloquence and devotion to England, gave him an almost unexampled popularity among all classes of readers. His *Ballad of Agincourt* is the best war-song of his age, if not of English literature, and its companion piece, *To the Virginian Voyage,* is scarcely less stirring. He lived past the third decade of the new century, and became a leader and friend to the younger Spenserians, Browne, Drummond, and Wither.

ANONYMOUS (1513?)

England, be glad

England, be glad, pluck up thy lusty heart!
Help now thy king, thy king, and take his part,
  And take his part

Against the Frenchmen in the field to fight
In the quarrel of the church, and of the right;
With spears and shields on goodly horses light,
Bows and arrows to put them all to flight,
>> To put them all to flight.
>> Help now thy king!

ANONYMOUS (Early 16th Century)

Western wind

Western wind, when will thou blow?
The small rain down can rain!—
Christ, if my love were in my arms
And I in my bed again!

KING HENRY THE EIGHTH (1491–1547)

Pastime with good company

Pastime with good company
I love, and shall until I die.
Grutch who list, but none deny,
So God be pleased, thus live will I.
For my pastance,
Hunt, sing, and dance,
My heart is set.
>> All goodly sport
>> For my comfort
Who shall me let?

Youth must have some dalliance,
Of good or ill some pastance;
Company methinks the best,
All thoughts and fancies to digest.
For idleness

light] mount Bows] With bows small] fine Grutch] Grouch, be glum pastance]
pastime All . . . let?] Who shall hinder me from . . . ?

Is chief mistress
Of vices all;
    Then who can say
    But mirth and play
Is best of all?

Company with honesty
Is virtue, vices to flee;
Company is good and ill,
But every man hath his free will.
The best ensue,
The worst eschew!
My mind shall be,
    Virtue to use,
    Vice to refuse;
Thus shall I use me.

Green groweth the holly

Green groweth the holly, so doth the ivy;
Though winter blasts blow never so high,
Green groweth the holly.

As the holly groweth green
    And never changeth hue,
So I am, ever hath been,
    Unto my lady true.
      Green groweth, &c.

Ah! the holly groweth green,
    With ivy all alone,
When flowerès cannot be seen
    And green-wood leaves be gone.
      Green groweth, &c.

Now unto my lady
    Promise to her I make:
From all other only
    To her I me betake.
      Green groweth, &c.

ensue] seek   Thus . . . use me] This shall be my custom   me betake] turn

Adieu, mine own lady,
 Adieu, my speciàl,
Who hath my heart truly,
 Be sure, and ever shall.
  Green groweth, &c.

WILLIAM CORNISH (14-?–1523)

Ah, Robin

'Ah, Robin, gentle Robin,
Tell me how thy leman doth;
And thou shalt know of mine.'

'My lady is unkind, I wis!'
'Alack! why is she so?'
'She loveth another better than me
And yet she will say no.'

'I can not think such doubleness,
For I find women true;
In faith, my lady loveth me well
She will change for no new.'

JOHN HEYWOOD (*c.* 1497–*c.* 1580)

A Praise of his Lady

Give place, you ladies, and be gone,
Boast not yourselves at all,
For here at hand approacheth one
Whose face will stain you all.
 The virtue of her lively looks
Excels the precious stone;
I wish to have none other books
To read or look upon.
 In each of her two crystal eyes

leman] sweetheart   I wis] certainly   say no] deny it   stain] eclipse

Smileth a naked boy;
It would you all in heart suffice
To see that lamp of joy.

I think nature hath lost the mold
Where she her shape did take,
Or else I doubt if nature could
So fair a creature make.

She may be well compared
Unto the phoenix kind,
Whose like was never seen nor heard,
That any man can find.

In life she is Diana chaste,
In truth, Penelope;
In word and eke in deed steadfast—
What will you more we say?

If all the world were sought so far,
Who could find such a wight?
Her beauty twinkleth like a star
Within the frosty night.

Her rosial color comes and goes
With such a comely grace,
More readier too than doth the rose
Within her lively face.

At Bacchus' feast none shall her meet,
Ne at no wanton play;
Nor gazing in an open street
Nor gadding as a stray.

The modest mirth that she doth use
Is mixed with shamefastness.
All vice she doth wholly refuse,
And hateth idleness.

O Lord, it is a world to see
How virtue can repair
And deck her in such honesty,
Whom nature made so fair.

Truly, she doth as far exceed

naked boy] Cupid   eke] also   wight] human being   Ne] Nor   she doth
use] is her custom   repair] adorn

Our women nowadays
As doth the gillyflower a weed,
And more, a thousand ways.
    How might I do to get a graff
Of this unspotted tree,
For all the rest are plain but chaff,
Which seem good corn to be.
    This gift alone I shall her give
When death doth what he can:
Her honest fame shall ever live
Within the mouth of man.

GEORGE BOLEYN, VISCOUNT ROCHFORD? (d. 1536)

O death, rock me asleep

O death, O death, rock me asleep,
Bring me to quiet rest;
Let pass my weary, guiltless ghost
Out of my care-full breast.
    Toll on, thou passing bell,
    Ring out my doleful knell;
    Thy sound my death abroad will tell,
        For I must die,
        There is no remedy.

    My pains, my pains, who can express?
Alas, they are so strong!
My dolors will not suffer strength
My life for to prolong.
    Toll on, &c.

    Alone, alone in prison strong
I wail my destiny.
Woe worth this cruel hap that I
Must taste this misery!
    Toll on, &c.

graff] scion

Farewell, farewell, my pleasures past,
Welcome, my present pain!
I feel my torment so increase
That life can not remain.
    Cease now, thou passing bell,
    Ring out my doleful knoll;
    For thou my death dost tell:
    Lord, pity thou my soul!
        Death doth draw nigh;
        Sound dolefully,
        For now I die,
        I die, I die!

SIR THOMAS WYATT (c. 1503–1542)

Rondeau

What? No, perdie! ye may be sure;
Think not to make me to your lure
With words and cheer so contrarying,
Sweet and sour contraweighing;
Too much it were still to endure.

Truth is tried where craft is in ure;
But though ye have had my heartès cure,
Trow ye I dote withoutè ending?
    What? No, perdie!

Though that with pain I do procure
For to forget that once was pure,
Within my heart shall still that thing
Unstable, unsure and wavering,
Be in my mind without recure?
    What? No, perdie!

perdie] a mild oath, literally 'by God'   make] draw   ure] use   Trow] Think
procure] endeavor   that] that which   still] ever   recure] cure

Whoso list to hunt

Whoso list to hunt, I know where is an hind,
But as for me—alas, I may no more.
The vain travail hath wearied me so sore,
I am of them that farthest come behind.
Yet may I, by no means, my wearied mind
Draw from the deer; but as she fleeth afore
Fainting I follow. I leave off therefore,
Since in a net I seek to hold the wind.
Who list her hunt, I put him out of doubt,
As well as I, may spend his time in vain.
And graven with diàmonds in letters plain
There is written, her fair neck round about:
    Noli me tangere, for Caesar's I am,
    And wildè for to hold, though I seem tame.

A Renouncing of Love

Farewell, love, and all thy laws forever,
Thy baited hooks shall tangle me no more;
Senec and Plato call me from thy lore
To perfect wealth, my wit for to endeavor;
In blindè error when I did persever,
Thy sharp repulse that pricketh aye so sore
Taught me in trifles that I set no store,
But 'scape forth thence, since liberty is lever.
Therefore, farewell! Go trouble younger hearts,
And in me claim no more authority;
With idle youth go use thy property,
And thereon spend thy many brittle darts.
    For hitherto though I have lost my time,
    Me list no longer rotten boughs to climb.

Description of the Contrarious Passions in a Lover

I find no peace, and all my war is done;
I fear and hope; I burn, and freeze like ice;

Noli me tangere] 'Touch me not'   lever] liefer, dearer   Me list] I choose

I fly aloft, yet can I not arise;
And naught I have, and all the world I season.
That locks nor looseth holdeth me in prison,
And holds me not, yet can I 'scape nowise;
Nor lets me live, nor die, at my devise,
And yet of death it giveth me occasion.
Without eye, I see; without tongue, I plain;
I wish to perish, yet I ask for health;
I love another, and thus I hate myself;
I feed me in sorrow, and laugh in all my pain.
  Lo, thus displeaseth me both death and life,
  And my delight is causer of this strife.

The Lover Compareth his State to a Ship in Perilous Storm Tossed on the Sea

My galley chargèd with forgetfulness
Thorough sharp seas, in winter nights, doth pass
'Tween rock and rock; and eke my foe, alas,
That is my lord, steereth with cruelness;
And every hour, a thought in readiness,
As though that death were light in such a case.
An endless wind doth tear the sail apace,
Of forcèd sighs and trusty fearfulness;
A rain of tears, a cloud of dark disdain,
Have done the wearied cords great hinderance;
Wreathèd with error and with ignorance,
The stars be hid that led me to this pain;
  Drowned is reason, that should be my comfort,
  And I remain despairing of the port.

Of his Love Called Anna

What word is that, that changeth not
Though it be turned, and made in twain?
It is mine Anna, God it wot,
The only causer of my pain,

season] seize   That] That which   devise] command   plain] complain

My love that meedeth with disdain.
Yet is it loved—what will you more?
It is my salve, and eke my sore.

A Description of Such a One as he would Love

A face that should content me wondrous well
Should not be fair, but lovely to behold,
Of lively look, all grief for to repel,
With right good grace, so would I that it should
Speak without word such words as none can tell;
The tress also should be of crispèd gold.
With wit, and these, perchance I might be tied,
And knit again with knot that should not slide.

*The Lover Showeth how he is Forsaken of Such as he
Sometime Enjoyed*

They flee from me, that sometime did me seek,
With naked foot stalking within my chamber.
Once have I seen them gentle, tame, and meek,
That now are wild, and do not once remember
That sometime they have put themselves in danger
To take bread at my hand; and now they range,
Busily seeking in continual change.
Thanked be fortune it hath been otherwise,
Twenty times better; but once especiàl,
In thin array, after a pleasant guise,
When her loose gown did from her shoulders fall,
And she me caught in her arms long and small,
And therewithal so sweetly did me kiss
And softly said, 'Dear heart, how like you this?'
It was no dream, for I lay broad a-waking.
But all is turned now, through my gentleness,
Into a bitter fashion of forsaking;
And I have leave to go, of her goodness,

meedeth] rewardeth   danger] captivity   small] slim

And she also to use newfangleness.
But since that I unkindly so am served,
How like you this? what hath she now deserved?

The Lover Complaineth the Unkindness of his Love

My lute, awake, perform the last
Labor that thou and I shall wast,
And end that I have now begun;
And when this song is sung and past,
My lute, be still, for I have done.

As to be heard where ear is none,
As lead to grave in marble stone,
My song may pierce her heart as soon.
Should we then sigh, or sing, or moan?
No, no, my lute, for I have done.

The rocks do not so cruelly
Repulse the waves continually,
As she my suit and affectiòn;
So that I am past remedy,
Whereby my lute and I have done.

Proud of the spoil that thou hast got
Of simple hearts, through lovè's shot,
By whom unkind thou hast them won,
Think not he hath his bow forgot,
Although my lute and I have done.

Vengeance shall fall on thy disdain,
That makest but game on earnest pain;
Think not alone under the sun
Unquit to cause thy lovers plain,
Although my lute and I have done.

May chance thee lie withered and old,
In winter nights that are so cold,
Plaining in vain unto the moon;
Thy wishes then dare not be told.
Care then who list, for I have done.

wast] waste   that (lines 3, 38)] that which   grave] engrave   Unquit] Unrequited

And then may chance thee to repent
The time that thou hast lost and spent
To cause thy lovers sigh and swoon;
Then shalt thou know beauty but lent,
And wish and want as I have done.
Now cease, my lute, this is the last
Labor that thou and I shall wast,
And ended is that we begun.
Now is this song both sung and past,
My lute, be still, for I have done.

And wilt thou leave me thus?

And wilt thou leave me thus?
Say nay, say nay! For shame,
To save thee from the blame
Of all my grief and grame.
And wilt thou leave me thus?
Say nay, say nay.

And wilt thou leave me thus,
That hath loved thee so long
In wealth and woe among?
And is thy heart so strong
As for to leave me thus?
Say nay, say nay.

And wilt thou leave me thus,
That hath given thee my heart,
Never for to depart
Neither for pain nor smart;
And wilt thou leave me thus?
Say nay, say nay.

And wilt thou leave me thus,
And have no more pity
Of him that loveth thee?

grame] sorrow

Alas, thy cruelty!
And wilt thou leave me thus?
Say nay, say nay!

Forget not yet

Forget not yet the tried intent
Of such a truth as I have meant,
My great travail, so gladly spent,
    Forget not yet.

Forget not yet when first began
The weary life ye know, since whan
The suit, the service none tell can,
    Forget not yet.

Forget not yet the great assays,
The cruel wrong, the scornful ways;
The painful patience in denays,
    Forget not yet.

Forget not yet, forget not this,
How long ago hath been, and is,
The mind that never meant amiss,—
    Forget not yet.

Forget not, then, thine own approved,
The which so long hath thee so loved,
Whose steadfast faith yet never moved,
    Forget not this.

Blame not my lute

Blame not my lute, for he must sound
  Of this or that as liketh me;
For lack of wit the lute is bound
  To give such tunes as pleaseth me;

denays] denials

Though my songs be somewhat strange,
And speaks such words as touch thy change,
   Blame not my lute!

My lute, alas, doth not offend,
  Though that perforce he must agree
To sound such tunes as I intend
  To sing to them that heareth me;
Then though my songs be somewhat plain,
And toucheth some that use to feign,
   Blame not my lute!

My lute and strings may not deny,
  But as I strike they must obey;
Break not them then so wrongfully,
  But wreak thyself some other way;
And though the songs which I indite
Do quit thy change with rightful spite,
   Blame not my lute!

Spite asketh spite, and changing change,
  And falsèd faith must needs be known;
The faults so great, the case so strange,
  Of right it must abroad be blown;
Then since that by thine own desart
My songs do tell how true thou art,
   Blame not my lute!

Blame but thyself that hast misdone,
  And well deservèd to have blame;
Change thou thy way, so evil begun,
  And then my lute shall sound that same;
But if till then my fingers play
By thy desert their wonted way,
   Blame not my lute!

Farewell, unknown! for though thou break
  My strings in spite with great disdain,
Yet have I found out, for thy sake,

quit] requite   By] About

Strings for to string my lute again:
And if, perchance, this seely rhyme
Do make thee blush at any time,
Blame not my lute!

HENRY HOWARD, EARL OF SURREY (1517?–1547)

Description of Spring, Wherein Each Thing Renews Save Only the Lover

The soote season that bud and bloom forth brings
With green hath clad the hill and eke the vale,
The nightingale with feathers new, she sings,
The turtle to her make hath told her tale.
Summer is come, for every spray now springs,
The hart hath hung his old head on the pale,
The buck in brake his winter coat he flings,
The fishes float with new repairèd scale,
The adder all her slough away she slings,
The swift swallow pursueth the flyès smale,
The busy bee her honey now she mings;
Winter is worn, that was the flowers' bale;
    And thus I see, among these pleasant things
    Each care decays,—and yet my sorrow springs.

A Complaint by Night of the Lover Not Beloved

Alas, so all things now do hold their peace,
Heaven and earth disturbèd in nothing;
The beasts, the air, the birds their song do cease,
The nightè's chare the stars about doth bring;
Calm is the sea, the waves work less and less:
So am not I, whom love, alas, doth wring,
Bringing before my face the great increase
Of my desires, whereat I weep and sing
In joy and woe, as in a doubtful ease.

seely] simple   soote] sweet   make] mate   head] antlers   pale] paling, fence
mings] compounds   chare] chariot

For my sweet thoughts sometime do pleasure bring,
But by and by the cause of my dis-ease
Gives me a pang that inwardly doth sting,
  When that I think what grief it is again
  To live and lack the thing should rid my pain.

Complaint of a Lover Rebuked

Love that liveth and reigneth in my thought,
That built his seat within my captive breast,
Clad in the arms wherein with me he fought,
Oft in my face he doth his banner rest.
She that me taught to love and suffer pain,
My doubtful hope and eke my hot desire
With shamefast cloak to shadow and refrain,
Her smiling grace converteth straight to ire;
And coward Love then to the heart apace
Taketh his flight, whereas he lurks and plains
His purpose lost, and dare not show his face.
For my lord's guilt thus faultless bide I pains;
  Yet from my lord shall not my foot remove:
  Swect is his death that takes his end by love.

Vow to Love Faithfully, Howsoever He Be Rewarded

Set me whereas the sun doth parch the green,
Or where his beams do not dissolve the ice,
In temperate heat where he is felt and seen,
In presence pressed of people, mad or wise;
Set me in high or yet in low degree,
In longest night or in the shortest day,
In clearest sky or where clouds thickest be,
In lusty youth or when my hairs are gray;
Set me in heaven, in earth, or else in hell,
In hill, or dale, or in the foaming flood;
Thrall or at large, alive whereso I dwell,

should rid] which should rid   whereas] where   presence] company

Sick or in health, in evil fame or good:
Hers will I be, and only with this thought
Content myself although my chance be naught.

The Frailty and Hurtfulness of Beauty

Brittle beauty that nature made so frail,
Whereof the gift is small, and short the season,
Flow'ring today, tomorrow apt to fail,
Tickle treasure, abhorred of reason,
Dangerous to deal with, vain, of none avail,
Costly in keeping, passed not worth two peason,
Slipper in sliding as is an eelè's tail,
Hard to attain, once gotten not geason,
Jewel of jeopardy that peril doth assail,
False and untrue, enticèd oft to treason,
En'my to youth—that most may I bewail!
Ah, bitter sweet! infecting as the poison,
    Thou farest as fruit that with the frost is taken:
    Today ready ripe, tomorrow all to-shaken.

Complaint of the Absence of Her Lover Being upon the Sea

O happy dames, that may embrace
    The fruit of your delight,
Help to bewail the woeful case
    And eke the heavy plight
Of me, that wonted to rejoice
The fortune of my pleasant choice:
Good ladies, help to fill my mourning voice.

In ship, freight with rememberance
    Of thoughts and pleasures past,
He sails that hath in governance
    My life while it will last:
With scalding sighs, for lack of gale,
Furthering his hope, that is his sail,
Toward me, the sweet port of his avail.

Tickle] Precarious   treasure] probably trisyllabic   peason] peas   not geason]
nothing extraordinary   to-shaken] shaken to pieces   avail] effort

Alas! how oft in dreams I see
 Those eyes that were my food;
Which sometime so delighted me,
 That yet they do me good:
Wherewith I wake with his return,
Whose absent flame did make me burn:
But when I find the lack, Lord, how I mourn!

When other lovers in arms across
 Rejoice their chief delight,
Drownèd in tears, to mourn my loss
 I stand the bitter night
In my window, where I may see
Before the winds how the clouds flee:
Lo, what a mariner love hath made me!

And in green waves when the salt flood
 Doth rise by rage of wind;
A thousand fancies in that mood
 Assail my restless mind.
Alas! now drencheth my sweet foe,
That with the spoil of my heart did go,
And left me; but, alas! why did he so?

And when the seas wax calm again
 To chase fro me annoy,
My doubtful hope doth cause me plain:
 So dread cuts off my joy.
Thus is my wealth mingled with woe,
And of each thought a doubt doth grow;
Now he comes! Will he come? Alas, no, no!

The Things that Cause a Quiet Life

 My friend, the things that do attain
The happy life be these, I find:
The riches left, not got with pain,
The fruitful ground, the quiet mind;

drencheth] drowneth plain] lament

The equal friend—no grudge, no strife;
No charge of rule, nor governance;
Without disease, the healthy life,
The household of continuance;

The mean diet, no dainty fare;
Wisdom joined with simpleness;
The night dischargèd of all care,
Where wine the wit may not oppress;

The faithful wife, without debate;
Such sleeps as may beguile the night:
Content thyself with thine estate,
Neither wish death, nor fear his might.

ANONYMOUS (*c.* 1550)

Thou sleepest fast

Thou sleepest fast, and I with woeful heart
Stand here alone sighing and cannot fly;
Thou sleepest fast, when cruel Love his dart
On me doth cast, alas, so painfully!
Thou sleepest fast, and I, all full of smart,
To thee, my foe, in vain do call and cry:
And yet, methinkès, though thou sleepest fast
Thou dreamest still which way my life to wast.

JOHN HARINGTON, THE ELDER (*c.* 1554)

A Sonnet made on Isabella Markham

Whence comes my love? O heart, disclose!
'Twas from cheeks that shame the rose,
From lips that spoil the ruby's praise,

of continuance] permanent, settled   mean] moderate   *Thou sleepest fast*] First
printed by Ault, in his *Elizabethan Lyrics,* 1925. Reprinted with his kind permission.   wast] waste   *Sonnet*] See p. 41.

From eyes that mock the diamond's blaze.
Whence comes my woe? as freely own—
Ah, me!—'twas from a heart like stone.

The blushing cheek speaks modest mind;
The lips, befitting words most kind.
The eye does tempt to love's desire,
And seems to say 'tis Cupid's fire.
Yet all so fair, but speak my moan,
Since naught doth say the heart of stone.

Why thus, my love, so kind bespeak
Sweet lip, sweet eye, sweet blushing cheek,
Yet not a heart to save my pain?
O Venus! take thy gifts again;
Make not so fair to cause our moan,
Or make a heart that's like our own!

THOMAS, LORD VAUX (1510–1556)

The Aged Lover Renounceth Love

I loathe that I did love;
    In youth that I thought sweet,
As time requires for my behove,
    Methinks they are not meet.

My lusts they do me leave,
    My fancies all be fled,
And tract of time begins to weave
    Grey hairs upon my head.

For age with stealing steps
    Hath clawed me with his clutch,
And lusty life, away she leaps
    As there had been none such.

I loathe, etc. (stanzas 1, 3, 8)] *Cf.* the grave-digger's song, *Hamlet* V. i.   that]
what   tract] course

My muse doth not delight
  Me as she did before;
My hand and pen are not in plight,
  As they have been of yore.

For reason me denies
  This youthly idle rhyme;
And day by day to me she cries,
  'Leave off these toys in time.'

The wrinkles in my brow,
  The furrows in my face
Say, limping age will lodge him now
  Where youth must give him place.

The harbinger of death,
  To me I see him ride,
The cough, the cold, the gasping breath
  Doth bid me to provide

A pickaxe and a spade,
  And eke a shrouding sheet,
A house of clay for to be made
  For such a guest most meet.

Methinks I hear the clerk
  That knolls the care-full knell,
And bids me leave my woeful work,
  Ere nature me compel.

My keepers knit the knot
  That youth did laugh to scorn,
Of me that clean shall be forgot
  As I had not been born.

Thus must I youth give up,
  Whose badge I long did wear;
To them I yield the wanton cup
  That better may it bear.

plight] trim

Lo, here the barèd skull
  By whose bald sign I know
That stooping age away shall pull
  Which youthful years did sow.

For beauty with her band
  These crooked cares hath wrought,
And shippèd me into the land
  From whence I first was brought.

And ye that bide behind,
  Have ye none other trust:
As ye of clay were cast by kind,
  So shall ye waste to dust.

ANONYMOUS (before 1557)

The Lover in Liberty Smileth at Them in Thraldom,
that Sometime Scorned his Bondage

At liberty I sit and see
  Them, that have erst laughed me to scorn,
Whipped with the whip that scourgèd me:
  And now they ban that they were born.

I see them sit full soberly
  And think their earnest looks to hide;
Now, in themselves, they cannot spy
  That they ere this in me have spied.

I see them sitting all alone,
  Marking the steps, each word and look;
And now they tread where I have gone,
  The painful path that I forsook.

Now I see well I saw no whit
  When they saw well that now are blind;
But happy hap hath made me quit,
  And just judgmènt hath them assigned.

by kind] by nature   erst] once upon a time   ban] curse   quit] free

I see them wander all alone,
 And tread full fast, in dreadful doubt,
The self-same path that I have gone:
 Blessèd be hap that brought me out!

At liberty all this I see,
 And say no word but 'Erst!' among,
Smiling at them that laughed at me:
 Lo, such is hap! Mark well my song!

ANONYMOUS (before 1557–8)

If ever I marry

If ever I marry, I'll marry a maid;
To marry a widow, I am sore afraid:
For maids they are simple, and never will grutch,
But widows full oft, as they say, know too much.

A maid is so sweet, and so gentle of kind,
That a maid is the wife I will choose to my mind;
A widow is froward, and never will yield;
Or if such there be, you will meet them but seeld.

A maid ne'er complaineth, do what-so you will;
But what you mean well, a widow takes ill:
A widow will make you a drudge and a slave,
And, cost ne'er so much, she will ever go brave.

A maid is so modest, she seemeth a rose
When first it beginneth the bud to unclose;
But a widow full-blowen full often deceives,
And the next wind that bloweth shakes down all her
 leaves.

That widows be lovely I never gainsay,
But too well all their beauty they know to display;

among] all the while seeld] seldom brave] finely dressed

But a maid hath so great hidden beauty in store,
She can spare to a widow, yet never be poor.

Then, if ever I marry, give me a fresh maid,
If to marry with any I be not afraid;
But to marry with any, it asketh much care;
And some bachelors hold they are best as they are.

QUEEN ELIZABETH (1533–1603)

When I was fair and young

When I was fair and young, and favor gracèd me,
  Of many was I sought, their mistress for to be;
But I did scorn them all, and answered them therefore,
  'Go, go, go, seek some otherwhere,
    Impòrtune me no more!'

How many weeping eyes I made to pine with woe,
  How many sighing hearts, I have no skill to show;
Yet I the prouder grew, and answered them therefore,
  'Go, go, go, seek some otherwhere,
    Impòrtune me no more!'

Then spake fair Venus' son, that proud victorious boy,
  And said: 'Fine dame, since that you be so coy,
I will so pluck your plumes that you shall say no more,
  Go, go, go, seek some otherwhere,
    Impòrtune me no more!'

When he had spake these words, such change grew in my
    breast
  That neither night nor day since that, I could take any
    rest.
Then lo! I did repent that I had said before,
  'Go, go, go, seek some otherwhere,
    Impòrtune me no more!'

GEORGE TURBERVILLE (*c.* 1540–*c.* 1595)

The Lover to the Thames

Thou stately stream that with the swelling tide
'Gainst London walls incessantly dost beat,
Thou Thames, I say, where barge and boat doth ride,
And snow-white swans do fish for needful meat:
　Whenso my love, of force or pleasure, shall
Flit on thy flood as custom is to do,
Seek not with dread her courage to appal,
But calm thy tide, and smoothly let it go,
As she may joy, arrived to siker shore,
To pass the pleasant stream she did before.
　To welter up and surge in wrathful wise,
As did the flood where Helle drenchèd was,
Would but procure defame of thee to rise:
Wherefore let all such ruthless rigor pass,
So wish I that thou may'st with bending side
Have power for aye in wonted gulf to glide.

Others as Fair, but not so Faithful

I sundry see, for beauty's gloss,
　That with my mistress may compare,
But few I find for true good-will
　That to their friends so friendly are.

Look, what she says I may assure
　Myself thereof: she will not feign;
What others speak is hard to trust,
　They measure all their words by gain.

Her looks declare her loving mind;
　Her count'nance and her heart agree;
When others laugh they look as smooth
　But love not half so well as she.

The grief is hers when I am griped,
　My finger's ache is her dis-ease;

As] That　siker] secure　flood] the Hellespont

With me though others mourn to sight
    Yet are their hearts at quiet ease.

So that I mark in Cupid's court
    Are many fair and fresh to see;
Each where is sown Dame Beauty's seed,
    But fair and faithful few there be.

To his Friend

I wot full well that beauty cannot last;
No rose that springs but lightly doth decay,
And feature like a lily leaf doth waste,
Or as the cowslip in the midst of May;
I know that tract of time doth conquer all,
And beauty's buds like fading flowers do fall.

That famous dame, fair Helen, lost her hue
When withered age with wrinkles changed her cheeks,
Her lovely looks did loathsomeness ensue
That was the *A per se* of all the Greeks.
And sundry moe that were as fair as she,
Yet Helen was as fresh as fresh might be.

No force for that: I price your beauty light
If so I find you steadfast in good will.
Though few there are that do in age delight,
I was your friend, and so do purpose still;
No change of looks shall breed my change of love,
Nor beauty's want my first good will remove.

THOMAS HOWELL (*c.* 1568)

The Red Rose

Whenas the mildest month
    Of jolly June doth spring,

tract] course   Her . . . ensue] Loathsomeness followed . . .   *A per se*] first and
best   moe] more   force] matter

And gardens green with happy hue
Their famous fruits do bring,
When eke the lustiest time
Reviveth youthly blood,
Then springs the finest featured flower
In border fair that stood:
Which moveth me to say,
In time of pleasant year,
Of all the pleasant flowers in June
The red rose hath no peer.

GEORGE GASCOIGNE (*c.* 1542–1577)

A Strange Passion of a Lover

Amid my bale I bathe in bliss,
  I swim in heaven, I sink in hell;
I find amends for every miss
  And yet my moan no tongue can tell.
I live and love, what would you more?
As never lover lived before.

I laugh sometimes with little lust,
  So jest I oft and feel no joy;
Mine ease is builded all on trust,
  And yet mistrust breeds mine annoy.
I live and lack, I lack and have,
I have and miss the thing I crave.

These things seem strange, yet are they true;
  Believe me, sweet, my state is such,
One pleasure which I would eschew
  Both slakes my grief and breeds my grutch.
So doth one pain which I would shun
Renew my joys, where grief begun.

Then like the lark that passed the night
  In heavy sleep, with cares oppressed,
Yet when she spies the pleasant light

She sends sweet notes from out her breast:
So sing I now because I think
How joys approach when sorrows shrink.

And as fair Philomene, again,
    Can watch and sing when other sleep,
And taketh pleasure in her pain
    To wray the woe that makes her weep:
So sing I now for to bewray
The loathsome life I lead alway.

The which to thee, dear wench, I write,
    That know'st my mirth, but not my moan.
I pray God grant thee deep delight,
    To live in joys when I am gone.
I cannot live, it will not be,
I die to think to part from thee.

The Lullaby of a Lover

Sing lullaby, as women do,
Wherewith they bring their babes to rest,
And lullaby can I sing too
As womanly as can the best.
With lullaby they still the child,
And if I be not much beguiled,
Full many wanton babes have I
Which must be stilled with lullaby.

First, lullaby my youthful years,
It is now time to go to bed,
For crooked age and hoary hairs
Have won the haven within my head;
With lullaby, then, youth be still,
With lullaby, content thy will,
Since courage quails and comes behind,
Go sleep, and so beguile thy mind.

(be)wray] reveal

Next, lullaby my gazing eyes,
Which wonted were to glance apace.
For every glass may now suffice
To show the furrows in my face;
With lullaby, then, wink awhile,
With lullaby, your looks beguile,
Let no fair face nor beauty bright
Entice you eft with vain delight.

And lullaby, my wanton will,
Let reason's rule now reign thy thought,
Since all too late I find by skill
How dear I have thy fancies bought;
With lullaby, now take thine ease,
With lullaby, thy doubts appease;
For trust to this, if thou be still,
My body shall obey thy will.

Eke, lullaby my loving boy,
My little Robin, take thy rest;
Since age is cold and nothing coy,
Keep close thy coin, for so is best;
With lullaby, be thou content,
With lullaby, thy lusts relent,
Let others pay which have moe pence,
Thou art too poor for such expense.

Thus, lullaby, my youth, mine eyes,
My will, my ware, and all that was!
I can no moe delays devise,
But welcome pain, let pleasure pass;
With lullaby, now take your leave,
With lullaby, your dreams deceive,
And when you rise with waking eye,
Remember then this lullaby.

wink] close   eft] hereafter   coy] lascivious

Ferdinando Ieronimi's Sonnet

The stately dames of Rome their pearls did wear
About their necks to beautify their name:
But she whom I do serve, her pearls doth bear
Close in her mouth, and, smiling, show the same.
No wonder, then, though every word she speaks
A jewel seem in judgment of the wise,
Since that her sugared tongue the passage breaks
Between two rocks, bedecked with pearls of price.
Her hair of gold, her front of ivory—
A bloody heart within so white a breast!—
Her teeth of pearl, lips ruby, crystal eye,
Needs must I honor her above the rest,
    Since she is formèd of none other mould
    But ruby, crystal, ivory, pearl, and gold.

GEORGE WHETSTONE (*c.* 1544–1587)

A Gentlewoman Forsweareth Hereafter to be Won
with Flattering Promises

Give me my work, that I may sit and sew,
And so escape the trains of trustless men:
I find too true, by witness of my woe,
How that fair words with faithless works they blen,
    Much siren-like, with sweet enticing call,
    We silly dames to witch and wray in thrall.

O cruel friend, whose false of faith I rue,
Thou forcest me to count all men unjust;
For if that vow or oath might make one true
Thou usèd'st such as well might force to trust:
    But I, betrayed by too far trusting thee,
    Will henceforth take fair words even as they be.

I will be deaf, though thousands sue for grace,
My sight as dim, if sights in silence plead;

front] forehead   mould] material   blen] blend   wray in thrall] betray into
servitude   false] breach

Salt tears no ruth within my heart shall place,
For this shall be my song and daily rede:
　Poor I, that lived in thraldom linked, of yore,
　Unbound at length, will learn to love no more.

HUMPHREY GIFFORD (*c.* 1580)

For Soldiers

Ye buds of Brutus' land, courageous youths, now play your
　　parts,
Unto your tackle stand, abide the brunt with valiant hearts!
For news is carried to and fro that we must forth to warfare
　　go,
Men muster now in every place, and soldiers are pressed forth
　　apace.
Faint not, spend blood, to do your Queen and country good!
Fair words, good pay, will make men cast all care away.

The time of war is come: prepare your corslet, spear, and
　　shield.
Methinks I hear the drum strike doleful marches to the field;
Tantarà, tantarà! the trumpets sound, which makes our hearts
　　with joy abound;
The roaring guns are heard afar, and every thing denounceth
　　war.
Serve God, stand stout, bold courage brings this gear about;
Fear not, forth run, faint heart fair lady never won.

Ye curious carpet knights, that spend the time in sport and
　　play,
Abroad, and see new sights! your country's cause calls you
　　away.
Do not, to make your ladies game, bring blemish to your
　　worthy name,

rede] resolve   Brutus' land] Britain, of which Brutus was the legendary founder
pressed] drafted   denounceth] announceth   gear] business   make . . . game]
provide . . . pleasure

Away to field and win renown! with courage beat your
   enemies down!
Stout hearts gain praise when dastards sail in slander's seas.
Hap what hap shall, we sure shall die but once for all.

Alarm methinks they cry. Be packing, mates, be gone with
   speed!
Our foes are very nigh; shame have that man that shrinks
   at need!
Unto it boldly let us stand, God will give right the upper
   hand;
Our cause is good, we need not doubt. In sign of courage
   give a shout!
March forth, be strong, good hap will come ere it be long;
Shrink not, fight well, for lusty lads must bear the bell.

All you that will shun evil must dwell in warfare every day,
The world, the flesh, and devil always do seek our souls' decay:
Strive with these foes with all your might, so shall you fight
   a worthy fight.
That conquest doth deserve most praise where vice do yield
   to virtue's ways.
Beat down foul sin! a worthy crown then shall ye win!
If we live well, in heaven with Christ our souls shall dwell.

From *A Delectable Dream*

['A foe to womankind' sings]

A woman's face is full of wiles,
   Her tears are like the crocodile;
With outward cheer on thee she smiles
   When in her heart she thinks thee ill.
Her tongue still chats of this and that,
   Than aspen leaf it wags more fast;
And as she talks she knows not what,
   There issues many a truthless blast.

bear the bell] lead, be foremost

Thou far dost take thy mark amiss
  If thou think faith in them to find.
The weathercock more constant is,
  Which turns about with every wind.
O, how in pity they abound!
  Their heart is mild like marble stone;
If in thyself no hope be found,
  Be sure of them thou gettest none.
I know some pepper-nosèd dame
  Will term me fool and saucy jack,
That dare their credit so defame
  And lay such slanders on their back.
What though on me they pour their spite?
  I may not use the glozer's trade:
I cannot say the crow is white,
  But needs must call a spade a spade.

EDWARD DE VERE, EARL OF OXFORD (1550–1604)

Were I a king

Were I a king I could command content;
  Were I obscure, unknown should be my cares;
And were I dead, no thoughts should me torment,
  Nor words, nor wrongs, nor loves, nor hopes, nor fears.
A doubtful choice, of three things one to crave,
A kingdom, or a cottage, or a grave.

CHIDIOCK TICHBORNE (d. 1586)

Elegy

My prime of youth is but a frost of cares,
My feast of joy is but a dish of pain,
My crop of corn is but a field of tares,
And all my goods is but vain hope of gain;
The day is fled, and yet I saw no sun,
And now I live, and yet my life is done.

glozer's] flatterer's

The spring is past and yet I have not sprung,
The trees are dead, and yet my leaves be green,
My youth is past and yet I am but young,
I was in world and yet I was not seen;
My thread is cut and yet it is not spun,
And now I live, and yet my life is done.

I sought for death and found it in the womb,
I looked for life and knew it was a shade,
I trod the earth and knew it was my tomb,
And now I die, and now I was but made;
The glass is full, and now the glass is run,
And now I live, and now my life is done.

SIR EDWARD DYER (d. 1607)

My mind to me a kingdom is

My mind to me a kingdom is,
Such perfect joy therein I find,
That it excels all other bliss
That world affords or grows by kind:
  Though much I want which most would have,
  Yet still my mind forbids to crave.

No princely pomp, no wealthy store,
No force to win the victory,
No wily wit to salve a sore,
No shape to feed a loving eye;
  To none of these I yield as thrall:
  For why? my mind doth serve for all.

I see how plenty suffers oft,
And hasty climbers soon do fall:
I see that those which are aloft
Mishap doth threaten most of all:
  They get with toil, they keep with fear;
  Such cares my mind could never bear.

Content I live, this is my stay:
I seek no more than may suffice,

by kind] by nature   For why] Because

I press to bear no haughty sway;
Look, what I lack my mind supplies:
  Lo, thus I triumph like a king,
  Content with that my mind doth bring.

Some have too much, yet still do crave,
I little have, and seek no more:
They are but poor, though much they have,
And I am rich with little store:
  They poor, I rich; they beg, I give;
  They lack, I leave; they pine, I live.

I laugh not at another's loss,
I grudge not at another's gain:
No worldly waves my mind can toss,
My state at one doth still remain:
  I fear no foe, I fawn no friend,
  I loathe not life, nor dread no end.

Some weigh their pleasure by their lust,
Their wisdom by their rage of will;
Their treasure is their only trust,
A cloakèd craft their store of skill;
  But all the pleasure that I find
  Is to maintain a quiet mind.

My wealth is health and perfect ease,
My conscience clear my chief defense:
I neither seek by bribes to please,
Nor by desert to breed offence:
  Thus do I live, thus will I die;
  Would all did so, as well as I.

SIR WALTER RALEIGH (*c.* 1552–1618)

The Lie

Go, soul, the body's guest,
Upon a thankless arrant.
Fear not to touch the best;

with that] with what   *The Lie*] Five stanzas are omitted.   arrant] errand

The truth shall be thy warrant:
  Go, since I needs must die,
  And give the world the lie.

Say to the court, it glows
And shines like rotten wood;
Say to the church, it shows
What's good, and doth no good:
  If church and court reply,
  Then give them both the lie.

Tell men of high condition
That manage the estate,
Their purpose is ambition,
Their practice only hate:
  And if they once reply,
  Then give them all the lie.

Tell zeal it wants devotion;
Tell love it is but lust;
Tell time it meets but motion;
Tell flesh it is but dust:
  And wish them not reply,
  For thou must give the lie.

Tell wit how much it wrangles
In tickle points of niceness;
Tell wisdom she entangles
Herself in over-wiseness:
  And when they do reply,
  Straight give them both the lie.

Tell fortune of her blindness·
Tell nature of decay;
Tell friendship of unkindness;
Tell justice of delay:
  And if they will reply,
  Then give them all the lie.

estate] government

Tell arts they have no soundness,
But vary by esteeming;
Tell schools they want profoundness,
And stand too much on seeming:
    If arts and schools reply,
    Give arts and schools the lie.

So when thou hast, as I
Commanded thee, done blabbing,
Because to give the lie
Deserves no less than stabbing,
    Stab at thee he that will,
    No stab thy soul can kill.

To the Queen

Our passions are most like to floods and streams:
    The shallow murmur, but the deep are dumb;
So, when affections yield discourse, it seems
    The bottom is but shallow whence they come.
They that are rich in words must needs discover
That they are poor in that which makes a lover.

Wrong not, dear empress of my heart,
    The merit of true passion,
With thinking that he feels no smart
    That sues for no compassion;
Since, if my plaints serve not to prove
    The conquest of your beauty,
It comes not from defect of love,
    But from excess of duty.

For knowing that I sue to serve
    A saint of such perfection
As all desire—but none deserve—
    A place in her affection,
I rather choose to want relief
    Than venture the revealing;

When glory recommends the grief,
　Despair distrusts the healing.

Thus those desires that aim too high
　For any mortal lover,
When reason cannot make them die,
　Discretion will them cover.
Yet, when discretion doth bereave
　The plaints that they should utter,
Then your discretion may perceive
　That silence is a suitor.

Silence in love bewrays more woe
　Than words though ne'er so witty;
A beggar that is dumb, you know,
　Deserveth double pity.
Then misconceive not, dearest heart,
　My true, though secret passion;
He smarteth most that hides his smart,
　And sues for no compassion.

The Passionate Man's Pilgrimage

Give me my scallop-shell of quiet,
　My staff of faith to walk upon,
My scrip of joy, immortal diet,
　My bottle of salvatiòn,
My gown of glory, hope's true gage;
And thus I'll take my pilgrimage.

Blood must be my body's balmer,
　No other balm will there be given;
Whilst my soul, like a white palmer,
　Travels to the land of heaven;
Over the silver mountains,
Where spring the nectar fountains:
　　And there I'll kiss
　　The bowl of bliss,

scallop-shell] badge of the pilgrim's vocation　　scrip] wallet　　balmer] embalmer

And drink my eternal fill
On every milken hill.
My soul will be a-dry before,
But after, it will ne'er thirst more.

And by the happy blissful way
  More peaceful pilgrims I shall see,
That have shook off their rags of clay
  And go appareled fresh like me.
        I'll bring them first
        To slake their thirst
And then to taste those nectar suckets,
        At the clear wells
        Where sweetness dwells
Drawn up by saints in crystal buckets.

And when our bottles and all we
Are filled with immortality,
Then the holy paths we'll travel,
Strewed with rubies thick as gravel;
Ceilings of diamonds, sapphire floors,
High walls of coral, and pearl bowers.

From thence to heaven's bribeless hall,
Where no corrupted voices brawl,
No conscience molten into gold,
Nor forged accusers bought and sold,
No cause deferred, nor vain-spent journey,
For there Christ is the King's Attorney,
Who pleads for all without degrees,
And he hath angels, but no fees.

When the grand twelve-million jury
Of our sins, with sinful fury,
'Gainst our souls black verdicts give,
Christ pleads his death, and then we live,
Be thou my speaker, taintless pleader,

milken] running with milk and honey   suckets] sweetmeats   angels] a play on
angel, a gold coin

Unblotted lawyer, true proceeder!
Thou mov'st salvation even for alms;
Not with a bribèd lawyer's palms.

And this is my eternal plea
To him that made heaven, earth, and sea,
Seeing my flesh must die so soon,
And want a head to dine next noon,
Just at the stroke, when my veins start and spread,
Set on my soul an everlasting head.
Then am I ready, like a palmer fit
To tread those blest paths which before I writ.

The Author's Epitaph, made by Himself

Even such is time, which takes in trust
    Our youth, our joys, and all we have,
And pays us but with age and dust;
    Who, in the dark and silent grave,
When we have wandered all our ways,
Shuts up the story of our days;
And from which earth, and grave, and dust
The Lord shall raise me up, I trust!

FRANCIS BACON (1561–1626)

On the Life of Man

The world's a bubble, and the life of man
    Less than a span;
In his conception wretched: from the womb
    So to the tomb;
Curs'd from the cradle, and brought up to years
    With cares and fears.
Who then to frail mortality shall trust
But limns the water, or but writes in dust.

Yet since with sorrow here we live oppressed,
    What life is best?

Courts are but only superficial schools
　　To dandle fools;
The rural parts are turned into a den
　　Of savage men;
And where's a city from all vice so free
But may be termed the worst of all the three?

Domestic cares afflict the husband's bed,
　　Or pains, his head;
Those that live single take it for a curse,
　　Or do things worse;
Some would have children; those that have them moan
　　Or wish them gone;
What is it, then, to have or have no wife
But single thraldom or a double strife?

Our own affections still at home to please
　　Is a disease;
To cross the sea to any foreign soil,
　　Perils and toil;
Wars with their noise affright us; when they cease
　　We're worse in peace.
What then remains, but that we still should cry
Not to be born, or being born, to die?

MICHAEL DRAYTON (1563-1631)

To the Virginian Voyage

You brave heroic minds
Worthy your country's name,
　That honor still pursue,
　Go, and subdue,
Whilst loit'ring hinds
Lurk here at home, with shame.

Britons, you stay too long;
Quickly aboard bestow you,
　And with a merry gale

Swell your stretched sail,
With vows as strong
As the winds that blow you.

Your course securely steer,
West and by south forth keep,
 Rocks, lee-shores, nor shoals,
 When Æolus scowls,
You need not fear,
So absolute the deep.

And cheerfully at sea,
Success you still entice,
 To get the pearl and gold,
 And ours to hold,
Virginià,
Earth's only paradise,

Where nature hath in store
Fowl, venison, and fish,
 And the fruitful'st soil,
 Without your toil,
Three harvests more,
All greater than your wish;

And the ambitious vine
Crowns with his purple mass,
 The cedar reaching high
 To kiss the sky,
The cypress, pine,
And useful sassafras,

To whom the golden age
Still nature's laws doth give,
 No other cares that tend,
 But them to defend
From winter's age,
That long there doth not live.

soil] *Sc.* 'hath in store.'

Whenas the luscious smell
Of that delicious land,
  Above the seas that flows,
  The clear wind throws,
Your hearts to swell
Approaching the dear strand,

In kenning of the shore,
Thanks to God first given,
  O you, the happi'st men,
  Be frolic then,
Let cannons roar,
Frighting the wide heaven.

And in regions far
Such heroes bring ye forth
  As those from whom we came,
  And plant our name
Under that star
Not known unto our north.

And as there plenty grows
Of laurel everywhere,
  Apollo's sacred tree,
  You it may see
A poet's brows
To crown, that may sing there.

Thy voyages attend,
Industrious Hakluỳt,
  Whose reading shall enflame
  Men to seek fame,
And much commend
To after times thy wit.

His Ballad of Agincourt

Fair stood the wind for France,
When we our sails advance,

advance] hoist

Nor now to prove our chance
　Longer will tarry;
But putting to the main,
At Caux, the mouth of Seine,
With all his martial train,
　Landed King Harry.

And taking many a fort,
Furnished in warlike sort,
Marcheth tow'rds Agincourt
　In happy hour;
Skirmishing day by day
With those that stopped his way,
Where the French general lay
　With all his power:

Which in his height of pride,
King Henry to deride,
His ransom to provide
　To the king sending;
Which he neglects the while,
As from a nation vile,
Yet with an angry smile,
　Their fall portending;

And, turning to his men,
Quoth our brave Henry then,
'Though they to one be ten,
　Be not amazèd;
Yet have we well begun;
Battles so bravely won
Have ever to the sun
　By fame been raisèd.

'And for myself,' quoth he,
'This my full rest shall be,
England ne'er mourn for me,
　Nor more esteem me.

Which in] Who in　　amazèd] confused by fear　　rest] resolve

Victor I will remain,
Or on this earth lie slain,
Never shall she sustain
    Loss to redeem me.

'Poitiers and Crecy tell,
When most their pride did swell,
Under our swords they fell;
    No less our skill is
Than when our grandsire great,
Claiming the regal seat,
By many a warlike feat
    Lopped the French lilies.'

The Duke of York so dread,
The eager vaward led;
With the main Henry sped,
    Amongst his henchmen.
Excester had the rear,
A braver man not there.
O Lord! how hot they were
    On the false Frenchmen!

They now to fight are gone;
Armor on armor shone,
Drum now to drum did groan,
    To hear was wonder;
That with the cries they make
The very earth did shake,
Trumpet to trumpet spake,
    Thunder to thunder.

Well it thine age became,
O noble Erpingham,
Which didst the signal aim
    To our hid forces;
When from a meadow by,
Like a storm suddenly

vaward] vanguard   main] main army

The English archery
  Stuck the French horses,

With Spanish yew so strong,
Arrows a cloth-yard long,
That like to serpents stong,
  Piercing the weather;
None from his fellow starts,
But playing manly parts,
And like true English hearts
  Stuck close together.

When down their bows they threw,
And forth their bilbows drew,
And on the French they flew,
  Not one was tardy;
Arms were from shoulders sent,
Scalps to the teeth were rent,
Down the French peasants went,
  Our men were hardy.

This while our noble king,
His broad sword brandishing,
Down the French host did ding,
  As to o'erwhelm it;
And many a deep wound lent,
His arms with blood besprent,
And many a cruel dent
  Bruisèd his helmet.

Gloster, that duke so good,
Next of the royal blood,
For famous England stood,
  With his brave brother;
Clarence, in steel so bright,
Though but a maiden knight,
Yet in that furious fight
  Scarce such another.

Piercing the weather] Shooting straight despite the wind   bilbows] swords

Warwick in blood did wade,
Oxford the foe invade,
And cruel slaughter made,
  Still as they ran up;
Suffolk his axe did ply,
Beaumont and Willoughby
Bare them right doughtily,
  Ferrers and Fanhope.

Upon St. Crispin's day
Fought was this noble fray,
Which fame did not delay
  To England to carry;
O when shall Englishmen,
With such acts fill a pen?
Or England breed again
  Such a King Harry?

SIR HENRY WOTTON (1568–1639)

The Character of a Happy Life

How happy is he born or taught
  That serveth not another's will;
Whose armor is his honest thought
  And simple truth his highest skill;

Whose passions not his masters are;
  Whose soul is still prepared for death,
Untied unto the world with care
  Of princes' grace, or vulgar breath;

Who envies none whom chance doth raise
  Or vice; who never understood
The deepest wounds are given by praise,
  By rule of state but not of good;

Who hath his life from rumors freed,
  Whose conscience is his strong retreat;
Whose state can neither flatterers feed,
  Nor ruin make accusers great;

Who God doth late and early pray
  More of his grace than goods to send,
And entertains the harmless day
  With a well-chosen book or friend,—

This man is free from servile bands
  Of hope to rise or fear to fall;
Lord of himself, though not of lands,
  And having nothing, yet hath all.

II
THE PASTORALISTS
Chiefly
1580–1590

THE PASTORALISTS

Though Wyatt and Surrey and the other poets of *Tottel's Miscellany* long continued to be popular with readers, they inspired no new writers of importance. The first twenty years of Elizabeth's reign advanced the lyric no further than the occasionally debonair egotism of Gascoigne. About the year 1580, however, it was given a new and vital impetus by two poets of first-rate importance, Spenser and Sidney. Their early success in work inspired by Italian and French pastorals established the pastoral as the dominant mode of the decade 1580–1590, in the work of such men as Breton, Lodge, and Greene, and gave it a popularity which continued through the succeeding decade, as shown in its use by Barnfield, Marlowe, Munday, Constable, Drayton, and Shakespeare himself. In 1600 a great many of the finest pastoral lyrics were assembled by John Bodenham in his *England's Helicon,* which marks the climax of the popularity of this vein in the lyric; though, as we shall see in Section VIII, the influence of Spenser was so enduring that pastoralism met with a fruitful revival in the seventeenth century. Thus, the pastoral fashion had not only a long-continued and pervasive influence, but also the honor of touching off the great lyrical outburst and of inspiring those typically joyous, youthful, pagan songs which have made the age immortal.

The pastoral is not a form but a literary convention, a way of representing—or disguising—life. It dreams of a golden age, of a time and clime happier than our own, when in a land of perpetual summer peace, untroubled save by the vague menace of storm, winter, and the waiting wolf, men young and strong and women always fair conversed and loved in grove and pasture, surrounded by their fleecy flocks. As practised first by Theocritus two thousand years ago in his idylls of the singing matches and debates of Sicilian peasants, it is possible to credit the pastoral with some

107

approach to reality. But in the *Georgics* and *Bucolics* of Vergil an element of unreality entered; and in Vergil's followers, the Italian Mantuan and the French Marot, the models chiefly followed by Spenser, its original nature had become so complicated by allegory and other conventions that it was highly artificial. Its artificiality could be only increased by transplanting it to England. Yet it caught on at once, and indeed has never ceased to be popular. Its artificiality is both its weakness and its charm.

So far as any particular form was associated with the pastoral, it was that of the eclogue, a dialogue between shepherds, narrative or descriptive in content. But the pastoral convention was by no means confined to the eclogue. It was adopted also in romances such as Lodge's *Rosalynde,* in plays such as Peele's *Arraignment of Paris,* Lyly's *Galathea,* and Fletcher's *Faithful Shepherdess,* and in other forms. The pastoral lyric, evolved naturally as an incidental adornment of the eclogue, pastoral romance, or pastoral drama, achieved at times an independent existence, in the course of which it became more at home in English surroundings. The lullaby, the marriage song, and the elegy frequently assumed a pastoral tone, and, since shepherds are natural philosophers, the lyric of this sort was used to express democratic feeling and the contentment which is to be found in country surroundings as opposed to the complicated and restless life of the city and the court.

The two great sponsors of the mode were friends, and admirers of each other's poetry. Edmund Spenser was born in 1552. His parents were apparently not well-to-do, though connected with other branches of the family in higher places. With assistance from the authorities of each institution, Spenser attended the Merchant Tailors' School and Pembroke College, Cambridge. At Pembroke he made the acquaintance of Gabriel Harvey, who tried to interest him in his crusade for reforming English versification according to the quantitative system, later the purpose of the Areopagus, a loosely organized if not entirely legendary fellowship of which Sidney was the chief ornament and Harvey the guiding spirit. After graduation, Spenser passed some years in study and travel and, in October, 1579, found himself under the patronage of the

Earl of Leicester in London. Here he had some acquaintance with Sidney and his circle, and published anonymously his *Shepherds' Calendar* 'containing twelve allegories proportionable to the twelve months', which is dedicated to Sidney.

The Shepherds' Calendar borrowed its title from the French *Kalendrier des Bergers,* a sort of popular almanac widely known in English translation. For the implied comparison between the course of human life and the course of the year Spenser may owe something to Marot. From the handling of the allegory and details of workmanship it is apparent that he was acquainted with the pastorals of Mantuan, one of the foremost Latin poets of the Italian Renaissance. But the success of the *Calendar,* and the enthusiasm with which it was hailed are undoubtedly due to the fact that in Spenser there had arisen at last an English artist great enough to transcend the foreign models with which he worked. His alone is the device of alternation from plaintive to gay, from homely to ideal, which makes the *Calendar* continuously interesting. His alone is the undertone of serious thought involved in the allegory, his alone the vivid and musical style and the variety of rime patterns. For the first time, moreover, foreign models are deliberately 'Englished.' The four-beat meter of *Perigot and Willie's Roundelay,* with its syllabic freedom, is based on the oldest English versification. And especially the archaic language—fortunately condemned by Sidney, so that later poets did not imitate it—bespeaks Spenser's allegiance to Chaucer and to the literature of his own land. Spenser's alone are the long and stately lyrics of the *Calendar.* The canzon pastoral in honor of Elizabeth, and the dirge for Dido, in the April and November eclogues respectively, are masterpieces. Together with the later *Epithalamion* and *Prothalamion,* they constitute his distinctive contribution to the pastoral lyric and are among the most notable of its triumphs.

Sir Philip Sidney was so idealized by his age, and concentrated in a relatively brief lifetime so much activity, social, diplomatic, military, as well as intellectual and artistic, that it is difficult to estimate him solely as a lyric poet, and to credit the excellence of the best of his work. He was the *beau ideal* of an English gentleman. Of his youth his devoted friend Fulke Greville reports that

he had 'such staidness of mind, lovely and familiar gravity, as carried grace and reverence above greater years. His talk ever of
knowledge, and his very play tending to enrich his mind.' At
Oxford 'he cultivated not one art, or one science, but the whole
circle of arts and sciences.' He traveled beyond the seas, witnessed
and nearly suffered in the Massacre of St. Bartholomew, took lessons
in horsemanship in Vienna, held intercourse with the brightest
spirits of Venice, Padua, and Paris, became on his return the darling
of the English court, was Ambassador to Vienna, broke a lance in
the last great English tournament, was restrained by the Queen
herself from going on an expedition with Drake to South America,
and died heroically in battle against the Spaniards in the Nether-
lands. Yet so firmly was he grounded in the tradition of the
gentleman who is also a scholar and a poet, that he found time
to write the most notable critical essay of his time, *The Defence
of Poesy,* the first and one of the best of the sonnet sequences (see
p. 168ff.), and a long, leisurely pastoral romance, *The Arcadia,*
which shared with and even overshadowed Spenser's *Shepherds'
Calendar* in immediate influence upon the pastoral lyrists.

The reasons for Sidney's influence cannot be fully illustrated in
an anthology of the present scope. They lie rather in the potency
of his example among his poetic fellows by reason of his personality
and achievements and in the popularity of his prose romance as
a whole. Dyer and Greville in particular were doubtless drawn
into the fashion by their close friendship with Sidney. *The Arcadia*
is full of pastoral lyrics, but Sidney himself was dissatisfied with
them, and we share his feeling. Many of them are experiments
growing out of Harvey's Areopagus and Sidney's own wide acquaintance with Italian poetry. A single example (p. 125) is
quoted as earnest of what, infrequently, they are at their best. Perfection of form and fullness of inspiration was to come to Sidney
in the sonnet vein. Nonetheless, the lyrics of the *Arcadia* were
largely instrumental in casting the pastoral spell over English
poetry for two decades.

To get a true picture of the wide popularity of the pastoral it
is only necessary to contemplate the heterogeneous group of poets
who produced excellent work in this kind. The pastoral conven-

tion and the ideas connected with it seem to have been in the
very air of the time and so to have affected all sorts and conditions
of men: Bartholomew Young, known principally as a translator;
the Earl of Essex, a brilliant courtier, a favorite of Elizabeth, who
wrote little verse of any kind; Christopher Marlowe, dramatist and
secret agent, whose single known venture into the field probably
was and is its most popular piece; Raleigh, courtier and adventurer,
who could turn his hand to many different kinds of writing but
is seldom playful; Shakespeare, ever sensitive to public taste; Edmund Bolton, Catholic poet, antiquarian, and literary critic;
Anthony Munday, voluminous author of plays, pageants, romances,
pamphlets, and ballads; Henry Constable, sonneteer and devotional lyrist, whose four pastoral pieces in the *Helicon* are all in
this vein that we have of his; Sir Henry Wotton, traveler, diplo-
mat, friend of Donne and Isaac Walton, who seems to have been
so caught by the pastoral manner in the nineties that he returned
to it at the end of his long career.

Amid such plenty as is found in the pastoral lyric the culling
out of the best is a thankless task. But it would seem that the
verdict of posterity has fallen upon Breton, Lodge, and Greene in
the eighties, and Barnfield and Drayton in the next decade. Breton,
Lodge, and Greene were University men. Breton, the step-son
of George Gascoigne, later enjoyed the patronage of the Countess
of Pembroke. He wrote a great deal, in verse and prose, hastily
and with a fatal facility. His pastorals are the best things he
wrote and among the best that we have. He is particularly happy
in adapting the artificiality of the fashion to English feeling and
the English countryside, as in the charming bit of description beginning 'Who can live in heart so glad' (p. 136). Lodge, a law
student, soldier, writer and, later, a prominent physician of London,
distinguished himself in the writing of verse satire and pastoral
prose romances, the latter containing songs of enchanting freshness and melody. Greene, romancer, playwright, pamphleteer, remembered for his wild life and sordid death, somehow contrived
to bring into the pastoral a depth of feeling which ennobles it
without destroying its delicacy and charm. As to Barnfield, suffice
it to say that his ode *As it fell upon a day* was long thought to be

Shakespeare's and deserves the compliment. Drayton cannot here be adequately represented. His long, exquisite 'nymphalls' mark him as the greatest of the followers of Spenser.

As mentioned above, the Elizabethan pastoral lyric which is probably best known and liked today, Marlowe's *Come live with me and be my love,* seems to have held the same position in its own time. It is possible to gauge the contemporary popularity of Elizabethan lyrics with some accuracy by noting the frequency with which they appeared in miscellanies, song-books, and manuscript commonplace books, and also by the number of imitations and 'answers' which they elicited. *Come live with me* inspired in addition to Raleigh's 'answer,' imitations by Donne (*The Bait*) and Herrick (*To Phyllis, to Love and Live with Him*); it is quoted in *The Merry Wives of Windsor,* III. i. 17–20, and echoed by Barnfield in his *Affectionate Shepherd.* Another popular piece was *As you came from the holy land,* which occurs in several versions. It is attributed to Sir Walter Raleigh on the basis of the initials 'Sr. W. R.' appended to a manuscript copy, and its descant upon true love is by no means unworthy of him, though the attribution is not certain. It is quoted in *The Knight of the Burning Pestle* and in *Hans Beerpot, his Invisible Comedy;* and the second stanza seems to have suggested Ophelia's 'How should I your true love know?' (*Hamlet,* IV. v. 23ff).

It should not be forgotten that some of the most perfect of English pastoral lyrics are to be found in the drama. Especially to be read for purposes of comparison is Shakespeare's *When icicles hang by the wall* (p. 231), in which the mode doffs all disguise and appears in honest English homespun. Thus, while the prevalence of the mode was due to Spenser and Sidney, its complete assimilation and finest development is to be sought elsewhere: in the amorous verse of the romances of Lodge and Greene, in the idylls of Breton, in individual poems of Marlowe, Constable, Munday, and Barnfield, and in the plays of Peele, Shakespeare, and Dekker. Here, in the perfection of the *genre,* its simplicity and insouciance, its music and metrical felicity, its sweet pathos and tenderness, its delicate artificiality, are united with a genuine joy in the beauty of nature.

But the proper sphere of the Elizabethan pastoralists is not reality. As Dowden [1] has said, 'They do not need ideas, or abstractions, or memories of the past or hopes for the future: it suffices them to be in presence of a bed of roses, or an arbour of eglantine, or the gold hair of a girl, or her clear eyes, bright lips, and little cloven chin, her fair, shadowed throat, and budding breasts. She shall be a shepherdess, and the passionate shepherd will cull the treasures of earth, and of the heaven of the gods of Greece and Rome to lay before her feet.' In a word, the pastoralists manifest that passionate delight in beauty which forms the inspiring motive of all true Renaissance poets.

For the preservation of many of the best pastorals as well as of sonnets and madrigals in the ensuing decade we are indebted to the continued publication of miscellanies, a custom established, as we have seen, by Tottel's *Songs and Sonnets*. As the number of those who read poetry increased, the practice of keeping commonplace books, made necessary by the real or affected reluctance of courtiers and gentlemen to permit their poems to appear in print, increased with it; and from time to time the best of these were printed. *Britton's Bower of Delights,* a pirated work including, among much else, poems of Nicholas Breton, appeared in 1591. *The Phoenix Nest* (1593) is the first to represent the new group, Spenser, Sidney, Watson, Breton, Lodge, and Raleigh, including poems of the latter two not printed elsewhere. Its editor, R. S., of the Inner Temple, is unknown. *The Passionate Pilgrim* 'by W. Shakespeare' (1599) is another pirated work containing poetry by Shakespeare, Barnfield, Griffin, Raleigh, Marlowe, and others. *England's Helicon,* projected by John Bodenham, published in 1600, is perhaps the richest and most representative of all. The series closes in 1602 with Francis Davison's admirable *Poetical Rhapsody*. Less strictly anthologies are the appendix to Chester's *Love's Martyr, The Turtle and the Phoenix* (1601), which contains poems by Shakespeare, Jonson, Marston, and Chapman, and collections of extracts like *Belvedere, or The Garden of the Muses,* and *England's Parnassus*. Munday's *Banquet of Dainty Conceits,* an inferior production published in 1588, and Breton's *Arbor of*

---

[1] *The Academy,* September 2, 1876, p. 231.

Amorous Devices (1593–4) are the work of their respective editors, who appear to have traded on titles usually employed to convey the idea of an anthology. After the death of the Queen few new miscellanies appeared, although as in the case of the sonnet-series, the old miscellanies continued to be re-published. Such miscellanies as were printed in the reign of James are mostly indiscriminate collections of ballads, lyrics, and occasional verse. The lyrical anthology went out of fashion and other collections, especially those of songs and madrigals, generally with the music attached, took their place in the popular esteem.

The best of the Elizabethan miscellanies were the product of educated literary taste and selection, and in them, especially in *The Phoenix Nest, England's Helicon,* and Davison's *Poetical Rhapsody,* will be found much of the choicest lyrical poetry prior to the accession of James I, including, besides a considerable body of verse the authorship of which it is difficult or impossible to identify, work by almost every important lyrical poet of the age. The *Poetical Rhapsody* contains an especially large proportion of new work, that of the editor himself as well as of the admirable poet A. W., whoever he may have been, being especially worthy to stand with the work of Sir John Davies, Donne, Sir Henry Wotton, and Campion in the dawn of a new century and a new poetic generation.

EDMUND SPENSER (1552?–1599)

Hobbinol's Lay of Fair Elisa,
Queen of Shepherds

Ye dainty nymphs, that in this blessèd brook
    Do bathe your breast,
Forsake your wat'ry bowers, and hither look,
    At my request;
And eke you virgins that on Parnasse dwell,
Whence floweth Helicon, the learnèd well,
    Help me to blaze

eke] also

Her worthy praise
Which in her sex doth all excel.

Of fair Elisa be your silver song,
      That blessèd wight;
The flower of virgins, may she flourish long,
      In princely plight.
For she is Syrinx' daughter without spot,
Which Pan, the shepherds' god, of her begot;
      So sprung her grace
      Of heavenly race,
No mortal blemish may her blot.

See where she sits upon the grassy green,
      (O seemly sight!)
Y-clad in scarlet, like a maiden queen,
      And ermines white;
Upon her head a crimson coronet
With damask roses and daffadillies set;
      Bay leaves between,
      And primroses green,
Embellish the sweet violet.

Tell me, have ye seen her angelic face,
      Like Phœbe fair?
Her heavenly 'haviòr, her princely grace,
      Can you well compare?
The red rose medled with the white y-fere,
In either cheek depeincten lively chere.
      Her modest eye,
      Her majesty,
Where have you seen the like but there?

I saw Phœbus thrust out his golden head,
      Upon her to gaze:
But when he saw how broad her beams did spread,
      It did him amaze.

wight] being   plight] state   medled] mingled   y-fere] together   depeincten]
depict   chere] mood

He blushed to see another Sun below,
Ne durst again his fiery face out show:
 Let him, if he dare,
 His brightness compare
With hers, to have the overthrow.

Show thyself, Cynthia, with thy silver rays,
 And be not abashed;
When she the beams of her beauty displays,
 O how art thou dashed?
But I will not match her with Latona's seed,
Such folly great sorrow to Niobe did breed.
 Now she is a stone,
 And makes daily moan,
Warning all other to take heed.

Pan may be proud, that ever he begot
 Such a bellibone,
And Syrinx rejoice, that ever was her lot
 To bear such an one.
Soon as my younglings cryen for the dam,
To her will I offer a milkwhite lamb:
 She is my goddess plain,
 And I her shepherds' swain,
Albeit forswonk and forswat I am.

I see Calliope speed her to the place,
 Where my goddess shines,
And after her the other Muses trace,
 With their violines.
Been they not bay branches which they do bear
All for Elisa in her hand to wear?
 So sweetly they play,
 And sing all the way,
That it a heaven is to hear.

Lo, how finely the Graces can it foot
 To the instrument;

Ne] Nor bellibone] goodly one forswonk] tired forswat] sweaty

They dancen deftly, and singen soote,
    In their merriment.
Wants not a fourth Grace to make the dance even?
Let that room to my lady be yeven.
    She shall be a Grace,
    To fill the fourth place,
And reign with the rest in heaven.

And whither runs this bevy of ladies bright,
    Ranged in a row?
They been all Ladies of the Lake behight,
    That unto her go.
Chloris, that is the chiefest nymph of all,
Of olive branches bears a coronal:
    Olives been for peace,
    When wars do surcease:
Such for a princess been principal.

Ye shepherds' daughters, that dwell on the green,
    Hie you there apace;
Let none come there but that virgins been,
    To adorn her grace.
And when you come, whereas she is in place,
See that your rudeness do not you disgrace:
    Bind your fillets fast,
    And gird in your wast,
For more finesse, with a tawdry lace.

Bring hither the pink and purple columbine,
    With gillyflowers:
Bring coronatiòns, and sops-in-wine
    Worn of paramours.
Strew me the ground with daffadowndillies,
And cowslips, and kingcups, and lovèd lilies:
    The pretty paunce,
    And the chevisaunce,
Shall match with the fair flower delice.

soote] sweet   yeven] given   behight] called   wast] waist   sops-in-wine]
pinks   paramours] lovers   paunce] pansy   chevisaunce] an unidentified flower,
perhaps the wallflower

Now rise up, Elisa, deckèd as thou art
    In royal array;
And now ye dainty damsels may depart,
    Each one her way.
I fear I have troubled your troupes too long:
Let Dame Elisa thank you for her song;
    And if you come hether
    When damsons I gether,
I will part them all you among.

Perigot and Willie's Roundelay

It fell upon a holy eve,
    Hey, ho, holiday!
When holy fathers wont to shrive;
    Now 'ginneth this roundelay.
Sitting upon a hill so high,
    Hey, ho, the high hill!
The while my flock did feed thereby;
    The while the shepherd self did spill;
I saw the bouncing bellibone,
    Hey, ho, bonibell!
Tripping over the dale alone,
    She can trip it very well!
Well deckèd in a frock of gray,
    Hey, ho, gray is greete!
And in a kirtle of green saye,
    The green is for maidens meet.
A chapelet on her head she wore,
    Hey, ho, chapèlet!
Of sweet violets therein was store,
    She sweeter than the violet.
My sheep did leave their wonted food,
    Hey, ho, silly sheep!
And gazed on her as they were wood,
    Wood as he that did them keep!

Title] They sing in turn.   spill] come to grief   bellibone, bonibell] beautiful and good   is greete] is for weeping   saye] a fine cloth   wood] mad

As the bonilass passed by,
  Hey, ho, bonilass!
She roved at me with glancing eye,
  As clear as the crystal glass:
All as the sunny beam so bright,
  Hey, ho, the sunbeam!
Glanceth from Phoebus' face forthright,
  So love into thy heart did stream:
Or as the thunder cleaves the clouds,
  Hey, ho, the thunder!
Wherein the lightsome levin shrouds,
  So cleaves thy soul asunder:
Or as Dame Cynthia's silver ray,
  Hey, ho, the moonlight!
Upon the glittering wave doth play,
  Such play is a piteous plight.
The glance into my heart did glide;
  Hey, ho, the glider!
Therewith my soul was sharply gryde,
  Such wounds soon waxen wider.
Hasting to wrench the arrow out,
  Hey, ho, Perigot!
I left the head in my heart-root,
  It was a desperate shot.
There it rankleth, aye more and more,
  Hey, ho, the arrow!
Ne can I find salve for my sore:
  Love is a cureless sorrow.
And though my bale with death I bought,
  Hey, ho, heavy cheer!
Yet should thilk lass not from my thought,
  So you may buy gold too dear.
But whether in painful love I pine,
  Hey, ho, pinching pain!
Or thrive in wealth, she shall be mine,
  But if thou can her obtain.

roved] took a practice shot   levin] lightning   gryde] pierced   desperate] dangerous   thilk] this

And if for graceless grief I die,
Hey, ho, graceless grief!
Witness she slew me with her eye,
Let thy folly be the prief.
And you that saw it, simple sheep,
Hey, ho, the fair flock!
For prief thereof, my death shall weep,
And moan with many a mock.
So learned I love on a holy eve,
Hey, ho, holiday!
That ever since my heart did grieve,
Now endeth our roundelay.

Prothalamion

Calm was the day, and through the trembling air
Sweet-breathing Zephyrus did softly play
A gentle spirit, that lightly did delay
Hot Titan's beams, which then did glister fair;
When I (whom sullen care,
Through discontent of my long fruitless stay
In princes' court, and expectation vain
Of idle hopes, which still do fly away
Like empty shadows, did afflict my brain)
Walked forth to ease my pain
Along the shore of silver-streaming Thames;
Whose rutty bank, the which his river hems,
Was painted all with variable flowers,
And all the meads adorned with dainty gems,
Fit to deck maidens' bowers,
And crown their paramours
Against the bridal day, which is not long:
   Sweet Thames, run softly, till I end my song.

There, in a meadow, by the river's side,
A flock of nymphs I chancèd to espy,
All lovely daughters of the flood thereby,
With goodly greenish locks, all loose untied

graceless grief] grief from lack of her favor   prief] proof   glister] glitter

As each had been a bride;
And each one had a little wicker basket
Made of fine twigs, entrailèd curiously,
In which they gathered flowers to fill their flasket,
And with fine fingers cropped full feateously
The tender stalks on high.
Of every sort which in that meadow grew
They gathered some; the violet, pallid blue,
The little daisy, that at evening closes,
The virgin lily, and the primrose true,
With store of vermeil roses,
To deck their bridegrooms' posies
Against the bridal day, which was not long:
  Sweet Thames, run softly, till I end my song.

With that I saw two swans of goodly hue
Come softly swimming down along the lee;
Two fairer birds I yet did never see;
The snow which doth the top of Pindus strew
Did never whiter shew,
Nor Jove himself, when he a swan would be
For love of Leda, whiter did appear;
Yet Leda was, they say, as white as he,
Yet not so white as these, nor nothing near;
So purely white they were,
That even the gentle stream the which them bare
Seemed foul to them, and bade his billows spare
To wet their silken feathers, lest they might
Soil their fair plumes with water not so fair,
And mar their beauties bright,
That shone as heaven's light,
Against their bridal day, which was not long:
  Sweet Thames, run softly, till I end my song.

Eftsoons the nymphs, which now had flowers their fill,
Ran all in haste to see that silver brood,
As they came floating on the crystal flood;

entrailèd] interwoven   flasket] a long, shallow basket   feateously] dexterously
lee] river   to them] compared to them   Eftsoons] Forthwith

Whom when they saw, they stood amazèd still,
Their wond'ring eyes to fill;
Them seemed they never saw a sight so fair,
Of fowls so lovely that they sure did deem
Them heavenly born, or to be that same pair
Which through the sky draw Venus' silver team;
For sure they did not seem
To be begot of any earthly seed,
But rather angels, or of angels' breed;
Yet were they bred of summer's heat, they say,
In sweetest season, when each flower and weed
The earth did fresh array;
So fresh they seemed as day,
Even as their bridal day, which was not long:
   Sweet Thames, run softly, till I end my song.

Then forth they all out of their baskets drew
Great store of flowers, the honor of the field,
That to the sense did fragrant odors yield,
All which upon those goodly birds they threw,
And all the waves did strew,
That like old Peneus' waters they did seem,
When down along by pleasant Tempe's shore,
Scatt'red with flowers, through Thessaly they stream,
That they appear, through lilies' plenteous store,
Like a bride's chamber-floor.
Two of those nymphs meanwhile two garlands bound
Of freshest flowers which in that mead they found,
The which presenting all in trim array,
Their snowy foreheads therewithal they crowned;
Whilst one did sing this lay
Prepared against that day,
Against their bridal day, which was not long:
   Sweet Thames, run softly, till I end my song.

'Ye gentle birds, the world's fair ornament,
And heaven's glory, whom this happy hour

Them seemed] It seemed to them   summer's heat] a play on Somerset, the sur-
name of the ladies whose marriage the poem celebrates

Doth lead unto your lovers' blissful bower,
Joy may you have, and gentle heart's content
Of your love's couplement;
And let fair Venus, that is queen of love,
With her heart-quelling son upon you smile,
Whose smile, they say, hath virtue to remove
All love's dislike, and friendship's faulty guile
For ever to assoil.
Let endless peace your steadfast hearts accord,
And blessèd plenty wait upon your board;
And let your bed with pleasures chaste abound,
That fruitful issue may to you afford
Which may your foes confound,
And make your joys redound
Upon your bridal day, which is not long:
   Sweet Thames, run softly, till I end my song.'

So ended she; and all the rest around
To her redoubled that her undersong,
Which said, their bridal day should not be long:
And gentle Echo from the neighbor ground
Their accents did resound.
So forth those joyous birds did pass along
Adown the lee, that to them murmured low,
As he would speak, but that he lacked a tongue,
Yet did by signs his glad affection show,
Making his stream run slow.
And all the fowl which in his flood did dwell
'Gan flock about these twain that did excel
The rest so far as Cynthia doth shend
The lesser stars. So they, enrangèd well,
Did on those two attend,
And their best service lend
Against their wedding-day, which was not long:
   Sweet Thames, run softly, till I end my song.

At length they all to merry London came,
To merry London, my most kindly nurse,

couplement] marriage   assoil] dispel   shend] shame by superiority

That to me gave this life's first native source,
Though from another place I take my name,
An house of ancient fame:
There when they came, whereas those bricky towers,
The which on Thames' broad agèd back do ride,
Where now the studious lawyers have their bowers
There whilom wont the Templar Knights to bide,
Till they decayed through pride:
Next whereunto there stands a stately place,
Where oft I gainèd gifts and goodly grace
Of that great lord which therein wont to dwell,
Whose want too well now feels my friendless case:
But ah! here fits not well
Old woes, but joys, to tell
Against the bridal day, which is not long:
   Sweet Thames, run softly, till I end my song.

Yet therein now doth lodge a noble peer,
Great England's glory, and the world's wide wonder,
Whose dreadful name late through all Spain did thunder,
And Hercules' two pillars standing near
Did make to quake and fear:
Fair branch of honor, flower of chivalry!
That fillest England with thy triumphs' fame,
Joy have thou of thy noble victory,
And endless happiness of thine own name
That promiseth the same;
That through thy prowess and victorious arms,
Thy country may be freed from foreign harms,
And great Eliza's glorious name may ring
Through all the world, filled with thy wide alarms,
Which some brave Muse may sing
To ages following
Upon the bridal day, which is not long:
   Sweet Thames, run softly, till I end my song.

From those high towers, this noble lord issuing,
Like radiant Hesper when his golden hair

whereas] where   There whilom] Where once   feels . . . case] case . . . feels

In th' ocean billows he hath bathèd fair,
Descended to the river's open viewing,
With a great train ensuing.
Above the rest were goodly to be seen
Two gentle knights of lovely face and feature,
Beseeming well the bower of any queen,
With gifts of wit and ornaments of nature
Fit for so goodly stature,
That like the twins of Jove they seemed in sight,
Which deck the baldrick of the heavens bright.
They two, forth pacing to the river's side,
Received those two fair brides, their loves' delight;
Which, at th' appointed tide,
Each one did make his bride,
Against their bridal day, which is not long:
    Sweet Thames, run softly, till I end my song.

SIR PHILIP SIDNEY (1554–1586)

Rural Poesy

O words, which fall like summer dew on me!
  O breath, more sweet than is the growing bean!
O tongue, in which all honeyed liquors be!
  O voice, that doth the thrush in shrillness stain!—
    Do you say still, this is her promise due,
    That she is mine, as I to her am true.

Gay hair, more gay than straw when harvest lies!
  Lips, red and plump as cherry's ruddy side!
Eyes fair and great, like fair great ox's eyes!
  O breast, in which two white sheep swell in pride!—
    Join you with me to seal this promise due,
    That she be mine, as I to her am true.

But thou white skin, as white as curds well pressed,
  So smooth as, sleekstone like, it smooths each part!

ensuing] following   feature] form   tide] time   shrillness] high pitch   stain]
eclipse   So smooth as] So smooth that   sleekstone] a polishing stone

And thou dear flesh, as soft as wool new dressed,
And yet as hard as brawn made hard by art!—
    First four but say, next four their saying seal;
    But you must pay the gage of promised weal.

THOMAS LODGE (*c.* 1557–1625)

The earth, late choked with showers

The earth, late choked with showers,
    Is now arrayed in green,
Her bosom springs with flowers,
    The air dissolves her teen;
        The heavens laugh at her glory,
        Yet bide I sad and sorry.

The woods are decked with leaves,
    And trees are clothèd gay,
And Flora, crowned with sheaves,
    With oaken boughs doth play;
        Where I am clad in black,
        The token of my wrack.

The birds upon the trees
    Do sing with pleasant voices,
And chant in their degrees
    Their loves and lucky choices;
        When I, whilst they are singing,
        With sighs mine arms am wringing.

The thrushes seek the shade,
    And I my fatal grave;
Their flight to heaven is made,
    My walk on earth I have;
        They free, I thrall; they jolly,
        I sad and pensive wholly.

First . . . seal] a proverb   teen] grief   Where] Whereas

Rosalind's Madrigal

Love in my bosom like a bee,
    Doth suck his sweet;
Now with his wings he plays with me,
    Now with his feet.
      Within mine eyes he makes his nest,
      His bed amidst my tender breast,
      My kisses are his daily feast;
      And yet he robs me of my rest:
        Ah, wanton, will ye?

And if I sleep, then percheth he
    With pretty flight,
And makes his pillow of my knee
    The livelong night.
      Strike I my lute, he tunes the string,
      He music plays if so I sing,
      He lends me every lovely thing;
      Yet cruel he my heart doth sting:
        Whist, wanton, still ye!

Else I with roses every day
    Will whip you hence,
And bind you, when you long to play,
    For your offence;
      I'll shut mine eyes to keep you in,
      I'll make you fast it for your sin,
      I'll count your power not worth a pin:
      Alas, what hereby shall I win,
        If he gainsay me?

What if I beat the wanton boy
    With many a rod?
He will repay me with annoy,
    Because a god.
      Then sit thou safely on my knee,
      And let thy bower my bosom be,

if so] if

Lurk in mine eyes, I like of thee;
O Cupid, so thou pity me,
    Spare not, but play thee.

Rosalind's Description

Like to the clear in highest sphere
    Where all imperial glory shines,
Of selfsame color is her hair
    Whether unfolded or in twines:
        Heigh ho, fair Rosaline!
Her eyes are sapphires set in snow,
    Refining heaven by every wink;
The gods do fear whenas they glow,
    And I do tremble when I think:
        Heigh ho, would she were mine!

Her cheeks are like the blushing cloud
    That beautifies Aurora's face,
Or like the silver crimson shroud
    That Phœbus' smiling looks doth grace:
        Heigh ho, fair Rosaline!
Her lips are like two budded roses
    Whom ranks of lilies neighbor nigh,
Within which bounds she balm incloses
    Apt to entice a deity:
        Heigh ho, would she were mine!

Her neck like to a stately tower
    Where love himself imprisoned lies,
To watch for glances every hour
    From her divine and sacred eyes:
        Heigh ho, fair Rosaline!
Her paps are centres of delight,
    Her breasts are orbs of heavenly frame,
Where Nature molds the dew of light
    To feed perfection with the same:
        Heigh ho, would she were mine!

like of] like   clear] clearness

With orient pearl, with ruby red,
    With marble white, with sapphire blue
Her body every way is fed,
    Yet soft in touch and sweet in view:
        Heigh ho, fair Rosaline!
Nature herself her shape admires;
    The gods are wounded in her sight;
And Love forsakes his heavenly fires
    And at her eyes his brand doth light:
        Heigh ho, would she were mine!

Then muse not, nymphs, though I bemoan
    The absence of fair Rosaline,
Since for her fair there is fairer none,
    Nor for her virtues so divine:
        Heigh ho, fair Rosaline;
Heigh ho, my heart! would God that she were mine!

Phœbe's Sonnet

'Downe-a-downe, downe-a-downe!'
    Thus Phyllis sung
By fancy once distressèd:
'Whoso by foolish love are stung,
    Are worthily oppressèd.
And so sing I, and so sing I,
    With a downe, with a downe,
        With a downe, with a downe,
        A downe, a-downe.'

When Love was first begot
    And by the mover's will
Did fall to human lot
    His solace to fulfill,
Devoid of all deceit,
    A chaste and holy fire
Did quicken man's conceit,
    And woman's breast inspire.

in her sight] by sight of her   her fair] her beauty   conceit] fancy

The gods that saw the good
That mortals did approve,
With kind and holy mood,
Began to talk of Love.
Downe-a-downe, &c.

But during this accord,
A wonder strange to hear;
Whilst Love in deed and word
Most faithful did appear,
False Semblance came in place,
By Jealousy attended,
And with a double face
Both Love and Fancy blended.
Which makes the gods forsake,
And men from fancy fly,
And maidens scorn a make,
Forsooth and so will I.
Downe-a-downe, &c.

BARTHOLOMEW YOUNG (d. 1598)

The Nymph Selvagia her Song

Shepherd, who can pass such wrong,
And a life in woes so deep,
Which to live is too too long,
As it is too short to weep?

Grievous sighs in vain I waste,
Leesing my affiance, and
I perceive my hope at last
With a candle in the hand.

What time then to hope among
Bitter hopes that ever sleep,
When this life is too too long,
As it is too short to weep?

make] mate   Leesing] Losing

This grief, which I feel so rife,
  Wretch, I do deserve as hire;
Since I came to put my life
  In the hands of my desire.

Then cease not my plaints so strong:
  For, though life her course doth keep,
It is not to live so long,
  As it is too short to weep.

ANTHONY MUNDAY (1553–1603)

Fedele's Song

I serve a mistress whiter than the snow,
  Straighter than cedar, brighter than the glass,
Finer in trip and swifter than the roe,
  More pleasant than the field of flowering grass;
More gladsome to my withering joys that fade
Than winter's sun or summer's cooling shade.

Sweeter than swelling grape of ripest wine,
  Softer than feathers of the fairest swan,
Smoother than jet, more stately than the pine,
  Fresher than poplar, smaller than my span,
Clearer than beauty's fiery-pointed beam
Or icy crust of crystal's frozen stream.

Yet is she curster than the bear by kind,
  And harder-hearted than the agèd oak,
More glib than oil, more fickle than the wind,
  Stiffer than steel, no sooner bent but broke.
Lo, thus my service is a lasting sore;
Yet will I serve, although I die therefore.

To Colin Clout

Beauty sat bathing by a spring,
  Where fairest shades did hide her;

curster] more cross-grained   glib] slippery

The winds blew calm, the birds did sing,
  The cool streams ran beside her.
My wanton thoughts enticed mine eye
  To see what was forbidden,
But better memory said, fie!
  So vain desire was chidden.
    Hey, nonny, nonny, &c.

Into a slumber then I fell,
  When fond imagination
Seemèd to see, but could not tell
  Her feature or her fashion.
But even as babes in dreams do smile,
  And sometime fall a-weeping,
So I awaked, as wise this while,
  As when I fell a-sleeping.
    Hey, nonny, nonny, &c.

FULKE GREVILLE, LORD BROOKE (1554–1628)

Of his Cynthia

Away with these self-loving lads,
Whom Cupid's arrow never glads.
Away, poor souls that sigh and weep,
In love of them that lie and sleep;
  For Cupid is a meadow god,
  And forceth none to kiss the rod.

God Cupid's shaft, like destiny,
Doth either good or ill decree.
Desert is born out of his bow,
Reward upon his feet doth go.
  What fools are they that have not known
  That Love likes no laws but his own?

My songs they be of Cynthia's praise,
I wear her rings on holy-days,
On every tree I write her name,

And every day I read the same.
   Where honor Cupid's rival is,
   There miracles are seen of his.

If Cynthia crave her ring of me,
I blot her name out of the tree.
If doubt do darken things held dear,
Then well fare nothing once a year!
   For many run, but one must win;
   Fools only hedge the cuckoo in.

The worth that worthiness should move
Is love, which is the due of love.
And love as well the shepherd can
As can the mighty nobleman.
   Sweet nymph, 'tis true you worthy be,
   Yet without love, naught worth to me.

NICHOLAS BRETON (1545?–1626?)

Olden Love-Making

In time of yore when shepherds dwelt
   Upon the mountain rocks,
And simple people never felt
   The pain of lovers' mocks;
But little birds would carry tales
   'Twixt Susan and her sweeting,
And all the dainty nightingales
   Did sing at lovers' meeting:
Then might you see what looks did pass
   Where shepherds did assemble,
And where the life of true love was
   When hearts could not dissemble.

Then 'yea' and 'nay' was thought an oath
   That was not to be doubted,
And when it came to 'faith' and 'troth'
   We were not to be flouted.

Then did they talk of curds and cream,
  Of butter, cheese, and milk,
There was no speech of sunny beam
  Nor of the golden silk.
Then for a gift a row of pins,
  A purse, a pair of knives,
Was all the way that love begins;
  And so the shepherd wives.

But now we have so much ado,
  And are so sore aggrievèd,
That when we go about to woo
  We cannot be believèd;
Such choice of jewels, rings, and chains,
  That may but favor move,
And such intolerable pains
  Ere one can hit on love;
That if I still shall bide this life
  'Twixt love and deadly hate,
I will go learn the country life
  Or leave the lover's state.

Phyllida and Corydon

In the merry month of May,
In a morn by break of day,
Forth I walked by the wood side,
Whenas May was in his pride.
There I spièd all alone,
Phyllida and Corydon.
Much ado there was, God wot!
He would love and she would not.
She said, never man was true;
He said, none was false to you.
He said, he had loved her long;
She said, love should have no wrong.
Corydon would kiss her then;
She said, maids must kiss no men,

Till they did for good and all;
Then she made the shepherd call
All the heavens to witness truth:
Never loved a truer youth.
Thus with many a pretty oath,
Yea and nay, and faith and troth,
Such as silly shepherds use
When they will not love abuse,
Love, which had been long deluded,
Was with kisses sweet concluded;
And Phyllida, with garlands gay,
Was made the Lady of the May.

Corydon's Supplication to Phyllis

Sweet Phyllis, if a silly swain
    May sue to thee for grace,
See not thy loving shepherd slain
    With looking on thy face;

But think what power thou hast got
    Upon my flock and me:
Thou seest they now regard me not,
    But all do follow thee.

And if I have so far presumed
    With prying in thine eyes,
Yet let not comfort be consumed
    That in thy pity lies;

But as thou art that Phyllis fair,
    That fortune favor gives,
So let not love die in despair
    That in thy favor lives.

The deer do browse upon the briar,
    The birds do pick the cherries;
And will not Beauty grant Desire
    One handful of her berries?

silly] simple   abuse] deceive   favor gives] makes handsome

If so it be that thou hast sworn
That none shall look on thee,
Yet let me know thou dost not scorn
To cast a look on me.

But if thy beauty make thee proud,
Think then what is ordained;
The heavens have never yet allowed
That love should be disdained.

Then lest the fates that favor love
Should curse thee for unkind,
Let me report for thy behove
The honor of thy mind;

Let Corydon with full consent
Set down what he hath seen,
That Phyllida with Love's content
Is sworn the shepherds' queen.

From *The Passionate Shepherd*

Pastoral III

Who can live in heart so glad
As the merry country lad?
Who upon a fair green balk
May at pleasure sit and walk,
And amid the azure skies
See the morning sun arise,
While he hears in every spring
How the birds do chirp and sing;
Or before the hounds in cry
See the hare go stealing by;
Or along the shallow brook,
Angling with a baited hook,
See the fishes leap and play

Pastoral III] The opening lines. It continues in a more conventional strain.   balk]
strip of unplowed ground   spring] tree, grove

In a blessèd sunny day;
Or to hear the partridge call
Till she have her covey all;
Or to see the subtle fox
How the villain plies the box;
After feeding on his prey,
How he closely sneaks away,
Through the hedge and down the furrow
Till he gets into his burrow;
Then the bee to gather honey,
And the little black-haired coney,
On a bank for sunny place,
With her forefeet wash her face,—
Are not these, with thousands moe
Than the courts of kings do know,
The true pleasing spirit's sights
That may breed true love's delights?

ROBERT GREENE (1558–1592)

Sephestia's Song to Her Child

Weep not, my wanton, smile upon my knee,
When thou art old there's grief enough for thee.
    Mother's wag, pretty boy,
    Father's sorrow, father's joy;
    When thy father first did see
    Such a boy by him and me,
    He was glad, I was woe,
    Fortune changèd made him so,
    When he left his pretty boy,
    Last his sorrow, first his joy.

Weep not, my wanton, smile upon my knee,
When thou art old there's grief enough for thee.

plies the box] plays a trick; perhaps, runs along the box (hedge), or veers (boxing
the compass). The figure from gaming given in the *New English Dictionary* is distasteful in a pastoral; some kind of 'dodge' is implied.   closely] covertly   coney]
rabbit   moe] more

Streaming tears that never stint,
Like pearl drops from a flint,
Fell by course from his eyes,
That one another's place supplies;
Thus he grieved in every part,
Tears of blood fell from his heart,
When he left his pretty boy,
Father's sorrow, father's joy.

Weep not, my wanton, smile upon my knee,
When thou art old there's grief enough for thee.
The wanton smiled, father wept,
Mother cried, baby leapt;
More he crowed, more we cried,
Nature could not sorrow hide:
He must go, he must kiss
Child and mother, baby bliss,
For he left his pretty boy,
Father's sorrow, father's joy.
Weep not, my wanton, smile upon my knee,
When thou art old there's grief enough for thee.

Doron's Description of Samela

Like to Diana in her summer weed,
  Girt with a crimson robe of brightest dye,
    Goes fair Samela;
Whiter than be the flocks that straggling feed,
  When washed by Arethusa Fount they lie,
    Is fair Samela;

As fair Aurora in her morning-gray,
  Decked with the ruddy glister of her love,
    Is fair Samela:
Like lovely Thetis on a calmèd day,
  Whenas her brightness Neptune's fancy move,
    Shines fair Samela;

by course] in a stream   one . . . supplies] *I.e.*, the tears fell unceasingly   bliss]
bless

Her tresses gold, her eyes like glassy streams,
  Her teeth are pearl, the breasts are ivory
      Of fair Samela;
Her cheeks like rose and lily yield forth gleams,
  Her brow's bright arches framed of ebony;
      Thus fair Samela

Passeth fair Venus in her bravest hue,
  And Juno in the show of majesty,
      For she's Samela;
Pallas in wit, all three, if you well view,
  For beauty, wit, and matchless dignity
      Yield to Samela.

Doron's Jig

Through the shrubs as I can crack
  For my lambs' little ones,
  'Mongst many pretty ones—
Nymphs, I mean,—whose hair was black
    As the crow,
    Like the snow
Her face and brows shined, I ween;
  I saw a little one,
  A bonny pretty one,
As bright, buxom, and as sheen
    As was she
    On her knee
That lulled the god whose arrows warms
  Such merry little ones,
  Such fair-faced pretty ones,
As dally in Love's chiefest harms.
    Such was mine,
    Whose gray eyne
Made me love. I 'gan to woo
  This sweet little one,
  This bonny pretty one;

crack] break   sheen] beautiful   eyne] eyes

I wooed hard, a day or two,
　　Till she bade,
　　'Be not sad,
Woo no more, I am thine own,
　　Thy dearest little one,
　　Thy truest pretty one.'
Thus was faith and firm love shown
　　As behoves
　　Shepherds' loves.

The Shepherd's Wife's Song

Ah, what is love? It is a pretty thing,
As sweet unto a shepherd as a king,
　　　And sweeter too:
For kings have cares that wait upon a crown,
And cares can make the sweetest love to frown.
　　　Ah then, ah then,
If country loves such sweet desires do gain,
What lady would not love a shepherd swain?

His flocks are folded, he comes home at night,
As merry as a king in his delight,
　　　And merrier too:
For kings bethink them what the state require,
Where shepherds careless carol by the fire.
　　　Ah then, ah then,
If country loves such sweet desires do gain,
What lady would not love a shepherd swain?

He kisseth first, then sits as blithe to eat
His cream and curds as doth the king his meat,
　　　And blither too:
For kings have often fears when they do sup,
Where shepherds dread no poison in their cup.
　　　Ah then, ah then,
If country loves such sweet desires do gain,
What lady would not love a shepherd swain?

To bed he goes, as wanton then, I ween,
As is a king in dalliance with a queen,—
     More wanton too:
For kings have many griefs, affects to move,
Where shepherds have no greater grief than love.
     Ah then, ah then,
If country loves such sweet desires do gain,
What lady would not love a shepherd swain?

Upon his couch of straw he sleeps as sound,
As doth the king upon his beds of down,—
     More sounder too:
For cares cause kings full oft their sleep to spill,
Where weary shepherds lie and snort their fill.
     Ah then, ah then,
If country loves such sweet desires do gain,
What lady would not love a shepherd swain?

Thus with his wife he spends the year, as blithe
As doth the king at every tide or sithe,
     And blither too:
For kings have wars and broils to take in hand,
Where shepherds laugh and love upon the land.
     Ah then, ah then,
If country loves such sweet desires do gain,
What lady would not love a shepherd swain?

Maesia's Song

Sweet are the thoughts that savor of content,
  The quiet mind is richer than a crown;
Sweet are the nights in careless slumber spent,
  The poor estate scorns fortune's angry frown:
Such sweet content, such minds, such sleep, such bliss,
Beggars enjoy, when princes oft do miss.

The homely house that harbors quiet rest,
  The cottage that affords no pride nor care,

affects] feelings   spill] lose   snort] sleep heavily   sithe] occasion

The mean that 'grees with country music best,
  The sweet consort of mirth and modest fare,
Obscurèd life sets down a type of bliss:
A mind content both crown and kingdom is.

Philomela's Ode that she Sung in her Arbor

Sitting by a river's side
Where a silent stream did glide,
Muse I did of many things
That the mind in quiet brings.
I 'gan think how some men deem
Gold their god; and some esteem
Honor is the chief content
That to man in life is lent;
And some others do contend
Quiet none like to a friend;
Others hold there is no wealth
Comparèd to a perfect health;
Some man's mind in quiet stands
When he is lord of many lands:
But I did sigh, and said all this
Was but a shade of perfect bliss;
And in my thoughts I did approve
Naught so sweet as is true love.
Love 'twixt lovers passeth these,
When mouth kisseth and heart 'grees,
With folded arms and lips meeting,
Each soul another sweetly greeting;
For by the breath the soul fleeteth
And soul with soul in kissing meeteth.
If love be so sweet a thing,
That such happy bliss doth bring,
Happy is love's sugared thrall;
But unhappy maidens all,
Who esteem your virgin blisses

mean] the middle part, here metaphorical   'gan] began; perhaps simply did
folded] interlocked

Sweeter than a wife's sweet kisses.
No such quiet to the mind
As true love with kisses kind;
But if a kiss prove unchaste,
Then is true love quite disgraced.
Though love be sweet, learn this of me:
No love sweet but honesty.

SIR EDWARD DYER (d. 1607)

Alas, my heart

Alas, my heart, mine eye hath wrongèd thee:
　Presumptuous eye, to gaze on Phyllis' face,
Whose heavenly eye no mortal man may see
　But he must die, or purchase Phyllis' grace.
　　Poor Corydon! the nymph, whose eye doth move thee,
　　Doth love to draw, but is not drawn to love thee.

Her beauty, nature's pride and shepherds' praise;
　Her eye, the heavenly planet of my life;
Her matchless wit and grace her fame displays,
　As if that Jove had made her for his wife:
　　Only her eyes shoot fiery darts to kill,
　　Yet is her heart as cold as Caucase hill.

My wings too weak to fly against the sun,
　Mine eyes unable to sustain her light,
My heart doth yield that I am quite undone—
　Thus hath fair Phyllis slain me with her sight:
　　My bud is blasted, withered is my leaf,
　　And all my corn is rotted in the sheaf.

Phyllis, the golden fetter of my mind!
　My fancy's idol and my vital power!
Goddess of nymphs and honor of thy kind!
　This age's phoenix, beauty's richest bower!—
　　Poor Corydon for love of thee must die,
　　Thy beauty's thrall, and conquest of thine eye.

Leave, Corydon, to plough the barren field,
Thy buds of hope are blasted with disgrace;
For Phyllis' looks no hearty love do yield,
Nor can she love, for all her lovely face.
Die, Corydon! the spoil of Phyllis' eye;
She cannot love, and therefore thou must die!

HENRY CHETTLE (*c.* 1560–*c.* 1607)

Damelus' Song to His Diaphenia

Diaphenia, like the daffadowndilly,
White as the sun, fair as the lily,
   Heigh ho, how I do love thee!
I do love thee as my lambs
Are belovèd of their dams;
   How blest were I if thou wouldst prove me!

Diaphenia, like the spreading roses,
That in thy sweets all sweets encloses,
   Fair sweet, how I do love thee!
I do love thee as each flower
Loves the sun's life-giving power;
   For dead, thy breath to life might move me.

Diaphenia, like to all things blessèd,
When all thy praises are expressèd,
   Dear joy, how I do love thee!
As the birds do love the spring,
Or the bees their careful king:
   Then in requite, sweet virgin, love me.

RICHARD BARNFIELD (1574–1627)

The Unknown Shepherd's Complaint

My flocks feed not, my ewes breed not,
My rams speed not, all is amiss;

Henry Chettle] This poem is usually credited to Henry Constable. See E. K.
Chambers, *Oxford Book of Sixteenth Century Verse*, p. 884, note.   requite] requital

Love is denying, faith is defying,
Heart's renying, causer of this.
All my merry jigs are quite forgot,
All my lady's love is lost, God wot;
Where her faith was firmly fixed in love,
There a nay is placed without remove.
  One silly cross wrought all my loss,
  O frowning Fortune, cursèd fickle dame,
  For now I see inconstancy
  More in women than in men remain.

In black mourn I, all fears scorn I,
Love hath forlorn me, living in thrall;
Heart is bleeding, all help needing,
O, cruel speeding, fraughted with gall.
My shepherd's pipe can sound no deal,
My wether's bell rings doleful knell.
My curtail dog that wont to have played
Plays not at all, but seems afraid;
  With sighs so deep, procures to weep
  In howling wise to see my doleful plight:
  How sighs resound through heartless ground
  Like a thousand vanquished men in bloody fight.

Clear wells spring not, sweet birds sing not,
Green plants bring not forth their dye;
Herds stand weeping, flocks all sleeping,
Nymphs back peeping fearfully.
All our pleasure known to us poor swains,
All our merry meeting on the plains,
All our evening sports from us are fled,
All our love is lost, for Love is dead.
  Farewell, sweet Love, thy like ne'er was
  For sweet content, the cause of all my moan.
  Poor Corydon must live alone,—
  Other help for him I see that there is none.

renying] apostasy   curtail] dock-tailed   procures] manages

An Ode

As it fell upon a day
In the merry month of May,
Sitting in a pleasant shade,
Which a grove of myrtles made,
Beasts did leap and birds did sing,
Trees did grow and plants did spring;
Every thing did banish moan,
Save the nightingale alone:
She, poor bird, as all forlorn,
Lean'd her breast up-till a thorn.
And there sung the doleful'st ditty
That to hear it was great pity.
'Fie, fie, fie!' now would she cry;
'Tereu, tereu!' by and by;
That to hear her so complain
Scarce I could from tears refrain,
For her griefs, so lively shown,
Made me think upon mine own.
Ah! thought I, thou mourn'st in vain,
None takes pity on thy pain:
Senseless trees, they cannot hear thee,
Ruthless bears, they will not cheer thee.
King Pandion, he is dead,
All thy friends are lapped in lead,
All thy fellow birds do sing
Careless of thy sorrowing.
Whilst as fickle fortune smiled,
Thou and I were both beguiled.
Every one that flatters thee
Is no friend in misery;
Words are easy, like the wind,
Faithful friends are hard to find.
Every man will be thy friend
Whilst thou hast wherewith to spend;
But if store of crowns be scant
No man will supply thy want.

up-till] against

If that one be prodigal,
Bountiful they will him call.
And with such-like flattering
Pity but he were a king.
If he be addict to vice
Quickly him they will entice;
If to women he be bent
They have at commandèment.
But if fortune once do frown,
Then farewell his great renown;
They that fawned on him before
Use his company no more.
He that is thy friend indeed,
He will help thee in thy need:
If thou sorrow, he will weep;
If thou wake, he cannot sleep.
Thus of every grief in heart
He with thee doth bear a part.
These are certain signs to know
Faithful friend from flatt'ring foe.

ROBERT DEVEREUX, EARL OF ESSEX (1566–1601)

A Passion

Happy were he could finish forth his fate
    In some unhaunted desert, most obscure
From all society, from love and hate
    Of worldly folk, there might he sleep secure;
There wake again, and give God ever praise,
    Content with hips and haws and brambleberry,
In contemplation passing still his days,
    And change of holy thoughts to make him merry.
That when he dies, his tomb might be a bush,
Where harmless robin dwells with gentle thrush.

They have] *I.e.*, They have women.   Use] Frequent   forth] out   hips and
haws] berries of the wild rose and hawthorn   robin] perhaps a play on Robin for
Robert, the poet's name

CHRISTOPHER MARLOWE (1564–1593)

The Passionate Shepherd to His Love

Come live with me, and be my love,
And we will all the pleasures prove,
That hills and valleys, dales and fields,
And all the craggy mountains yields.

And we will sit upon the rocks,
Seeing the shepherds feed their flocks
By shallow rivers, to whose falls
Melodious birds sing madrigals.

And I will make thee beds of roses,
And a thousand fragrant posies,
A cap of flowers and a kirtle
Embroidered all with leaves of myrtle;

A gown made of the finest wool
Which from our pretty lambs we pull;
Fair-linèd slippers for the cold,
With buckles of the purest gold;

A belt of straw and ivy buds,
With coral clasps and amber studs:
An if these pictures may thee move,
Come live with me and be my love.

The shepherd swains shall dance and sing
For thy delight each May morning:
If these delights thy mind may move,
Then live with me and be my love.

SIR WALTER RALEIGH (c. 1552–1618)

The Nymph's Reply

If all the world and love were young,
And truth in every shepherd's tongue,
These pretty pleasures might me move
To live with thee and be thy love.

An if] If

Time drives the flocks from field to fold,
When rivers rage and rocks grow cold;
And Philomel becometh dumb;
The rest complains of cares to come.

The flowers do fade, and wanton fields
To wayward winter reckoning yields;
A honey tongue, a heart of gall,
Is fancy's spring, but sorrow's fall.

Thy gowns, thy shoes, thy beds of roses,
Thy cap, thy kirtle, and thy posies
Soon break, soon wither, soon forgotten,
In folly ripe, in reason rotten.

Thy belt of straw and ivy buds,
Thy coral clasps and amber studs,
All these in me no means can move
To come to thee and be thy love.

But could youth last, and love still breed,
Had joys no date, nor age no need,
Then these delights my mind might move
To live with thee and be thy love.

As you came from the holy land

'As you came from the holy land
  Of Walsinghame,
Met you not with my true love
  By the way as you came?'

'How shall I know your true love,
  That have met many one,
As I went to the holy land,
  That have come, that have gone?'

'She is neither white nor brown,
  But as the heavens fair;
There is none hath a form so divine,
  In the earth or the air.'

'Such an one did I meet, good sir,
   Such an angelic face,
Who like a queen, like a nymph did appear
   By her gait, by her grace.'

'She hath left me here all alone,
   All alone, as unknown,
Who sometimes did me lead with herself,
   And me loved as her own.'

'What's the cause that she leaves you alone,
   And a new way doth take,
Who loved you once as her own,
   And her joy did you make?'

'I have loved her all my youth,
   But now, old as you see,
Love likes not the falling fruit,
   From the witherèd tree.

'Know that love is a careless child,
   And forgets promise past;
He is blind, he is deaf, when he list,
   And in faith never fast.

'His desire is a dureless content
   And a trustless joy;
He is won with a world of despair,
   And is lost with a toy.

'Of women-kind such indeed is the love,
   Or the word love, abused,
Under which many childish desires
   And conceits are excused.

'But true love is a durable fire
   In the mind ever burning
Never sick, never old, never dead,
   From itself never turning.'

dureless] transient

A Description of Love

Now what is love? I pray thee tell.
It is that fountain and that well
Where pleasure and repentance dwell;
It is perhaps that saucing bell
That tolls all in to heaven or hell:
And this is love, as I hear tell.

Yet what is love? I pray thee say.
It is a work on holy-day;
It is December matched with May;
When lusty bloods, in fresh array,
Hear ten months after of the play:
And this is love, as I hear say.

Yet what is love? I pray thee sain.
It is a sunshine mixed with rain;
It is a tooth-ache, or like pain;
It is a game where none doth gain;
The lass saith no, and would full fain:
And this is love, as I hear sain.

Yet what is love? I pray thee say.
It is a yea, it is a nay,
A pretty kind of sporting fray;
It is a thing will soon away;
Then take the vantage while you may:
And this is love, as I hear say.

Yet what is love? I pray thee show.
A thing that creeps, it cannot go;
A prize that passeth to and fro;
A thing for one, a thing for mo;
And he that proves must find it so:
And this is love, sweet friend, I trow.

saucing] sacring, during Mass   sain] say   go] walk   proves] tries   trow] believe

WILLIAM SHAKESPEARE (1564–1616)

Crabbed age and youth

Crabbed age and youth
  Cannot live together;
Youth is full of pleasance,
  Age is full of care:
Youth like summer morn,
  Age like winter weather;
Youth like summer brave,
  Age like winter bare.
Youth is full of sport,
Age's breath is short;
  Youth is nimble, age is lame:
Youth is hot and bold,
Age is weak and cold;
  Youth is wild, and age is tame.
Age, I do abhor thee,
Youth, I do adore thee;
  O, my love, my love is young!
Age, I do defy thee;
O, sweet shepherd! hie thee,
  For methinks thou stays too long.

MICHAEL DRAYTON (1563–1631)

From *The Shepherd's Garland* (*Eclogue IX*)

The Roundelay

Batt. Gorbo, as thou cam'st this way
  By yonder little hill,
Or as thou through the fields didst stray,
  Saw'st thou my Daffodil?

She's in a frock of Lincoln green
  Which color likes her sight,
And never hath her beauty seen
  But through a veil of white;

brave] in fine array   seen] been seen, appeared

Than roses richer to behold,
That trim up lovers' bowers,
The pansy and the marigold,
Though Phœbus' paramours.

Gorbo. Thou well describ'st the daffodil;
It is not full an hour
Since by the spring, near yonder hill,
I saw that lovely flower.

Batt. Yet my fair flower thou didst not meet,
Nor news of her didst bring,
And yet my Daffodil's more sweet
Than that by yonder spring.

Gorbo. I saw a shepherd that doth keep
In yonder field of lilies,
Was making, as he fed his sheep,
A wreath of daffodillies.

Batt. Yet, Gorbo, thou delud'st me still,
My flower thou didst not see,
For know, my pretty Daffodil
Is worn of none but me.

To show itself but near her seat
No lily is so bold,
Except to shade her from the heat,
Or keep her from the cold.

Gorbo. Through yonder vale as I did pass,
Descending from the hill,
I met a smirking bonny lass,
They call her Daffodil;

Whose presence, as along she went,
The pretty flowers did greet,
As though their heads they downward bent
With homage to her feet.

richer] *Sc.* 'she is.'   The] Than the   keep] keep his flock   Was] Who was
smirking] smiling

And all the shepherds that were nigh,
From top of every hill,
Unto the valleys loud did cry,
'There goes sweet Daffodil.'

Batt. Ay, gentle shepherd, now with joy
Thou all my flocks dost fill;
That's she alone, kind shepherd's boy,
Let us to Daffodil.

EDMUND BOLTON (*c.* 1575–*c.* 1633)

A Palinode

As withereth the primrose by the river,
As fadeth summer's sun from gliding fountains,
As vanisheth the light-blown bubble ever,
As melteth snow upon the mossy mountains:
So melts, so vanisheth, so fades, so withers
The rose, the shine, the bubble, and the snow,
Of praise, pomp, glory, joy, which short life gathers,—
Fair praise, vain pomp, sweet glory, brittle joy.
The withered primrose by the mourning river,
The faded summer's sun from weeping fountains,
The light-blown bubble, vanishèd for ever,
The molten snow upon the naked mountains,
    Are emblems that the treasures we uplay
    Soon wither, vanish, fade, and melt away.

For as the snow, whose lawn did overspread
Th' ambitious hills which giant-like did threat
To pierce the heaven with their aspiring head,
Naked and bare doth leave their craggy seat;
Whenas the bubble, which did empty fly
The dalliance of the undiscernèd wind
On whose calm rolling waves it did rely,
Hath shipwreck made where it did dalliance find;
And when the sunshine which dissolved the snow,

Colored the bubble with a pleasant vary,
And made the rathe and timely primrose grow,
Swarth clouds withdrawn, which longer time do tarry:
   O, what is praise, pomp, glory, joy, but so
   As shine by fountains, bubbles, flowers, or snow?

SIR JOHN WOTTON (*c.* 1600)

Damætas' Jig

Jolly shepherd, shepherd on a hill,
   On a hill so merrily,
   On a hill so cheerily,
Fear not, shepherd, there to pipe thy fill,
Fill every dale, fill every plain:
   Both sing and say, 'Love feels no pain.'

Jolly shepherd, shepherd on a green,
   On a green so merrily,
   On a green so cheerily,
Be thy voice shrill, be thy mirth seen,
Heard to each swain, seen to each trull:
   Both sing and say, 'Love's joy is full.'

Jolly shepherd, shepherd in the sun,
   In the sun so merrily,
   In the sun so cheerily,
Sing forth thy songs, and let thy rhymes run
Down to the dales, to the hills above:
   Both sing and say, 'No life to love.'

Jolly shepherd, shepherd in the shade,
   In the shade so merrily,
   In the shade so cheerily,
Joy in thy life, life of shepherd's trade,
Joy in thy love, love full of glee:
   Both sing and say, 'Sweet love for me.'

vary] play of color   rathe] early   trull] girl   No life] No end

Jolly shepherd, shepherd here or there,
　　Here or there so merrily,
　　Here or there so cheerily,
Or in thy chat, either at thy cheer,
In every jig, in every lay
　　Both sing and say, 'Love lasts for aye.'

Jolly shepherd, shepherd Daphnis' love,
　　Daphnis' love so merrily,
　　Daphnis' love so cheerily,
Let thy fancy never more remove,
Fancy be fixed, fixed not to fleet:
　　Still sing and say, 'Love's yoke is sweet.'

SIR HENRY WOTTON (1568–1639)

A Description of the Spring

And now all nature seemed in love:
The lusty sap began to move;
New juice did stir the embracing vines,
And birds had drawn their valentines;
The jealous trout, that low did lie,
Rose at a well-dissembled fly;
There stood my friend, with patient skill
Attending of his trembling quill.
Already were the eaves possessed
With the swift pilgrim's daubèd nest:
The groves already did rejoice
In Philomel's triumphing voice.
The showers were short, the weather mild,
The morning fresh, the evening smiled.
Joan takes her neat-rubbed pail, and now
She trips to milk the sand-red cow;
Where, for some sturdy football swain,
Joan strokes a sillabub or twain.
The fields and gardens were beset

still] ever　　jealous] suspicious　　quill] float　　pilgrim's] swallow's　　strokes] milks

With tulip, crocus, violet;
And now, though late, the modest rose
Did more than half a blush disclose.
Thus all looked gay, all full of cheer,
To welcome the new-liveried year.

III

THE SONNETEERS

Chiefly
1590–1600

THE SONNETEERS

The decade from 1590 to 1600 was the period of the sonnet, the vogue of which was the most excessive, and the shortest-lived, of the poetic fashions of the age. Raised to unprecedented popularity by the publication of Sidney's *Astrophel and Stella* in 1591, sonneting had begun to encounter unfavorable criticism by 1595, and by the end of Elizabeth's reign its glory had departed, except among the little group of admirers of Spenser who were responsible for the revival of the pastoral. The noble example of Donne's *Holy Sonnets* preserved the sonnet as a form for devotional writing. Scattered later sequences like Habington's *Castara,* though erotic in content, eschew the sonnet form.

The introduction of the quatorzain into English by Wyatt, and Surrey's adaptation of the strict Italian scheme to one better suited to the genius of the English language and habit of thought have already been described.[1] The example of these two pioneers was not widely followed. After the publication of Tottel's *Songs and Sonnets,* the term 'sonnet' appears from time to time in new works but chiefly in its generalized sense of 'a little song.' Gascoigne, whose flair for such matters is evinced in his critical essay, *Certain Notes of Introduction concerning the Making of Verse and Rime in English,* recalled the stricter definition of the form both by precept and example, including in his *Posies* (1575) some thirty sonnets, among them one which follows the strict Italian rime scheme. It also appears that in 1569, Spenser, though but seventeen, had already interested himself in the translation of sonnets from Du Bellay and, indirectly, from Petrarch.

But the kind of sonneteering which was to catch the fancy of both poets and public in England was the writing of a number of

[1] See p. 40 and pp. 51–2.

sonnets in sequence, in the manner of Petrarch, the series being addressed to some mistress real or ideal. For the establishment of this fashion Sidney is responsible. Plausible conjectures as to the date of composition of his *Astrophel and Stella* place it at much the same time as the *Arcadia,* in the years 1580-1-2, and it is thus the earliest amatory sequence. Like Petrarch's to Laura, Sidney's sequence had the additional attraction that the reader could believe if he wished—as many did and do—that it was actually the reflection of his love for the Lady Penelope Devereux, whom he lost by some sort of indecision and who then contracted an unhappy marriage with Lord Rich. To maintain this proposition with respect to the sequence as a whole would be small compliment to Stella, since a good number of the sonnets appear clearly to be literary exercises; and a knowledge that the best of them were addressed to her could neither increase nor diminish the impression they convey of artistic sincerity. Their keynote is in the last line of the first sonnet: 'Fool,' said my muse to me, 'look in thy heart and write!' In them is heard unmistakably for the first time that individual note, that intense and passionate cry of the poet's very heart that was to be the distinctive mark of the great literature of Elizabeth. With the sonnets from *Astrophel and Stella* belong certain others found in Sidney's miscellaneous works and several fine love-poems not in sonnet form.

Next to Sidney as a pioneer of sonneting must be mentioned Thomas Watson, whose *Hecatompathia, or a Passionate Century of Love,* was published in 1582. Like Sidney, Watson modeled his form and material on various Italian and Latin authors, but chiefly on Petrarch. As will be seen from the two 'passions' subsequently quoted, however, he did not use the fourteen-line form. Moreover, his *Passionate Century* is less a true sequence than Sidney's, and for this reason as well as for his deficiency in poetic fire, it seems likely that Watson's published work had less influence than Sidney's *Astrophel* circulated in manuscript.

Certainly it is safe to attribute to Sidney's influence the probably contemporaneous poetizing of his friend Fulke Greville, published much later (1633), with other work, under the title of *Cælica.* Greville's work has keenness, intellectual thrust, condensation of

style, and a new and independent spirit. He was one of the earliest
sonneteers to widen the range of lyric themes to include non-erotic
sentiment, and he shows a tendency to abandon the classical imagery
and allusion which make so much of the sonnet writing seem ornate
and over-elaborate. Earlier publication, or a wider circulation of
his work in manuscript, might have exercised a salutary discipline
upon the sonneteers.

In some of the songs of Robert Greene from romances written
toward the end of the eighties it is difficult not to feel the influence
of the new Petrarchanism. Such pieces as *Ah, were she pitiful as
she is fair* and *Fair is my love for April in her face* are not in sonnet
form, and for that reason alone it is tempting to include them with
the pastoral. But their spirit is subtly different. It is the spirit of
the Petrarchan lover. With them belongs the Earl of Oxford's
If women could be fair and yet not fond, also published in the late
eighties. Raleigh's *Methought I saw the grave where Laura lay,*
included as part of the dedicatory matter in Spenser's *Faery Queen*
(1590), is a good early example of the extension of the sonnet form
to occasional verse, for which its convenient length later made it
widely used.

With the quasi-surreptitious publication of *Astrophel and Stella*
in 1591 came the deluge. The printer included with those of Sidney
'sundry other rare sonnets of divers noblemen and gentlemen,' notably twenty-seven by Samuel Daniel, who was then traveling abroad.
Daniel resented this premature publication of his work and in the
following year put forth a fuller edition, under the title of *Delia.*
Constable's *Diana* appeared in the same year and enjoyed a remarkable popularity. Sonneteering became a craze and sequence after
sequence in repeated editions issued from the press. After Sidney,
Daniel, and Constable, the last of whom also wrote *Spiritual Sonnets to the Honor of God and his Saints,* probably the first religious
sequence, came Lodge's *Phyllis,* Watson's *Tears of Fancy,* Barnes's
Parthenophil and Parthenophe (a mixture of lyric forms, as were
many of these collections), Drayton's *Idea,* and Dr. Giles Fletcher's
Licia. In 1594 appeared Percy's *Cœlia* and the anonymous
Zepheria; in 1595, Barnfield's *Cynthia,* Chapman's *A Coronet for
his Mistress Philosophy,* probably the earliest attempt to write a

sonnet-sequence neither devotional nor amatory, *Emaricdulfe* by
E. C., and Barnes's *A Divine Century of Spiritual Sonnets;* in 1596,
Griffin's *Fidessa,* Smith's *Chloris,* Lynche's *Diella,* and, crowning
the year, Spenser's *Amoretti.* In 1597, *Laura* by Robert Tofte, though
not strictly in the sonnet form, belongs to the tradition. Sonnets
of Shakespeare were well known, as Meres tells us, before 1598.
Breton's *The Soul's Harmony* appeared in 1600, Sir John Davies'
Sonnets to Philomel in Davison's *Poetical Rhapsody,* in 1602. Individual sonnets of such men as Joshua Sylvester, Charles Best, and
Dyer were printed in the miscellanies. Practically every poet of
consequence and assuredly every poetaster attempted the form. One
scholar interested in such matters has declared that over 3000 sonnets were printed during the period. How many others perished in
manuscript or a-borning can never be known. But the printed
total alone is enough to assure us that seldom before or since has any
form of poetry had so concentrated and extraordinary a vogue.
And this enthusiasm as expressed in mere quantity helps to explain
the obvious faults of the Elizabethan sonneteers as well as their
excellence when at their best.

   In quality the Elizabethan sonnet has been aptly described as a
strange medley of splendor and dullness. The latter is no more
than we should expect of so sudden a flood of composition, much of
it doubtless hasty, in a difficult and restricted form, and for the most
part on a single theme. Though a few of the sequences, such as
Astrophel and Stella, Spenser's *Amoretti,* and E. C.'s *Emaricdulfe,*
seem written to a real woman realistically described and actually beloved of the poet, others like Fletcher's *Licia,* Lodge's *Phyllis,* and
both of Watson's sequences are, and were intended to be, no more
than translations or literary exercises. Much of the tediousness of
the style is due to a single cause: the tireless repetition of a few
conventional images and ideas. The cruel fair one, with hair of
twisted gold, roses in her cheeks, suns in her eyes, but ice in her
heart; her lover, ever faithful, racked by extremes of bale and bliss,
heaven and hell, hope and fear, fire and ice, humbly comparing his
state to that of a ship tossed upon the sea, longing for sleep,
exulting in the thought that his love shall in his immortal verse live
ever young—only the best of the sonneteers in the best of their son-

nets escape completely such familiar Petrarchan trappings. And even in these the conventions are not so much discarded as authenticated by the power of genuine feeling.

As for the splendor of their poetical merit, five of the sequences stand out above the rest, all of them amatory. Sidney's *Astrophel and Stella,* as has been said, is a worthy exemplar of the fashion, ranking in beauty and sincere passion with all but the best of its great successors, Daniel's *Delia,* Drayton's *Idea,* the *Amoretti* of Spenser, and the *Sonnets* of Shakespeare. Samuel Daniel, an Oxford man, protégé of the Countess of Pembroke, and later maker of masques under King James, was styled by Browne 'well-languaged Daniel,' and though lacking the fire—not always the imagination—of his master Sidney, was deservedly popular for the purity, smoothness, and dignity of his style. Drayton, whose sound workmanship and honest enthusiasm enabled him to achieve success and esteem in practically every kind of poetry popular in his day, was lured at the height of the fashion into imitation of the French poets, as well as of Daniel, Sidney, and Shakespeare. His best sonnets, such as the ever-popular *Since there's no help, come let us kiss and part,* seem to have been written long after the wane of the fashion. In them he displays an energy and feeling for the dramatic which have led to fruitless efforts to identify his mistress Idea with Anne Goodere, the daughter of his patron. Spenser's *Amoretti* is among the few sequences indubitably addressed to an actual woman, having been written during his courtship of Elizabeth Boyle, whom he married in 1594. They express in lofty but conventional terms the moods of courtship and the triumph of love. Taken as a whole, they are disappointing. Their course of true love runs too smooth; their adoration of virginity seems too high a mood to be captured in fourteen lines. Spenser's muse was more at home in the 'linkèd sweetness long drawn out,' the prolonged and melodious fervor, of the *Prothalamion.* It was reserved for Shakespeare to crown the sonnet fashion with the brooding thought, god-like passion, and rich music peculiarly his own. Through the long controversy occasioned by the extremes of great poetry and trivial fooling through which his sonnets run, the unsatisfactory arrangement in which they were printed, and the in-

vincible anonymity of the persons addressed, most lovers of Elizabethan poetry and of Shakespeare have clung to the opinion of
Wordsworth when he said, 'In none of Shakespeare's writings is
found in equal compass a greater number of felicitous feelings
exquisitely expressed.' The sequence of 154 sonnets falls into two
general groups, those addressed to a handsome young man, the
author's friend, usually identified as his patron, the Earl of
Southampton, (1–126) and those addressed to an unknown dark
lady (127–152). Of neither of these personages are we likely
ever to know more than Shakespeare himself tells us in the 144th
sonnet:

> Two loves I have, of comfort and despair,
> Which like two spirits do suggest me still;
> The better angel is a man right fair,
> The worser spirit a woman colored ill;
> To win me soon to hell, my female evil
> Tempteth my better angel from my side,
> And would corrupt my saint to be a devil,
> Wooing his purity with her foul pride;
> And whether that my angel be turned fiend,
> Suspect I may but not directly tell;
> But being both from me, both to each friend,
> I guess one angel in another's hell.
>   Yet this shall I ne'er know, but live in doubt,
>   Till my bad angel fire my good one out.

Such was the story, if there was a story, of Shakespeare's *Sonnets*.
Its tragic undertones are evident. A minor group, sonnets 76–86,
omitting 81, allude clearly to a rival poet, who is no more identi-
fiable than the other persons. It is interesting to note that the
majority of the golden sonnets which elevate the series to its place
with the greatest of poetry are in the group addressed to the man.
They should be read without the slightest association of abnormal
psychology, as expressions of a passion by no means unknown to
the choicer spirits of our time, but commoner and more vocal in
the more primitive society of the sixteenth century—the passion
of friendship.

The dependence of the sonneteers upon foreign models, Italian and French, in particular upon Petrarch, Ronsard, and Desportes, from the latter of whom new borrowings are being continually discovered, inevitably lessened their repute even in their own time. Sidney early voiced his criticism of such dependence, however little he may have been free from it. It was not so much the dishonesty of the procedure that he objected to. The crime of plagiarism had not as yet been invented; the spirit of the age in matters of literary ownership was entirely different from ours. Watson was at considerable pains to indicate his sources, and Lodge, who, to do him justice, was poet enough to transcend the material he worked with, publicly praised his favorite, Desportes, whose poetical writings, he says, are 'for the most part Englished and ordinarily in everybody's hands.' But as new sonnet-sequences continued to pour forth, the soundness of Sidney's criticism of the unoriginality of sonnet writing became increasingly evident in the prevalence of 'conceits,' over-ingenious efforts to deck a too-familiar sentiment or subject in new and striking figures of speech. The conceit takes two forms, frequently combined, and both established by Sidney himself: (1) the hyperbole, as where he says that the ink he spills runs of its own volition into Stella's name, and (2) the extended comparison, in which a lover's fate is likened in detail to a ship tossed upon the sea; or his beloved's face to the façade of a palace —the lintel, her brow, being alabaster crowned with gold; the door, her mouth, red porphyry locked with pearls; the porches, which endure the name of cheeks, of red and white marble. The efforts of lesser sonneteers to outdo such amorous excesses of their masters led to an increasing chorus of criticism, satire, and parody. Chapman in his *Muses that sing love's sensual empery* (p. 194) rebukes the sonneteers for their preoccupation with fleshly love. Sir John Davies in his *Gulling Sonnets* (p. 208) deliberately carries the conceit to ridiculous extremes. Shakespeare himself protests, in a little gem of honest love poetry, 'My mistress' eyes are nothing like the sun,' and Jonson, Davies of Hereford, and others joined in after their fashion with criticism, burlesque, and satire. Such signs foretold the waning of the sonnet craze.

The intensive cultivation of the sonnet form was, on the whole, beneficial to the lyric. It demanded of the Elizabethans a technique which they needed to acquire: greater skill in the minutiae of form, stricter unity of thought, and, to preserve the dignified tread of its decasyllables, more careful molding of each line as a part of the whole. In the hands of genius the sonnet reached an artistic height which was not surpassed until the conception of its scope was widened and the beauty of the stricter Petrarchan form was reasserted by Milton, to be practised later by Wordsworth and Rossetti.

SIR PHILIP SIDNEY (1554–1586)

A Ditty

My true love hath my heart and I have his,
By just exchange one for another given;
I hold his dear, and mine he cannot miss,
There never was a better bargain driven.
   My true love hath my heart and I have his.

His heart in me keeps him and me in one,
My heart in him his thoughts and senses guides;
He loves my heart, for once it was his own,
I cherish his, because in me it bides.
   My true love hath my heart and I have his.

From *Astrophel and Stella*

I

Loving in truth, and fain in verse my love to show,
That she, dear she, might take some pleasure of my pain,
Pleasure might cause her read, reading might make her
   know,
Knowledge might pity win, and pity grace obtain,—
I sought fit words to paint the blackest face of woe;
Studying inventions fine, her wits to entertain,
Oft turning others' leaves to see if thence would flow

miss] do without

Some fresh and fruitful showers upon my sunburnt brain.
But words came halting forth, wanting invention's stay;
Invention, Nature's child, fled step-dame Study's blows,
And others' feet still seemed but strangers in my way.
Thus, great with child to speak, and helpless in my throes,
   Biting my truant pen, beating myself for spite,
    'Fool', said my muse to me, 'look in thy heart and write!'

II

Not at first sight, nor yet with a dribbed shot,
Love gave the wound, which while I breathe will bleed;
But known worth did in mine of time proceed,
Till by degrees it had full conquest got.
I saw and liked; I liked but lovèd not;
I loved, but straight did not what love decreed;
At length to love's decrees I, forced, agreed,
Yet with repining at so partial lot.
Now even that footstep of lost liberty
Is gone, and now, like slave-born Muscovite,
I call it praise to suffer tyranny;
And now employ the remnant of my wit
   To make myself believe that all is well,
    While, with a feeling skill, I paint my hell.

VII

When nature made her chief work, Stella's eyes,
In color black why wrapped she beams so bright?
Would she in beamy black, like painter wise,
Frame daintiest luster mixed of shades and light?
Or did she else that sober hue devise
In object best to knit and strength our sight,
Lest, if no veil these brave gleams did disguise,
They, sunlike, should more dazzle than delight?
Or would she her miraculous power show,
That, whereas black seems beauty's contrary,
She even in black doth make all beauties flow?

dribbed] weak, or poorly aimed   mine] undermine   partial] unfair

Both so, and thus,—she, minding Love should be
    Placed ever there, gave him this mourning weed
    To honor all their deaths who for her bleed.

XI

In truth, O Love, with what a boyish kind
Thou dost proceed in thy most serious ways,
That when the heav'n to thee his best displays,
Yet of that best thou leav'st the best behind!
For, like a child, that some fair book doth find,
With gilded leaves or colored vellum plays,
Or, at the most, on some fine picture stays,
But never heeds the fruit of writer's mind;
So, when thou saw'st, in nature's cabinet,
Stella, thou straight look'dst babies in her eyes;
In her cheeks' pit thou didst thy pitfold set,
And in her breast, bo-peep or couching, lies,
    Playing and shining in each outward part,
    But, fool, seek'st not to get into her heart.

XXXI

With how sad steps, O moon, thou climb'st the skies!
How silently, and with how wan a face!
What! may it be that even in heav'nly place
That busy archer his sharp arrows tries?
Sure, if that long-with-love-acquainted eyes
Can judge of love, thou feel'st a lover's case;
I read it in thy looks: thy languished grace
To me, that feel the like, thy state descries.
Then, ev'n of fellowship, O moon, tell me,
Is constant love deemed there but want of wit?
Are beauties there as proud as here they be?
Do they above love to be loved, and yet
    Those lovers scorn whom that love doth possess?
    Do they call virtue there ungratefulness?

minding] intending   kind] fashion   lies] liest   descries] reveals   virtue . . .
ungratefulness] ungratefulness . . . a virtue

XXXIX

Come sleep! O sleep, the certain knot of peace,
The baiting place of wit, the balm of woe,
The poor man's wealth, the prisoner's release,
Th' indifferent judge between the high and low;
With shield of proof shield me from out the prease
Of those fierce darts despair at me doth throw;
O make in me those civil wars to cease;
I will good tribute pay, if thou do so.
Take thou of me smooth pillows, sweetest bed,
A chamber deaf to noise and blind to light,
A rosy garland and a weary head;
And if these things, as being thine by right,
   Move not thy heavy grace, thou shalt in me,
   Livelier than elsewhere, Stella's image see.

XLI

Having this day my horse, my hand, my lance
Guided so well that I obtained the prize,
Both by the judgment of the English eyes
And of some sent from that sweet enemy, France;
Horsemen my skill in horsemanship advance,
Town-folks my strength; a daintier judge applies
His praise to sleight which from good use doth rise;
Some lucky wits impute it but to chance;
Others, because of both sides I do take
My blood from them who did excel in this,
Think nature me a man of arms did make.
How far they shot awry! The true cause is,
   Stella looked on, and from her heav'nly face
   Sent forth the beams which made so fair my race.

baiting] To 'bait' was to pause for rest and refreshment.   indifferent] impartial
prease] press   rosy] implying comfort and hope, but perhaps also 'silent,' with a
suggestion of 'under the rose'   use] practice

LIV

Because I breathe not love to every one,
Nor do not use set colors for to wear,
Nor nourish special locks of vowèd hair,
Nor give each speech a full point of a groan,
The courtly nymphs, acquainted with the moan
Of them who in their lips love's standard bear,
'What, he!' say they of me, 'Now I dare swear
He cannot love; no, no, let him alone.'
And think so still, so Stella know my mind!
Profess indeed I do not Cupid's art;
But you, fair maids, at length this true shall find,
That his right badge is but worn in the heart;
   Dumb swans, not chatt'ring pies, do lovers prove;
   They love indeed who quake to say they love.

First Song

Doubt you to whom my Muse these notes intendeth,
Which now my breast o'ercharged to music lendeth?
   To you, to you, all song of praise is due,
Only in you my song begins and endeth.

Who hath the eyes which marry state with pleasure?
Who keeps the key of Nature's chiefest treasure?
   To you, to you, all song of praise is due,
Only for you the heaven forgat all measure.

Who hath the lips where wit in fairness reigneth?
Who womankind at once both decks and staineth?
   To you, to you, all song of praise is due,
Only by you Cupid his crown maintaineth.

Who hath the feet whose step of sweetness planteth?
Who else, for whom Fame worthy trumpets wanteth?
   To you, to you, all song of praise is due,
Only to you her scepter Venus granteth.

state] dignity   pleasure] vivacity   staineth] puts to disadvantage

Who hath the breast whose milk doth passions nourish?
Whose grace is such that when it chides doth cherish?
   To you, to you, all song of praise is due,
Only through you the tree of life doth flourish.

Who hath the hand which without stroke subdueth?
Who long-dead beauty with increase reneweth?
   To you, to you, all song of praise is due,
Only at you all envy hopeless rueth.

Who hath the hair which loosest fastest tieth?
Who makes a man live then glad when he dieth?
   To you, to you, all song of praise is due,
Only of you the flatterer never lieth.   .

Who hath the voice which soul from senses sunders?   ·
Whose force but yours the bolts of beauty thunders?
   To you, to you, all song of praise is due,
Only with you not miracles are wonders.

Doubt you to whom my Muse these notes intendeth,
Which now my breast o'ercharged to music lendeth?
   To you, to you, all song of praise is due,
Only in you my song begins and endeth.

LXIV

No more, my dear, no more these counsels try;
O, give my passions leave to run their race;
Let Fortune lay on me her worst disgrace;
Let folk o'ercharged with brain against me cry;
Let clouds bedim my face, break in mine eye;
Let me no steps but of lost labor trace;
Let all the earth with scorn recount my case,
But do not will me from my love to fly.
I do not envy Aristotle's wit,
Nor do aspire to Cæsar's bleeding fame;

reneweth] reincarnates   rueth] laments   not miracles are] miracles are not

Nor aught do care though some above me sit;
Nor hope nor wish another course to frame,
  But that which once may win thy cruel heart;
  Thou art my wit, and thou my virtue art.

XC

Stella, think not that I by verse seek fame,
Who seek, who hope, who love, who live but thee;
Thine eyes my pride, thy lips mine history;
If thou praise not, all other praise is shame.
Nor so ambitious am I as to frame
A nest for my young praise in laurel tree;
In truth, I swear I wish not there should be
Graved in mine epitaph a poet's name.
Ne, if I would, could I just title make,
That any laud to me thereof should grow,
Without my plumes from others' wings I take;
For nothing from my wit or will doth flow,
  Since all my words thy beauty doth endite,
  And love doth hold my hand and makes me write.

Ring out your bells

Ring out your bells, let mourning shows be spread;
    For Love is dead:
    All Love is dead, infected
With plague of deep disdain:
    Worth, as naught worth, rejected,
And Faith fair scorn doth gain.
    From so ungrateful fancy,
    From such a female franzy,
    From them that use men thus.
    Good Lord, deliver us!

Weep, neighbors, weep; do you not hear it said
    That Love is dead?
    His death-bed, peacock's folly,

Graved] Engraved   Ne] Nor   Without] Unless   endite] inspire the writing of

His winding-sheet is shame,
　His will, false-seeming holy,
His sole exec'tor, blame. &c.

Let dirge be sung, and trentals rightly read,
　　For Love is dead;
　Sir Wrong his tomb ordaineth:
My mistress' marble heart,
　Which epitaph containeth,
'Her eyes were once his dart.' &c.

Alas, I lie: rage hath this error bred;
　　Love is not dead;
　Love is not dead, but sleepeth
In her unmatchèd mind,
　Where she his counsel keepeth,
Till due deserts she find.
　　Therefore from so vile fancy,
　　To call such wit a franzy,
　　Who Love can temper thus,
　　Good Lord, deliver us!

Leave me, O love

Leave me, O love which reachest but to dust;
And thou, my mind, aspire to higher things;
Grow rich in that which never taketh rust:
Whatever fades but fading pleasure brings.
Draw in thy beams, and humble all thy might
To that sweet yoke where lasting freedoms be;
Which breaks the clouds and opens forth the light,
That doth both shine and give us sight to see.
O take fast hold; let that light be thy guide
In this small course which birth draws out to death,
And think how evil becometh him to slide,
Who seeketh heav'n, and comes of heav'nly breath.
　Then farewell, world; thy uttermost I see;
　Eternal love, maintain thy life in me.

trentals] masses for the dead

Wooing Stuff

Faint amorist, what! dost thou think
To taste love's honey, and not drink
One dram of gall? or to devour
A world of sweet and taste no sour?
Dost thou ever think to enter
The Elysian fields, that dar'st not venture
In Charon's barge? a lover's mind
Must use to sail with every wind.
He that loves, and fears to try,
Learns his mistress to deny.
Doth she chide thee? 'tis to shew it
That thy coldness makes her do it.
Is she silent? is she mute?
Silence fully grants thy suit.
Doth she pout, and leave the room?
Then she goes to bid thee come.
Is she sick? Why then be sure
She invites thee to the cure.
Doth she cross thy suit with 'No'?
Tush, she loves to hear thee woo.
Doth she call the faith of man
In question? Nay, she loves thee than;
And if e'er she makes a blot,
She's lost if that thou hit'st her not.
He that after ten denials
Dares attempt no farther trials,
Hath no warrant to acquire
The dainties of his chaste desire.

THOMAS WATSON (c. 1557–1592)

From *Hecatompathia*

Passion XXXVII

If Jove himself be subject unto love
And range the woods to find a mortal prey;

use] be accustomed   Learns] Teaches   if that] if

If Neptune from the seas himself remove,
  And seek on sands with earthly wights to play:
    Then may I love my peerless choice by right,
    Who far excels each other mortal wight.

If Pluto could by love be drawn from hell,
  To yield himself a silly virgin's thrall;
If Phœbus could vouchsafe on earth to dwell,
  To win a rustic maid unto his call:
    Then how much more should I adore the sight
    Of her, in whom the heav'ns themselves delight?

If country Pan might follow nymphs in chase,
  And yet through love remain devoid of blame;
If satyrs were excused for seeking grace
  To joy the fruits of any mortal dame:
    Then, why should I once doubt to love her still
    On whom ne gods nor men can gaze their fill?

Passion C. My Love Is Past

Resolved to dust entombed here lieth Love,
  Through fault of her, who here herself should lie;
He struck her breast, but all in vain did prove
  To fire the ice: and doubting by and by
    His brand had lost his force, he 'gan to try
    Upon himself; which trial made him die.

In sooth no force; let those lament that lust,
  I'll sing a carol song for obsequy;
For towards me his dealings were unjust,
  And cause of all my passèd misery:
    The Fates, I think, seeing what I had passed,
    In my behalf wrought this revenge at last.

But somewhat more to pacify my mind,
  By illing him, through whom I lived a slave,
I'll cast his ashes to the open wind,

wights] beings   prove] endeavor   doubting] fearing   his force] its force   no
force] no matter   lust] list, wish   illing] harming, speaking ill of

Or write this epitaph upon his grave:
    'Here lieth Love, of Mars the bastard son,
    Whose foolish fault to death himself hath done.'

FULKE GREVILLE, LORD BROOKE (1554–1628)

From *Cælica*

XVII

Cynthia, whose glories are at full forever,
Whose beauties draw forth tears, and kindle fires,—
Fires, which kindled once are quenchèd never,
So beyond hope your worth bears up desires,—
Why cast you clouds on your sweet-looking eyes?
Are you afraid they show me too much pleasure?
Strong nature decks the grave wherein it lies,
Excellence can never be expressed in measure.
Are you afraid because my heart adores you,
The world will think I hold Endymion's place?
Hippolytus, sweet Cynthia, kneeled before you,
Yet did you not come down to kiss his face.
    Angels enjoy the heavens' inward choirs:
    Star-gazers only multiply desires.

XXII

I, with whose colors Myra dressed her head,
    I, that wore posies of her own hand-making,
I, that mine own name in the chimneys read
    By Myra finely wrought ere I was waking:
Must I look on, in hope time coming may
With change bring back my turn again to play?

I, that on Sunday at the church-stile found
    A garland sweet with true-love knots in flowers,
Which I to wear about mine arm was bound,

Fires] dissyllabic   it] the hope of pleasure   chimneys] fire-place, or mantelpiece

That èach of us might know that all was ours:
Must I now lead an idle life in wishes,
And follow Cupid for his loaves and fishes?

I, that did wear the ring her mother left,
  I, for whose love she gloried to be blamed,
I, with whose eyes her eyes committed theft,
  I, who did make her blush when I was named:
Must I lose ring, flowers, blush, theft, and go naked,
Watching with sighs till dead love be awakèd?

I, that when drowsy Argus fell asleep,
  Like Jealousy o'erwatchèd with Desire,
Was ever warnèd modesty to keep
  While her breath speaking kindled nature's fire:
Must I look on a-cold while others warm them?
Do Vulcan's brothers in such fine nets arm them?

Was it for this that I might Myra see
  Washing the water with her beauties white?
Yet would she never write her love to me:
  Thinks wit of change while thoughts are in delight?
Mad girls must safely love, as they may leave:
No man can print a kiss; lines may deceive.

LV

Cynthia, because your horns look divers ways,
  Now darkened to the east, now to the west,
Then at full glory once in thirty days,
  Sense doth believe that change is nature's rest.
Poor earth, that dare presume to judge the sky:
  Cynthia is ever round, and never varies;
Shadows and distance do abuse the eye,
  And in abusèd sense truth oft miscarries:
Yet who this language to the people speaks,
Opinion's empire, sense's idol, breaks.

o'erwatchèd with] outwaited by   Vulcan's brothers] those who entrap lovers
as . . . leave] that they may stop   abuse] deceive

LXXXVII

The earth, with thunder torn, with fire blasted,
With waters drowned, with windy palsy shaken,
Cannot for this with heaven be distasted,
Since thunder, rain, and winds from earth are taken.
Man, torn with love, with inward furies blasted,
Drowned with despair, with fleshly lustings shaken,
Cannot for this with heaven be distasted:
Love, fury, lustings out of man are taken.
Then man, endure thyself, those clouds will vanish;
Life is a top which whipping sorrow driveth,
Wisdom must bear what our flesh cannot banish,
The humble lead, the stubborn bootless striveth:
  Or, man, forsake thyself, to heaven turn thee,
  Her flames enlighten nature, never burn thee.

LXXXVIII

Whenas man's life, the light of human lust,
  In socket of his earthly lanthorn burns,
That all his glory unto ashes must,
  And generations to corruption turns,
Then fond desires that only fear their end,
Do vainly wish for life, but to amend.

But when this life is from the body fled,
  To see itself in that eternal glass,
Where time doth end, and thoughts accuse the dead,
  Where all to come is one with all that was,
Then living men ask how he left his breath,
That while he livèd never thought of death.

ROBERT GREENE (1558–1592)

Ah, were she pitiful as she is fair

Ah, were she pitiful as she is fair,
  Or but as mild as she is seeming so,

must] must turn   fond] foolish   living] here, 'immortal'

Then were my hopes greater than my despair,
　Then all the world were heaven, nothing woe.
Ah, were her heart relenting as her hand,
　That seems to melt even with the mildest touch,
Then knew I where to seat me in a land,
　Under [the] wide heavens, but yet not such.
So as she shows, she seems the budding rose,
　Yet sweeter far than is an earthly flower,
Sovereign of beauty, like the spray she grows,
　Compassed she is with thorns and cankered bower,
Yet were she willing to be plucked and worn,
She would be gathered, though she grew on thorn.

Ah, when she sings, all music else be still,
　For none must be comparèd to her note;
Ne'er breathed such glee from Philomela's bill,
　Nor from the morning singer's swelling throat.
Ah, when she riseth from her blissful bed,
　She comforts all the world, as doth the sun,
And at her sight the night's foul vapor's fled;
　When she is set, the gladsome day is done.
O glorious sun, imagine me the west,
Shine in my arms, and set thou in my breast!

Fair is my love for April in her face

Fair is my love for April in her face,
　Her lovely breasts September claims his part,
And lordly Jùly in her eyes takes place,
　But cold December dwelleth in her heart;
Blest be the months that set my thoughts on fire,
Accurst that month that hindereth my desire.

Like Phœbus' fire, so sparkle both her eyes;
　As air perfumed with amber in her breath,
Like swelling waves, her lovely teats do rise,

such] so benign as she   Under . . . such] See p. 38.   shows] appears
cankered] crabbed   bower] arbor, branches

As earth her heart, cold, dateth me to death:
Ay me, poor man, that on the earth do live,
When unkind earth death and despair doth give.

In pomp sits mercy seated in her face;
  Love 'twixt her breasts his trophies doth imprint;
Her eyes shine favor, courtesy, and grace,
  But touch her heart, ah, that is framed of flint!
Therefore my harvest in the grass bears grain;
The rock will wear, washed with a winter's rain.

Menaphon's Song

Some say Love,
Foolish Love,
  Doth rule and govern all the gods:
I say Love,
Inconstant Love,
  Sets men's senses far at odds.
Some swear Love,
Smooth-faced Love,
  Is sweetest sweet that men can have:
I say Love,
Soùr Love,
  Makes virtue yield as beauty's slave.
A bitter sweet, a folly worst of all,
That forceth wisdom to be folly's thrall!

Love is sweet.
Wherein sweet?
  In fading pleasures that do pain.
Beauty sweet:
Is that sweet
  That yieldeth sorrow for a gain?
If Love's sweet,
Herein sweet,
  That minute's joys are monthly woes:
'Tis not sweet,

That is sweet
  Nowhere but where repentance grows.
Then love who list, if beauty be so sour;
Labor for me, Love rest in prince's bower.

Cupid abroad was 'lated in the night

Cupid abroad was 'lated in the night,
  His wings were wet with ranging in the rain;
Harbor he sought, to me he took his flight
  To dry his plumes. I heard the boy complain;
    I oped the door and granted his desire,
    I rose myself, and made the wag a fire.

Looking more narrow by the fire's flame,
  I spied his quiver hanging by his back.
Doubting the boy might my misfortune frame,
  I would have gone, for fear of further wrack;
    But what I drad did me, poor wretch, betide,
    For forth he drew an arrow from his side.

He pierced the quick, and I began to start,—
  A pleasing wound but that it was too high;
His shaft procured a sharp yet sugared smart.
  Away he flew, for why, his wings were dry;
    But left the arrow sticking in my breast,
    That sore I grieved I welcomed such a guest.

EDWARD DE VERE, EARL OF OXFORD (1550–1604)

If women could be fair

If women could be fair and yet not fond,
  Or that their love were firm, not fickle still,
I would not marvel that they make men bond
  By service long to purchase their good will;

---

wag] young rascal   fire's] dissyllabic   drad] dreaded   fond] foolish   **still**] ever

But when I see how frail those creatures are,
I muse that men forget themselves so far.

To mark the choice they make, and how they change,
   How oft from Phœbus they do flee to Pan;
Unsettled still, like haggards wild they range,
   These gentle birds that fly from man to man,—
Who would not scorn and shake them from the fist,
And let them fly, fair fools, which way they list?

Yet for disport we fawn and flatter both,
   To pass the time when nothing else can please,
And train them to our lure with subtle oath,
   Till, weary of their wiles, ourselves we ease;
And then we say when we their fancy try,
'To play with fools, O what a fool was I!'

SIR WALTER RALEIGH (c. 1552–1618)

A Vision upon this Conceit of the Faery Queen

Methought I saw the grave where Laura lay,
Within that temple where the vestal flame
Was wont to burn; and passing by that way
To see that buried dust of living fame,
Whose tomb fair Love and fairer Virtue kept,
All suddenly I saw the Faery Queen;
At whose approach the soul of Petrarch wept,
And from thenceforth those graces were not seen,
For they this Queen attended; in whose stead
Oblivion laid him down on Laura's hearse.
Hereat the hardest stones were seen to bleed,
And groans of buried ghosts the heavens did pierce;
   Where Homer's sprite did tremble all for grief,
   And cursed th' access of that celestial thief.

haggards] untamed hawks   *Conceit*] *Conception*. The sonnet appeared in Spenser's
Faery Queen, 1590.   sprite] spirit   access] coming

SAMUEL DANIEL (*c.* 1563–1619)

From *Delia*

XVIII

Restore thy tresses to the golden ore,
Yield Cytherea's son those arcs of love,
Bequeath the heavens the stars that I adore,
And to the orient do thy pearls re-move,
Yield thy hands' pride unto the ivory white,
To Arabian odors give thy breathing sweet,
Restore thy blush unto Aurora bright,
To Thetis give the honor of thy feet;
Let Venus have thy graces her resigned,
And thy sweet voice give back unto the spheres;
But yet restore thy fierce and cruel mind
To Hyrcan tigers and to ruthless bears;
   Yield to the marble thy hard heart again:
   So shalt thou cease to plague, and I to pain.

XXXI

Look, Delia, how we esteem the half-blown rose,
The image of thy blush and summer's honor,
Whilst in her tender green she doth enclose
That pure, sweet beauty time bestows upon her.
No sooner spreads her glory to the air,
But straight her full-blown pride is in declining;
She then is scorned that late adorned the fair:
So clouds thy beauty after fairest shining.
No April can revive thy withered flowers,
Whose blooming grace adorns thy glory now;
Swift, speedy time, feathered with flying hours,
Dissolves the beauty of the fairest brow.
   O let not, then, such riches waste in vain,
   But love whilst that thou may'st be loved again.

arcs] eyebrows, to be used as bows   her] to her   fair] fair one   whilst that]
whilst

XLII

Beauty, sweet love, is like the morning dew,
Whose short refresh upon the tender green
Cheers for a time, but till the sun doth shew,
And straight 'tis gone as it had never been.
Soon doth it fade that makes the fairest flourish,
Short is the glory of the blushing rose,
The hue which thou so carefully dost nourish,
Yet which at length thou must be forced to lose.
When thou surcharged with burthen of thy years,
Shalt bend thy wrinkles homeward to the earth,
And that in beauty's lease expired appears
The date of age, the Calends of our death—
    But ah! no more, this must not be foretold,
    For women grieve to think they must be old.

XLV

Care-charmer Sleep, son of the sable Night,
Brother to Death, in silent darkness born:
Relieve my languish and restore the light;
With dark forgetting of my cares return,
And let the day be time enough to mourn
The shipwreck of my ill-adventured youth:
Let waking eyes suffice to wail their scorn
Without the torment of the night's untruth.
Cease, dreams, the images of day-desires,
To model forth the passions of the morrow;
Never let rising sun approve you liars,
To add more grief to aggravate my sorrow.
    Still let me sleep, embracing clouds in vain,
    And never wake to feel the day's disdain.

XLVI

Let others sing of knights and paladins
In agèd accents and untimely words,

refresh] refreshing   flourish] flowering   And that] And when   approve] prove
untimely] old-fashioned

Paint shadows in imaginary lines
Which well the reach of their high wits records;
But I must sing of thee, and those fair eyes
Authentic shall my verse in time to come,
When yet th' unborn shall say, 'Lo, where she lies,
Whose beauty made him speak that else was dumb.'
These are the arks, the trophies I erect,
That fortify thy name against old age;
And these thy sacred virtues must protect
Against the dark, and time's consuming rage.
   Though th' error of my youth in them appear,
   Suffice, they show I lived and loved thee dear.

An Ode

Now 'each creature joys the other,
   Passing happy days and hours;
One bird reports unto another
   In the fall of silver showers,
Whilst the earth, our common mother,
   Hath her bosom decked with flowers,

Whilst the greatest torch of heaven
   With bright rays warms Flora's lap,
Making nights and days both even,
   Cheering plants with fresher sap:
My field of flowers quite bereaven,
   Wants refresh of better hap.

Echo, daughter of the air,
   Babbling guest of rocks and hills,
Knows the name of my fierce fair,
   And sounds the accents of my ills.
Each thing pities my despair,
   Whilst that she her lover kills,

Whilst that she, O cruel maid,
   Doth me and my love despise;
My life's flourish is decayed,

Authentic shall] Shall authenticate   reports] re-echoes   fair] fair one

That depended on her eyes:
But her will must be obeyed,
And well he ends, for love who dies.

EDMUND SPENSER (1552?–1599)

From *Amoretti*

XXXVII

What guile is this, that those her golden tresses
She doth attire under a net of gold;
And with sly skill so cunningly them dresses,
That which is gold or hair may scarce be told?
Is it that men's frail eyes, which gaze too bold,
She may entangle in that golden snare;
And, being caught, may craftily enfold
Their weaker hearts, which are not well aware?
Take heed, therefore, mine eyes, how ye do stare
Henceforth too rashly on that guileful net,
In which, if ever ye entrappèd are,
Out of her bands ye by no means shall get.
  Fondness it were for any, being free,
  To covet fetters, though they golden be.

LV

So oft as I her beauty do behold,
And therewith do her cruelty compare,
I marvel of what substance was the mould,
The which her made at once so cruel fair.
Not earth, for her high thoughts more heavenly are;
Not water, for her love doth burn like fire;
Not air, for she is not so light or rare;
Not fire, for she doth freeze with faint desire.
Then needs another element inquire
Whereof she mote be made—that is, the sky;

Fondness] Foolishness   mote] might

For to the heaven her haughty looks aspire,
And eke her mind is pure immortal high.
　Then, sith to heaven ye likened are the best,
　Be like in mercy as in all the rest.

LXX

Fresh spring, the herald of love's mighty king,
In whose coat armor richly are displayed
All sorts of flowers, the which on earth do spring,
In goodly colors gloriously arrayed—
Go to my love, where she is careless laid,
Yet in her winter's bower not well awake;
Tell her the joyous time will not be stayed
Unless she do him by the forelock take;
Bid her therefore herself soon ready make,
To wait on Love amongst his lovely crew,
Where every one that misseth then her make
Shall be by him amerced with penance due.
　Make haste, therefore, sweet love, whilst it is prime,
　For none can call again the passèd time.

LXXV

One day I wrote her name upon the strand,
But came the waves and washèd it away:
Again I wrote it with a second hand,
But came the tide and made my pains his prey.
'Vain man,' said she, 'that dost in vain essay
A mortal thing so to immortalize;
For I myself shall, like to this, decay,
And eke my name be wipèd out likewise.'
'Not so,' quod I, 'let baser things devise
To die in dust, but you shall live by fame;
My verse your virtues rare shall èternize,

eke] also　sith] since　her make] her mate　amerced] punished　devise] resolve

And in the heavens write your glorious name:
Where, whenas death shall all the world subdue,
Our love shall live, and later life renew.'

LXXXI

Fair is my love, when her fair golden hairs
With the loose wind ye waving chance to mark;
Fair, when the rose in her red cheeks appears,
Or in her eyes the fire of love does spark.
Fair, when her breast, like a rich-laden bark,
With precious merchandise she forth doth lay;
Fair, when that cloud of pride, which oft doth dark
Her goodly light, with smiles she drives away.
But fairest she, when so she doth display
The gate with pearls and rubies richly dight,
Through which her words so wise do make their way
To bear the message of her gentle sprite.
  The rest be works of nature's wonderment,
  But this the work of heart's astonishment.

THOMAS LODGE (*c.* 1557–1625)

From *Phyllis*

XIII

Love guards the roses of thy lips
  And flies about them like a bee;
If I approach he forward skips,
  And if I kiss he stingeth me.

Love in thine eyes doth build his bower,
  And sleeps within their pretty shine;
And if I look the boy will lour,
  And from their orbs shoot shafts divine.

dight] adorned   sprite] spirit

Love works thy heart within his fire,
　　And in my tears doth firm the same;
And if I 'tempt it, will retire,
　　And of my plaints doth make a game.

Love, let me cull her choicest flowers,
　　And pity me, and calm her eye,
Make soft her heart, dissolve her lours,
　　Then will I praise thy deity.

But if thou do not, Love, I'll truly serve her
In spite of thee, and by firm faith deserve her.

XV

My Phyllis hath the morning sun
　　At first to look upon her,
And Phyllis hath morn-waking birds
　　Her risings for to honor.
My Phyllis hath prime-feathered flowers
　　That smile when she treads on them,
And Phyllis hath a gallant flock
　　That leaps since she doth own them.
But Phyllis hath so hard a heart—
　　Alas, that she should have it!—
As yields no mercy to desert
　　Nor grace to those that crave it.
Sweet sun, when thou look'st on,
　　Pray her regard my moan;
Sweet birds, when you sing to her,
　　To yield some pity woo her;
Sweet flowers, whenas she treads on,
　　Tell her, her beauty deads one;
And if in life her love she nill agree me,
Pray her, before I die she will come see me.

firm] harden by cooling　　'tempt] try to obtain　　whenas . . . on] when she
treads on you　　nill] will not

Accurst be Love

Accurst be Love, and those that trust his trains!
    He tastes the fruit whilst others toil,
    He brings the lamp, we lend the oil,
    He sows distress, we yield him soil,
    He wageth war, we bide the foil.

Accurst be Love, and those that trust his trains!
    He lays the trap, we seek the snare,
    He threateneth death, we speak him fair,
    He coins deceits, we foster care,
    He favoreth pride, we count it rare.

Accurst be Love, and those that trust his trains!
    He seemeth blind, yet wounds with art,
    He vows content, he pays with smart,
    He swears relief, yet kills the heart,
    He calls for truth, yet scorns desart.
Accurst be Love, and those that trust his trains!
Whose heaven is hell, whose perfect joys are pains.

For pity, pretty eyes, surcease

For pity, pretty eyes, surcease
To give me war, and grant me peace.
Triumphant eyes, why bear you arms
Against a heart that thinks no harms?
A heart already quite appalled,
A heart that yields and is enthralled?
Kill rebels, proudly that resist,
Not those that in true faith persist,
And conquered serve your deity.—
Will you, alas! command me die?
Then die I yours, and death my cross;
But unto you pertains the loss.

foil] repulse, defeat

BARNABE BARNES (*c.* 1569–1609)

From *Parthenophil and Parthenophe*

LXVI

Ah, sweet Content, where is thy mild abode?
Is it with shepherds and light-hearted swains,
Which sing upon the downs and pipe abroad,
Tending their flocks and cattle on the plains?
Ah, sweet Content, where dost thou safely rest?
In heaven with angels which the praises sing
Of him that made and rules at his behest
The minds and hearts of every living thing?
Ah, sweet Content, where doth thine harbor hold?
Is it in churches with religious men
Which please the gods with prayèrs manifold,
And in their studies meditate it then?
    Whether thou dost in heaven or earth appear,
    Be where thou wilt, thou wilt not harbor here!

E. C. (*c.* 1595)

From *Emaricdulfe*

XXIX

My heart is like a ship on Neptune's back;
Thy beauty is the sea where my ship saileth;
Thy frowns the surges are that threat my wrack,
Thy smiles the winds that on my sails soft galeth.
Long tossed betwixt fair hope and foul despair,
My sea-sick heart, arrivèd on thy shore—
Thy love, I mean—begs that he may repair
His broken vessel with thy bounteous store.
Dido relieved Æneas in distress,
And lent him love, and gave to him her heart;
If half such bounty thou to me express,

galeth] bloweth   foul] ugly

From thy fair shore I never will depart,
But thank kind fortune that my course did sort
To suffer shipwreck on so swect a port.

GEORGE CHAPMAN (1559?–1634)

From *A Coronet for his Mistress Philosophy*

I

Muses that sing love's sensual empery,
And lovers kindling your enragèd fires
At Cupid's bonfires burning in the eye,
Blown with the empty breath of vain desires;
You that prefer the painted cabinet
Before the wealthy jewels it doth store ye,
That all your joys in dying figures set,
And stain the living substance of your glory:
Abjure those joys, abhor their memory,
And let my love the honored subject be
Of love, and honor's còmplete history;
Your eyes were never yet let in to see
  The majesty and riches of the mind,
  But dwell in darkness; for your god is blind.

BARTHOLOMEW GRIFFIN (d. 1602)

From *Fidessa*

XXXV

I have not spent the April of my time,
The sweet of youth, in plotting in the air,
But do at first adventure seek to climb,
Whilst flowers of blooming years are green and fair.
I am no leaving of all-withering age,
I have not suffered many winter lours;

sort] allot   empery] sovereignty   dying] perishable

I feel no storm unless my love do rage,
And then in grief I spend both days and hours.
This yet doth comfort, that my flower lasted
Until it did approach my sun too near,
And then, alas, untimely was it blasted,
So soon as once thy beauty did appear.
   But after all, my comfort rests in this,
   That for thy sake my youth decayèd is.

RICHARD LYNCHE (*c.* 1596)

From *Diella*

IV

What sugared terms, what all-persuading art,
What sweet mellifluous words, what wounding looks
Love used for his admittance to my heart!
Such eloquence was never read in books.
He promised pleasure, rest, and endless joy,
Fruition of the fairest she alive.
His pleasure, pain; rest, trouble; joy, annoy,
Have I since found, which me of bliss deprive.
The Trojan horse thus have I now let in,
Wherein enclosed these armèd men were placed:
Bright eyes, fair cheeks, sweet lips, and milk-white skin;
These foes my life have overthrown and razed.
   Fair outward shows prove inwardly the worst,
   Love looketh fair, but lovers are accurst.

ROBERT TOFTE (d. 1620)

From *Laura*

VII

When she was born she came with smiling eye
Laughing into the world, a sign of glee;
When I was born, to her quite contrary,

Wailing I came into the world to see.
   Then mark this wonder strange: what nature gave,
   From first to th' last this fashion kept we have.
She in my sad laments doth take great joy;
I, through her laughing, die, and languish must
Unless that love, to save me from this 'noy,
Do unto me, unworthy, show so just
   As for to change her laughter into pain,
   And my complaints into her joy again.

VIII

In love his kingdom great two fools there be:
My lady's one, myself the other am.
The fond behavior of both which to see,
Whoso but nicely marks will say the same.
Foolish our thoughts are; foolish our desire;
Foolish our hearts in fancy's flame to fry;
Foolish to burn in love's hot scorching fire,—
But what! Fools are we none. My tongue doth lie.
   For who most foolish is and fond, in love,
   More wiser far than others oft doth prove.

WILLIAM SHAKESPEARE (1564–1616)

From *Sonnets*

XII

When I do count the clock that tells the time,
And see the brave day sunk in hideous night;
When I behold the violet past prime,
And sable curls all silvered o'er with white;
When lofty trees I see barren of leaves,
Which erst from heat did canopy the herd,
And summer's green all girded up in sheaves,
Borne on the bier with white and bristly beard;
   Then of thy beauty do I question make,

Unless that] Unless   brave] splendid   erst] formerly

That thou among the wastes of time must go,
Since sweets and beauties do themselves forsake,
And die as fast as they see others grow;
  And nothing 'gainst time's scythe can make defence,
  Save breed, to brave him, when he takes thee hence.

XVIII

Shall I compare thee to a summer's day?
Thou art more lovely and more temperate:
Rough winds do shake the darling buds of May,
And summer's lease hath all too short a date.
Sometime too hot the eye of heaven shines,
And often is his gold complexion dimmed;
And every fair from fair sometime declines,
By chance, or nature's changing course, untrimmed:
But thy eternal summer shall not fade,
Nor lose possession of that fair thou owest;
Nor shall death brag thou wander'st in his shade
When in eternal lines to time thou growest.
  So long as men can breathe, or eyes can see,
  So long lives this, and this gives life to thee.

XXIX

When in disgrace with fortune and men's eyes,
I all alone beweep my outcast state,
And trouble deaf heaven with my bootless cries,
And look upon myself, and curse my fate,
Wishing me like to one more rich in hope,
Featured like him, like him with friends possessed,
Desiring this man's art, and that man's scope,
With what I most enjoy contented least;
Yet in these thoughts myself almost despising,
Haply I think on thee, and then my state,
Like to the lark at break of day arising
From sullen earth, sings hymns at heaven's gate:
  For thy sweet love remembered such wealth brings,
  That then I scorn to change my state with kings.

fair] beauty   untrimmed] undecked   owest] hast   to time] forever

XXX

When to the sessions of sweet silent thought
I summon up remembrance of things past,
I sigh the lack of many a thing I sought,
And with old woes new wail my dear time's waste;
Then can I drown an eye, unused to flow,
For precious friends hid in death's dateless night,
And weep afresh love's long since canceled woe,
And moan th' expense of many a vanished sight.
Then can I grieve at grievances fore-gone,
And heavily from woe to woe tell o'er
The sad account of fore-bemoanèd moan,
Which I new pay, as if not paid before:
But if the while I think on thee, dear friend,
All losses are restored, and sorrows end.

XXXIII

Full many a glorious morning have I seen
Flatter the mountain tops with sovereign eye,
Kissing with golden face the meadows green,
Gilding pale streams with heavenly alchemy;
Anon permit the basest clouds to ride
With ugly rack on his celestial face,
And from the forlorn world his visage hide,
Stealing unseen to west with this disgrace.
Even so my sun one early morn did shine,
With all triumphant splendor on my brow;
But out, alack! he was but one hour mine,
The region cloud hath masked him from me now:
Yet him for this my love no whit disdaineth;
Suns of the world may stain, when heaven's sun,
staineth.

LX

Like as the waves make towards the pebbled shore,
So do our minutes hasten to their end;

expense] loss   rack] cloud-mass driven by the wind in the upper air   region
cloud] the rack   stain] lose luster

Each changing place with that which goes before,
In sequent toil all forwards do contend.
Nativity, once in the main of light,
Crawls to maturity, wherewith being crowned,
Crooked eclipses 'gainst his glory fight,
And time that gave doth now his gift confound.
Time doth transfix the flourish set on youth,
And delves the parallels in beauty's brow;
Feeds on the rarities of nature's truth,
And nothing stands but for his scythe to mow:
  And yet to times in hope my verse shall stand,
  Praising thy worth, despite his cruel hand.

LXIV

When I have seen by time's fell hand defaced
The rich proud cost of out-worn buried age;
When sometime lofty towers I see down rased,
And brass eternal slave to mortal rage:
When I have seen the hungry ocean gain
Advantage on the kingdom of the shore,
And the firm soil win of the wat'ry main,
Increasing store with loss, and loss with store:
When I have seen such interchange of state,
Or state itself confounded to decay,
Ruin hath taught me thus to ruminate:
That time will come and take my love away.
  This thought is as a death, which cannot choose
  But weep to have that which it fears to lose.

LXXI

No longer mourn for me when I am dead,
Than you shall hear the surly sullen bell
Give warning to the world that I am fled
From this vile world, with vilest worms to dwell:
Nay, if you read this line, remember not
The hand that writ it; for I love you so

once] when once   main of light] the world   transfix] pierce   flourish] adornment, gloss

That I in your sweet thoughts would be forgot,
If thinking on me then should make you woe.
O if, I say, you look upon this verse,
When I perhaps compounded am with clay,
Do not so much as my poor name rehearse,
But let your love even with my life decay,
   Lest the wise world should look into your moan,
   And mock you with me after I am gone.

LXXIII

That time of year thou may'st in me behold,
When yellow leaves, or none, or few, do hang
Upon those boughs which shake against the cold,
Bare ruined choirs, where late the sweet birds sang.
In me thou see'st the twilight of such day
As after sunset fadeth in the west,
Which by and by black night doth take away,
Death's second self, that seals up all in rest:
In me thou see'st the glowing of such fire,
That on the ashes of his youth doth lie,
As the death-bed whereon it must expire,
Consumed with that which it was nourished by.
   This thou perceiv'st, which makes thy love more strong,
   To love that well which thou must leave ere long.

CIV

To me, fair friend, you never can be old,
For as you were when first your eye I eyed,
Such seems your beauty still. Three winters cold
Have from the forests shook three summers' pride;
Three beauteous springs to yellow autumn turned,
In process of the seasons have I seen;
Three April perfumes in three hot Junes burned,
Since first I saw you fresh, which yet are green.
Ah! yet doth beauty, like a dial hand,
Steal from his figure, and no pace perceived;
So your sweet hue, which methinks still doth stand,

Hath motion, and mine eye may be deceived;
  For fear of which, hear this, thou age unbred:
  Ere you were born was beauty's summer dead.

CVI

When in the chronicle of wasted time
I see descriptions of the fairest wights,
And beauty making beautiful old rhyme,
In praise of ladies dead, and lovely knights;
Then in the blazon of sweet beauty's best
Of hand, of foot, of lip, of eye, of brow,
I see their antique pen would have expressed
Even such a beauty as you master now.
So all their praises are but prophecies
Of this our time, all you prefiguring;
And for they looked but with divining eyes,
They had not skill enough your worth to sing:
  For we, which now behold these present days,
  Have eyes to wonder, but lack tongues to praise.

CXVI

Let me not to the marriage of true minds
Admit impediments: love is not love,
Which alters when it alteration finds,
Or bends with the remover to remove:
O no! it is an ever-fixèd mark,
That looks on tempests, and is never shaken;
It is the star to every wand'ring bark,
Whose worth's unknown, although his height be taken.
Love 's not Time's fool, though rosy lips and cheeks
Within his bending sickle's compass come;
Love alters not with his brief hours and weeks,

master] possess   And for] And because   divining] conjecturing   skill] cause remover] changeable, fickle one   worth] excellence; perhaps, in a star, magnitude or astrological influence   height] elevation; 'we may know something about love, or a star, but not the full value of either.'

But bears it out even to the edge of doom.
If this be error, and upon me proved,
I never writ, nor no man ever loved.

CXXIX

The expense of spirit in a waste of shame
Is lust in action; and till action, lust
Is perjured, murderous, bloody, full of blame,
Savage, extreme, rude, cruel, not to trust;
Enjoyed no sooner but despisèd straight;
Past reason hunted; and no sooner had,
Past reason hated, as a swallowed bait,
On purpose laid to make the taker mad—
Mad in pursuit, and in possession so;
Had, having, and in quest to have, extreme;
A bliss in proof,—and proved, a very woe;
Before, a joy proposed; behind, a dream.
    All this the world well knows; yet none knows well
    To shun the heaven that leads men to this hell.

CXXX

My mistress' eyes are nothing like the sun;
Coral is far more red than her lips' red:
If snow be white, why then her breasts are dun;
If hairs be wires, black wires grow on her head.
I have seen roses damasked, red and white,
But no such roses see I in her cheeks;
And in some perfumes is there more delight
Than in the breath that from my mistress reeks.
I love to hear her speak, yet well I know
That music hath a far more pleasing sound;
I grant I never saw a goddess go:
My mistress, when she walks, treads on the ground.
    And yet, by heaven, I think my love as rare
    As any she belied with false compare.

The . . . action] Lust in action is . . .   expense] expending   straight] immediately   knows well] knows well how   damasked] deep pink   reeks] emanates   go] walk

RICHARD BARNFIELD (1574–1627)

In Praise of Music and Poetry

If music and sweet poetry agree,
As they must needs, the sister and the brother,
Then must the love be great 'twixt thee and me,
Because thou lov'st the one, and I the other.
Dowland to thee is dear, whose heavenly touch
Upon the lute doth ravish human sense;
Spenser to me, whose deep conceit is such
As, passing all conceit, needs no defence.
Thou lov'st to hear the sweet melodious sound
That Phœbus' lute, the queen of music, makes;
And I in deep delight am chiefly drowned
Whenas himself to singing he betakes.
  One god is god of both, as poets feign;
  One knight loves both, and both in thee remain.

JOSHUA SYLVESTER (1563–1618)

Sonnet

Were I as base as is the lowly plain,
And you, my love, as high as heaven above,
Yet should the thoughts of me, your humble swain,
Ascend to heaven in honor of my love.
Were I as high as heaven above the plain,
And you, my love, as humble and as low
As are the deepest bottoms of the main,
Wheresoe'er you were, with you my love should go.
Were you the earth, dear love, and I the skies,
My love should shine on you like to the sun,
And look upon you with ten thousand eyes,
Till heaven waxed blind and till the world were dun.
  Wheresoe'er I am, below, or else above you,
  Wheresoe'er you are, my heart shall truly love you.

conceit] imagination   Joshua Sylvester] Sylvester's authorship of the poem is queried
by E. K. Chambers, *The Oxford Book of Sixteenth Century Verse*, p. 887, note.
dun] dark

CHARLES BEST (*c.* 1570–1627)

A Sonnet of the Moon

Look how the pale queen of the silent night
Doth cause the ocean to attend upon her;
And he, as long as she is in his sight,
With her full tide is ready her to honor.
But when the silver wagon of the moon
Is mounted up so high he cannot follow,
The sea calls home his crystal waves to moan,
And with low ebb doth manifest his sorrow.
So you that are the sovereign of my heart
Have all my joys attending on your will;
My joys, low-ebbing when you do depart,
When you return, their tide my heart doth fill.
   So as you come and as you do depart,
   Joys ebb and flow within my tender heart.

SIR EDWARD DYER (d. 1607)

The lowest trees have tops

The lowest trees have tops, the ant her gall,
   The fly her spleen, the little spark his heat;
The slender hairs cast shadows, though but small,
   And bees have stings, although they be not great.
Seas have their source, and so have shallow springs,
And love is love, in beggars as in kings.

Where waters smoothest run, there deepest are the fords;
   The dial stirs, yet none perceives it move;
The firmest faith is found in fewest words;
   The turtles do not sing, and yet they love.
True hearts have ears and eyes, no tongues to speak;
They hear and see, and sigh—and then they break.

MICHAEL DRAYTON (1563–1631)

From *Idea*

IV

Bright star of beauty, on whose eye-lids sit
A thousand nymph-like and enamored graces,
The goddesses of memory and wit,
Which there in order take their several places;
In whose dear bosom, sweet, delicious Love
Lays down his quiver, which he once did bear,
Since he that blessèd paradise did prove,
And leaves his mother's lap to sport him there.
Let others strive to entertain with words,
My soul is of a braver mettle made;
I hold that vile which vulgar wit affords,
In me's that faith which time cannot invade:
   Let what I praise be still made good by you,
   Be you most worthy, whilst I am most true.

XX

An evil spirit, your beauty, haunts me still,
Wherewith, alas, I have been long possessed,
Which ceaseth not to tempt me to each ill,
Nor gives me once but one poor minute's rest;
In me it speaks, whether I sleep or wake,
And when by means to drive it out I try,
With greater torments then it me doth take,
And tortures me in most extremity;
Before my face it lays down my despairs,
And hastes me on unto a sudden death,
Now tempting me to drown myself in tears,
And then in sighing to give up my breath.
   Thus am I still provoked to every evil
   By this good-wicked spirit, sweet angel-devil.

LXI

Since there's no help, come, let us kiss and part;
Nay, I have done, you get no more of me,
And I am glad, yea, glad with all my heart
That thus so cleanly I myself can free;
Shake hands forever, cancel all our vows,
And when we meet at any time again,
Be it not seen in either of our brows
That we one jot of former love retain.—
Now at the last gasp of love's latest breath,
When, his pulse failing, passion speechless lies,
When faith is kneeling by his bed of death,
And innocence is closing up his eyes,
    Now if thou would'st, when all have given him over,
    From death to life thou might'st him yet recover.

The Crier

Good folk, for gold or hire,
But help me to a crier;
For my poor heart is run astray
After two eyes that passed this way.
    Oyez, oyez, oyez!
    If there be any man
    In town or country can
    Bring me my heart again,
    I'll please him for his pain.
And by these marks I will you show
That only I this heart do owe:
    It is a wounded heart,
    Wherein yet sticks the dart;
Ev'ry piece sore hurt throughout it;
Faith and *troth* writ round about it.
It was a tame heart and a dear,
    And never used to roam;
But, having got this haunt, I fear

pain] pains   owe] own   haunt] habit

'Twill hard-ly stay at home.
For God's sake, walking by the way,
    If you my heart do see,
Either impound it for a stray,
    Or send it back to me.

Canzonet

To his Coy Love

I pray thee leave, love me no more,
    Call home the heart you gave me;
I but in vain that saint adore,
    That can, but will not save me.
These poor half-kisses kill me quite;
    Was ever man thus servèd,
Amidst an ocean of delight
    For pleasure to be stervèd?

Show me no more those snowy breasts,
    With azure riverets branchèd,
Where, whilst mine eye with plenty feasts,
    Yet is my thirst not staunchèd.
O, Tantalus! thy pains ne'er tell,
    By me thou art prevented;
'Tis nothing to be plagued in hell,
    But thus in heaven tormented!

Clip me no more in those dear arms,
    Nor thy life's comfort call me;
O, these are but too powerful charms,
    And do but more enthrall me.
But see how patient I am grown
    In all this coil about thee:
Come, nice thing, let thy heart alone,
    I cannot live without thee.

stervèd] starved   prevented] anticipated   clip] embrace   coil] fuss   nice] coy

SIR JOHN DAVIES (1569–1626)

From *Gulling Sonnets*

IV

The hardness of her heart and truth of mine
When the all-seeing eyes of heaven did see,
They straight concluded that by power divine
To other forms our hearts should turnèd be.
Then hers, as hard as flint, a flint became,
And mine, as true as steel, to steel was turned;
And then between our hearts sprang forth the flame
Of kindest love, which unextinguished burned.
And long the sacred lamp of mutual love
Incessantly did burn in glory bright,
Until my folly did her fury move
To recompense my service with despite;
   And to put out with snuffers of her pride
   The lamp of love which else had never died.

JOHN DAVIES OF HEREFORD (1565?–1618)

*The Author, loving these homely meats specially, viz., Cream,
Pancakes, Buttered Pippin-pies (laugh, good people) and
Tobacco, writ to that worthy and virtuous gentlewoman
whom he calls Mistress, as followeth*

If there were, O! an Hellespont of cream
Between us, milk-white mistress, I would swim
To you, to show to both my love's extreme,
Leander-like,—yea! dive from brim to brim.
But met I with a buttered pippin-pie
Floating upon 't, that would I make my boat
To waft me to you without jeopardy,
Though sea-sick I might be while it did float.
Yet if a storm should rise, by night or day,
Of sugar-snows and hail of caraways,

Then, if I found a pancake in my way,
It like a plank should bring me to your kays;
   Which having found, if they tobacco kept,
   The smoke should dry me well before I slept.

kays] quays

IV

LYRICS IN PLAYS
1560–1642

LYRICS IN PLAYS

The waning of the sonnet fashion coincides in time with the close of the sixteenth century and of Elizabeth's reign. Before proceeding to illustrate the work of those poets who belong in spirit or in date to the seventeenth century, it has seemed wise to assemble from both centuries some specimens of the lyrics which appeared in plays. As will be seen in reading the selections, this medium engaged the attention of authors who appear in nearly all the other sections, and the lyrics frequently reflect the poetic fashions contemporary with the plays in which they appeared. It will be noticed that the majority of the pieces here quoted are songs, the composition of which was encouraged by the fact that plays were performed by boy actors of the Queen's Chapel and other companies in which there were trained musicians. Also, music was an essential feature of the masques presented at court or in the houses of the nobility, and the authors of such entertainments—Jonson, Daniel and others—naturally composed songs for them. But the drama found occasional use for the spoken lyric also. In *Love's Labour's Lost,* Shakespeare not only introduces two sonnets proper, which were published separately in *The Passionate Pilgrim* as poems by him, but uses the sonnet form in dialogue in several instances. There are two sonnets in *Romeo and Juliet,* one in *All's Well,* and one in *Henry V.* (It will be noticed that all these plays are early, *All's Well* being the only one that falls after 1600. After this Shakespeare did not use the sonnet in his plays.) The familiar figure of the poet reading his verses aloud or reciting them to his mistress is employed by Jonson (p. 248). Thus the use of independent lyrics in the plays was not strictly limited to song.

In this section we have to do with a lyric tradition older than that of the sonnet or the pastoral, a tradition originating in the

213

liturgical plays of the tenth century and continuing unbroken throughout the development of the drama. With the rise of secular plays, especially when presented by boy companies of trained singers, the custom gained in popularity and importance, so that many plays have at least one song and some as many as a dozen. When, as is sometimes the case, all the songs are given to the same character, we may suspect that the company could boast of but one trained singer, and it is seldom that more than three characters in a play have songs. Three-men's songs seem to have been especially popular; Dekker makes special mention in the dedicatory address to his *Shoemakers' Holiday* of the fact that his play contains two of them. Songs in dialogue are frequent.

Some poets—Fletcher, Dekker, Peele are examples—wrote no other lyrics than those in their plays. Nashe's best lyric (p. 228), one of the great utterances of our literature, is found in his masque-like *Summer's Last Will and Testament,* and Shirley's reputation as a lyric poet of high rank owes much to a single song in a play (p. 263). Shakespeare wrote for plays at least half a dozen of the world's finest lyrics. The prevalence in Elizabethan drama of this appeal to the contemporary passion for music is shown by the existence in play-texts of stage-directions calling for songs although the songs themselves are not given, the gaps presumably being filled in the performance with well-known songs or songs from other men's works. A single play of Marston's contains thirteen such stage-directions.

The function of song in the secular drama was originally to amuse. Its first appearance is as a complementary, and sometimes even extraneous, form of entertainment added to comedy. The earliest song of high quality in a tragedy is that in Peele's *David and Bethsabe* (p. 226), and it, while of a serious sweetness, is not precisely tragic in import. But in *Ralph Roister Doister,* the first regular English comedy, the schoolmaster-author, Nicholas Udall, introduces half a dozen songs which owe nothing to his Latin model, Plautus. Especially at the end of a comedy, it was conventional for the company to join in some merry catch, often supplemented with a dance, before kneeling to ask God's blessing on the Queen.

In certain scenes and situations, moreover, singing lent a realistic touch. What more natural than that Hodge and Diccon, sitting down to drink, should lift their lusty voices in praise of ale, that cobblers and grave-diggers should sing at their work, or gipsies around their fire roar out a catch? For such occasions any good song in keeping with the spirit of the action would do, and the dramatist, if he had not time to compose one, could rely upon the stage-manager to insert something suitable. But as a more effective dramaturgy was developed, the playwrights were quick to perceive the possibilities of song for a variety of other and more organic uses: the bridging of a time-interval; the creation of suspense, foreshadowing, atmosphere; the revelation of character, and even the conveying to one of the characters on the stage, or to the audience, of something essential to the plot itself. A song could be devised which would not only seem natural in a given situation but could also, by the meaning of its words and the spirit of its music, subserve one of these additional purposes, or several of them at once. The song which the peddler warbles on the road can also reveal that he is a sophisticated rogue. That Desdemona should sing softly to herself while preparing for the night in the intimacy of her chamber is natural and realistic enough, but that, unaware that she is to die, she should sing *The Willow Song,* with its undertone of tragedy, sharpens the irony of her singing at all and foreshadows the dreadful scene of her murder, which follows. Meanwhile, by lengthening the scene, the song has aided in the creation of suspense. That Portia's servants should sing whilst Bassanio comments on the caskets to himself is good stage technique: Portia may well desire it to ease the almost unbearable tension of the moment and it holds the attention of the audience during the, for them, less dramatic interval during which he walks from gold casket to silver, from silver to lead, and hesitates before each. But may not a musical reminder that true love is not a thing of the eyes (p. 232) help him to make the correct choice, lead, even if we doubt the ingenious suggestion that the sound of 'bred' and 'head' coupled in singing with the *l*-sound of the burden, actually caused the word 'lead' to echo in his ear? Many of the songs in the plays, then, have a more integral part than that of mere entertainment, and a study of them in their setting is most revealing as to the subtle effectiveness of certain scenes, and the constructive ingenuity of the dramatists.

On the other hand, in seventeenth-century comedy of manners and in Restoration drama, the lyrics are quite as frequently in contrast with the tone of the play. Jonson's

> Come, my Celia, let us prove,
> While we may, the sports of love;

is so perfectly in the key of those courtly invitations to dalliance which are challenges, provocations, rather than serious attacks upon virtue, that we are rather surprised to find Volpone using it as prelude to an actual attempt at seduction. The song of Volpone's dwarf, *Fools, they are the only nation,* fits the play but is an epigram, satiric rather than lyrical. Heywood, Dryden, and others put lyrics in various contemporary veins into the mouths of Roman soldiers, Mexican women—whomever the plot calls for.

It is also most interesting to see, in a representative selection of lyrics from drama, chronologically arranged, how consistently they reflect the changing lyrical fashions, even when the drama in its appeal to a different audience diverges from them. The songs of Lyly and Peele partake of the pastoral and classical spirit preceding 1590, echoed in the following decade by those of *Love's Labour's Lost, As You Like It,* and Dekker's *Patient Grissill. Who is Sylvia* and *O mistress mine* say with exquisite perfection what the sonneteers, hampered by Italianate convention, were trying to say; while a decade later the dirge from *Cymbeline* has already something of the somberness, the dying fall, of seventeenth-century utterance, a note that deepens in the dirge from Ford's *Broken Heart* and Shirley's *The glories of our blood and state.* The homespun good fellowship of prentices and journeymen with homespun verse to match is in the 'Three-Men's Songs' of Dekker's *Shoemakers' Holiday;* classicism of form and theme is at its height in such a lyric as Jonson's *See the chariot at hand here of love,* though he inserted it in a cynical comedy of contemporary manners; a foretaste of the playful mockery of the cavaliers is heard in the songs of *The Poetaster* and *Volpone.* The school of coarse, rowdy, realistic comedy could hardly have a better token than Middleton's

Come, my dainty doxies, or the sentimentalism of Beaumont and Fletcher than *Lay a garland on my hearse.* It is not altogether fancy to see in Fletcher's *Drink today and drown all sorrow* an epitome of Cavalier hedonism, or in Webster's dirge from *The White Devil,* or Massinger's *Why art thou slow, thou rest of trouble, death?* the essence of the rich, strange melancholy of later tragedy. Finally, we have in Suckling's *Why so pale and wan?* and Habington's *Fine young folly* the perfection of the elegant cynicism of the Cavalier. To complete the picture from later sections, Milton's songs in *Comus* have the leisurely sweetness of revived Spenserianism, and the songs of Dryden's plays, though well above the level of their time, show the conventionalized Cavalier attitudes of Restoration and later verse.

As to the comparative achievement of the various dramatists in the lyric, the first of its masters was John Lyly, unless we suppose the songs published with his plays to be later interpolations by another hand. Lyly had an unusual opportunity in the performance of his plays by the trained child musicians of the Queen's Chapel, and it is pleasant to believe that he proved himself equal to it by composing charming songs and placing them effectively in the plays. It has been objected that he wrote epigrams rather than lyrics, but the many readers who admire his best-known song, *Cupid and my Campaspe,* would be loath to deny it the possibility of genuine emotion, however playfully expressed. Certainly no such criticism could be leveled at Thomas Nashe, who has left us, though few, some of the purest—and saddest—lyrics in our tongue. Though it can hardly be an accident that these poems were written in a plague year and that the refrain of one of them, 'Lord have mercy on us,' was the official inscription which, with a cross, was affixed to the doors of 'visited houses,' they have a quality above occasion, even so terrible a one as the plague. They are universal laments for beauty that must die.

As to Shakespeare, the lyrics in his plays, like everything else that he touched, are beyond comparison in beauty and variety. Both in metrical effect: in the treacherous trochaic measure of the witch songs from *Macbeth,* or the intricate variation of movement and line-length within the stanza in *Come away, come away, death,* and in theme: in the exquisite feeling of *O mistress mine,* that distillation of all poems of young love that ever were, or in the beauty wed to strangeness of *Full fathom five,* he is here undisputed king. Next to him, perhaps, in absolute quality as in fecundity is his collaborator, John Fletcher, who displays something of the same mastery of expression combined with a complete absence of effort. Fletcher is not startling nor very original, perhaps, but he has done what many have tried and failed to do: he has united all but perfect beauty to all but perfect naturalness. And not far below him stands Jonson. Despite the railings of those critics who, confusing Jonson's theories and manners with his poetry, pronounce the latter to be harsh, stiff, and heavy, these qualities are precisely as demonstrable as Jonson's enmity toward Shakespeare. Both are the purest figments of the imagination. As Lowell remarks, 'Ben, with all his principles off, could soar and sing with the best of them.' He could also soar with his principles on, quite possibly because of them. Many of his lyrics, especially those in the masques, are nearly perfect in their kind, and the reason for their perfection is to be found in the happy conjunction of a choice lyrical gift with the cultivated taste of genuine scholarship. There are, as Lowell goes on to say, strains in his lyrics which Herrick, the most Catullian of poets since Catullus, could imitate but never match.

With such men to follow, it is amazing what lyrics the lesser dramatists produced: Thomas Dekker, whose life was spent in alternation between the debtors' jail and the lower London theaters in unremitting drudgery under pawn-broking Henslowe, could yet sing like a lark of sweet content and country glee; Anthony Munday, obscure literary hack, reeling out volume after volume of ordinary verse and yet more ordinary prose, reached once or twice a rare level; Thomas Heywood, facile and most productive of dramatists, was visited at moments by the golden touch of lyric inspiration. Even in translations, such as that of Thomas Mabbe from the Spanish *Celestina,* we find songs which are graceful and charming in their own right. From Chapman and Marston alone of them all is it difficult to get a lyric which is not at once good and representative. From all the rest comes music of varying melody and compass: the dainty lightness of Lyly; the sweet sincerity of

Dekker; the delicate, erotic sentiment of Beaumont and Fletcher; the weird and fanciful sorrow of Webster; the classical symmetry and nicety of Jonson; the rich variety and perfect mastery of Shakespeare.

The most striking characteristic of the lyrics from plays is the variety of the themes which they bring within the range of the lyric. It is of them and not of the pastoral or the sonnet that we think when we say that the scope of this old poetry was the scope of life itself. The reader who turns from that roaring tavern bacchanal *Back and side go bare* to the winsomeness of *Ye little birds that sit and sing;* from the droning of Tom Tyler, typical of the 'jigging veins of riming mother wits' so arrogantly laughed off the stage by Marlowe, to the sprightly urbanity of *If I freely may discover;* from a courtly compliment for Campaspe to a riotous gipsy thing like *Come, my dainty doxies;* from the tinkling laughter of a lover and his lass in the springtime to the rich resonance of *The glories of our blood and state* will hardly be tempted to call the Elizabethan lyric 'limited in scope.'

From WILLIAM STEVENSON'S *Gammer Gurton's Needle*

[II. Prologue.   Hodge and Diccon drinking.   *First a song.*]

Back and side go bare, go bare,
  Both foot and hand go cold;
But, belly, God send thee good ale enough,
  Whether it be new or old.

I cannot eat but little meat,
  My stomach is not good;
But sure I think that I can drink
  With him that wears a hood.
Though I go bare, take ye no care,
  I am nothing a-cold;
I stuff my skin so full within
  Of jolly good ale and old.
    Back and side go bare, &c.

I love no roast but a nutbrown toast,
    And a crab laid in the fire;
A little bread shall do me stead,
    Much bread I not desire.
No frost nor snow, no wind, I trow,
    Can hurt me if I would,
I am so wrapped, and throughly lapped
    Of jolly good ale and old.
      Back and side go bare, &c.

And Tib my wife, that as her life
    Loveth well good ale to seek,
Full oft drinks she, till ye may see
    The tears run down her cheeks.
Then doth she troll to me the bowl,
    Even as a maltworm should,
And saith, 'Sweetheart, I took my part
    Of this jolly good ale and old.'
      Back and side go bare, &c.

Now let them drink, till they nod and wink,
    Even as good fellows should do;
They shall not miss to have the bliss
    Good ale doth bring men to;
And all poor souls that have scoured bowls
    Or have them lustily trolled,
God save the lives of them and their wives,
    Whether they be young or old.
      Back and side go bare, &c.

From *Tom Tyler and his Wife*

[Scene I. Tom Tyler cometh in singing.]

The proverb reporteth, no man can deny,
That wedding and hanging is destiny.

crab] crab apple   do me stead] be enough, fill my need   trow] think   troll] pass
wink] close the eyes

I am a poor tiler in simple array,
And get a poor living, but eightpence a day,
My wife as I get it, doth spend it away;
    And 'I cannot help it,' she saith; wot ye why?
    For wedding and hanging is destiny.

I thought when I wed her, she had been a sheep,
At board to be friendly, to sleep when I sleep.
She loves so unkindly, she makes me to weep;
    But I dare say nothing, God wot; wot ye why?
    For wedding and hanging is destiny.

Besides this unkindness whereof my grief grows,
I think few tilers are matched with such shrows;
Before she leaves brawling, she falls to deal blows
    Which early and late doth cause me cry
    That wedding and hanging is destiny.

The more that I please her, the worse she doth like me,
The more I forbear her, the more she doth strike me,
The more that I get her, the more she doth glike me;
    Woe worth this ill fortune that maketh me cry
    That wedding and hanging is destiny.

If I had been hangèd when I had been married,
My torments had ended, though I had miscarried;
If I had been warnèd, then would I have tarried;
    But now—all too lately—I feel and cry
    That wedding and hanging is destiny.

From JOHN PICKERING's *Horestes*

[The muster of Horestes' men. Haltersick sings.]

    Farewell, adieu, that courtly life,
    To war we tend to go;
    It is good sport to see the strife
    Of soldiers in a row.

shrows] shrews   glike] trick

How merrily they forward march
These enemies to slay,
With hey, trim, and trixie too,
Their banners they display.

Now shall we have the golden cheats,
When others want the same;
And soldiers have full many feats
Their enemies to tame;
  With cocking here, and booming there,
  They break their foe's array;
  And lusty lads amid the fields
  Their ensigns do display.

The drum and flute play lustily,
The trumpet blows amain,
And venturous knights courageously
Do march before their train
  With spears in rest, so lively dressed
  In armor bright and gay;
  With hey, trim, and trixie too,
  Their banners they display.

From JOHN LYLY's *Alexander and Campaspe*

[III. v. Alexander's palace. Apelles, a painter in love with Campaspe,
sings.]

Cupid and my Campaspe played
At cards for kisses; Cupid paid.
He stakes his quiver, bow, and arrows,
His mother's doves and team of sparrows,
Loses them too; then down he throws
The coral of his lip, the rose
Growing on's cheek (but none knows how),
With these the crystal of his brow,
And then the dimple of his chin:
All these did my Campaspe win.

cheats] spoils   cocking] *I.e.,* their firearms.

At last he set her both his eyes;
She won, and Cupid blind did rise.
O Love! has she done this to thee?
What shall, alas, become of me?

From JOHN LYLY's *Sapho and Phao*

[IV. iv. Vulcan's smithy. He sings, while they make the arrows.]

My shag-hair Cyclops, come, let's ply
Our Lemnian hammers lustily.
By my wife's sparrows,
I swear these arrows,
Shall singing fly
Through many a wanton's eye.
These headed are with golden blisses,
These silver ones feathered with kisses;
    But this of lead
    Strikes a clown dead,
    When in a dance
    He falls in a trance,
To see his black-brow lass not buss him,
And then whines out for death t' untruss him.
So, so, our work being done, let's play,
Holiday, boys, cry holiday.

From JOHN LYLY's *Midas*

[V. iii. (The end of the play.) *They sing all.*]

Sing to Apollo, god of day,
Whose golden beams with morning play,
And make her eyes so brightly shine,
Aurora's face is called divine;
Sing to Phœbus and that throne
Of diamonds which he sits upon.
   Io, pæans let us sing
   To physic's and to poesy's king!

set] bet   untruss him] loosen his clothing

Crown all his altars with bright fire,
Laurels bind about his lyre,
A Daphnean coronet for his head,
The Muses dance about his bed;
When on his ravishing lute he plays,
Strew his temple round with bays.
   Io, pæans let us sing
   To the glittering Delian king!

From GEORGE PEELE's *Arraignment of Paris*

[I. ii. The vale of Ida. Paris, in love with Œnone, sings with her.]

Œnone.   Fair and fair, and twice so fair,
     As fair as any may be,
    The fairest shepherd on our green,
     A love for any lady.

Paris.   Fair and fair, and twice so fair,
     As fair as any may be,
    Thy love is fair for thee alone
    And for no other lady.

Œnone.   My love is fair, my love is gay,
    As fresh as been the flowers in May,
    And of my love my roundelay,
    My merry, merry roundelay,
     Concludes with Cupid's curse:
    They that do change old love for new
    Pray gods they change for worse!

Ambo simul.   *They that do change, &c.*

Œnone.   Fair and fair, and twice so fair,
     As fair as any may be,
    The fairest shepherd on our green,
     A love for any lady.

Paris.   Fair and fair, and twice so fair,
     As fair as any may be,
    Thy love is fair for thee alone
    And for no other lady.

Œnone.   My love can pipe, my love can sing,
    My love can many a pretty thing,

Ambo simul.] *Together.*

And of his lovely praises ring
My merry, merry roundelays.
Amen to Cupid's curse:
They that do change old love for new
Pray gods they change for worse!
Ambo simul. They that do change, &c.

From GEORGE PEELE's *Polyhymnia*

[Sung before Elizabeth, as preface to the ceremonies on the resignation
of Sir Henry Lee as the Queen's Champion]

His golden locks time hath to silver turned;
   O time too swift, O swiftness never ceasing!
His youth 'gainst time and age hath ever spurned,
   But spurned in vain: youth waneth by increasing.
Beauty, strength, youth, are flowers but fading seen;
Duty, faith, love, are roots, and ever green.

His helmet now shall make a hive for bees,
   And, lovers' sonnets turned to holy psalms,
A man-at-arms must now serve on his knees,
   And feed on prayèrs, which are age his alms;
But though from court to cottage he depart,
His saint is sure of his unspotted heart.

And when he saddest sits in homely cell,
   He'll teach his swains this carol for a song:
'Blest be the hearts that wish my sovereign well,
   Curst be the souls that think her any wrong!
Goddess, allow this agèd man his right,
To be your beadsman now, that was your knight.'

From GEORGE PEELE's *Old Wives' Tale*

[The smith's cottage, before Madge begins her tale.
Fantastic. Sirrah Frolic, I am sure thou are not with-
out some round or other.
Frolic. Else think you me ill brought up.
                              They sing.]

age his] age's

Whenas the rye reach to the chin,
And chopcherry, chopcherry ripe within,
Strawberries swimming in the cream,
And schoolboys playing in the stream;
Then O, then O, then O, my true love said,
Till that time come again,
She could not live a maid.

From GEORGE PEELE's *David and Bethsabe*

[Scene I. Bethsabe bathing. She sings.]

Hot sun, cool fire, tempered with sweet air,
Black shade, fair nurse, shadow my white hair.
Shine, sun; burn, fire; breathe, air, and ease me;
Black shade, fair nurse, shroud me and please me;
Shadow, my sweet nurse, keep me from burning,
Make not my glad cause cause of mourning.
  Let not my beauty's fire
  Inflame unstaid desire,
  Nor pierce any bright eye
  That wandereth lightly.

From *Locrine*

[II. iii. Enter Strumbo, Dorothy, Trumpart, cobbling shoes and singing.]

Trum. We cobblers lead a merry life,
All. Dan, dan, dan, dan;
Strum. Void of all envy and of strife,
All. Dan diddle dan.
Dor. Our ease is great, our labor small,
All. Dan, dan, dan, dan;
Strum. And yet our gains be much withal,
All. Dan diddle dan.
Dor. With this art so fine and fair,
All. Dan, dan, dan, dan;

Whenas] When white] fair unstaid] unrestrained *Locrine*] attributed hesitantly by Chambers to Charles Tilney (d. 1586)

Trum. No occupation may compare,
All. Dan diddle dan.
Strum. For merry pastime and joyful glee,
Dan, dan, dan, dan;
Dor. Most happy men we cobblers be,
Dan diddle dan.
Trum. The can stands full of nappy ale,
Dan, dan, dan, dan;
Strum. In our shop still withouten fail,
Dan diddle dan.
Dor. This is our meat, this is our food,
Dan, dan, dan, dan;
Trum. This brings us to a merry mood,
Dan diddle dan;
Strum. This makes us work for company,
Dan, dan, dan, dan;
Dor. To pull the tankards cheerfully,
Dan diddle dan.
Trum. Drink to thy husband, Dorothy,
Dan, dan, dan, dan;
Dor. Why, then, my Strumbo, there's to thee,
Dan diddle dan.
Strum. Drink thou the rest, Trumpart, amain,
Dan, dan, dan, dan;
Dor. When that is gone, we'll fill't again,
Dan diddle dan.

From THOMAS NASHE's *Summer's Last Will and Testament*

[Enter Ver with his train, singing.]

Spring, the sweet spring, is the year's pleasant king;
Then blooms each thing, then maids dance in a ring,
Cold doth not sting, the pretty birds do sing
Cuckoo, jug-jug, pu-we, to-witta-woo!

nappy] heady   still] always   for company] for company's sake   pull] drink
Ver] See p. 230.

The palm and may make country houses gay,
Lambs frisk and play, the shepherds pipe all day,
And we hear aye birds tune this merry lay:
  Cuckoo, jug-jug, pu-we, to-witta-woo!

The fields breathe sweet, the daisies kiss our feet,
Young lovers meet, old wives a-sunning sit;
In every street these tunes our ears do greet:
  Cuckoo, jug-jug, pu-we, to-witta-woo!
    Spring, the sweet spring!

[*Summer.* Sing me some doleful ditty to the lute,
That may complain of my approaching death.]

Adieu, farewell earth's bliss,
This world uncertain is;
Fond are life's lustful joys,
Death proves them all but toys.
None from his darts can fly:
I am sick, I must die.
  Lord, have mercy on us!

Rich men, trust not in wealth,
Gold cannot buy you health;
Physic himself must fade,   .
All things to end are made.
The plague full swift goes by;
I am sick, I must die.
  Lord, have mercy on us!

Beauty is but a flower
Which wrinkles will devour:
Brightness falls from the air,
Queens have died young and fair,
Dust hath closed Helen's eye.
I am sick, I must die.
  Lord, have mercy on us!

palm] branches   may] hawthorn buds   Fond] Foolish

Strength stoops unto the grave,
Worms feed on Hector brave,
Swords may not fight with fate.
Earth still holds ope her gate;
Come! come! the bells do cry.
I am sick, I must die.
    Lord, have mercy on us!

Wit with his wantonness
Tasteth death's bitterness;
Hell's executioner
Hath no ears for to hear
What vain art can reply.
I am sick, I must die.
    Lord, have mercy on us!

Haste, therefore, each degree,
To welcome destiny.
Heaven is our heritage,
Earth but a player's stage;
Mount we unto the sky.
I am sick, I must die.
    Lord, have mercy on us!

From WILLIAM SHAKESPEARE'S *Two Gentlemen of Verona*

[IV. ii. Under Sylvia's window. Thurio and musicians serenade her.]

Who is Silvia? what is she,
    That all our swains commend her?
Holy, fair, and wise is she;
    The heaven such grace did lend her,
That she might admirèd be.

Is she kind as she is fair?
    For beauty lives with kindness.
Love doth to her eyes repair,
    To help him of his blindness;
And being helped, inhabits there.

Then to Silvia let us sing,
    That Silvia is excelling;
She excels each mortal thing,
    Upon the dull earth dwelling:
To her let us garlands bring.

From WILLIAM SHAKESPEARE's *Love's Labour's Lost*

[IV. iii. The King of Navarre's Park. Dumain, in love, declaims an ode.]

On a day—alack the day!—
Love, whose month is ever May,
Spied a blossom passing fair
Playing in the wanton air:
Through the velvet leaves the wind
All unseen, can passage find;
That the lover, sick to death,
Wished himself the heaven's breath.
'Air,' quoth he, 'thy cheeks may blow:
Air, would I might triumph so!
But, alack, my hand is sworn
Ne'er to pluck thee from thy thorn:
Vow, alack, for youth unmeet,
Youth so apt to pluck a sweet.
Do not call it sin in me
That I am forsworn for thee:
Thou for whom Jove would swear
Juno but an Ethiope were;
And deny himself for Jove,
Turning mortal for thy love.'

[V. ii. (The end of the play.)
Armado (*to the King*). Will you hear the dialogue that the two learned men have compiled in praise of the owl and the cuckoo?
King. Call them forth quickly.
Armado. This side is Hiems, Winter, this Ver, the Spring. Ver, begin.]

can] could

Spring.

When daisies pied and violets blue
    And lady-smocks all silver-white
And cuckoo-buds of yellow hue
    Do paint the meadows with delight,
The cuckoo then, on every tree,
    Mocks married men, for thus sings he:
            'Cuckoo!
Cuckoo, cuckoo!' O word of fear!
Unpleasing to a married ear.

When shepherds pipe on oaten straws,
    And merry larks are ploughmen's clocks,
When turtles tread, and rooks, and daws,
    And maidens bleach their summer smocks,
The cuckoo then, on every tree,
    Mocks married men, for thus sings he:
        ·   'Cuckoo!
Cuckoo, cuckoo!' O word of fear!
Unpleasing to a married ear.

Winter.

When icicles hang by the wall,
    And Dick the shepherd blows his nail,
And Tom bears logs into the hall,
    And milk comes frozen home in pail;
When blood is nipped, and ways be foul,
    Then nightly sings the staring owl,
            'To-who!
Tu-whit, to-who!' a merry note,
While greasy Joan doth keel the pot.

When all aloud the wind doth blow,
    And coughing drowns the parson's saw,
    And birds sit brooding in the snow,

pied] variegated   turtles] turtledoves   blows his nail] breathes on his finger-ends,
to warm them   foul] muddy   keel] cool, stir to prevent from boiling over   saw]
discourse, perhaps here trite saying, proverb

And Marian's nose looks red and raw;
When roasted crabs hiss in the bowl,
Then nightly sings the staring owl,
'To-who!
Tu-whit, to-who!' a merry note,
While greasy Joan doth keel the pot.

From WILLIAM SHAKESPEARE's *Merchant of Venice*

[III. ii. A room in Portia's house. Music, whilst Bassanio comments
on the caskets to himself.]

Tell me, where is fancy bred,
Or in the heart, or in the head?
How begot, how nourishèd?
Reply, reply.

It is engendered in the eyes,
With gazing fed; and fancy dies
In the cradle where it lies.
Let us all ring fancy's knell;
I'll begin it—Ding, dong, bell.
Ding, dong, bell.

From WILLIAM SHAKESPEARE's *As You Like It*

[II. v. The Forest. Enter Amiens, Jaques, and others. *Amiens sings.*]

Under the greenwood tree
Who loves to lie with me,
And turn his merry note
Unto the sweet bird's throat,
Come hither, come hither, come hither!
Here shall he see
No enemy
But winter and rough weather.

Who doth ambition shun,
And loves to live i' the sun,
Seeking the food he eats,

crabs] crab apples   fancy] love   turn] adapt   throat] song

And pleased with what he gets,
Come hither, come hither, come hither!
Here shall he see
No enemy
But winter and rough weather.

[II. vii. The Forest.
Duke Senior. Give us some music; and, good cousin, sing.

Amiens sings.]

Blow, blow, thou winter wind,
Thou art not so unkind
As man's ingratitude;
Thy tooth is not so keen,
Because thou art not seen,
Although thy breath be rude.
Heigh, ho! sing, heigh, ho! unto the green holly.
Most friendship is feigning, most loving mere folly.
Then, heigh, ho! the holly!
This life is most jolly.

Freeze, freeze, thou bitter sky,
That dost not bite so nigh
As benefits forgot:
Though thou the waters warp,
Thy sting is not so sharp,
As friend remembered not.
Heigh, ho! sing, &c.

[V. iii. The Forest.
Touchstone. Come, sit, sit, and a song. *Two pages sing.*]

It was a lover and his lass,
With a hey, and a ho, and a hey nonino,
That o'er the green corn-field did pass
In the spring time, the only pretty ring time,
When birds do sing, hey ding a ding, ding;
Sweet lovers love the spring.

Between the acres of the rye,
    With a hey, and a ho, and a hey nonino,
These pretty country folks would lie,
    In spring time, &c.

This carol they began that hour,
    With a hey, and a ho, and a hey nonino,
How that a life was but a flower,
    In spring time, &c.

And therefore take the present time,
    With a hey, and a ho, and a hey nonino,
For love is crownèd with the prime
    In spring time, &c.

From WILLIAM SHAKESPEARE's *Twelfth Night*

[II. iii.   Olivia's house.
Sir Andrew.   Now, a song.   *Feste sings.*]

O, mistress mine, where are you roaming?
O, stay and hear; your true love's coming,
    That can sing both high and low:
Trip no further, pretty sweeting,
Journeys end in lovers meeting,
    Every wise man's son doth know.

What is love? 'Tis not hereafter;
Present mirth hath present laughter;
    What 's to come is still unsure:
In delay there lies no plenty,
Then come kiss me, sweet and twenty,
    Youth 's a stuff will not endure.

[II. iv.   The Duke's palace.
Duke.   Prithee, sing.   *Clown sings.*]

Come away, come away, death,
And in sad cypress let me be laid;
    Fly away, fly away, breath;

cypress] branches strewn on the coffin

I am slain by a fair cruel maid.
My shroud of white, stuck all with yew,
    O, prepare it!
My part of death, no one so true
    Did share it.

    Not a flower, not a flower sweet,
On my black coffin let there be strown;
    Not a friend, not a friend greet
My poor corpse, where my bones shall be thrown:
A thousand thousand sighs to save,
    Lay me, O! where
Sad true lover never find my grave,
    To weep there.

From WILLIAM SHAKESPEARE's *Measure for Measure*

[IV. i. The moated grange at St. Luke's. Enter Mariana and a boy. The boy sings.]

    Take, O, take those lips away
      That so sweetly were forsworn;
    And those eyes, the break of day,
      Lights that do mislead the morn:
    But my kisses bring again,
      Bring again;
    Seals of love, but sealed in vain,
      Sealed in vain.

From WILLIAM SHAKESPEARE's *Macbeth*

[IV. i. A cavern. In the middle a boiling cauldron. Thunder. Enter the three witches. They sing.]

1 Witch. Thrice the brinded cat hath mewed.

2 Witch. Thrice, and once the hedge-pig whined.

3 Witch. Harpier cries; 'tis time, 'tis time.

brinded] striped   Harpier] Harpy

1 Witch. Round about the cauldron go;
In the poisoned entrails throw.
Toad, that under cold stone
Days and nights has thirty-one
Sweltered venom sleeping got,
Boil thou first i' the charmèd pot!

All. Double, double, toil and trouble;
Fire burn, and cauldron bubble.

2 Witch. Fillet of a fenny snake,
In the cauldron boil and bake;
Eye of newt and toe of frog,
Wool of bat and tongue of dog,
Adder's fork and blind-worm's sting,
Lizard's leg and owlets's wing,
For a charm of powerful trouble,
Like a hell-broth boil and bubble.

All. Double, double, toil and trouble;
Fire burn, and cauldron bubble.

3 Witch. Scale of dragon, tooth of wolf,
Witch's mummy, maw and gulf
Of the ravined salt-sea shark,
Root of hemlock digged i' th' dark,
Liver of blaspheming Jew,
Gall of goat, and slips of yew
Slivered in the moon's eclipse,
Nose of Turk and Tartar's lips,
Finger of birth-strangled babe
Ditch-delivered by a drab,
Make the gruel thick and slab:
Add thereto a tiger's chaudron,
For th' ingredients of our cau'dron.

All. Double, double, toil and trouble;
Fire burn, and cauldron bubble.

Sweltered] Exuded like sweat   fenny] fen-   fork] forked tongue, supposed to be the
sting   blind-worm] a reptile, supposed dangerous   mummy] gum prepared from
a dead body   gulf] voracious belly   ravined] glutted   slab] viscid   chaudron]
entrails

2 Witch.   Cool it with a baboon's blood,
        Then the charm is firm and good.

From WILLIAM SHAKESPEARE's *Cymbeline*

[II. iii. An antechamber adjoining Imogen's apartment. ·Enter Cloten, lords, and musicians.

Cloten. First, a very excellent good-conceited thing; after, a wonderful sweet air with admirable rich words to it: and then let her consider.]

Hark, hark! the lark at heaven's gate sings,
    And Phœbus 'gins arise,
His steeds to water at those springs
    On chaliced flowers that lies;
And winking Mary-buds begin
    To ope their golden eyes;
With every thing that pretty is,
    My lady sweet, arise;
        Arise, arise!

[IV. ii. Wales. Before the cave. Enter Arvirague, with Imogen as dead. He and Guiderius sing.]

Fear no more the heat o' the sun,
    Nor the furious winter's rages;
Thou thy worldly task hast done,
    Home art gone, and ta'en thy wages:
Golden lads and girls all must,
    As chimney-sweepers, come to dust.

Fear no more the frown o' the great,
    Thou art past the tyrant's stroke;
Care no more to clothe and eat;
    To thee the reed is as the oak:
The scepter, learning, physic, must
All follow this, and come to dust.

chaliced] cup-shaped   Mary-buds] marigold buds

Fear no more the lightning-flash,
Nor th' all-dreaded thunder-stone;
Fear not slander, censure rash;
Thou hast finished joy and moan:
All lovers young, all lovers must
Consign to thee, and come to dust.

No exorciser harm thee!
Nor no witchcraft charm thee!
Ghost unlaid forbear thee!
Nothing ill come near thee!
Quiet consummation have,
And renownèd be thy grave!

From WILLIAM SHAKESPEARE's *Winter's Tale*

[IV. iv.   The shepherd's cottage.   Enter Autolycus, singing.]

Lawn as white as driven snow;
Cyprus black as e'er was crow;
Gloves as sweet as damask roses;
Masks for faces and for noses;
Bugle-bracelet, necklace amber,
Perfume for a lady's chamber;
Golden quoifs and stomachers,
For my lads to give their dears;
Pins, and poking-sticks of steel,
What maids lack from head to heel.
Come buy of me, come! come buy, come buy!
Buy, lads, or else your lasses cry.
Come buy!

thunder-stone] thunderbolt   censure rash] hasty judgment   Consign to thee] Accept thy fate   exorciser] one who calls up spirits   consummation] death   Cyprus] Crape   Bugle-bracelet] made of tube-shaped, black glass beads   quoifs] caps poking-sticks] rods used for stiffening the plaits of ruffs; steel ones, the latest and best kind, were applied hot.

From WILLIAM SHAKESPEARE'S *Tempest*

[I. ii.   The island, before Prospero's cell.   Ariel sings.]

Full fathom five thy father lies,
    Of his bones are coral made,
Those are pearls that were his eyes:
    Nothing of him that doth fade,
But doth suffer a sea-change
Into something rich and strange.
Sea-nymphs hourly ring his knell:
    Ding-dong.
Hark! now I hear them—Ding-dong, bell.

From WILLIAM SHAKESPEARE and JOHN FLETCHER'S
Two Noble Kinsmen

[I. i.   Athens, before the temple.   A bridal procession enters.   A boy
    sings.]

Roses, their sharp spines being gone,
Not royal in their smells alone,
    But in their hue;
Maiden pinks, of odor faint,
Daisies smell-less, yet most quaint,
    And sweet thyme true;

Primrose, first-born child of Ver,
Merry spring-time's harbinger,
    With her bells dim;
Oxlips in their cradles growing,
Marigolds on deathbeds blowing,
    Larks'-heels trim—

All dear Nature's children sweet,
Lie 'fore bride and bridegroom's feet,
    Blessing their sense!

Larks'-heels] Larkspurs

Not an angel of the air,
Bird melodious, or bird fair,
    Be absent hence!

The crow, the sland'rous cuckoo, nor
The boding raven, nor chough hoar
    Nor chattering pie,
May on our bride-house perch or sing,
Or with them any discord bring,
    But from it fly.

From ANTHONY MUNDAY and HENRY CHETTLE'S
Death of Robert, Earl of Huntingdon

[I. iii. A priory.
King. After Earl Robert's timeless burial,
Fall to your wood-songs, yeomen bold.]

Weep, weep, ye woodmen, wail,
    Your hands with sorrow wring;
Your master Robin Hood lies dead,
    Therefore sigh as you sing.

Here lies his primer and his beads,
    His bent bow and his arrows keen,
His good sword and his holy cross:
    Now cast on flowers fresh and green.

And, as they fall, shed tears and say
    Well-a, well-a-day! well-a, well-a-day!
Thus cast ye flowers, and sing,
    And on to Wakefield take your way.

timeless] untimely   primer] book of devotion

From Thomas Dekker's *Shoemakers' Holiday*

[V. iv.   A 'three-men's song' to entertain the shoemakers at Eyre's banquet.]

Cold's the wind, and wet's the rain,
    Saint Hugh be our good speed;
Ill is the weather that bringeth no gain,
    Nor helps good hearts in need.

Troll the bowl, the jolly nut-brown bowl,
    And here, kind mate, to thee;
Let's sing a dirge for Saint Hugh's soul,
    And down it merrily.

Down-a-down, hey, down-a-down,
    Hey derry derry down-a-down;
    (*Close with the tenor boy.*)
Ho! well done, to me let come,
    Ring compass, gentle joy.

Troll the bowl, &c.   (*As often as there be men to*
    drink.
At last, when all have drunk, this verse:)

Cold's the wind, and wet's the rain,
    Saint Hugh be our good speed;
Ill is the weather that bringeth no gain,
    Nor helps good hearts in need.

From Thomas Dekker's *Patient Grissill*

[I. i.   The country near Saluzzo. Ianiculo, a basket maker, and Babulo, his servant, beguile their labor with a song.]

Art thou poor, yet hast thou golden slumbers?
    O sweet content!

Troll] Pass around   *Close . . .*] This and the succeeding parenthesis are directions to the singers.   Ring compass] Ring a full peal   *Patient Grissill*] written by Dekker with Chettle and Haughton.   Most editors consider the songs Dekker's.

Art thou rich, yet is thy mind perplexèd?
O punishment!
Dost thou laugh to see how fools are vexèd
To add to golden numbers golden numbers?
O sweet content, O sweet, O sweet content!

Work apace, apace, apace, apace;
Honest labor bears a lovely face,
Then hey nonny nonny, hey nonny nonny.

Canst drink the waters of the crispèd spring?
O sweet content!
Swim'st thou in wealth, yet sink'st in thine own tears?
O punishment!
Then he that patiently want's burden bears,
No burden bears, but is a king, a king.
O sweet content, O sweet, O sweet content!

Work apace, apace, &c.

From THOMAS DEKKER and JOHN FORD's *Sun's Darling*

[III. i. The sun takes his seat above. Enter country fellows and
wenches. They sing.]

Haymakers, rakers, reapers, and mowers,
Wait on your summer-queen;
Dress up with musk-rose her eglantine bowers,
Daffodils strew the green;
Sing, dance, and play,
'Tis holiday;
The sun does bravely shine
On our ears of corn.
Rich as a pearl
Comes every girl:
This is mine! this is mine! this is mine!
Let us die, ere away they be borne.

crispèd] ruffled   bravely] beautifully

Bow to the sun, to our queen, and that fair one
    Come to behold our sports;
Each bonny lass here is counted a rare one,
    As those in princes' courts.
            These and we
            With country glee,
Will teach the woods to resound,
And the hills with Echo's hollo:
            Skipping lambs
            Their bleating dams,
    'Mongst kids shall trip it round;
For joy thus our wenches we follow.

Wind, jolly huntsmen, your neat bugles shrilly,
    Hounds make a lusty cry;
Spring up, you falconers, the partridges freely,
    Then let your brave hawks fly.
            Horses amain,
            Over ridge, over plain,
    The dogs have the stag in chase:
'Tis a sport to content a king.
            So ho ho! through the skies
            How the proud bird flies,
    And sousing kills with a grace!
Now the deer falls; hark, how they ring!

From BEN JONSON's *Cynthia's Revels*

[I. ii. A fountain in Gargaphie, a fustian country.
Echo. Vouchsafe me, I may . . . sing some mourning strain
Over his (Narcissus') wat'ry hearse.]

Slow, slow, fresh fount, keep time with my salt tears;
    Yet slower yet, O faintly, gentle springs;
List to the heavy part the music bears,
    Woe weeps out her division when she sings.
            Droop herbs and flowers,

Spring up] Flush   sousing] swooping   division] musical variation

Fall grief in showers;
Our beauties are not ours;
  O, I could still,
Like melting snow upon some craggy hill,
  Drop, drop, drop, drop,
Since nature's pride is now a withered daffodil.

[V. vi. Cynthia's court. Hesperus, Cynthia, and others. They sing
a hymn to Diana.]

.   Queen and Huntress, chaste and fair,
    Now the sun is laid to sleep,
Seated in thy silver chair,
    State in wonted manner keep:
      Hesperus entreats thy light,
      Goddess excellently bright.

Earth, let not thy envious shade
    Dare itself to interpose;
Cynthia's shining orb was made
    Heaven to clear when day did close:
      Bless us then with wishèd sight,
      Goddess excellently bright.

Lay thy bow of pearl apart
    And thy crystal-shining quiver;
Give unto the flying hart
    Space to breathe, how short soever:
      Thou that mak'st a day of night,
      Goddess excellently bright.

From BEN JONSON's *Poetaster*

[II. ii. Albius's house in Rome.
Gallus. O, this contention is excellent. What is't you sing, sir?
Crispinus. *If I freely may discover, &c.* Sir, I'll sing that.]

If I freely may discover
What would please me in my lover:

clear] brighten   discover] reveal

I would have her fair and witty,
Savoring more of court than city;
A little proud, but full of pity;
Light and humorous in her toying,
Oft building hopes and soon destroying;
Long, but sweet, in the enjoying;
Neither too easy, nor too hard,
All extremes I would have barred.

She should be allowed her passions,
So they were but used as fashions;
    Sometimes froward, and then frowning,
    Sometimes sickish, and then swowning,
    Every fit with change still crowning.
    Purely jealous I would have her;
    Then only constant when I crave her,
    'Tis a virtue should not save her.
Thus, nor her delicates would cloy me,
Neither her peevishness annoy me.

From BEN JONSON's *Particular Entertainment of the Queen
and Prince at Althrope, 1603*

[Scene I. The park at Althrope. A satyr sings.]

This is Mab, the mistress-fairy,
That doth nightly rob the dairy,
And can hurt or help the churning
As she please, without discerning;

She that pinches country wenches
If they rub not clean their benches,
And with sharper nails remembers
When they rake not up their embers;
But if so they chance to feast her,
In a shoe she drops a tester.

save her] keep her mine   delicates] pleasurable qualities   discerning] being seen
tester] sixpence

This is she that empties cradles,
Takes out children, puts in ladles;
Trains forth midwives in their slumber
With a sieve the holes to number;
And then leads them from her burrows
Home through ponds and water-furrows.

She can start our franklin's daughters
In their sleep with shrieks and laughters,
And on sweet Saint Annè's night
Feed them with a promised sight,
Some of husbands, some of lovers,
Which an empty dream discovers.

From BEN JONSON's *Volpone*

[III. vii.   A room in Volpone's house.   Sung by Volpone, who is attempting to seduce Celia.]

Come, my Celia, let us prove
While we can, the sports of love;
Time will not be ours forever,
He at length our good will sever.
Spend not then his gifts in vain;
Suns that set may rise again,
But if once we lose this light,
'Tis with us perpetual night.
Why should we defer our joys?
Fame and rumor are but toys.
Cannot we delude the eyes
Of a few poor household spies?
Or his easier ears beguile,
Thus removèd by our wile?
'Tis no sin love's fruits to steal;
But the sweet thefts to reveal,
To be taken, to be seen,
These have crimes accounted been.

Trains] Lures   franklin] farmer   discovers] reveals

From BEN JONSON's *Silent Woman*

[I. i. Clerimont's house in London.
Clerimont. A pox of her . . . piec'd beauty:
I have made a song . . . o' the subject.]

Song

Still to be neat, still to be dressed
As you were going to a feast;
Still to be powdered, still perfumed:
Lady, it is to be presumed,
Though art's hid causes are not found,
All is not sweet, all is not sound.

Give me a look, give me a face
That makes simplicity a grace;
Robes loosely flowing, hair as free:
Such sweet neglect more taketh me
Than all th' adulteries of art;
They strike mine eyes, but not my heart.

From BEN JONSON's *Pan's Anniversary*

[The scene is Arcadia. After the antimasque, a hymn is sung by
nymphs and Arcadians.]

Of Pan we sing, the best of singers, Pan,
    That taught us swains how first to tune our lays,
And on the pipe more airs than Phœbus can.
    Hear, O you groves, and hills resound his praise.

Of Pan we sing, the best of leaders, Pan,
    That leads the Naiads and the Dryads forth,
And to their dances more than Hermes can.
    Hear, O you groves, and hills resound his worth.

piec'd] patched up   Still] Always   As] As if   can] can play

Of Pan we sing, the best of hunters, Pan,
That drives the hart to seek unusèd ways,
And in the chase more than Silvanus can.
Hear, O you groves, and hills resound his praise.

Of Pan we sing, the best of shepherds, Pan,
That keeps our flocks and us, and both leads forth
To better pastures than great Pales can.
Hear, O you groves, and hills resound his worth;
And, while his powers and praises thus we sing,
The valleys let rebound and all the rivers ring.

From BEN JONSON's *The Devil is an Ass*

[II. ii. Manly's chambers in Lincoln's Inn, opposite Fitzdottrel's house.
Wittipol speaks from Manly's window to Mrs. Fitzdottrel at
her window.]

The Triumph of Charis

See the chariot at hand here of love,
Wherein my lady rideth!
Each that draws is a swan or a dove,
And well the car love guideth.
As she goes, all hearts do duty
Unto her beauty;
And, enamored, do wish, so they might
But enjoy such a sight,
That they still were to run by her side,
Thorough swords, thorough seas, whither she would ride.

Do but look on her eyes, they do light
All that love's world compriseth!
Do but look on her hair, it is bright
As love's star when it riseth!
Do but mark, her forehead's smoother
Than words that soothe her!

Triumph] *Triumphal Procession*   See, etc.] The first stanza is from *Underwoods*
(1640).   Thorough] Through

And from her arched brows such a grace
 Sheds itself through the face,
As alone there triùmphs to the life
All the gain, all the good, of the elements' strife.

Have you seen but a bright lily grow
 Before rude hands have touched it?
Have you marked but the fall o' the snow
 Before the soil hath smutched it?
Have you felt the wool o' the beaver?
 Or swan's down ever?
Or have smelt o' the bud o' the brier
 Or the nard i' the fire?
Or have tasted the bag o' the bee?
O so white, O so soft, O so sweet is she!

From BEN JONSON's *Sad Shepherd*

[I. i.   Robin Hood's bower.   Æglamour, the sad shepherd, sings of
 Earine.]

Here she was wont to go, and here, and here!
Just where those daisies, pinks, and violets grow:
The world may find the spring by following her;
For other print her airy steps ne'er left.
Her treading would not bend a blade of grass,
Or shake the downy blow-ball from his stalk;
But like the soft west-wind she shot along,
And where she went, the flowers took thickest root,
As she had sowed them with her odorous foot.

[Karolin, the kind shepherd, sings.]

Though I am young and cannot tell
 Either what death or love is well,

As] That   elements] the four elements (hot, cold, moist, dry) which according to
ancient physics composed all matter, and were in constant strife   nard] an aromatic
herb or ointment   blow-ball] seed head   his] its   As] As if

Yet I have heard they both bear darts,
  And both do aim at human hearts.
And then again I have been told
  Love wounds with heat, as death with cold;
So that I fear they do but bring
  Extremes to touch, and mean one thing.

As in a ruin we it call
  One thing to be blown up, or fall;
Or to our end, like way may have
  By a flash of lightning or a wave;
So love's inflamèd shaft or brand
  May kill as soon as death's cold hand,
Except love's fires the virtue have
  To fright the frost out of the grave.

From THOMAS MIDDLETON's *Blurt, Master Constable*

[V. ii.   Imperia's house in Venice.   She sings to Fontinelle, her French
  lover.]

Love for such a cherry lip
  Would be glad to pawn his arrows;
Venus here to take a sip
  Would sell her doves and team of sparrows.
      But they shall not so;
        Hey nonny, nonny no!
      None but I this lip must owe;
        Hey nonny, nonny no!

Did Jove see this wanton eye,
  Ganymede must wait no longer;
Phœbe here one night did lie,
  Would change her face and look much younger.
      But they shall not so;
        Hey nonny, nonny no!

owe] own   wait] attend as cup-bearer   did] if she did

None but I this lip must owe;
Hey nonny, nonny no!

From THOMAS MIDDLETON's *More Dissemblers Besides Women*

[IV. i. Near Milan. Enter Gipsy Captain with a company of gipsies,
male and female, singing.]

Captain. Come, my dainty doxies,
My dells, my dells most dear,
We have neither house nor land,
Yet never want good cheer.
All. We never want good cheer.
Captain. We take no care for candle-rents.
2 Gipsy. We lie. *3 Gipsy.* We snort.
Captain. We sport in tents,
Then rouse betimes and steal our dinners.
Our store is never taken
Without pigs, hens, or bacon,
And that's good meat for sinners.
At wakes and fairs we cozen
Poor country folks by dozen;
If one have money, he disburses;
Whilst some tell fortunes, some pick purses;
Rather than be out of use,
We'll steal garters, hose or shoes,
Boots, or spurs with jingling rowels,
Shirts or napkins, smocks or towels.
Come live with us, come live with us,
All you that love your eases;
He that's a gipsy
May be drunk or tipsy
At what hour he pleases.
All. We laugh, we quaff, we roar, we scuffle,
We cheat, we drab, we filch, we shuffle.

doxies, dells] sweethearts   candle-rents] house-rent money   snort] snore   shuffle]
are shifty, evasive

From THOMAS HEYWOOD's *Rape of Lucrece*

[IV. ii.   A Roman camp.   Morning.   Officers enter, and one of them
sings.]

Pack, clouds, away! and welcome, day!
  With night we banish sorrow;
Sweet air, blow soft; mount, lark, aloft,
  To give my love good-morrow.
Wings from the wind to please her mind,
  Notes from the lark I'll borrow;
Bird, prune thy wing, nightingale, sing,
  To give my love good-morrow;
    To give my love good-morrow,
    Notes from them all I'll borrow.

Wake from thy rest, robin redbreast,
  Sing birds in every furrow;
And from each bill let music shrill
  Give my fair love good-morrow.
Blackbird and thrush in every bush,
  Stare, linnet, and cock-sparrow,
You pretty elves, amongst yourselves
  Sing my fair love good-morrow;
    To give my love good-morrow
    Sing birds in every furrow.

From JOHN MARSTON's *Dutch Courtesan*

[V. i.   Beatrice's chamber.
    Enter young Freeville, disguised, to Beatrice.   He sings.]

O love, how strangely sweet
  Are thy weak passions,
That love and joy should meet
  In self-same fashions.

Pack] Be off   prune] preen·   Stare] Starling

O, who can tell
   The cause why this should move?
But only this:
   No reason ask of love.

From *The Fair Maid of the Exchange*

[III. i. London. A street. Frank, in love with Phyllis, sings.]

Ye little birds that sit and sing
   Amidst the shady valleys,
And see how Phyllis sweetly walks
   Within her garden-alleys;
Go, pretty birds, about her bower;
Sing, pretty birds, she may not lour;
Ah, me! methinks I see her frown,
   Ye pretty wantons, warble.

Go, tell her through your chirping bills,
   As you by me are bidden,
To her is only known my love,
   Which from the world is hidden.
Go, pretty birds, and tell her so;
See that your notes strain not too low,
For still, methinks, I see her frown,
   Ye pretty wantons, warble.

Go, tune your voices' harmony,
   And sing, I am her lover;
Strain loud and sweet, that every note
   With sweet content may move her:
And she that hath the sweetest voice,
Tell her I will not change my choice;
Yet still, methinks, I see her frown,
   Ye pretty wantons, warble.

she may] that she may   strain] sing

O, fly! make haste! see, see, she falls
  Into a pretty slumber;
Sing round about her rosy bed,
  That waking she may wonder.
Say to her, 'tis her lover true
That sendeth love to you, to you;
And when you hear her kind reply,
  Return with pleasant warblings.

From FRANCIS BEAUMONT's *Knight of the Burning Pestle*

[III. i. Waltham Forest. Night. Jasper and Luce are lost.]

Jasp.　　Tell me, dearest, what is love?
Luce.　　'Tis a lightning from above;
　　　　　'Tis an arrow, 'tis a fire,
　　　　　'Tis a boy they call Desire.
　　　　　　　'Tis a smile
　　　　　　　Doth beguile
Jasp.　　The poor hearts of men that prove.

　　　　　Tell me more, are women true?
Luce.　　Some love change, and so do you.
Jasp.　　Are they fair, and never kind?
Luce.　　Yes, when men turn with the wind.
Jasp.　　　Are they forward?
Luce.　　　Ever toward
　　　　　Those that love, to love anew.

From FRANCIS BEAUMONT's *Masque of the Inner Temple*

[The first song, when the priests of Jove descend, and the knights follow
them.]

　　　　Shake off your heavy trance,
　　　　　And leap into a dance
　　　　Such as no mortals use to tread:

prove] try it　　Yes, when] Sometimes kind, whereas　　use] are accustomed

Fit only for Apollo
To play to, for the moon to lead,
And all the stars to follow!

From FRANCIS BEAUMONT and JOHN FLETCHER's
Maid's Tragedy

[I. ii.   The second song in Evadne's bridal masque.]

Hold back thy hours, dark Night, till we have done;
    The day will come too soon;
Young maids will curse thee, if thou steal'st away
And leav'st their losses open to the day:
    Stay, stay, and hide
The blushes of the bride.

Stay, gentle Night, and with thy darkness cover
    The kisses of her lover;
Stay, and confound her tears and her shrill cryings,
Her weak denials, vows, and often-dyings;
    Stay, and hide all:
But help not, though she call.

[II. i.   The ante-room to Evadne's bed-chamber.   Aspatia sings.]

Lay a garland on my hearse
    Of the dismal yew;
Maidens, willow branches bear;
    Say I dièd true.

My love was false, but I was firm
    From my hour of birth;
Upon my buried body lie
    Lightly, gentle earth.

From JOHN FLETCHER's *Faithful Shepherdess*

[III. i.   The Holy Well.   The God of the River sings to Amoret.]

Do not fear to put thy feet
Naked in the river sweet;
Think not leech, or newt, or toad

Will bite thy foot when thou hast trod;
Nor let the water rising high,
As thou wad'st in, make thee cry
And sob; but ever live with me,
And not a wave shall trouble thee.

From JOHN FLETCHER's *Nice Valour*

[III. i. Genoa. The court. To banish Cupid, the passionate mad
man sings.]

Hence, all you vain delights,
As short as are the nights
  Wherein you spend your folly:
There's naught in this life sweet
If man were wise to see't,
  But only melancholy,
  O sweetest melancholy!

Welcome, folded arms and fixèd eyes,
A sigh that piercing mortifies,
A look that's fastened to the ground,
A tongue chained up without a sound.

Fountain heads, and pathless groves,
Places which pale passion loves;
Moonlight walks, when all the fowls
Are warmly housed, save bats and owls;
  A midnight bell, a parting groan,
  These are the sounds we feed upon.
Then stretch our bones in a still, gloomy valley;
Nothing's so dainty sweet as lovely melancholy.

From JOHN FLETCHER's *Bloody Brother*

[II. ii. The palace of Rollo, duke of Normandy. Enter the Master
Cook, Butler, etc., with a jack of beer.]

Drink today, and drown all sorrow,
You shall perhaps not do it tomorrow.

mortifies] kills   jack] a leathern jug

Best, while you have it, use your breath;
There is no drinking after death.

Wine works the heart up, wakes the wit;
There is no cure 'gainst age but it.
It helps the headache, cough, and tisic,
And is for all diseases physic.

Then let us swill, boys, for our health;
Who drinks well, loves the commonwealth.
And he that will to bed go sober,
Falls with the leaf still in October.

From JOHN FLETCHER's *Valentinian*

[II. iv. Rome. The emperor's palace. Three noble panders sing as
Lucina, the chaste, abused wife of Maximus, enters.]

Now the lusty spring is seen;
    Golden yellow, gaudy blue,
    Daintily invite the view.
Everywhere on every green
Roses blushing as they blow,
    And enticing men to pull,
Lilies whiter than the snow
    Woodbines of sweet honey full:
        All love's emblems, and all cry,
        'Ladies, if not plucked we die.'

Yet the lusty spring hath stayed;
    Blushing red and purest white
    Daintily to love invite
Every woman, every maid.
Cherries kissing as they grow,
    And inviting men to taste,
Apples even ripe below,

tisic] consumption   physic] medicine   swill] drink freely   even] evenly

Winding gently to the waist:
All love's emblems, and all cry,
'Ladies, if not plucked we die.'

[V. viii. Attendants at the banquet sing, while the traitor Maximus
drinks wine that Eudoxia has secretly poisoned.]

God Lyæus, ever young,
Ever honored, ever sung,
Stained with blood of lusty grapes,
In a thousand lusty shapes,
Dance upon the mazer's brim,
In the crimson liquor swim;
From thy plenteous hand divine,
Let a river run with wine:
 God of youth, let this day here
 Enter neither care nor fear.

From SAMUEL DANIEL's *Tethys' Festival*

[Tethys and her nymphs repose upon a mount, while a chorus sings.]

Are they shadows that we see?
 And can shadows pleasure give?
Pleasures only shadows be,
 Cast by bodies we conceive,
And are made the things we deem·
In those figures which they seem.

But these pleasures vanish fast
 Which by shadows are expressed:
Pleasures are not, if they last,
 In their passing is their best:
Glory is most bright and gay·
In a flash, and so away.

Winding] Curving mazer] bowl

Feed apace then, greedy eyes,
  On the wonder you behold;
Take it sudden as it flies,
  Though you take it not to hold:
When your eyes have done their part,
Thought must length it in the heart.

From JOHN WEBSTER's *White Devil*

[V. iv. Padua. Brachiano's palace. Cornelia, distracted, sings at the
  winding of her son Marcello's corse.]

Call for the robin redbreast and the wren,
Since o'er shady groves they hover,
And with leaves and flowers do cover
The friendless bodies of unburied men.
Call unto his funeral dole
The ant, the field-mouse, and the mole,
To rear him hillocks that shall keep him warm,
And, when gay tombs are robbed, sustain no harm;
But keep the wolf far thence, that's foe to men,
For with his nails he'll dig them up again.

From THOMAS MAY's *Old Couple*

[III. i. Earthworm's house.
Dotterel. 'Tis but a sonnet, gentlemen, that I fitted
To my fair mistress here.   *He reads.*]

Dear, do not your fair beauty wrong
In thinking still you are too young;
The rose and lilies in your cheek
Flourish, and no more ripeness seek;
Your cherry lip, red, soft, and sweet,
Proclaims such fruit for taste most meet;
Then lose no time, for love has wings
And flies away from agèd things.

length] prolong   dole] mourning

From John Ford's *Broken Heart*

[V. iii. (The end of the play.)   A Temple.
Calantha.   Command the voices . . . now to sing the song I fitted for
my end.   *Men sing.*]

All.　　　　Glories, pleasures, pomps, delights, and ease
　　　　　　　　Can but please
　　　　　　Outward senses, when the mind
　　　　　　Is or untroubled or by peace refined.
I Voice.　　Crowns may flourish and decay,
　　　　　　Beauties shine, but fade away.
II Voice.　　Youth may revel, yet it must
　　　　　　Lie down in a bed of dust.
III Voice.　Earthly honors flow and waste,
　　　　　　Time alone doth change and last.
All.　　　　Sorrows mingled with contents prepare
　　　　　　　　Rest for care;
　　　　　　Love only reigns in death; though art
　　　　　　Can find no comfort for a broken heart.

From James Mabbe's *Celestina*

[Actus XIX.   Pleberio's garden.   Melibea awaits Calisto.
Melibea (*to Lucrecia, her companion*).   Hear me, now, I will sing
alone.]

　　　　You birds whose warblings prove
　　　　　　Aurora draweth near,
　　　　Go fly and tell my love
　　　　　　That I expect him here.

　　　　The night doth posting move,
　　　　　　Yet comes he not again:
　　　　God grant some other love
　　　　　　Do not my love detain.

You birds, etc.] From the Spanish of Rojas.   See p. 167.   posting] swiftly

From Philip Massinger's *Emperor of the East*

[V. iii. Constantinople. A room in the palace. Enter the Empress
Eudocia in sackcloth, her hair loose. She sings.]

Why art thou slow, thou rest of trouble, Death,
    To stop a wretch's breath,
That calls on thee, and offers her sad heart
    A prey unto thy dart?
I am nor young nor fair; be, therefore, bold:
    Sorrow hath made me old,
Deformed, and wrinkled; all that I can crave
    Is quiet in my grave.

Such as live happy, hold long life a jewel;
    But to me thou art cruel
If thou end not my tedious misery
    And I soon cease to be.
Strike, and strike home, then! pity unto me,
In one short hour's delay, is tyranny.

From Sir John Suckling's *Aglaura*

[IV. ii. Persia. The court.
Orsames. A little foolish counsel, madam, I gave a friend of mine when
he was falling into a consumption.]

Why so pale and wan, fond lover?
    Prithee why so pale?
Will, when looking well can't move her,
    Looking ill prevail?
    Prithee why so pale?

Why so dull and mute, young sinner?
    Prithee why so mute?
Will, when speaking well can't win her,
    Saying nothing do 't?
    Prithee why so mute?

Quit, quit, for shame! this will not move,
This cannot take her;
If of herself she will not love,
Nothing can make her:
The devil take her!

From William Habington's *Queen of Arragon*

[IV. i.   Arragon.   The gardens of the court.   Sanmartino's dwarf
sings while his master awaits Cleantha.]

Fine young folly, though you were
That fair beauty I did swear,
    Yet you ne'er could reach my heart;
For we courtiers learn at school
Only with your sex to fool;
    Y' are not worth the serious part.

When I sigh and kiss your hand,
Cross my arms and wondering stand,
    Holding parley with your eye,
Then dilate on my desires,
Swear the sun ne'er shot such fires—
    All is but a handsome lie.

When I eye your curl or lace,
Gentle soul, you think your face
    Straight some murder doth commit;
And your virtue doth begin
To grow scrupulous of my sin,
    When I talk to show my wit.

Therefore, madam, wear no cloud,
Nor to check my love grow proud;
    For in sooth I much do doubt
'Tis the powder in your hair,
Not your breath, perfumes the air,
    And your clothes that set you out.

Quit] Leave, cease

Yet though truth has this confessed,
And I vow I love in jest,
    When I next begin to court
And protest an amorous flame,
You will swear I in earnest am.
    Bedlam! this is pretty sport.

From JAMES SHIRLEY's *Contention of Ajax and Ulysses*

[The third (last) scene. Calchas sings in the funeral procession of Ajax.]

The glories of our blood and state
    Are shadows, not substantial things;
There is no armor against fate;
    Death lays his icy hand on kings.
        Scepter and crown
        Must tumble down,
And in the dust be equal made
With the poor crooked scythe and spade.

Some men with swords may reap the field,
    And plant fresh laurels where they kill;
But their strong nerves at last must yield,
    They tame but one another still.
        Early or late,
        They stoop to fate,
And must give up their murmuring breath,
When they, pale captives, creep to death.

The garlands wither on your brow,
    Then boast no more your mighty deeds;
Upon death's purple altar now,
    See where the victor-victim bleeds.
        Your heads must come
        To the cold tomb;
Only the actions of the just
Smell sweet and blossom in their dust.

blood and state] lineage and rank

V

LYRICS IN SONG-BOOKS

1584–1700

LYRICS IN SONG-BOOKS

The present section, like the preceding one, is a collection of lyrics specialized in use, and covers a considerable portion of the entire period under discussion. We are here concerned with those lyrics which were primarily intended to be sung. As with the lyrics in plays, it will be interesting to note the appearance, here less frequent, of poets whose work appears in other sections, and to see how the songs reflect the changing literary fashions of the time. The first selection given is dated 1584 and the first seven appeared before the turn of the century; the bulk of the selections falls between 1600 and 1620. It would, of course, be as futile to inquire when the popularity of song in England began as to inquire when it ended. It never has. But the two decades mentioned were certainly the time of its greatest popularity during our period. During the first of them alone (1600–1610) some thirty-five song-books of known date appeared. This seems to establish the fact that upon the decline of the fashion for sonnets the attention of the minor lyrists was directed chiefly to the writing of songs for music, and that these were for a time the ruling fashion.

For completeness in this section practically the entire book might well be included, since every popular lyric found its way sooner or later into the song-books. Many sonnets were set to music. Portions of poems circulated in manuscript often found their way into song-books before their authors published them. For example, stanzas 1 and 2 of Carew's *He that loves a rosy cheek* appeared first in Porter's *Madrigals* (1632), and may have been written for music. In other words, we have here to do with a genuinely national fashion. In the oft-quoted words of Chappell,[1]

---

[1] W. Chappell, *Popular Music of the Olden Time,* vol. 1, p. 98. Chappell and Co., London, 1855–9.

During the long reign of Elizabeth music seems to have been in universal cultivation as well as universal esteem. Not only was it a necessary qualification for ladies and gentlemen, but even the City of London advertised the musical ability of boys educated in Bridewell and Christ's Hospital as a mode of recommending them as servants, apprentices, or husbandmen. . . . Tinkers sang catches; milkmaids sang ballads; carters whistled. Each trade, and even the beggars, had their special song. The base viol hung in the drawing room for the amusement of waiting visitors; and the lute, cittern and virginals, for the amusement of waiting customers, were the necessary furniture of the barber's shop. They had music at dinner, music at supper, music at weddings, music at funerals, music at dawn, music at night. . . . He who felt not in some degree its soothing influences was viewed as a morose, unsocial being, whose converse ought to be shunned and regarded with suspicion and distrust.

The Queen herself dined in state to the accompaniment of kettledrums and trumpets and was proud of her technical skill on the virginals.

A long and honorable list of trained musicians and composers bears witness to the artistic cultivation of music both vocal and instrumental, and representative specimens from the considerable body of their compositions which has been handed down to us have of recent years attracted increasing interest in performance by symphony orchestras and ballets. The term 'musician' meant creative artist and composer. The modern musician who lives only by his skill on some one instrument or in singing was apparently little known and, where known, was placed in the category of masters of fencing or dancing. Such men as William Byrd, the earliest and most famous of composers of music for songs and part-songs; John Wilbye, sometimes called the greatest of English madrigalist composers; Thomas Morley, whose *First Book of Airs,* 1600, contains the original setting of Shakespeare's *It was a lover and his lass;* and John Dowland, the celebrated lutenist, whose fame extended to the Continent, were products of long special training, usually culminating in the taking of the Doctor's degree in Music at Oxford or Cambridge. The estimation in which musicians were held may be seen in Barnfield's sonnet *To Music and Poetry* (p. 203). Other nations, notably Italy and Germany, have long since outstripped England in music, and an entirely new school has gone on to achievements undreamed of in this simple age of lute and virginal, of madrigals and three-part catches. But the period from 1400 to the rise of Italian music with Palestrina in the latter half of the sixteenth century is designated by historians of European music as 'The English Period.' And the music of the age which followed, namely that which falls within the centuries covered by this book, has historical value as well as a perennial charm. We are here concerned with the popularity of a sister art because of the impetus which it gave to the writing of lyrics to be set to music, for the Elizabethans were very particular as to the artistic quality of the words of their songs and did not consider, as we seem to do, that any nonsense is good enough to sing.

We cannot but suppose that music influenced the quantity and the quality of the lyric poetry produced for singing. Two chief types of song were popular, the madrigal and the air. The madrigal was a polyphonic composition without instrumental accompaniment in which four, five, or six voices, often entering successively, sang independent melodies at the same time. The words of each part consisted of the same basic text, but with internal repetitions (sometimes doubling its length) which differed from those in some or all of the other parts. Thus different words were often sung simultaneously, or the same words to different rhythms. Naturally, so complex a performance required a brief, direct, and simple poem as its groundwork (pp. 278, 293, 457, 463). The air was a composition for solo voice or several voices in unison, accompanied by the lute or other instrument. It was generally a single musical idea, the parts conforming more or less to a single rhythm corresponding to the meter of the verse. The air gave prominence to the words and kept the stanzas entire and was thus suited to the performance of longer poems in which the structure of the stanzas and of the music was repeated. It is likely that the writers of airs had an even greater effect upon the lyric than the madrigalists.

Whether a poet wrote his lyric for already existing music or a composer fitted a tune to existing words, the interrelation of the two arts was clearly salutary for both. In the first case, since the tune in itself was somewhat fixed in shape, the lyric could not be shapeless. In the second, the composer had before him a structure which he could not help respecting. The chief fault of modern popular music, the sacrifice of the rhythm of the words to that of the music, though not entirely unknown, is rare in Elizabethan song.

The Elizabethan song-book commonly supplied both music and words, printed either in separate parts of alto, bass, and so on, or with the parts so arranged on the page that three or four singers might sit on opposite sides of the table, each facing his own part. The earliest collection of English madrigals is probably William Byrd's *Psalms, Sonnets and Songs* (1588), though the word 'madrigal' appears for the first time in Nicholas Yonge's *Musa Transalpina* of the same year. Thomas Watson's *First Set of Italian Madrigals* followed in 1590, and these three collections, with the *Canzonets* (1593) and *Madrigals for Four Voices* (1594) of Thomas Morley, set abroach the great flood of song-books referred to above. The most interesting point about them for our present purpose, namely the authorship of the lyrics they contained, is a matter much in dispute. Generally, only the names of the writers of music are given and, at times, not even these, the name on the title-page being that of the collector or publisher of the volume. Hence the question arises how far the composers of the day were their own poets. Were they, as many have supposed, responsible only for the music, or were the poems and the music generally conceived simultaneously? Critics inclining to the latter view urge the 'detailed parallelism in matter of successive stanzas in the airs, through which the same music fits them all' and 'the uniformity of poetical style which at times accompanies the musical work of the same composer,' though the latter could also be explained if a single composer and a single poet were working together. In general, it would appear that composers, framing their music 'to the life of the words,' set popular poems which fell into their hands from any source. A few are known to have attempted both words and music, but with less success in one or the other; the airs of Morley and Dowland, for example, are better than their verses. On the other hand, in the work of the greatest composer of the time, Thomas Campion, the two arts are ideally joined.

Thomas Campion, a member of a well-to-do middle class family, attended Cambridge without taking a degree, entered Gray's Inn, though he was not apparently called to the Bar, and later took a medical degree, presumably on the Continent. His first acknowledged verse was in Latin, but in 1601 he published in English a *Book of Airs* containing two groups of his poems, the first set to airs composed by himself, the second to airs of Philip Rosseter, his life-long friend, later the manager of a company of boy actors under the patronage of James's Queen. Campion's *Observations in the Art of English Poesy* (1602) is a plea for the quantitative classical system of versification, coupled with an attack on 'the vulgar and inartistic custom of riming,' an attack which drew from Daniel an answer pointing out the inconsistency of his position, since Campion's 'commendable rimes have given to the world the best notice of his worth.' Campion continued to publish his *Books of Airs,* the fourth and last of which appeared but three years before his death in 1620; and his technical treatise on harmony, *A New Way of Making Four Parts in Counterpoint* (1613) was for many years the standard textbook on the subject.

In verse Campion was a belated Elizabethan. His style retains definite, though unobtrusive, traces of Euphuistic balance and antithesis. Above all, his inspiration was classical. His ease and purity of diction and perfect taste were learned at the fountain-head of Catullus and Anacreon. He achieved by conscious experimentation an infinite variety of cadence without sacrificing the appearance of spontaneity. Only occasionally does he attain to that depth and finality that mark great poetry, but he belongs with Herrick and Ben Jonson in lighter vein, as one of the best classical lyrists in the language.

The list of Jacobean and later seventeenth-century composers and collectors of music is a long one: Thomas Weelkes, Giles Farnaby, Robert Jones, Thomas Ravenscroft, Michael Este, Thomas Bateson, Francis Pilkington, Tobias Hume, Richard Allison, Thomas Ford, Martin Peerson, John Wilbye, Henry and William Lawes, John Wilson, Henry Playford, and Dr. John Blow are a few of the most active. While song-books did not continue to be published in such volume as during the reign of James, there is a steady flow of them throughout the period, many, like those of Lawes, being republished several times. As versification became more regular, the madrigal disappeared and the air with lute accompaniment was increasingly devoted to emphasizing the rhythm and meaning of the verse.

In the song-books will be found poetry on every theme and in every fashion represented elsewhere in the two centuries under consideration, and every degree of lyric perfection from the general level to the rarest heights. Our selections begin with an excellent old ballad which found its way into Clement Robinson's miscellany, *A Handful of Pleasant Delights* (1584), but had undoubtedly been popular for many years before. Though above the average in quality, it calls to mind the great mass of popular poetry known as 'broadsides,' made by those 'base ballad makers' so despised of more educated poets, printed in black letter on a single sheet with a crude wood-cut, and hawked in the streets for a penny, exactly as cheap paper reprints of the lyrics of Tin Pan Alley are today. It will be recalled that the peddler Autolycus carried ballads in his pack as a sideline, to the delight of the country wenches. A still more popular broadside, too long to reprint in its entirety, was entitled *A New Courtly Sonnet of the Lady Greensleeves*. It is twice mentioned by Shakespeare and is usually included, with its quaint and delightful music, in modern collections of Elizabethan songs. *Greensleeves* belongs to that class described by Autolycus[2] as 'doleful ballads against the hard hearts of maids.' It begins

> Alas, my love, ye do me wrong
>   To cast me off discourteously;
> And I have lovèd you so long,
>   Delighting in your company.

and continues verse by verse with a long list of things the faithful lover has given her: kerchiefs, a petticoat, jewels, a smock of silk, a girdle of gold so red, a purse, a pincase, crimson stockings all of silk, white pumps, a green gown, garters fringèd with the gold, and men to wait upon her. The refrain,

[2] *Winter's Tale* IV. iii.

> Greensleeves was all my joy,
> Greensleeves was my delight;
> Greensleeves was my heart of gold,
> And who but Lady Greensleeves?

has music of a pleasant lilt in the first three lines, then sinks back into the wailing minor again. The jigging vein of the broadside was artistically imitated by Campion in such pieces as *Fain would I wed a fair young man.*

The song early dons the pastoral disguise in *While that the sun with his beams hot* (p. 275), and resumes it later in *Camella fair tripped o'er the plain* (p. 304), and *On a time the amorous Silvy* (p. 307), which parallel in time the Spenserian revival. The sonnet strain is strong in Campion's *When thou must home to shades of underground* (p. 283), and *There is a garden in her face* (p. 287). The epigram of courtly compliment was especially popular, as in *Lady, when I behold the roses sprouting* (p. 278), *Thrice toss those oaken ashes in the air* (p. 286), *Drink to me only with thine eyes* (the familiar musical setting of this is eighteenth-century), and *I saw fair Chloris* (p. 309), the latter one of the most popular of all seventeenth-century poems, being found, according to Ault, in three song-books, eleven miscellanies, and eighteen manuscripts. The Cavalier, taught by Donne and Jonson to flout the mistress the Petrarchans had adored, sings *Think'st thou, Kate, to put me down?* (p. 297), *Once did my thoughts both ebb and flow* (p. 300), and *When, Celia, I intend to flatter you* (p. 315), an attitude which crystallizes into downright rudeness, however urbanely expressed, in Restoration pieces like *Sabina has a thousand charms* (p. 317). Religious devotion, rarely absent from the song-books, is illustrated in *A stranger here* (p. 304), *Upon my lap my sovereign sits* (p. 308), and that little masterpiece of homely beauty, *Yet if his majesty, our sovereign lord* (p. 314). After the Restoration this graver note, with or without the accent of piety, is still frequently heard, in keeping with the serious undertone of the age. At the other end of the scale, the witty japes so common in later miscellanies were set to music as in *If all be true that I do think* (p. 312), and *Ye gods, you gave to me a wife* (p. 317). As always, popular song took on the color of its time.

In theme, if not in quality, it had something to add. The lyrics in song-books, like those in the plays, expand and diversify the scope of lyric sentiment. The perennial theme of true love, minus all pastoral masquerade or Italianate embroidery, is˙ here at its best, in songs that have deservedly outlived their age: *Fain would I change that note* (p. 295), *There is a lady sweet and kind* (p. 297), *Dear, if you change* (p. 277), and *Follow your saint* (p. 282). Music itself is exquisitely apostrophized by Herrick in *Charm me asleep* (now best known in a setting by Brahms, adapted from a Gregorian chant). *Now winter nights enlarge* (p. 285), *Maids to bed* (p. 303), and *Sister, awake* (p. 294), are little realistic pictures of domestic life and customs. There are songs for beggars, for soldiers, for mariners. By its alliance with music, most democratic of the arts, the lyric gained in universal appeal.

ANONYMOUS (Before 1600)

A Proper Song

Fain would I have a pretty thing
  To give unto my lady:
I name no thing, nor I mean no thing,
  But as pretty a thing as may be.

Twenty journeys would I make,
  And twenty ways would hie me,
To make adventure for her sake,
  To set some matter by me:
    But I would fain have a pretty thing, &c.

Some do long for pretty knacks,
  And some for strange devices:
God send me that my lady lacks,
  I care not what the price is. *Thus, &c.*

A Proper Song] One stanza is omitted.   *Proper*] Goodly

I walk the town and tread the street,
  In every corner seeking:
The pretty thing I cannot meet,
  That's for my lady's liking. *Fain, &c.*

The mercers pull me, going by,
  The silk-wives say, 'What lack ye?'
'The thing you have not,' then say I,
  'Ye foolish fools, go pack ye!' *But, &c.*

'It is not all the silk in Cheap,
  Nor all the golden treasure,
Nor twenty bushels on a heap
  Can do my lady pleasure.' *But, &c.*

The gravers of the golden shows
  With jewels do beset me;
The sempsters in the shops that sews,
  They do nothing but let me. *But, &c.*

But were it in the wit of man
  By any means to make it,
I could for money buy it than,
  And say 'Fair lady, take it.' *Thus, &c.*

O lady, what a luck is this,
  That my good willing misseth
To find what pretty thing it is
  That my good lady wisheth.
Thus fain would I have had this pretty thing
  To give unto my lady:
I said no harm, nor I meant no harm,
  But as pretty a thing as may be.

While that the sun

While that the sun with his beams hot
  Scorchèd the fruits in vale and mountain,
Philon, the shepherd, late forgot,

mercers] cloth merchants   silk-wives] women who sell silk   go pack ye] be off
Cheap] Cheapside   gravers] engravers, goldsmiths   sempsters] seamstresses   let]
hinder   than] then

Sitting beside a crystal fountain
In shadow of a green oak tree,
Upon his pipe this song played he:
 Adieu love, adieu love, untrue love,
 Untrue love, untrue love, adieu love;
 Your mind is light, soon lost for new love.

So long as I was in your sight,
 I was your heart, your soul, your treasure;
And evermore you sobbed and sighed,
 Burning in flames beyond all measure:
Three days endured your love to me,
And it was lost in other three.
 Adieu love, &c.

Another shepherd you did see,
 To whom your heart was soon enchainèd;
Full soon your love was leapt from me,
 Full soon my place he had obtainèd:
Soon came a third, your love to win;
And we were out and he was in.
 Adieu love, &c.

Sure you have made me passing glad
 That you your mind so soon removèd,
Before that I the leisure had
 To choose you for my best belovèd:
For all my love was past and done
Two days before it was begun.
 Adieu love, &c.

Sing we and chant it

Sing we and chant it
While love doth grant it.
 Fa la la!
Not long youth lasteth,
And old age hasteth.

Now is best leisure
To take our pleasure.
Fa la la!

All things invite us
Now to delight us,
Fa la la!
Hence, care, be packing!
No mirth be lacking!
Let spare no treasure
To live in pleasure.
Fa la la!

Dear, if you change

Dear, if you change, I'll never choose again;
  Sweet, if you shrink, I'll never think of love;
Fair, if you fail, I'll judge all beauty vain;
  Wise, if too weak, moe wits I'll never prove.
Dear, sweet, fair, wise, change, shrink, nor be not weak;
And, on my faith, my faith shall never break!

Earth with her flowers shall sooner heaven adorn;
  Heaven her bright stars through earth's dim globe shall
    move;
Fire heat shall lose, and frosts of flames be born;
  Air, made to shine, as black as hell shall prove.
Earth, heaven, fire, air, the world transformed shall view,
Ere I prove false to faith, or strange to you.

Brown is my love

Brown is my love, but graceful;
  And each renownèd whiteness,
Matched with thy lovely brown, loseth its brightness.

Fair is my love, but scornful;
  Yet have I seen despisèd
Dainty white lilies, and sad flowers well prizèd.

moe] more   prove] put to the test   change, shrink] neither change nor shrink

Lady, when I behold

Lady, when I behold the roses sprouting,
Which, clad in damask mantles, deck the arbors,
And then behold your lips, where sweet love harbors,
My eyes present me with a double doubting:
For viewing both alike, hard-ly my mind supposes,
Whether the roses be your lips, or your lips the roses.

Thrice blessèd be the giver

Thrice blessèd be the giver
That gave sweet Love that golden quiver,
And live he long among the gods anointed
That made the arrow-heads sharp-pointed:
If either of them both had quailèd,
She of my love and I of hers had failèd.

Madrigal

Faustina hath the fairer face,
And Phyllida the feater grace;
    Both have mine eye enrichèd:
This sings full sweetly with her voice;
Her fingers make as sweet a noise:
    Both have mine ear bewitchèd.
Ay me! sith Fates have so provided,
My heart, alas, must be divided.

FRANCIS DAVISON (c. 1575–c. 1619)

Madrigal I: To Cupid

Love, if a god thou art,
    Then evermore thou must
    Be merciful and just.

damask] deep pink, of velvety texture   supposes] guesses · feater] daintier   Her]
The other's   sith] since

If thou be just, O wherefore doth thy dart
Would mine alone, and not my lady's heart?

If merciful, then why
    Am I to pain reserved,
    Who have thee truly served;
While she, that by thy power sets not a fly,
Laughs thee to scorn, and lives in liberty?

Then, if a god thou wouldst accounted be,
Heal me like her, or else wound her like me.

Sweet, if you like and love me still

Sweet, if you like and love me still,
And yield me love for my good will,
And do not from your promise start
When your fair hand gave me your heart;
        If dear to you I be
        As you are dear to me,
Then yours I am and will be ever,
No time nor place my love shall sever,
But faithful still I will persèver,
        Like constant marble stone,
        Loving but you alone.

But if you favor moe than me,
Who love thee still, and none but thee;
If others do the harvest gain ·
That's due to me for all my pain;
        If that you love to range
        And oft to chop and change,
Then get you some new-fangled mate;
My doting love shall turn to hate,
Esteeming you,—though too too late—
        Not worth a pebble stone,
        Loving not me alone.

sets] cares   still] ever   start] withdraw

THOMAS CAMPION (1567–1620)

What if a day

What if a day, or a month, or a year
  Crown thy delights with a thousand sweet contentings;
Cannot a chance of a night or an hour
  Cross thy desires with as many sad tormentings?
      Fortune, honor, beauty, youth,
        Are but blossoms dying;
      Wanton pleasure, doting love,
        Are but shadows flying.
          All our joys
          Are but toys,
        Idle thoughts deceiving.
          None have power
          Of an hour
        In their lives' bereaving.

Earth's but a point to the world; and a man
  Is but a point to the earth's comparèd centure.
Shall then the point of a point be so vain
  As to triumph in a silly point's adventure?
      All is hazard that we have,
        There is nothing biding;
      Days of pleasure are like streams
        Through fair meadows gliding.
          Weal and woe,
          Time doth go,
        Time is never turning.
          Secret fates
          Guide our states
        Both in mirth and mourning.

My love bound me

My love bound me with a kiss
  That I should no longer stay;

In . . . bereaving] To delay the snatching away of our lives   centure] circumference   turning] turning back

When I felt so sweet a bliss
　　I had less power to pass away.
Alas! that women do not know
　Kisses make men loath to go.

Yes, she knows it but too well,
　　For I heard when Venus' dove
In her ear did softly tell
　　That kisses were the seals of love.
O, muse not then though it be so,
Kisses make men loath to go.

Wherefore did she thus inflame
　　My desires, heat my blood,
Instantly to quench the same
　　And starve whom she had given food?
I the common sense can show:
　Kisses make men loath to go.

Had she bid me go at first
　　It would ne'er have grieved my heart;
Hope delayed had been the worst.
　　But ah! to kiss and then to part!
How deep it struck; speak, gods, you know
Kisses make men loath to go.

My sweetest Lesbia

My sweetest Lesbia, let us live and love,
And though the sager sort our deeds reprove,
Let us not weigh them. Heaven's great lamps do dive
Into their west, and straight again revive;
But soon as once set is our little light,
Then must we sleep one ever-during night.

If all would lead their lives in love like me,
Then bloody swords and armor should not be;
No drum nor trumpet peaceful sleeps should move,

desires] trisyllabic   weigh] regard   ever-during] everlasting   move] rouse

Unless alarm came from the camp of love.
But fools do live, and waste their little light,
And seek with pain their ever-during night.

When timely death my life and fortune ends,
Let not my hearse be vexed with mourning friends,
But let all lovers, rich in triumph, come
And with sweet pastimes grace my happy tomb;
And Lesbia, close up thou my little light,
And crown with love my ever-during night.

When to her lute

When to her lute Corinna sings,
Her voice revives the leaden strings,
And doth in highest notes appear
As any challenged echo clear:
But when she doth of mourning speak,
E'en with her sighs the strings do break.

And as her lute doth live or die,
Led by her passion, so must I:
For when of pleasure she doth sing,
My thoughts enjoy a sudden spring;
But if she doth of sorrow speak,
E'en from my heart the strings do break.

Follow your saint

Follow your saint, follow with accents sweet;
Haste you, sad notes, fall at her flying feet.
There, wrapped in cloud of sorrow, pity move,
And tell the ravisher of my soul I perish for her love.
But if she scorns my never-ceasing pain,
Then burst with sighing in her sight and ne'er return again.

All that I sung still to her praise did tend;
Still she was first, still she my songs did end.
Yet she my love and music both doth fly,

still] always

The music that her echo is and beauty's sympathy.
Then let my notes pursue her scornful flight:
It shall suffice that they were breathed and died for her
  delight.

Thou art not fair

Thou art not fair for all thy red and white,
  For all those rosy ornaments in thee;
Thou art not sweet, though made of mere delight,
  Nor fair nor sweet, unless thou pity me.
I will not soothe thy fancies; thou shalt prove
That beauty is no beauty without love.

Yet love not me, nor seek thou to allure
  My thoughts with beauty, were it more divine;
Thy smiles and kisses I cannot endure,
  I'll not be wrapped up in those arms of thine.
Now show it, if thou be a woman right,—
Embrace and kiss and love me, in despite.

When thou must home

When thou must home to shades of underground,
  And there arrived, a new admirèd guest,
The beauteous spirits do engirt thee round,
  White Iope, blithe Helen, and the rest,
To hear the stories of thy finished love
From that smooth tongue whose music hell can move,

Then wilt thou speak of banqueting delights,
  Of masques and revels which sweet youth did make,
Of tourneys and great challenges of knights,
  And all these triumphs for thy beauty's sake;
When thou hast told these honors done to thee,
Then tell, O, tell how thou didst murder me.

mere] pure   soothe] humor, flatter   a woman right] truly feminine   hell can move] can stir the feelings of hell

Come, cheerful day

Come, cheerful day, part of my life, to me:
    For while thou view'st me with thy fading light,
Part of my life doth still depart with thee,
    And I still onward haste to my last night.
Time's fatal wings do ever forward fly:
So every day we live, a day we die.

But, O ye nights, ordained for barren rest,
    How are my days deprived of life in you,
When heavy sleep my soul hath dispossessed
    By feignèd death life sweetly to renew!
Part of my life, in that you life deny:
So every day we live, a day we die.

Come, you pretty false-eyed wanton

Come, you pretty false-eyed wanton,
    Leave your crafty smiling.
Think you to escape me now
    With slippery words beguiling?
No, you mocked me th' other day,
When you got loose, you fled away.
But since I have caught you now,
    I'll clip your wings for flying;
Smothering kisses fast I'll heap,
    And keep you so from crying.

Sooner may you count the stars,
    And number hail down-pouring,
Tell the osiers of the Thames,
    Or Goodwin Sands devouring,
Than the thick-showered kisses here,
Which now thy tired lips must bear.

in that you life deny] in denying life to renew it   Tell] Count

Such a harvest never was,
   So rich and full of pleasure;
But 'tis spent as soon as reaped,
   So trustless is love's treasure.

Would it were dumb midnight now,
   When all the world lies sleeping;
Would this place some desert were
   Which no man hath in keeping!
My desires should then be safe,
And when you cried then would I laugh;
But if aught might breed offence,
   Love only should be blamèd:
I would live your servant still,
   And you my saint unnamèd.

Now winter nights enlarge

Now winter nights enlarge
   The number of their hours;
And clouds their storms discharge
   Upon the airy towers.
Let now the chimneys blaze
   And cups o'erflow with wine,
Let well-tuned words amaze
   With harmony divine.
Now yellow waxen lights
   Shall wait on honey love,
While youthful revels, masques and courtly sights,
   Sleep's leaden spells remove.

This time doth well dispense
   With lovers' long discourse;
Much speech hath some defence,
   Though beauty no remorse.
All do not all things well:
   Some measures comely tread,

airy] lofty   dispense With] excuse   comely] becomingly

Some knotted riddles tell,
    Some poems smoothly read.
The summer hath his joys,
    And winter his delights;
Though love and all his pleasures are but toys
    They shorten tedious nights.

Thrice toss these oaken ashes

Thrice toss these oaken ashes in the air,
Thrice sit thou mute in this enchanted chair,
Then thrice three times tie up this true love's knot,
And murmur soft, 'She will, or she will not.'

Go burn these poisonous weeds in yon blue fire,
These screech-owl's feathers and this prickling briar,
This cypress gathered at a dead man's grave,
That all thy fears and cares an end may have.

Then come, you fairies, dance with me a round;
Melt her hard heart with your melodious sound.—
In vain are all the charms I can devise:
She hath an art to break them with her eyes.

Never love unless you can

Never love unless you can
Bear with all the faults of man;
Men sometimes will jealous be,
Though but little cause they see,
    And hang the head, as discontent,
    And speak what straight they will repent.

Men that but one saint adore
Make a show of love to more;
Beauty must be scorned in none,

knotted] knotty   his] its

Though but truly served in one;
  For what is courtship but disguise?
  True hearts may have dissembling eyes.

Men when their affairs require
Must a while themselves retire,
Sometimes hunt, and sometimes hawk,
And not ever sit and talk.
  If these and such like you can bear,
  Then like, and love, and never fear.

There is a garden in her face

There is a garden in her face,
Where roses and white lilies grow;
  A heavenly paradise is that place,
Wherein all pleasant fruits do flow.
  There cherries grow which none may buy
  Till 'Cherry-ripe' themselves do cry.

Those cherries fairly do enclose
Of orient pearl a double row,
  Which when her lovely laughter shows,
They look like rosebuds filled with snow.
  Yet them nor peer nor prince can buy,
  Till 'Cherry-ripe' themselves do cry.

Her eyes like angels watch them still;
Her brows like bended bows do stand,
  Threatening with piercing frowns to kill
All that attempt with eye or hand
  Those sacred cherries to come nigh,
  Till 'Cherry-ripe' themselves do cry.

Love me or not

Love me or not, love her I must or die;
Leave me or not, follow her needs must I.

Cherry-ripe] the familiar street-vendor's cry   orient] lustrous   needs] necessarily

O that her grace would my wished comforts give!
How rich in her, how happy should I live!

All my desire, all my delight should be
Her to enjoy, her to unite to me;
Envy should cease, her would I love alone:
Who loves by looks is seldom true to one.

Could I enchant, and that it lawful were,
Her would I charm softly that none should hear;
But love enforced rarely yields firm content:
So would I love that neither should repent.

Fain would I wed

Fain would I wed a fair young man that day and night could
    please me,
When my mind or body grieved, that had the power to ease me.
Maids are full of longing thoughts that breed a bloodless
    sickness,
And that, oft I hear men say, is only cured by quickness.
Oft I have been wooed and praised, but never could be movèd;
Many for a day or so I have most dearly lovèd,
But this foolish mind of mine straight loathes the thing re-
    solvèd;
If to love be sin in me, that sin is soon absolvèd.
Sure I think I shall at last fly to some holy order;
When I once am settled there, then can I fly no farther.
Yet I would not die a maid, because I had a mother;
As I was by one brought forth, I would bring forth another.

A. W. (c. 1602)

In Praise of a Beggar's Life

Bright shines the sun; play, beggars, play!
Here's scraps enough to serve today.

quickness] vigor   straight] straightway   resolvèd] settled

What noise of viols is so sweet
  As when our merry clappers ring?
What mirth doth want where beggars meet?
  A beggar's life is for a king.
Eat, drink, and play; sleep when we list;
Go where we will, so stocks be missed.
    Bright shines, &c.

The world is ours, and ours alone;
  For we alone have world at will;
We purchase not, all is our own;
  Both fields and streets we beggars fill.
Nor care to get, nor fear to keep,
Did ever break a beggar's sleep.
    Bright shines, &c.

A hundred head of black and white
  Upon our downs securely feed;
If any dare his master bite
  He dies, therefore, as sure as Creed.
Thus beggars lord it as they please
And none but beggars live at ease.
    Bright shines, &c.

Sweet love, mine only treasure

Sweet love, mine only treasure,
  For service long unfeignèd,
  Wherein I naught have gainèd,
Vouchsafe this little pleasure,
  To tell me in what part
  My lady keeps my heart.

If in her hair so slender,
  Like golden nets entwinèd
  Which fire and art have finèd,

clappers] clack-dishes   missed] escaped   finèd] refined

Her thrall my heart I render
   Forever to abide
   With locks so dainty tied.

If in her eyes she bind it,
   Wherein that fire was framèd
   By which it is enflamèd,
I dare not look to find it:
   I only wish it sight
   To see that pleasant light.

But if her breast have deignèd
   With kindness to receive it,
   I am content to leave it
Though death thereby were gainèd:
   Then, lady, take your own
   That lives for you alone.

BEN JONSON (1572–1637)

To Celia

Drink to me only with thine eyes,
   And I will pledge with mine;
Or leave a kiss but in the cup,
   And I'll not look for wine.
The thirst that from the soul doth rise
   Doth ask a drink divine;
But might I of Jove's nectar sup,
   I would not change for thine.

I sent thee late a rosy wreath,
   Not so much honoring thee
As giving it a hope, that there
   It could not withered be;
But thou thereon didst only breathe
   And sent'st it back to me;
Since when it grows, and smells, I swear,
   Not of itself, but thee.

dainty] daintily

GEFFREY WHITNEY (1548?–1601?)

In crystal towers

In crystal towers and turrets richly set
  With glittering gems that shine against the sun,
In regal rooms of jasper and of jet,
  Content of mind not always likes to won;
But oftentimes it pleaseth her to stay
In simple cots, enclosed in walls of clay.

ANONYMOUS (c. 1600–c. 1620)

I saw my lady weep

I saw my lady weep,
And Sorrow proud to be advancèd so
In those fair eyes where all perfections keep.
  Her face was full of woe:
But such a woe, believe me, as wins more hearts
Than Mirth can do with her enticing parts.

Sorrow was there made fair,
And passion wise; tears a delightful thing;
Silence beyond all speech, a wisdom rare;
  She made her sighs to sing,
And all things with so sweet a sadness move
As made my heart at once both grieve and love.

O fairer than aught else
The world can show, leave off in time to grieve.
Enough, enough: your joyful look excels;
  Tears kill the heart, believe.
O strive not to be excellent in woe,
Which only breeds your beauty's overthrow.

Fine knacks for ladies

Fine knacks for ladies, cheap, choice, brave, and new!
  Good pennyworths! but money cannot move.

won] dwell   parts] qualities   leave off] cease   brave] fine   move] buy them

I keep a fair but for the fair to view;
  A beggar may be liberal of love.
Though all my wares be trash, the heart is true.

Great gifts are guiles and look for gifts again;
  My trifles come as treasures from my mind.
It is a precious jewel to be plain;
  Sometimes in shell the orient'st pearls we find.
Of others take a sheaf, of me a grain.

Within this pack, pins, points, laces, and gloves,
  And divers toys fitting a country fair;
But in my heart, where duty serves and loves,
  Turtles and twins, court's brood, a heavenly pair.
Happy the heart that thinks of no removes!

If fathers knew

If fathers knew but how to leave
  Their children wit as they do wealth,
And could constrain them to receive
  That physic which brings perfect health,
The world would not admiring stand
A woman's face and woman's hand.

Women confess they must obey,
  We men will needs be servants still;
We kiss their hands, and what they say
  We must commend, be 't never so ill:
Thus we, like fools, admiring stand
Her pretty foot and pretty hand.

We blame their pride, which we increase
  By making mountains of a mouse;
We praise because we know we please;

the fair] fair ones   points] laces for bodice, etc.   Turtles] Turtledoves   court's]
courtship's   removes] changes

Poor women are too credulous
To think that we admiring stand
Or foot, or face, or foolish hand.

Whether men do laugh or weep

Whether men do laugh or weep,
Whether they do wake or sleep,
Whether they die young or old,
Whether they feel heat or cold,
There is underneath the sun
Nothing in true earnest done.

All our pride is but a jest,
None are worst, and none are best;
Grief and joy, and hope and fear,
Play their pageants everywhere:
Vain opinion all doth sway,
And the world is but a play.

Powers above in clouds do sit,
Mocking our poor apish wit,
That so lamely with such state
Their high glory imitate.
No ill can be felt but pain,
And that happy men disdain.

A Madrigal

My love in her attire doth show her wit,
  It doth so well become her:
For ev'ry season she hath dressings fit,
  For winter, spring, and summer.
  No beauty she doth miss,
  When all her robes are on:
  But Beauty's self she is,
  When all her robes are gone.

Vain opinion] Empty reputation   miss] lack

Weep you no more, sad fountains

Weep you no more, sad fountains;
  What need you flow so fast?
Look how the snowy mountains
  Heaven's sun doth gently waste.
  But my sun's heavenly eyes
    View not your weeping,
    That now lies sleeping
  Softly, now softly lies
    Sleeping.

Sleep is a reconciling,
  A rest that peace begets.
Doth not the sun rise smiling
  When fair at even he sets?
  Rest you then, rest, sad eyes,
    Melt not in weeping
    While she lies sleeping
  Softly, now softly lies
    Sleeping.

Sister, awake

Sister, awake! close not your eyes,
  The day her light discloses,
And the bright morning doth arise
  Out of her bed of roses.

See, the clear sun, the world's bright eye,
  In at our window peeping:
Lo, how he blusheth to espy
  Us idle wenches sleeping.

Therefore, awake! make haste, I say,
  And let us, without staying,
All in our gowns of green so gay
  Into the park a-maying.

Your shining eyes

Your shining eyes and golden hair,
Your lily-rosèd lips most fair,
Your other beauties that excel,
Men cannot choose but like them well;
But when for them they say they'll die,
Believe them not, they do but lie.

The Soldier's Song

I sing the praise of honored wars,
The glory of well-gotten scars,
The bravery of glittering shields,
Of lusty hearts and famous fields;
For that is music worth the ear of Jove,
A sight for kings, and still the soldier's love.

Look! O, methinks I see
The grace of chivalry;
The colors are displayed,
The captains bright arrayed.
See, now the battle's ranged,
Bullets now thick are changed.
Hark! shots and wounds abound,
The drums alarum sound.
The captains cry: 'Za-za!'
The trumpets sound *ta-ra!*
O, this is music worth the ear of Jove,
A sight for kings, and still the soldier's love.

Fain would I change that note

Fain would I change that note
 To which fond love hath charmed me,
Long, long to sing by rote,
 Fancying that that harmed me.

bravery] brightness, splendor

Yet when this thought doth come,
'Love is the perfect sum
Of all delight,'
I have no other choice
Either for pen or voice,
To sing or write.

O love, they wrong thee much
That say thy sweet is bitter;
When thy ripe fruit is such
As nothing can be sweeter.
Fair house of joy and bliss
Where truest pleasure is,
I do adore thee.
I know thee what thou art,
I serve thee with my heart
And fall before thee.

If I could shut the gate against my thoughts

If I could shut the gate against my thoughts,
And keep out sorrow from this room within,
Or memory could cancel all the notes
Of my misdeeds, and I unthink my sin,
How free, how clear, how clean my soul should lie,
Discharged of such a loathsome company.

Or were there other rooms without my heart
That did not to my conscience join so near,
Where I might lodge the thoughts of sin apart,
That I might not their clamorous crying hear;
What peace, what joy, what ease should I possess,
Freed from their horrors that my soul oppress.

But O my Savior, who my refuge art,
Let thy dear mercies stand 'twixt them and me,
And be the wall to separate my heart
So that I may at length repose me free;
That peace, and joy, and rest may be within,
And I remain divided from my sin.

Why canst thou not

Why canst thou not, as others do,
  Look on me with unwounding eyes,
And yet look sweet, but yet not so,
  Smile, but not in killing wise?
Arm not thy graces to confound;
Only look, but do not wound.

Why should mine eyes see more in you
  Than they can see in all the rest?
For I can others' beauties view
  And not find my heart oppressed.
O, be as others are to me,
Or let me be more to thee!

There is a lady

There is a lady sweet and kind,
Was never face so pleased my mind;
I did but see her passing by,
And yet I love her till I die.

Her gesture, motion, and her smiles,
Her wit, her voice, my heart beguiles,—
Beguiles my heart, I know not why,
And yet I love her till I die.

Cupid is wingèd and doth range,
Her country so my love doth change:
But change she earth, or change she sky,
Yet will I love her till I die.

Think'st thou, Kate?

Think'st thou, Kate, to put me down
With a no or with a frown?
Since love holds my heart in bands,
I must do as love commands.

There is a lady] attributed to Thomas Ford (d. 1648), by Grierson, *Oxford Book of Seventeenth Century Verse*, p. 202.   Three stanzas are here omitted.

Love commands the hands to dare
When the tongue of speech is spare;
Chiefest lesson in love's school,
Put it in adventure, fool.

Fools are they that fainting flinch
For a squeak, a scratch, a pinch.
Women's words have double sense;
'Stand away!'—a simple fence!

If thy mistress swears she'll cry,
Fear her not; she'll swear and lie.
Such sweet oaths no sorrow bring
Till the prick of conscience sting.

Though my carriage be but careless

Though my carriage be but careless,
    Though my looks be of the sternest,
Yet my passions are compareless:
    When I love, I love in earnest.

No, my wits are not so wild,
    But a gentle soul may yoke me;
Nor my heart so hard compiled,
    But it melts if love provoke me.

Once I thought

Once I thought to die for love,
Till I found that women prove
    Traitors in their smiling.
They say men unconstant be,
But themselves love change we see,
Till new grows old, and old grows stale, and all is but be-
    guiling.

Put it in adventure] Risk it   a simple fence] an easy barrier; perhaps, a mere de-
fensive thrust   But] But that   compiled] constructed

We be three poor mariners

We be three poor mariners,
　　Newly come from the seas;
We spend our lives in jeopardy,
　　While others live at ease.
Shall we go dance the round, the round,
　　Shall we go dance the round?
And he that is a bully boy
　　Come pledge me on the ground.

We care not for those martial men
　　That do our states disdain;
But we care for the merchantmen
　　Which do our states maintain:
To them we dance the round, the round,
　　To them we dance the round;
And he that is a bully boy
　　Come pledge me on the ground.

Love not me for comely grace

Love not me for comely grace,
For my pleasing eye or face,
Nor for any outward part,—
No, nor for a constant heart,
For these may fail or turn to ill,
　　So thou and I shall sever.
Keep therefore a true woman's eye,
And love me still, but know not why;
So hast thou the same reason still
　　To dote upon me ever.

I live, and yet methinks I do not breathe

I live, and yet methinks I do not breathe;
I thirst and drink, I drink and thirst again;
I sleep and yet do dream I am awake;

bully boy] good fellow　　states] vocation(s)

I hope for that I have; I have and want:
I sing and sigh; I love and hate at once.
    O, tell me, restless soul, what uncouth jar
    Doth cause in store such want, in peace such war?

Risposta

There is a jewel which no Indian mines
Can buy, no chymic art can counterfeit;
It makes men rich in greatest poverty,
Makes water wine, turns wooden cups to gold,
The homely whistle to sweet music's strain:
    Seldom it comes, to few from heaven sent,
    That much-in-little, all-in-naught,—content.

Sweet, let me go!

Sweet, let me go! Sweet, let me go!
What do you mean to vex me so?
Cease, cease, cease your pleading force!
Do you think thus to extort remorse?
Now, now! no more! alas, you overbear me;
And I would cry, but some would hear, I fear me.

Once did my thoughts

Once did my thoughts both ebb and flow,
    As passion did them move;
Once did I hope, straight fear again,
    And then I was in love.

Once did I waking spend the night,
    And told how many minutes move,
Once did I wishing waste the day,
    And then I was in love.

---

that] that which   *Risposta*] *Answer* (Italian)   chymic art] alchemy   remorse]
pity   straight] straightway   told] counted

Once by my carving true love's knots,
  The weeping trees did prove
That wounds and tears were both our lots,
  And then I was in love.

Once did I breathe another's breath,
  And in my mistress move;
Once was I not mine own at all,
  And then I was in love.

Once wore I bracelets made of hair,
  And collars did approve,
Once were my clothes made out of wax,
  And then I was in love.

Once did I sonnet to my saint,
  My soul in number moved,
Once did I tell a thousand lies,
  And then in truth I loved.

Once in my ear did dangling hang
  A little turtledove;
Once, in a word, I was a fool,
  And then I was in love.

The sea hath many thousand sands

The sea hath many thousand sands,
  The sun hath motes as many;
The sky is full of stars, and love
  As full of woes as any:
Believe me, that do know the elf,
And make no trial by thyself.

It is in truth a pretty toy
  For babes to play withal;

---

did approve] 'went in for'   out of wax] perfectly   number] measure   withal]
with

But O the honeys of our youth
   Are oft our age's gall!
Self-proof in time will make thee know
He was a prophet told thee so:

A prophet that, Cassandra-like,
   Tells truth without belief,
For headstrong youth will run his race,
   Although his goal be grief;
Love's martyr, when his heat is past,
Proves Care's confessor at the last.

How many new years have grown old

How many new years have grown old
   Since first your servant old was new;
How many long hours have I told
   Since first my love was vowed to you;
And yet, alas, she doth not know
Whether her servant love or no.

How many walls as white as snow,
   And windows clear as any glass,
Have I conjùred to tell you so,
   Which faithfully performèd was;
And yet you'll swear you do not know
Whether your servant love or no.

How often hath my pale, lean face,
   With true charàcters of my love,
Petitionèd to you for grace,
   Whom neither sighs nor tears can move;
O cruel, yet do you not know
Whether your servant love or no.

And wanting oft a better token,
   I have been fain to send my heart,
Which now your cold disdain hath broken,

confessor] penitent

Nor can you heal't by any art:
O look upon't, and you shall know
Whether your servant love or no.

Crownèd with flowers

Crownèd with flowers I saw fair Amaryllis
    By Thyrsis sit, hard by a fount of crystal;
And with her hand, more white than snow or lilies,
    On sand she wrote, 'My faith shall be immortal':
And suddenly a storm of wind and weather
Blew all her faith and sand away together.

The Bellman's Song

Maids to bed and cover coal;
Let the mouse out of her hole;
Crickets in the chimney sing
Whilst the little bell doth ring:
If fast asleep, who can tell
When the clapper hits the bell?

Fair is the rose

Fair is the rose, yet fades with heat or cold;
Sweet are the violets, yet soon grow old;
The lily's white, yet in one day 'tis done;
White is the snow, yet melts against the sun:
So white, so sweet, was my fair mistress' face,
Yet altered quite in one short hour's space:
So short-lived beauty a vain gloss doth borrow,
Breathing delight today but none tomorrow.

The silver swan

The silver swan, who living had no note,
When death approached, unlocked her silent throat;
Leaning her breast against the reedy shore,

Thus sung her first and last, and sung no more:
'Farewell, all joys; O death, come close mine eyes;
More geese than swans now live, more fools than wise.'

A stranger here

A stranger here, as all my fathers were
   That went before, I wander to and fro;
From earth to heaven is my pilgrimage,
   A tedious way for flesh and blood to go.
O thou that art the way, pity the blind
And teach me how I may thy dwelling find.

Camella fair

Camella fair tripped o'er the plain,
   I followed quickly after;
Have overtaken her I would fain,
   And kissed her when I caught her.
But hope being passed her to obtain,
   'Camella!' loud I call:
She answered me with great disdain,
   'I will not kiss at all.'

Cupid, in a bed of roses

Cupid, in a bed of roses
   Sleeping, chancèd to be stung
   Of a bee that lay among
The flowers where he himself reposes;
And thus to his mother weeping
   Told that he this wound did take
   Of a little wingèd snake,
As he lay securely sleeping.
Cytherea smiling said
   That 'if so great sorrow spring
   From a silly bee's weak sting

As should make thee thus dismayed,
What anguish feel they, think'st thou, and what pain,
Whom thy empoisoned arrows cause complain?'

Her hair the net

Her hair the net of golden wire,
    Wherein my heart, led by my wandering eyes
    So fast entangled is that in no wise
It can, nor will, again retire;
    But rather will in that sweet bondage die
    Than break one hair to gain her liberty.

I heard a noise

I heard a noise and wishèd for a sight,
I looked aside and did a shadow see,
Whose substance was the sum of my delight;
It came unseen, and so it went from me.
    But yet conceit persuaded my intent
    There was a substance where the shadow went.

I did not play Narcissus in conceit,
I did not see my shadow in a spring:
I knew mine eyes were dimmed with no deceit,
I saw the shadow of some worthy thing:
    For, as I saw the shadow passing by,
    I had a glance of something in my eye.

But what it was, alas, I cannot tell,
Because of it I had no perfect view:
But as it was, by guess, I wish it well
And will until I see the same anew.
    Shadow, or she, or both, or choose you whether:
    Blest be the thing that brought the shadow hether!

retire] draw out   her liberty] liberty from her   conceit] imagination   intent]
judgment   whether] which

The Dance

Robin is a lovely lad,
No lass a smoother ever had.
Tommy hath a look as bright
As is the rosy morning light.
Tib is dark and brown of hue,
But like her color firm and true.
Jinny hath a lip to kiss
Wherein a spring of nectar is.
Simkin well his mirth can place
And words to win a woman's grace.
Sib is all in all to me,
There is no queen of love but she.
Let us in a lovers' round
Circle all this hallowed ground.
Softly, softly, trip and go,
The light-foot fairies jet it so.
Forward then and back again,
Here and there and everywhere,
Winding to and winding fro,
Skipping high and louting low.
And like lovers hand in hand
March around and make a stand.

Sweet Suffolk owl

Sweet Suffolk owl, so trimly dight
With feathers, like a lady bright,
Thou sing'st alone, sitting by night,
    'Te whit, te whoo!'
Thy note that forth so freely rolls,
With shrill command the mouse controls,
And sings a dirge for dying souls,
    'Te whit, te whoo!'

smoother] pleasanter   jet it] dance   louting] bowing   controls] dominates

Open the door!

'Open the door! Who's there within?
The fairest of thy mother's kin?
   O come, come, come abroad
And hear the shrill birds sing,
   The air with tunes that load.
It is too soon to go to rest,
The sun not midway yet to west;
   The day doth miss thee,
And will not part until it kiss thee.'

'Were I as fair as you pretend,
Yet to an unknown seld-seen friend
   I dare not ope the door;
To hear the sweet birds sing
Oft proves a dangerous thing.
The sun may run his wonted race
And yet not gaze on my poor face;
   The day may miss me:
Therefore depart, you shall not kiss me.'

Hey nonny no!

Hey nonny no!
Men are fools that wish to die!
Is 't not fine to dance and sing
When the bells of death do ring?
Is 't not fine to swim in wine,
And turn upon the toe
And sing hey nonny no,
When the winds do blow,
And the seas do flow?
Hey nonny no!

On a time

On a time the amorous Silvy
Said to her shepherd, 'Sweet, how do ye?

seld-seen] seldom-seen

Kiss me this once, and then God b' wi' ye,
     My sweetest dear!
Kiss me this once, and then God b' wi' ye,
For now the morning draweth near.'

With that, her fairest bosom showing,
Opening her lips, rich perfumes blowing,
She said, 'Now kiss me and be going,
     My sweetest dear!
Kiss me this once and then be going,
For now the morning draweth near.'

With that the shepherd waked from sleeping,
And spying where the day was peeping,
He said, 'Now take my soul in keeping,
     My sweetest dear!
Kiss me, and take my soul in keeping,
Since I must go, now day is near.'

RICHARD ROWLANDS (c. 1550–1620)

Our Blessed Lady's Lullaby

Upon my lap my sovereign sits
     And sucks upon my breast;
Meantime his love maintains my life
     And gives my sense her rest.
          Sing lullaby, my little boy,
          Sing lullaby, mine only joy.

When thou hast taken thy repast,
     Repose, my babe, on me;
So may thy mother and thy nurse
     Thy cradle also be.
          Sing lullaby, &c.

Rowlands] writing under the name of Richard Verstegan. See the *Dictionary of National Biography*.   *Lullaby*] the first four of twenty-four stanzas, as in Peerson's *Private Music* (1620)   sense] body

I grieve that duty doth not work
  All that my wishing would,
Because I would not be to thee
  But in the best I should.
    Sing lullaby, &c.

Yet as I am, and as I may,
  I must and will be thine,
Though all too little for thyself
  Vouchsafing to be mine.
    Sing lullaby, &c.

WILLIAM STRODE (1602–1645)

On Chloris Walking in the Snow

I saw fair Chloris walk alone
Whilst feathered rain came softly down,
And Jove descended from his tower
To court her in a silver shower;
The wanton snow flew to her breast
Like little birds unto their nest,
But overcome with whiteness there
For grief it thawed into a tear,
Thence falling on her garment hem
To deck her, froze into a gem.

THOMAS PHILIPOTT (*c.* 1632)

On a Spark of Fire Fixing on a Gentlewoman's Breast

Fair Julia sitting by the fire,
An amorous spark, with hot desire,
Flew to her breast, but could not melt
The chaste snow there; which when it felt,
And that resistance it did bide,

But in] Less than   for] in return for   *On a Spark*] an 'answer' to the preceding poem

For grief it blushed, and so it died.
Yet lest it should prove aught unkind,
It contrite ashes left behind.

FRANCIS QUARLES (1592–1644)

O, the fickle state of lovers

O, the fickle state of lovers!
A heart perplexed with hopes and fears
Today a world of joy discovers,
And tomorrow's drowned in tears:
  A lover's state's like April's weather,
  Rain and sunshine both together.

If his mistress do but smile,
A heaven of joy is in his heart;
If her brow but frown a while,
Hell can find no greater smart:
  In a lover's breast doth dwell
  Very heaven, or very hell.

ROBERT HERRICK (1591–1674)

To Music, to Becalm his Fever

Charm me asleep, and melt me so
  With thy delicious numbers,
That being ravished, hence I go
  Away in easy slumbers.
    Ease my sick head,
    And make my bed,
Thou powèr that canst sever
    From me this ill,
    And quickly still,
    Though thou not kill,
     My fever.

Thou sweetly canst convert the same
From a consuming fire
Into a gentle-licking flame,
And make it thus expire.
Then make me weep
My pains asleep,
And give me such reposes
That I, poor I,
May think thereby
I live and die
'Mongst roses.

Fall on me like a silent dew,
Or like those maiden showers
Which by the peep of day do strew
A baptime o'er the flowers.
Melt, melt my pains
With thy soft strains,
That having ease me given,
With full delight
I leave this light
And take my flight
For heaven.

HENRY REYNOLDS (c. 1632)

Was it a form?

Was it a form, a gait, a grace,
Was it their sweetness merely?
Was it the heaven of a bright face,
That made me love so dearly?

Was it a skin of silk and snow,
That soul and senses wounded?
Was 't any of these, or all of these,
Whereon my faith was founded?

baptime] baptism

Ah, no! 'twas a far deeper part
Than all the rest that won me:
'Twas a fair-clothed but feigning heart
I loved, and has undone me.

HENRY HARRINGTON (c. 1658)

Trust the form of airy things

Trust the form of airy things,
Or a siren when she sings,
Trust the sly hyena's voice,
Or of all distrust make choice,—
And believe these sooner then
Truth in women, faith in men.

KATHERINE PHILIPS (1631–1664)

Song

'Tis true our life is but a long disease,
Made up of reàl pain and seeming ease.
You stars, who these entangled fortunes give,
    O tell me why
    It is so hard to die,
      Yet such a task to live!

If with some pleasure we our griefs betray,
It costs us dearer than it can repay,
For time or fortune all things so devours,
    Our hopes are crossed,
    Or else the object lost,
      Ere we can call it ours.

HENRY ALDRICH (1647–1710)

If all be true that I do think

If all be true that I do think,
There are five reasons we should drink:

then] than

Good wine, a friend, or being dry,
Or lest we should be by and by;
Or any other reason why.

ANONYMOUS (After 1620)

When I behold

When I behold my mistress' face,
Where beauty hath her dwelling-place,
And see those seeing stars, her eyes,
In whom love's fire forever lies,
And hear her witty, charming words
Her sweet tongue to mine ear affords,
Me thinks he wants wit, ears, and eyes
Whom love makes not idolatrize.

When on mine eyes

When on mine eyes her eyes first shone,
      I all amazèd
      Steadily gazèd,
And she to make me more amazèd,
So caught, so wove four eyes in one
As who had with advisement seen us
Would have admired love's equal force between us.

But treason in those friend-like eyes,
      My heart first charming
      And then disarming,
So maimed it, ere it dreamed of harming,
As at her mercy now it lies,
And shows me, to my endless smart,
She loved but with her eyes, I with my heart.

witty] wise   amazèd] bewildered   admired] wondered at   As] That

Love in thy youth

Love in thy youth, fair maid, be wise;
  Old Time will make thee colder,
And though each morning new arise
  Yet we each day grow older.

Thou as heaven art fair and young,
  Thine eyes like twin stars shining:
But ere another day be sprung,
  All these will be declining;

Then winter comes with all his fears,
  And all thy sweets shall borrow;
Too late then wilt thou shower thy tears,
  And I too late shall sorrow.

Yet if his majesty our sovereign lord

Yet if his majesty our sovereign lord
    Should of his own accord
    Friendly himself invite,
And say 'I'll be your guest tomorrow night,'
How should we stir ourselves, call and command
All hands to work! 'Let no man idle stand.

'Set me fine Spanish tables in the hall,
    See they be fitted all;
    Let there be room to eat,
And order taken that there want no meat.
See every sconce and candlestick made bright,
That without tapers they may give a light.

'Look to the presence: are the carpets spread,
    ·The dazie o'er the head,
    The cushions in the chairs,

order taken] arrangement made   presence] presence-chamber   dazie] dais, canopy
over the throne

And all the candles lighted on the stairs?
Perfume the chambers, and in any case
Let each man give attendance in his place.'

Thus if the king were coming would we do,
     And 'twere good reason too;
       For 'tis a duteous thing
To show all honor to an earthly king,
And after all our travail and our cost,
So he be pleased, to think no labor lost.

But at the coming of the King of Heaven
     All's set at six and seven:
       We wallow in our sin,
Christ can not find a chamber in the inn.
We entertain him always like a stranger,
And, as at first, still lodge him in the manger.

When, Celia, I intend

When, Celia, I intend to flatter you,
And tell you lies to make you true,
       I swear
     There's none so fair,—
     And you believe it too.

Oft have I matched you with the rose, and said
No twins so like hath nature made;
       But 'tis
     Only in this,—
     You prick my hand, and fade.

Oft have I said there is no precious stone
But may be found in you alone;
       Though I
     No stone espy,—
     Unless your heart be one.

When I praise your skin, I quote the wool
That silkworms from their entrails pull,
 And show
 That new-fall'n snow
 Is not more beautiful.

Yet grow not proud by such hyperboles;
Were you as excellent as these,
 Whilst I
 Before you lie,
 They might be had with ease.

The Passing-Bell

Come, honest sexton, take thy spade,
And let my grave be quickly made;
Thou still art ready for the dead,
Like a kind host to make a bed.
I now am come to be thy guest;
Let me in some dark lodging rest,
For I am weary, full of pain,
And of my pilgrimage complain.
On heaven's decree I waiting lie,
And all my wishes are to die.
 Hark! hark! I hear my passing-bell,
 Farewell, my loving friends, farewell!

Make my cold bed, good sexton, deep,
That my poor bones may safely sleep
Until that sad and joyful day
When from above a voice shall say,
'Wake, all ye dead, lift up your eyes,
The great Creator bids you rise.'
Then do I hope, among the just,
To shake off this polluted dust;
And with new robes of glory dressed
To have access among the blest.
 Hark! hark! I hear my passing-bell,
 Farewell, my loving friends, farewell!

quote] refer to

Ye gods, you gave to me a wife

Ye gods, you gave to me a wife,
    Out of your wonted favor,
To be the comfort of my life,
    And I was glad to have her:
But if your providence divine
    For something else design her,
To obey your will at any time
    I'm ready to resign her.

Lost is my quiet

Lost is my quiet forever,
    Lost is life's happiest part;
Lost all my tender endeavor
    To touch an insensible heart.

But though my despair is past curing,
    And much undeserved is my fate,
I'll show by a patient enduring,
    My love is unmoved as her hate.

A Love-Song

Sabina has a thousand charms
    To captivate my heart;
Her lovely eyes are Cupid's arms,
    And every look a dart:
But when the beauteous idiot speaks,
    She cures me of my pain;
Her tongue the servile fetters breaks
    And frees her slave again.

Had nature to Sabina lent
    Beauty with reason crowned,
Each single shaft her eyes had sent
    Had given a mortal wound;

arms] weapons

Now though each hour she gains a heart,
And makes mankind her slave,
Yet like the Grecian hero's dart,
She heals the wounds she gave.

VI

DONNE AND THE METAPHYSICALS

Chiefly

c. 1591–*c*. 1601

and

1633–1650

DONNE AND THE METAPHYSICALS

John Donne belongs in date to the age of Elizabeth, in spirit to the seventeenth century. His *Songs and Sonets,* the most characteristic of his secular lyrics, were composed between 1591 and 1601. While every other poet in England was busily penning Petrarchan sonnets, Donne was perfecting in *Go and catch a falling star* a kind of mockery that was to laugh them from the poetic scene, and a new and sinewy technique to set at naught their artificial conventions; he was writing love poetry in the mood and accent of a new generation. Delayed by that indifference to publication which in the nineties still, though more rarely, characterized writers of Donne's social position, the appearance of his poems posthumously in 1633 came when a public was ready for them, and they became instantly and enormously popular. But as they had been widely circulated in manuscript, their fame was already known to many, and thus they helped to create the taste by which they were later to be appreciated. For the better understanding, then, of Donne and of his share in what was to come, it will be profitable to pause and consider what is implied by the spirit of the seventeenth century and how it contrasts with that of the age of Elizabeth.

Elizabethan literature is young in spirit; it seems the expression of a race who lived in the springtime of the world. Its moral soundness and health, its elevation of mood, its bright fancy, its voluptuous gloom and exuberant optimism are what we expect of spirited, happy young manhood; its very lapses from decorum are those of childhood, its extravagances, those of youth and heated blood. Three powerful influences—the Renaissance, the rising tide of their national fortunes, and the long reign of their great Queen —combined to create for Englishmen in the closing decades of the sixteenth century a sort of intellectual and emotional paradise. In the seventeenth century the race fell from its paradise into the realities of the modern world.

The search for truth which Bacon called 'the sovereign good of our nature' became the keynote of the new age. Many of the ideas which are the very substance of modern thought were evolved. Monarchy was overthrown, and restored—with a difference. Religion felt the first cold impact of science, and the Church suffered upheaval. Evidence for the shattering logic of Copernicus and Bruno could be seen through a telescope. If Heaven was not above man, was Hell under his feet? And if not, what became of the literal interpretation of the Scripture? If the stars were vast impersonal planets, ·what became of their astrological influence upon the affairs of men? The world itself, in that vast company—what was it but a fleck of unconsidered mud? The microscope added final proof to Harvey's theory of the circulation of the blood and revealed vast realms of living organisms never seen before. Man was overwhelmed by the universe these new instruments of thought and precision had opened up. Dismayed and saddened at first by the apparent downfall of all that he had believed in, he sought escape from the new realities in ways familiar enough to those who are thrown in contact with young men and women in the day of their disillusion: in beauty, in mysticism, in flippancy. Donne, himself a victim of 'the worst voluptuousness, which is an hydroptic immoderate desire of humane learning,' was the first poet of an age in which, as he says, the new philosophy called all in doubt.

The subjects of Donne's poems were identical with those of previous Elizabethan poetry: the old, first subjects—love and death. The effect of revolutionary novelty which his poems convey is due entirely to the poet's handling of his themes. Donne's was a nature of that rare sort in which thought and passion may co-exist, producing a mental state aptly described by Mr. T. S. Eliot as 'unified sensibility.' His was a mind in which emotion did not confuse and dissipate thought, as it does with most men, but on the contrary stimulated and clarified it. Thinking was to him a passionate experience; his mind was capable of passionate logic. In consequence, he brought to poetry a realistic insight, a ruthless, cynical, at times even brutal, probing of the emotion of love as

he knew it, and, at the same time, a weight of sincere feeling—
sometimes of bitterness, sometimes of joy in the deep contentment
of mutual love—that were as new as they were powerful.

In style as well as mood Donne represents a complete break
with the Petrarchan tradition. The cruelty and unfaithfulness of
womankind are no longer to be adored with humble lamenting,
but rather flayed with a devastating mockery. The Petrarchan
imagery drawn from familiar natural objects and equally familiar
mythology is supplanted by a new range of homely, vivid figures
drawn from alchemy, medicine, law, mathematics, and astronomy.
Nor can we doubt that the break was conscious and deliberate,
for in one of his satires he dismisses Ariosto, Ovid, and even
golden-mouthed Spenser as 'builders of Sleep's house.'

A further element of Donne's originality is his contempt for
mere form and the graces of diction, for alliteration, choice of
words for sound or smoothness, and regularity of rhythm. For
these he substitutes the homely and compelling movement of
colloquial speech, already familiar in the drama of the day but a
decided innovation in the lyric. The result is a new variety of
sound patterns, admirably adapted to the nature of his thought
and compelling when rightly read, but harsh-sounding to the
reader who, like Jonson, did not see what Donne was trying to do,
or who did not attend carefully to the punctuation.[1] Rightly heard,
these colloquial cadences add much to the pleasure of reading and
enhance the movement of the thought. They are especially note-
worthy in the explosive, often petulant, beginnings characteristic
of Donne:

> I wonder, by my troth, what thou and I
> Did till we loved.
>
> Busy old fool, unruly sun!

But the quality in Donne which most of all fascinated the
seventeenth-century mind was his dazzling wit, as expressed in
paradox, and especially in 'conceit.' It was his conceits which his
followers found most worthy of imitation, and which brought

[1] See p. 46.

him undeserved critical opprobrium as the leader of a 'metaphysical' school. We shall do well, therefore, to examine the Donnean conceit, and determine in what it differs from that of Sidney and the Elizabethans. We have already described the conceit as a figure of speech, either brief or extended, displaying excessive ingenuity or lack of taste, or both. The description is as applicable to Donne as to Sidney. Conceit is a kind of imagery, and, like all imagery, arises from the perception of a likeness, or likenesses, between different things. But whereas the fanciful and strained hyperboles of Sidney characteristically compare one physical object or process with another, Donne characteristically compares an object with an abstraction, especially a scientific or philosophical abstraction, or bases his comparison of two objects upon an abstract likeness. He has in unusual degree the power which Mr. T. S. Eliot postulates of all poets, that of 'amalgamating disparate experiences.' The likenesses he perceives are remote rather than familiar, logical rather than sensuous. It should be added that Donne employs the conceit of extended comparison with a sustained logic and a subtlety which were the natural outgrowth of a mind trained, as was his, on the medieval dialectic of the Jesuits. This sort of figure, especially when involving science in the comparison, constitutes a distinctive mark of his style.

As to far-fetchedness and bad taste, it would be idle to deny that both are found in Donne's practice of the conceit. When he writes

> Our hands were firmly cèmented
> With a fast balm, which thence did spring;
> Our eye-beams twisted and did thread
> Our eyes upon one double string;

few readers nowadays would hesitate to dismiss the figures as over-ingenious and ridiculous. But, as a recent critic reminds us, excesses of ingenuity are not in themselves more reprehensible than the excesses of sensation indulged in by the Petrarchans, and they are certainly more interesting.[2] Few readers nowadays would hesi-

---

[2] Joan Bennett, in *Four Metaphysical Poets*, p. 12ff. Cambridge University Press, 1934. This and allied matters are interestingly discussed.

tate to condemn the taste of those who admired the famous *Flea*. But the point at which good taste ends, or extravagance begins, is not a matter of definition, and opinions on individual cases differ surprisingly. Of the best of Donne's conceits let it be said that they do not seem like conceits at all, so naturally do they proceed from the bias of his mind, coupled with intensity of feeling. They leave us with a sense of our own blindness at not having seen the likenesses which, Donne convinces us, do exist, and with a sense of gratification at the insight of a mind which can go on discovering new facets of a comparison which we would have thought exhausted in the first stanza. Such triumphs as *A Valediction Forbidding Mourning* and *A Lecture upon the Shadow,* where the extravagance of the comparison is not only excused but justified by the intensity and sincerity of the feeling, have in store for the reader who gives himself to them a unique and unforgettable poetic experience.

The secular lyrics of Donne, those in the sections entitled *Songs and Sonets* and *Elegies* in the first edition (1633), are of uncertain date and arrangement. The order in which they appear in the following pages is that decided upon by Donne's foremost modern editor, Professor H. J. C. Grierson. The reader will find that they fall into several groups according to their mood and theme. In some of them, mockery of the shallowness and inconstancy of women is a pose as artificial as that of the humility of the Petrarchan lover. In others, and especially the *Elegies,* the best of which are too long to be quoted here, there is frank sensuality and cynical wit. Others record the delight of mutual love-making, sometimes, but not always, with a cynical aside upon its transiency and the inconstancy of the woman or of both parties. Still others idealize the marriage of true minds in which physical mating is the symbol of deep, true affection. In the case of a poet so intensely subjective as Donne, it is perhaps less dangerous than with another man to yield to the temptation of associating these groups with the successive stages of Donne's personal life, and especially of connecting the poems of true love with his romantic attachment and marriage to Anne More. Though the matter is beyond proof, internal evidence to support this arrangement is not altogether lacking, in that many of the *Elegies* seem extravagant and immature in workmanship, while in *The Good-Morrow, A Valediction Forbidding Mourning,* and *Sweetest love, I do not go,* three which we like to think were written to his wife, there is a serenity, an absence of fantasticality and paradox, and a perfection of workmanship, which accord with the idea that they were later work.

Donne is one of the most individualistic of English poets and he is correspondingly difficult to understand and appreciate. Historical considerations are of little avail, for he is neither the product of a school nor in any true sense the founder of one. He deepened the range of lyric poetry by reason of his poetic insight, his power of associating the familiar with the remote, of flashing light and meaning into what at first would appear to be merely commonplace. His poetry is intense, subtle, perverse, full of paradoxical reasoning, curious learning, and a sceptical philosophy of love and life. Witty, passionate, weighty, moving, frequently bizarre, at times even repulsive, it has never for long the harmonious simplicity of perfect beauty. But beauty there is, though fitfully, in lines and phrases that cannot be forgotten:

> A bracelet of bright hair about the bone,

> All other things to their destruction draw;
> Only our love hath no decay.

> Love is a growing, or full constant light;
> And his first minute, after noon, is night.

The intellectualized emotion which characterizes Donne's genius has won him the harshest of criticism and the most extravagant devotion. Because of the actuality of his style and the originality of his thought he gained a contemporary popularity which few lyric poets have ever rivaled; and few of his time have been the object of such continued and increasing interest in ours. Yet his readers, though surprisingly numerous, are comparatively few, for they must always be limited to the elect who can share his 'unified sensibility.' To these he will always be, in the words of Jonson, 'the first poet in the world in some things.'

To few men has come greatness of such diverse kinds. Donne was in his youth a poet of fleshly love, realistic, cynical, frequently voluptuous. He lived to become the most brilliant and moving preacher of his day. Yet the two phases of his career are not separable, but are clearly aspects of the same personality. The *Songs and Sonets* cannot but appear in a different light when we read of his later spirituality; and in his sermons and religious verse he continues to be a poet, the same poet as in the *Songs and Sonets*. Such terms as repentance and religious conversion seem inadequate when applied to the phenomenon of his later years. He belongs with those intense natures which can be transformed by experience, by suffering. The discord between his earlier and later life only *seems* more difficult to resolve because his extraordinary abilities carried him so far in such widely different directions.

The term 'metaphysical,' first applied in an adversely critical sense to the theory and work of Donne's imitators, has come with the clearer understanding and appreciation of Donne's genius to be accepted as a useful epithet to describe the nature of his poetry. It seems to have been first used about 1630 by William Drummond in a letter to a learned friend deploring the evil days upon which the Muse of Poetry had fallen:

In vain have some men of late, transformers of everything, consulted upon her reformation, and endeavored to abstract her to metaphysical ideas and scholastic quiddities, denuding her of her own habits and those ornaments with which she hath amused the world some thousand years.

To Drummond, 'metaphysical' probably meant little more than 'scientific,' and the passage is thus a recognizable description of Donnean poetry as it would appear to a Spenserian and a classicist, who would naturally resent above all the sloughing off of those familiar images drawn from nature and mythology. Quite possibly following Drummond, Dryden, in his *Discourse concerning Satire* (1693), uses the word in rebuking Donne for writing love poetry that is too hard for the ladies to understand:

[Donne] affects the metaphysics, not only in his satires, but in his amorous verses, where nature only should reign; and perplexes the minds of the fair sex with nice speculations of philosophy, when he should engage their hearts, and entertain them with the softnesses of love.

Finally the great Dr. Johnson, in his *Life of Cowley,* writes:

About the beginning of the 17th century appeared a race of writers that may be termed the metaphysical poets . . . [Their] wit may be considered as a kind of *discordia concors;* a combination of dissimilar images, or discovery of occult resemblances in things apparently unlike.

It may be that Johnson had studied Dryden's essay more carefully than the poetry to which he alludes, but his definition of the effect of the Donnean conceit is clear and just. His damning implication that Donne and his followers were wits rather than poets is modified somewhat when he continues:

If they frequently threw away their wit upon false conceits, they likewise sometimes struck out unexpected truth; if their conceits were far-fetched, they were often worth the carriage. To write on their plan it was at least necessary to read and think.

At all events, the term 'metaphysical' to describe the poetry of Donne and his imitators has since Johnson's use of it become a commonplace, much abused by critics who are dismayed to find themselves confronted with a poet like Donne who cannot be classified, or who desire to explain away anything in seventeenth-century poetry which they do not understand or like. It is chiefly dangerous, however, when used to link Donne chronologically and qualitatively with imitators like Cowley, who began writing after his death and more than three decades after the composition of his poetry, and thus to picture him as the founder of a school, and a malign influence on English poetry. To blame upon Donne all the excesses of the seventeenth-century conceit is to neglect the fact that the very force and pressure of the literary activity of the time, the exhaustion by the great Elizabethans of the normal range of imagery, had put every poet in precisely the same position from which Donne emerged triumphantly in his own way. The pre-occupation of the time with science made it a natural recourse to any poet in search of novelty, and many a one must have met the situation in the same way as Donne without in any true sense imitating him.

If, however, we dismiss the idea of a school and divest the term 'metaphysical' of its derogatory accent, using it in the Aristotelian sense of 'beyond the physical, abstract, subtle, supernatural,' what we should call today psychological, it may be usefully applied to some of Donne's intellectualized love verse and to some of the spiritual poetry of Herbert, Crashaw, and Vaughan. Donne's themes *are* metaphysical, even in some of the verse in which he seems most concerned with the physical. His images *are* metaphysical. The majority of his imitators had neither the mind for metaphysics nor the passion necessary to elevate them into poetry.

Donne is inimitable, but he was widely imitated, not only by the few in whom a similar weight of passion underlay the fantasticality and paradox, but by the many who had not his strength and originality. His example is thus responsible for a few of the successes of later seventeenth-century poetry and for many of its worst aberrations, such as the extravagant conceits of Cleveland and some of the religious poets, and the frigid love poetry of Cowley. Among the most successful of his followers were a number of men who knew him well, and these, with others who reveal his influence at its best, are represented in the present section. Since the example of Donne was quite as pervasive if not of such long continuance as that of Jonson, the metaphysical vein is to be found not only in the poets here grouped under that head but also among the 'sons of Ben,' the religious poets, and the Cavaliers. Jonson himself essayed the Donnean conceit in *On a Lover's Dust Made Sand for an Hour Glass* (p. 391), and Donne's truest disciple was probably George Herbert.

The poets chosen here as representing most clearly the influence of Donne in the secular lyric include, as has been said, a number of men who were close to him personally. The ode, *Absence, hear thou my protestation,* hesitantly attributed to one of his literary associates, John Hoskins, is so perfectly in the manner of Donne that it may well be his. Sir Henry Wotton, his friend from college days, is difficult to place in relation to any of the several fashions in poetry which he practised, partly because of the uncertain dating of his poems, which were not collected until twelve years after his death in 1639. He seems to have begun writing poetry about the same time as Donne and to have caught something of Donne's lighter mockery of women, as well as a little of his subtlety in comparison and his constructive excellence. Lord Herbert of Cherbury, elder brother of Donne's friend and protégé, George Herbert, was a metaphysical by the bent of his own mind, being a serious philosopher of considerable ability. He erred somewhat on the side of over-intellectualizing in his verses. His *If you do love as well as I* is one of the most skillful imitations of Donne's extended comparison, but lacks his intensity of feeling. Henry King, according to Walton, was Donne's dearest friend and the executor of his will. He was also, if Grierson's supposition is correct, the editor of the first edition of his poems. King was friendly with many other literary men, among them Ben Jonson, with whom his work has some similarity, especially in the use of the couplet. In fact, the most Donnean of King's poems here included, *My once dear love,* is written in the couplet form. William Habington, who was a Catholic, and was educated abroad, is usually spoken of as harking back to the poetry of the 1590's because in *Castara* he gained some popularity with a sequence of poems similar to the sonnet-series, though few of them are in sonnet form. Actually he seems to have been responsive to several of the poetical trends of the seventeenth century, the metaphysical among them. His *They meet with but unwholesome springs* is an answer to Donne's *Go and catch a falling star,* and his *To the World,* subtitled *The Perfection of Love,* has the very accent of the conquering insolence of some of Donne's exultant love-songs.

It was chiefly Cowley and Cleveland who brought the metaphysical vein into eventual disrepute by decking out commonplace thoughts in fantastically far-fetched comparisons. Their conceits delighted their own generation but a succeeding age found them tiresome.   In a selection of the present scope, of course, space cannot be spared to illustrate their tediousness.   Poems typical of Cowley's sincere boyish classicism and of Cleveland's highly-regarded virility are given, and touches will be found in them in which there is a manifest attempt at metaphysical subtlety.   For the rest, *We must not part as others do* and *Go, happy book* suggest the wide diffusion of the metaphysical vein around the mid-century, to authors unknown or very obscure; and the last selection, that of Katherine Philips, marks the probable limit of its popularity in the secular lyric, although in satire and devotion it can be traced to the end of the century.   But before its wane it was to inspire the secular as well as the devotional work of one more lyrist of high quality.

Andrew Marvell was a many-sided man and poet.   Son of the master of Kingston-upon-Hull Grammar School, he received there, and at Trinity College, Cambridge, a sound education which he improved by foreign travel.   He is said to have formed while in Rome a life-long friendship with Milton, who approved his classical scholarship.   Most of the lighter lyrics of Marvell belong to the years which he spent in travel and as tutor to the daughter of the famous Parliamentary general, Lord Fairfax.   From the famous gardens of the Fairfax seat in Yorkshire doubtless came the inspiration of Marvell's nature poetry, in which he stands next to Herrick in this age and at times above him.   In 1657, Marvell was appointed assistant to Milton in the latter's secretary-ship.   Later, as a member of Parliament, he became absorbed in politics and in writing verse of a different sort from love lyrics, expressing his admiration of Cromwell in elegy and ode, and becoming known as the daring and incorruptible satirist of Charles II and his dissolute life.   Though he never mentions Donne's name, and though his conceits are marked by quaintness and charm—what Lamb calls 'witty delicacy'—rather than by extravagance and grotesqueness, Marvell's *My love is of a birth as rare* is an extended conceit that Donne might well have written, and *Had we but world enough and time* is one of the most memorable of metaphysical love-poems.

JOHN DONNE (1572–1631)

Song

Go and catch a falling star,
    Get with child a mandrake root,
Tell me where all past years are,
    Or who cleft the devil's foot,
Teach me to hear mermaids singing,
Or to keep off envy's stinging,
        And find
        What wind
Serves to advance an honest mind.

If thou be'st born to strange sights,
    Things invisible go see,
Ride ten thousand days and nights,
    Till age snow white hairs on thee;
Thou, when thou return'st, wilt tell me
All strange wonders that befell thee,
        And swear
        Nowhere
Lives a woman true, and fair.

If thou find'st one, let me know,
    Such a pilgrimage were sweet;
Yet do not, I would not go,
    Though at next door we might meet;
Though she were true when you met her,
And last till you write your letter,
        Yet she
        Will be
False, ere I come, to two or three.

Woman's Constancy

Now thou hast loved me one whole day,
Tomorrow when thou leav'st, what wilt thou say?

mandrake] mandragora, the forked root of which was thought to resemble the human form

Wilt thou then antedate some new-made vow?
    Or say that now
We are not just those persons which we were?
Or, that oaths made in reverential fear
Of love, and his wrath, any may forswear?
Or, as true deaths true marriages untie,
So lovers' contracts, images of those,
Bind but till sleep, death's image, them unloose?
    Or, your own end to justify,
For having purposed change and falsehood, you
Can have no way but falsehood to be true?
Vain lunatic, against these 'scapes I could
    Dispute and conquer, if I would;
    Which I abstain to do,
For by tomorrow, I may think so too.

The Indifferent

'I can love both fair and brown,
Her whom abundance melts, and her whom want betrays,
Her who loves loneness best, and her who masks and plays,
Her whom the country formed, and whom the town,
Her who believes, and her who tries,
Her who still weeps with spongy eyes,
And her who is dry cork, and never cries;
I can love her and her, and you and you,
I can love any, so she be not true.

'Will no other vice content you?
Will it not serve your turn to do as did your mothers?
Or have you all old vices spent, and now would find out
    others?
Or doth a fear that men are true, torment you?
O, we are not, be not you so,
Let me, and do you, twenty know.
Rob me, but bind me not, and let me go.

antedate] assign to an earlier date   tries] tests

. Must I, who came to travail thorough you,
Grow your fixed subject, because you are true?'

Venus heard me sigh this song,
And by love's sweetest part, variety, she swore,
She heard not this till now, and that it should be so no more.
She went, examined, and returned ere long,
And said, 'Alas, some two or three
Poor heretics in love there be,
Which think to 'stablish dangerous constancy.
But I have told them, "Since you will be true,
You shall be true to them who are false to you." '

The Triple Fool

I am two fools, I know,
For loving, and for saying so
    In whining poetry;
But where's that wise man, that would not be I,
    If she would not deny?
Then as th' earth's inward, narrow, crooked lanes
Do purge sea-water's fretful salt away,
    I thought, if I could draw my pains,
Through rime's vexation, I should them allay.
Grief brought to numbers cannot be so fierce,
For he tames it that fetters it in verse.

But when I have done so,
Some man, his art and voice to show,
    Doth set and sing my pain,
And, by delighting many, frees again
    Grief, which verse did restrain.
To love and grief tribute of verse belongs,
But not of such as pleases when 'tis read,
    Both are increasèd by such songs:
For both their triumphs so are publishèd,
And I, which was two fools, do so grow three:
Who are a little wise, the best fools be.

thorough] through   set] set to music

Lovers' Infiniteness

If yet I have not all thy love,
Dear, I shall never have it all;
I cannot breathe one other sigh, to move,
Nor can entreat one other tear to fall,
And all my treasure, which should purchase thee,
Sighs, tears, and oaths, and letters, I have spent.
Yet no more can be due to me,
Than at the bargain made was meant;
If then thy gift of love were partiàl,
That some to me, some should to others fall,
    Dear, I shall never have thee all.

Or if then thou gavest me all,
All was but all, which thou hadst then;
But if in thy heart, since, there be or shall
New love created be, by other men
Which have their stocks entire, and can in tears,
In sighs, in oaths, and letters outbid me,
This new love may beget new fears,
For, this love was not vowed by thee.
And yet it was; thy gift being general,
The ground, thy heart, is mine; whatever shall
    Grow there, dear, I should have it all.

Yet I would not have all yet:
He that hath all can have no more,
And since my love doth every day admit
New growth, thou shouldst have new rewards in store;
Thou canst not every day give me thy heart;
If thou canst give it, then thou never gavest it:
Love's riddles are, that though thy heart depart,
It stays at home, and thou with losing savest it:
But we will have a way more liberal
Than changing hearts,—to join them; so we shall
    Be one, and one another's all.

Song

Sweetest love, I do not go
    For weariness of thee,
Nor in hope the world can show
    A fitter love for me;
        But since that I
Must die at last, 'tis best
To use myself in jest,
        Thus by feigned deaths to die.

Yesternight the sun went hence,
    And yet is here today;
He hath no desire nor sense,
    Nor half so short a way.
        Then fear not me,
But believe that I shall make
Speedier journeys, since I take
        More wings and spurs than he.

O how feeble is man's power,
    That, if good fortune fall,
Cannot add another hour,
    Nor a lost hour recall.
        But come bad chance,
And we join to it our strength,
And we teach it art and length,
        Itself o'er us t' advance.

When thou sigh'st, thou sigh'st not wind,
    But sigh'st my soul away;
When thou weep'st, unkindly kind,
    My life's blood doth decay.
        It cannot be
That thou lov'st me as thou say'st,
If in thine my life thou waste,
        That art the best of me.

use] accustom   fear not] do not be anxious about   come bad chance] let bad
chance come

Let not thy divining heart
   Forethink me any ill.
Destiny may take thy part
   And may thy fears fulfill;
     But think that we
   Are but turned aside to sleep:
   They who one another keep
     Alive, ne'er parted be.

The Anniversary

All kings, and all their favorites,
  All glory of honors, beauties, wits,
The sun itself, which makes times as they pass,
Is elder by a year now than it was
When thou and I first one another saw;
All other things to their destruction draw,
  Only our love hath no decay;
This, no tomorrow hath, nor yesterday;
Running, it never runs from us away,
But truly keeps his first, last, everlasting day.

Two graves must hide thine and my corse;
  If one might, death were no divorce.
Alas, as well as other princes, we,
Who prince enough in one another be,
Must leave at last in death, these eyes and ears,
Oft fed with true oaths and with sweet salt tears;
  But souls where nothing dwells but love—
All other thoughts being inmates—then shall prove
This, or a love increasèd there above,
When bodies to their graves, souls from their graves remove.

And then we shall be throughly blest,
  But we no more than all the rest;
Here upon earth, we are kings, and none but we
Can be such kings, nor of such subjects be.

his] its   inmates] foreigners   throughly] thoroughly

Who is so safe as we, where none can do
Treason to us, except one of us two?
    True and false fears let us refrain;
Let us love nobly, and live, and add again
Years and years unto years, till we attain
To write threescore: this is the second of our reign.

The Dream

Dear love, for nothing less than thee
Would I have broke this happy dream;
    It was a theme
For reason, much too strong for fantasy.
Therefore thou waked'st me wisely; yet
My dream thou brok'st not, but continued'st it:
Thou art so true, that thoughts of thee suffice
To make dreams truths and fables histories.
Enter these arms, for since thou thought'st it best
Not to dream all my dream, let's act the rest.

As lightning or a taper's light,
Thine eyes, and not thy noise, waked me.
    Yet I thought thee—
For thou lov'st truth—an angel at first sight;
But when I saw thou saw'st my heart,
And knew'st my thoughts, beyond an angel's art,
When thou knew'st what I dreamt, when thou knew'st
    when
Excess of joy would wake me, and cam'st then,
I must confess, it could not choose but be
Profane to think thee anything but thee.

Coming and staying showed thee thee,
But rising makes me doubt, that now
    Thou art not thou.
That love is weak, where fear's as strong as he;
'Tis not all spirit, pure and brave,

broke] broken off

If mixture it of fear, shame, honor, have.
Perchance as torches, which must ready be,
Men light and put out, so thou deal'st with me;
Thou cam'st to kindle, go'st to come: then I
Will dream that hope again, but else would die.

The Apparition

When by thy scorn, O murderess, I am dead,
And that thou think'st thee free
From all solicitation from me,
Then shall my ghost come to thy bed,
And thee, feigned vestal, in worse arms shall see;
Then thy sick taper will begin to wink,
And he, whose thou art then, being tired before,
Will, if thou stir, or pinch to wake him, think
    Thou call'st for more,
And in false sleep will from thee shrink;
And then, poor aspen wretch, neglected thou
Bathed in a cold quicksilver sweat wilt lie,
    A verier ghost than I;
What I will say, I will not tell thee now,
Lest that preserve thee; and since my love is spent,
I had rather thou should'st painfully repent,
Than by my threatenings rest still innocent.

The Broken Heart

He is stark mad, whoever says
    That he hath been in love an hour;
Yet not that love so soon decays,
    But that it can ten in less space devour.
Who will believe me if I swear
That I have had the plague a year?
    Who would not laugh at me if I should say
    I saw a flask of powder burn a day?

And that] And when, therefore,   not that] not because

Ah, what a trifle is a heart,
  If once into love's hands it come!
All other griefs allow a part
  To other griefs, and ask, themselves, but some;
They come to us, but us love draws,
He swallows us, and never chaws;
  By him, as by chained shot, whole ranks do die;
  He is the tyrant pike, our hearts the fry.

If 'twere not so, what did become
  Of my heart when I first saw thee?
I brought a heart into the room,
  But from the room I carried none with me;
If it had gone to thee, I know
Mine would have taught thine heart to show
  More pity unto me, but love, alas,
  At one first blow did shiver it as glass.

Yet nothing can to nothing fall,
  Nor any place be empty quite;
Therefore I think my breast hath all
  Those pieces still, though they be not unite;
And now as broken glasses show
A hundred lesser faces, so
  My rags of heart can like, wish, and adore,
  But after one such love, can love no more.

A Valediction Forbidding Mourning

As virtuous men pass mildly away,
  And whisper to their souls to go,
Whilst some of their sad friends do say
  'The breath goes now,' and some say 'No';

So let us melt, and make no noise,
  No tear-floods nor sigh-tempests move;
'Twere profanation of our joys
  To tell the laity our love.

Moving of th' earth brings harms and fears,
　Men reckon what it did and meant;
But trepidation of the spheres,
　Though greater far, is innocent.

Dull sublunary lovers' love,
　Whose soul is sense, cannot admit
Absence, because it doth remove
　Those things which elemented it.

But we, by a love so much refined
　That ourselves know not what it is,
Inter-assurèd of the mind,
　Care less eyes, lips, and hands to miss.

Our two souls, therefore, which are one,
　Though I must go, endure not yet
A breach, but an expansiòn,
　Like gold to airy thinness beat.

If they be two, they are two so
　As stiff twin compasses are two:
Thy soul, the fixed foot, makes no show
　To move, but doth if th' other do.

And though it in the center sit,
　Yet when the other far doth roam,
It leans and hearkens after it,
　And grows erect as that comes home.

Such wilt thou be to me, who must,
　Like th' other foot, obliquely run:
Thy firmness makes my circle just,
　And makes me end where I begun.

Love's Deity

I long to talk with some old lover's ghost,
　Who died before the god of love was born;

trepidation] oscillation　　　elemented it] were the basis of their love　　　beat] beaten

I cannot think that he, who then loved most,
    Sunk so low as to love one which did scorn.
But since this god produced a destiny,
And that vice-nature, custom, lets it be,
I must love her that loves not me.

Sure they which made him god meant not so much,
    Nor he in his young godhead practised it;
But when an even flame two hearts did touch,
    His office was indulgently to fit
Actives to passives; correspondency
Only, his subject was; it cannot be
Love, till I love her that loves me.

But every modern god will now extend
    His vast prerogative as far as Jove;
To rage, to lust, to write too, to commend,
    All is the purlieu of the god of love.
O were we wakened by this tyranny
To un-god this child again, it could not be
I should love her who loves not me.

Rebel and atheist, too, why murmur I,
    As though I felt the worst that Love could do?
Love might make me leave loving, or might try
    A deeper plague, to make her love me too,
Which, since she loves before, I am loath to see;
Falsehood is worse than hate; and that must be,
If she whom I love should love me.

The Funeral

Whoever comes to shroud me, do not harm
    Nor question much
That subtile wreath of hair which crowns my arm;
The mystery, the sign you must not touch,
    For 'tis my outward soul,

vice-nature] substitute for nature   purlieu] illicitly extended province   loves
before] already loves another

Viceroy to that, which then to heaven being gone,
    Will leave this to control
And keep these limbs, her provinces, from dissolutiòn.

For if the sinewy thread my brain lets fall
    Through every part,
Can tie those parts, and make me one of all,
These hairs, which upward grew, and strength and art
    Have from a better brain,
Can better do it; except she meant that I
    By this should know my pain,
As prisoners then are manacled, when they are condemned
    to die.

Whate'er she meant by it, bury it with me,
    For since I am
Love's martyr, it might breed idolatry
If into others' hands these relics came;
    As 'twas humility
To afford to it all that a soul can do,
    So 'tis some bravery,
That since you would have none of me, I bury some of you.

The Blossom

    Little think'st thou, poor flower,
    Whom I have watched six or seven days,
And seen thy birth, and seen what every hour
Gave to thy growth, thee to this height to raise,
And now dost laugh and triumph on this bough:
    Little think'st thou
That it will freeze anon, and that I shall
Tomorrow find thee fall'n, or not at all.

    Little think'st thou, poor heart,
    That labor'st yet to nestle thee,

sinewy thread] the spinal cord with its branching nerves   bravery] defiance
anon] forthwith

And think'st by hovering here to get a part
In a forbidden or forbidding tree,
And hop'st her stiffness by long siege to bow:
   Little think'st thou
That thou tomorrow, ere that sun doth wake,
Must with this sun and me a journey take.

 But thou which lov'st to be
  Subtile to plague thyself, wilt say,
'Alas, if you must go, what's that to me?
Here lies my business, and here I will stay.
You go to friends, whose love and means present
   Various content
To your eyes, ears, and tongue, and every part.
If then your body go, what need you a heart?'

 Well then, stay here; but know,
  When thou hast stayed and done thy most:
A naked thinking heart, that makes no show,
Is to a woman but a kind of ghost.
How shall she know my heart, or—having none—
   Know thee for one?
Practise may make her know some other part,
But take my word, she doth not know a heart.

 Meet me at London, then,
  Twenty days hence, and thou shalt see
Me fresher, and more fat, by being with men,
Than if I had stayed still with her and thee.
For God's sake, if you can, be you so too:
   I would give you
There to another friend, whom we shall find
As glad to have my body as my mind.

The Relic

When my grave is broke up again
Some second guest to entertain—
For graves have learned that woman-head

woman-head] womanhood

To be to more than one a bed—
　　And he that digs it, spies
A bracelet of bright hair about the bone,
　　Will he not let us alone,
And think that there a loving couple lies,
Who thought that this device might be some way
To make their souls, at the last busy day,
Meet at this grave and make a little stay?

　　If this fall in a time or land
　　Where mis-devotion doth command,
　　Then he that digs us up will bring
　　Us to the bishop and the king,
　　　To make us relics; then
Thou shalt be a Mary Magdalen, and I
　　A something else thereby;
All women shall adore us, and some men;
And since at such time miracles are sought,
I would have that age by this paper taught
What miracles we harmless lovers wrought.

　　First, we loved well and faithfully,
　　Yet knew not what we loved nor why;
　　Difference of sex no more we knew,
　　Than our guardian angels do;
　　　Coming and going, we
Perchance might kiss, but not between those meals;
　　Our hands ne'er touched the seals
Which nature, injured by late law, sets free.
These miracles we did; but now, alas,
All measure and all language I should pass,
Should I tell what a miracle she was.

The Expiration

So, so, break off this last lamenting kiss,
　　Which sucks two souls, and vapors both away;

vapors] dissipates in the form of vapor

Turn thou, ghost, that way and let me turn this,
    And let our selves benight our happiest day.
We asked none leave to love, nor will we owe
    Any so cheap a death as saying, go;

Go; and if that word have not quite killed thee,
    Ease me with death, by bidding me go too.
Or if it have, let my word work on me,
    And a just office on a murderer do,—
Except it be too late to kill me so,
    Being double dead, going and bidding go.

The Computation

For the first twenty years,—since yesterday—
I scarce believed thou could'st be gone away;
For forty more I fed on favors past,
And forty on hopes that thou would'st they might last.
Tears drowned one hundred and sighs blew out two;
A thousand, I did neither think nor do,
Or not divide, all being one thought of you;
Or in a thousand more, forgot that too.
Yet call not this long life, but think that I
Am, by being dead, immortal; can ghosts die?

A Lecture upon the Shadow

Stand still, and I will read to thee
A lecture, love, in love's philosophy.
    These three hours that we have spent
    Walking here, two shadows went
Along with us, which we ourselves produced;
    But, now the sun is just above our head,
    We do those shadows tread,
And to brave clearness all things are reduced.
    So whilst our infant loves did grow,
    Disguises did, and shadows, flow
    From us and our cares, but now 'tis not so.

benight] darken   brave] splendid

That love hath not attained the high'st degree,
Which is still diligent lest others see.

Except our loves at this noon stay,
We shall new shadows make the other way.
  As the first were made to blind
  Others, these which come behind
Will work upon ourselves, and blind our eyes.
  If our loves faint, and westwardly decline,
    To me thou falsely thine,
And I to thee, mine actions shall disguise.
  The morning shadows wear away,
  But these grow longer all the day;
But O, love's day is short, if love decay.

Love is a growing, or full constant light,
And his first minute, after noon, is night.

JOHN HOSKINS? (1566–1638)

Ode

Absence, hear thou my protestatiòn
      Against thy strength,
      Distance and length:
Do what thou canst for alteratiòn,
  For hearts of truest mettle
Absence doth join, and time doth settle.

Who loves a mistress of such quality,
      He soon hath found
      Affection's ground
Beyond time, place, and all mortality.
  To hearts that cannot vary
Absence is present, time doth tarry.

Hoskins] This poem occurs in several manuscripts of Donne and is thought by
many scholars to be his. Professor Grierson argues for Hoskins' authorship.

My senses want their outward motiòns,
　　Which now within
　　Reason doth win,
Redoubled in her secret notiòns:
　　Like rich men that take pleasure
In hiding, more than handling, treasure.

By absence this good means I gain,
　　That I can catch her,
　　Where none can watch her,
In some close corner of my brain:
　　There I embrace and kiss her;
And so I both enjoy and miss her.

SIR HENRY WOTTON (1568–1639)

An Elegy

O faithless world, and thy most faithless part,
　　A woman's heart,
The true shop of variety, where sits
　　Nothing but fits
And fevers of desire and pangs of love,
　　Which toys remove.
Why was she born to please? or I to trust
　　Words writ in dust,
Suffering her eyes to govern my despair,
　　My pain for air,
And fruit of time rewarded with untruth,
　　The food of youth.
Untrue she was, yet I believed her eyes,
　　Instructed spies,
Till I was taught that love was but a school
　　To breed a fool.
Or sought she more than triumphs of denial,
　　To see a trial
How far her smiles commanded my weakness?
　　Yield and confess:

close] secret

Excuse not now thy folly, nor her natùre;
    Blush and endure
As well thy shame as passions that were vain;
    And think thy gain
To know that love lodged in a woman's breast
    Is but a guest.

On his Mistress, Elizabeth of Bohemia

You meaner beauties of the night,
    That poorly satisfy our eyes
More by your number than your light,
    You common people of the skies,—
    What are you when the sun shall rise?

You curious chanters of the wood,
    That warble forth Dame Nature's lays,
Thinking your voices understood
    By your weak accents, what's your praise,
    When Philomel her voice shall raise?

You violets that first appear,
    By your pure purple mantles known
Like the proud virgins of the year,
    As if the spring were all your own,
    What are you when the rose is blown?

So, when my mistress shall be seen
    In form and beauty of her mind,
By virtue first, then choice, a queen,
    Tell me if she were not designed
    The eclipse and glory of her kind?

EDWARD, LORD HERBERT OF CHERBURY (1583–1648)

Madrigal

Dear, when I did from you remove,
I left my joy, but not my love:

curious] careful

That never can depart.
It neither higher can ascend,
    Nor lower bend;
Fixed in the center of my heart,
    As in his place,
And lodgèd so, how can it change,
    Or you grow strange?
Those are earth's properties and base.
Each where, as the bodies divine,
Heaven's lights and you to me will shine.

Of Black Beauty

Black beauty, which above that common light
    Whose power can no colors here renew
    But those which darkness can again subdue,
Dost still remain unvaried to the sight,
And like an object equal to the view,
    Art neither changed with day, nor hid with night;
    When all those colors which the world calls bright,
And which old poetry doth so pursue,
Are with the night so perishèd and gone
    That of their being there remains no mark,
Thou still abidest so entirely one,
    That we may know that blackness is a spark
Of light inàccessible, and alone
    Our darkness which can make us think it dark.

The Thought

If you do love as well as I,
Then every minute from your heart
    A thought doth part:
And wingèd with desire doth fly
Till it hath met, in a straight line,
    A thought of mine
So like to yours, we cannot know

his] its   which above] who above

Whether of both doth come, or go,
　　　Till we define
Which of us two that thought doth owe.

I say then that your thoughts which pass
Are not so much the thoughts you meant
　　　As those I sent:
For as my image in a glass
Belongs not to the glass you see
　　　But unto me,
So when your fancy is so clear
That you would think you saw me there,
　　　It needs must be
That it was I did first appear.

Likewise, when I send forth a thought,
My reason tells me, 'tis the same
　　　Which from you came,
And which your beauteous image wrought.
Thus while our thoughts by turns do lead,
　　　None can precede;
And thus, while in each other's mind
Such interchangèd forms we find,
　　　Our loves may plead
To be of more than vulgar kind.

May you then often think on me,
And by that thinking know 'tis true
　　　I thought on you;
I in the same belief will be:
While, by this mutual address,
　　　We will possess
A love must live, when we do die,
Which rare and secret property
　　　You will confess,
If you do love as well as I.

Whether of both] Which of the two　　owe] own　　I did] I who did　　must] which
must

HENRY KING (1592–1669)

Sonnet

Tell me no more how fair she is,
   I have no mind to hear
The story of that distant bliss
   I never shall come near:
By sad experience I have found
That her perfection is my wound.

And tell me not how fond I am
   To tempt a daring fate,
From whence no triumph ever came,
   But to repent too late:
There is some hope ere long I may
In silence dote myself away.

I ask no pity, Love, from thee,
   Nor will thy justice blame,
So that thou wilt not envy me
   The glory of my flame,
Which crowns my heart whene'er it dies,
In that it falls her sacrifice.

The Surrender

My once dear love, hapless that I no more
Must call thee so, the rich affection's store
That fed our hopes lies now exhaust and spent,
Like sums of treasure unto bankrupts lent.

We that did nothing study but the way
To love each other, with which thoughts the day
Rose with delight to us, and with them set,
Must learn the hateful art how to forget.

So that] Provided that

We that did nothing wish that heaven could give
Beyond ourselves, nor did desire to live
Beyond that wish, all these now cancel must
As if not writ in faith, but words and dust.

Yet witness those clear vows which lovers make,
Witness the chaste desires that never brake
Into unruly heats; witness that breast
Which in thy bosom anchored his whole rest;
'Tis no default in us, I dare acquite
Thy maiden faith, thy purpose fair and white
As thy pure self. Cross planets did envỳ
Us to each other, and heaven did untie
Faster than vows could bind. O, that the stars,
When lovers meet, should stand opposed in wars!

Since, then, some higher destinies command,
Let us not strive, nor labor to withstand
What is past help. The longest date of grief
Can never yield a hope of our relief;
And though we waste ourselves in moist laments,
Tears may drown us, but not our discontents.

Fold back our arms, take home our fruitless loves,
That must new fortunes try, like turtledoves
Dislodgèd from their haunts. We must in tears
Unwind a love knit up in many years.
In this last kiss I here surrender thee
Back to thyself, so thou again art free;
Thou in another, sad as that, re-send
The truest heart that lover e'er did lend.

Now turn from each. So fare our severed hearts
As the divorced soul from her body parts.

Sic Vita

Like to the falling of a star,
Or as the flights of eagles are,

brake] broke   acquite] acquit   Title] 'Such is life.'

Or like the fresh spring's gaudy hue,
Or silver drops of morning dew,
Or like a wind that chafes the flood,
Or bubbles which on water stood:
Even such is man, whose borrowed light
Is straight called in, and paid to night.
　　The wind blows out, the bubble dies;
　　The spring entombed in autumn lies;
　　The dew dries up, the star is shot;
　　The flight is past, and man forgot.

A Contemplation upon Flowers

Brave flowers, that I could gallant it like you,
　　And be as little vain!
You come abroad, and make a harmless shew,
　　And to your beds of earth again;
You are not proud, you know your birth:
For your embroidered garments are from earth.

You do obey your months and times, but I
　　Would have it ever spring;
My fate would know no winter, never die,
　　Nor think of such a thing.
O that I could my bed of earth but view,
And smile and look as cheerfully as you!

O teach me to see death and not to fear,
　　But rather to take truce.
How often have I seen you at a bier,
　　And there look fresh and spruce.
You fragrant flowers, then teach me, that my breath
Like yours may sweeten and perfume my death.

Brave] Handsome　　gallant it] play the dandy　　And to] And return to

WILLIAM HABINGTON (1605-1654)

To Roses in the Bosom of Castara

Ye blushing virgins happy are
  In the chaste nunnery of her breasts,
For he'd profane so chaste a fair
  Whoe'er should call them Cupid's nests.

Transplanted thus, how bright ye grow,
  How rich a perfume do ye yield!
In some close garden, cowslips so
  Are sweeter than i' th' open field.

In those white cloisters live secure
  From the rude blasts of wanton breath,
Each hour more innocent and pure,
  Till you shall wither into death.

Then that which living gave you room
  Your glorious sepulchre shall be.
There wants no marble for a tomb,
  Whose breast hath marble been to me.

To the World

The Perfection of Love

You who are earth and cannot rise
  Above your sense,
Boasting the envied wealth which lies
Bright in your mistress' lips or eyes,
  Betray a pitied eloquence.

That which doth join our souls, so light
  And quick doth move,
That like the eagle in his flight

fair] fair one   close] enclosed   sense] senses

It doth transcend all human sight,
Lost in the element of love.

You poets reach not this, who sing
The praise of dust
But kneaded, when by theft you bring
The rose and lily from the spring
T'' adorn the wrinkled face of lust.

When we speak love, nor art nor wit
We gloss upon;
Our souls engender, and beget
Ideas which you counterfeit
In your dull propagatiòn.

While time seven ages shall disperse
We'll talk of love,
And when our tongues hold no commèrce
Our thoughts shall mutually converse,
And yet the blood no rebel prove.

And though we be of several kind,
Fit for offence,
Yet are we so by love refined
From impure dross, we are all mind:
Death could not more have conquered sense.

How suddenly those flames expire
Which scorch our clay!
Prometheus-like when we steal fire
From heaven, 'tis endless and entire;
It may know age, but not decay.

Against *Them who Lay Unchastity to the Sex of* Women

They meet but with unwholesome springs
And summers which infectious are,

gloss upon] comment upon, use   several kind] opposite sexes

They hear but when the mermaid sings,
  And only see the falling star,
      Whoever dare
Affirm no woman chaste and fair.

Go cure your fevers, and you'll say
  The dog-days scorch not all the year;
In copper mines no longer stay
  But travel to the west, and there
      The right ones see,
And grant all gold's not alchemy.

What madman 'cause the glow-worm's flame
  Is cold, swears there's no warmth in fire?
'Cause some make forfeit of their name
  And slave themselves to man's desire,
      Shall the sex, free
From guilt, damned to the bondage be?

Nor grieve, Castara, though 'twere frail;
  Thy virtue then would brighter shine,
When thy example should prevail
  And every woman's faith be thine:
      And were there none,
'Tis majesty to rule alone.

Nox Nocti Indicat Scientiam

When I survey the bright
    Celestial sphere,
So rich with jewels hung, that night
Doth like an Ethiop bride appear,

My soul her wings doth spread,
    And heavenward flies,
The Almighty's mysteries to read
In the large volume of the skies.

right ones] true ones   'twere] the sex were   Title] 'Night unto night showeth knowledge.'

For the bright firmament
　　Shoots forth no flame
So silent, but is eloquent
In speaking the Creator's name.

　No unregarded star
　　Contracts its light
Into so small a character,
Removed far from our human sight,

　But, if we steadfast look,
　　We shall discern
In it, as in some holy book,
How man may heavenly knowledge learn.

　It tells the conqueror,
　　That far-stretched power
Which his proud dangers traffic for,
Is but the triumph of an hour;

　That from the farthest north
　　Some nation may,
Yet undiscovered, issue forth,
And o'er his new-got conquest sway.

　Some nation yet shut in
　　With hills of ice
May be let out to scourge his sin,
Till they shall equal him in vice.

　And then they likewise shall
　　Their ruin have;
For as yourselves your empires fall,
And every kingdom hath a grave.

　Thus those celestial fires,
　　Though seeming mute,
The fallacy of our desires
And all the pride of life confute.

sway] rule　　confute] bring to naught

For they have watched since first
The world had birth:
And found sin in itself accursed,
And nothing permanent on earth.

ABRAHAM COWLEY (1618–1667)

Of Myself

This only grant me, that my means may lie
Too low for envy, for contempt too high.
  Some honor I would have,
Not from great deeds, but good alone:
Th' unknown are better than ill-known;
  Rumor can ope the grave.
Acquaintance I would have, but when 't depends
Not on the number, but the choice of friends.

Books should, not business, entertain the light;
And sleep, as undisturbed as death, the night.
  My house a cottage, more
Than palace, and should fitting be
For all my use, no luxury.
  My garden painted o'er
With Nature's hand, not Art's; and pleasures yield
Horace might envy in his Sabine field.

Thus would I double my life's fading space,
For he that runs it well, twice runs his race.
  And in this true delight,
These unbought sports, this happy state,
I would not fear nor wish my fate,
  But boldly say each night:
'Tomorrow let my sun his beams display,
Or in clouds hide them; I have lived today.'

pleasures yield] should yield pleasures which

The Spring

Though you be absent here, I needs must say
The trees as beauteous are, and flowers as gay,
    As ever they were wont to be;
    Nay, the birds' rural music too
    Is as melodious and free
    As if they sung to pleasure you:
I saw a rosebud ope this morn; I'll swear
The blushing morning opened not more fair.

How could it be so fair, and you away?
How could the trees be beauteous, flowers so gay?
    Could they remember but last year,
    How you did them, they you delight,
    The sprouting leaves which saw you here
    And called their fellows to the sight
Would, looking round for the same sight in vain,
Creep back into their silent barks again.

Where'er you walked, trees were as reverend made
As when of old gods dwelt in every shade.
    Is't possible they should not know
    What loss of honor they sustain,
    That thus they smile and flourish now,
    And still their former pride retain?
Dull creatures! 'tis not without cause that she
Who fled the god of wit was made a tree.

In ancient times sure they much wiser were,
When they rejoiced the Thracian verse to hear;
    In vain did nature bid them stay
    When Orpheus had his song begun;
    They called their wondering roots away
    And bade them silent to him run.
How would those learnèd trees have followed you!
You would have drawn them, and their poet too.

But who can blame them now? For since you're gone
They're here the only fair, and shine alone.
    You did their natural rights invade;
    Wherever you did walk or sit,
    The thickest boughs could make no shade,
    Although the sun had granted it:
The fairest flowers could please no more, near you,
Than painted flowers, set next to them, could do.

Whene'er then you come hither, that shall be
The time which this to others is, to me.
    The little joys which here are now,
    The name of punishments do bear,
    When by their sight they let us know
    How we deprived of greater are.
'Tis you the best of seasons with you bring;
This is for beasts, and that for men, the spring.

The Wish

Well then; I now do plainly see
This busy world and I shall ne'er agree.
The very honey of all earthly joy
Does, of all meats, the soonest cloy;
    And they, methinks, deserve my pity
Who for it can endure the stings,
The crowd, and buzz, and murmurings
    Of this great hive, the city.

Ah yet, ere I descend to th' grave,
May I a small house and large garden have;
And a few friends, and many books, both true,
Both wise, and both delightful too!
    And since love ne'er will from me flee,
A mistress moderately fair,
And good as guardian angels are,
    Only beloved, and loving me!

O fountains! when in you shall I
Myself eased of unpeaceful thoughts espy?
O ficlds! O woods! when, when shall I be made
The happy tenant of your shade?
   Here's the spring-head of pleasure's flood;
Here's wealthy nature's treasury,
Where all the riches lie that she
   Has coined and stamped for good.

Pride and ambition here
Only in far-fetched metaphors appear;
Here naught but winds can hurtful murmurs scatter,
And naught but echo flatter.
   The gods, when they descended, hither
From heaven did always choose their way;
And therefore we may boldly say
   That 'tis the way too thither.

How happy here should I
And one dear she live, and embracing die!
She who is all the world, and can exclude
In deserts solitude.
   I should have then this only fear:
Lest men, when they my pleasures see,
Should hither throng to live like me,
   And so make a city here.

The Thief

Thou robb'st my days of business and delights,
   Of sleep thou robb'st my nights;
   Ah, lovely thief, what wilt thou do?
   What? rob me of heaven too?
   Even in my prayers thou hauntest me:
   And I, with wild idolatry,
Begin to God, and end them all to thee.

only] single

Is it a sin to love, that it should thus
  Like an ill conscience torture us?
  Whate'er I do, where'er I go—
  None guiltless e'er was haunted so!—
  Still, still, methinks, thy face I view,
  And still thy shape does me pursue,
As if, not you me, but I had murdered you.

From books I strive some remedy to take,
  But thy name all the letters make;
  Whate'er 'tis writ, I find thee there,
  Like points and commas everywhere.
  Me blessed for this let no man hold,
  For I, as Midas did of old,
Perish by turning everything to gold.

What do I seek, alas, or why do I
  Attempt in vain from thee to fly?
  For, making thee my deity,
  I gave thee then ubiquity.
  My pains resemble hell in this:
  The divine presence there too is,
But to torment men, not to give them bliss.

Drinking

  The thirsty earth soaks up the rain,
  And drinks, and gapes for drink again.
  The plants suck in the earth, and are
  With constant drinking fresh and fair.
  The sea itself, which one would think
  Should have but little need of drink,
  Drinks ten thousand rivers up,
  So filled that they o'erflow the cup.
  The busy sun—and one would guess
  By's drunken fiery face no less—
  Drinks up the sea, and when he has done,
  The moon and stars drink up the sun;

They drink and dance by their own light,
They drink and revel all the night.
Nothing in nature 's sober found,
But an eternal health goes round.
Fill up the bowl then, fill it high;
Fill all the glasses there, for why
Should every creature drink but I—
Why, man of morals, tell me why?

JOHN CLEVELAND (1613–1658)

Mark Antony

Whenas the nightingale chanted her vespers,
And the wild forester couched on the ground,
Venus invited me in th' evening whispers
Unto a fragrant field with roses crowned,
    Where she before had sent
    My wishes' complement,
    Unto my heart's content
    Played with me on the green.
        Never Mark Antony
        Dallied more wantonly
        With the fair Egyptian Queen.

First on her cherry cheeks I mine eyes feasted,
Thence fear of surfeiting made me retire;
Next on her warmer lips, which, when I tasted,
My duller spirits made active as fire.
    Then we began to dart,
    Each at another's heart,
    Arrows that knew no smart,
    Sweet lips and smiles between.
        Never, &c.

Wanting a glass to plait her amber tresses,
Which like a bracelet rich deckèd mine arm,
Gaudier than Juno wears whenas she graces

Jove with embraces more stately than warm;
   Then did she peep in mine
   Eyes' humor crystalline;
   I in her eyes was seen
   As if we one had been.
     Never, &c.

Mystical grammar of amorous glances;
Feeling of pulses, the physic of love;
Rhetorical courtings and musical dances;
Numb'ring of kisses arithmetic prove;
   Eyes like astronomy;
   Straight-limbed geometry;
   In her art's ingeny
   Our wits were sharp and keen.
     Never, &c.

ANONYMOUS (Before 1650)

We must not part as others do

We must not part as others do,
With sighs and tears, as we were two.
Though with these outward forms we part,
We keep each other in our heart.
What search hath found a being, where
I am not, if that thou be there?

True love hath wings, and can as soon
Survey the world, as sun and moon,
And everywhere our triumphs keep
Over absence, which makes others weep:
By which alone a power is given
To live on earth, as they in heaven.

humor] fluid, lens   physic] medical science, remedy   prove] proves, tests   in-
geny] cleverness   if that] if   keep] (love can) maintain

THOMAS BEAUMONT (Before 1650)

To his Mistress

Sending her the Arcadia

Go, happy book, and let my Candia see
In thee the emblem of herself and me.
When she surveys thy story,—thou shalt stand
Charmed in the whiter circle of her hand,
Rocked on the ivory cradle of her knee,
Her bright love-ruling stars bent over thee—
A Delphic fury in thy leaves shall swell
And all thy fictions turn to oracle.
For where thy quainter language draws each line
Of beauty's map, and by a skill divine
Upon it does each native grace confer,
They will appear descriptiòns of her.
And where thy amorous passions best discover
The rocky firmness of a constant lover,
They lively show those purer flames that rest
Still burning on the altar in my breast.
    So thou'rt her glass where she herself may see,
    And in true lovers' parts remember me.

ANDREW MARVELL (1621–1678)

The Coronet

When for the thorns with which I long, too long
    With many a piercing wound,
    My Savior's head have crowned,
I seek with garlands to redress that wrong,—
    Through every garden, every mead,
I gather flowers (my fruits are only flowers),
    Dismantling all the fragrant towers

To his Mistress] first reprinted by Ault in his Seventeenth Century Lyrics (1928),
reprinted here with his permission   the Arcadia] See p. 110.   quainter] finer
passions] outbursts   discover] reveal   towers] headdresses

That once adorned my shepherdess's head;
And now, when I have summed up all my store,
  Thinking (so I myself deceive),
  So rich a chaplet thence to weave
As never yet the King of Glory wore,
  Alas! I find the serpent old,
  That, twining in his speckled breast,
  About the flowers disguised does fold
  With wreaths of fame and interest.
Ah foolish man, that wouldst debase with them
And mortal glory, heaven's diadem!
But thou who only couldst the serpent tame,
Either his slipp'ry knots at once untie,
And disentangle all his winding snare;
Or shatter too with him my curious frame,
And let these wither—so that he may die—
Though set with skill, and chosen out with care:
That they while thou on both their spoils dost tread,
May crown thy feet, that could not crown thy head.

Bermudas

  Where the remote Bermudas ride
  In the ocean's bosom unespied,
  From a small boat, that rowed along,
  The listening winds received this song:

  'What should we do but sing his praise,
  That led us through the watery maze,
  Unto an isle so long unknown,
  And yet far kinder than our own?
  Where he the huge sea-monsters wracks,
  That lift the deep upon their backs,
  He lands us on a grassy stage,
  Safe from the storms' and prelates' rage.

twining in] coiling   curious] finely wrought   frame] the chaplet   these] the flowers   both their spoils] the ruin of the flowers and of the serpent   wracks] destroys   stage] bank, ledge

He gave us this eternal spring,
Which here enamels everything,
And sends the fowls to us, in care,
On daily visits through the air;
He hangs in shades the orange bright,
Like golden lamps in a green night,
And does in the pomegranates close
Jewels more rich than Ormus shows;
He makes the figs our mouths to meet,
And throws the melons at our feet;
But apples plants of such a price
No tree could ever bear them twice;
With cedars chosen by his hand
From Lebanon, he stores the land,
And makes the hollow seas, that roar,
Proclaim the ambergris on shore;
He cast (of which we rather boast)
The gospel's pearl upon our coast,
And in these rocks for us did frame
A temple, where to sound his name.
O let our voice his praise exalt,
Till it arrive at heaven's vault,
Which thence, perhaps, rebounding may
Echo beyond the Mexique bay.'

Thus sung they in the English boat,
A holy and a cheerful note;
And all the way to guide their chime
With falling oars they kept the time.

To his Coy Mistress

Had we but world enough and time,
This coyness, lady, were no crime.
We would sit down and think which way
To walk and pass our long love's day.

in care] in his care for us   Ormus] a city on the Persian Gulf, sacked by the
Portuguese   apples] presumably pineapples   rather] more justly   chime] rhythm

Thou by the Indian Ganges' side
Shouldst rubies find; I by the tide
Of Humber would complain. I would
Love you ten years before the Flood;
And you should, if you please, refuse
Till the conversion of the Jews.
My vegetable love should grow
Vaster than empires, and more slow;
An hundred years should go to praise
Thine eyes and on thy forehead gaze;
Two hundred to adore each breast,
But thirty thousand to the rest;
An age at least to every part,
And the last age should show your heart.
For, lady, you deserve this state,
Nor would I love at lower rate.

But at my back I always hear
Time's wingèd chariot hurrying near;
And yonder all before us lie
Deserts of vast eternity.
Thy beauty shall no more be found,
Nor, in thy marble vault, shall sound
My echoing song; then worms shall try
That long-preserved virginity;
And your quaint honor turn to dust,
And into ashes all my lust:
The grave's a fine and private place,
But none, I think, do there embrace.

Now therefore while the youthful hue
Sits on thy skin like morning glew,
And while thy willing soul transpires
At every pore with instant fires,
Now let us sport us while we may,
And now, like amorous birds of prey,
Rather at once our time devour

quaint] fastidious   glew] glow

Than languish in his slow-chapped power.
Let us roll all our strength, and all
Our sweetness up into one ball,
And tear our pleasures with rough strife
Thorough the iron gates of life:
Thus, though we cannot make our sun
Stand still, yet we will make him run.

The Fair Singer

To make a final conquest of all me,
Love did compose so sweet an enemy,
In whom both beauties to my death agree,
Joining themselves in fatal harmony;
That, while she with her eyes my heart does bind,
She with her voice might captivate my mind.

I could have fled from one but singly fair;
My disentangled soul itself might save,
Breaking the curlèd trammels of her hair;
But how should I avoid to be her slave
Whose subtle art invisibly can wreathe
My fetters of the very air I breathe?

It had been easy fighting in some plain,
Where victory might hang in equal choice;
But all resistance against her is vain
Who has th' advantage both of eyes and voice;
And all my forces needs must be undone,
She having gainèd both the wind and sun.

The Definition of Love

My love is of a birth as rare
As 'tis for object strange and high:
It was begotten by Despair
Upon Impossibility.

slow-chapped] slow-devouring   Thorough] Through

Magnanimous Despair alone
Could show me so divine a thing,
Where feeble Hope could ne'er have flown
But vainly flapped its tinsel wing.

And yet I quickly might arrive
Where my extended soul is fixed,
But fate does iron wedges drive,
And always crowds itself betwixt.

For fate with jealous eye doth see
Two perfect loves, nor lets them close:
Their union would her ruin be,
And her tyrannic power depose.

And therefore her decrees of steel
Us as the distant poles have placed,—
Though love's whole world on us doth wheel—
Not by themselves to be embraced.

Unless the giddy heaven fall,
And earth some new convulsion tear;
And, us to join, the world should all
Be cramped into a planisphere.

As lines, so loves oblique may well
Themselves in every angle greet:
But ours so truly parallel,
Though infinite can never meet.

Therefore the love which us doth bind,
But fate so enviously debars,
Is the conjunction of the mind,
And opposition of the stars.

The Mower to the Glow-Worms

Ye living lamps, by whose dear light
The nightingale does sit so late,
And studying all the summer night,
Her matchless songs does meditate;

close] join   planisphere] circular map

Ye country comets, that portend
No war nor prince's funeral,
Shining unto no higher end
Than to presage the grass's fall;

Ye glow-worms, whose officious flame
To wandering mowers shows the way,
That in the night have lost their aim,
And after foolish fires do stray;

Your courteous lights in vain you waste,
Since Juliana here is come;
For she my mind hath so displaced,
That I shall never find my home.

The Mower's Song

My mind was once the true survey
Of all these meadows fresh and gay,
And in the greenness of the grass
Did see its hopes as in a glass,—
When Juliana came, and she,
What I do to the grass, does to my thoughts and me.

But these, while I with sorrow pine,
Grew more luxuriant still, and fine,
That not one blade of grass you spied
But had a flower on either side,—
When Juliana came, and she,
What I do to the grass, does to my thoughts and me.

Unthankful meadows, could you so
A fellowship so true forego,
And in your gaudy May-games meet,
While I lay trodden under feet,—
When Juliana came, and she,
What I do to the grass, does to my thoughts and me?

officious] obliging   aim] destination   survey] picture   gaudy] gay

But what you in compassion ought,
Shall now by my revenge be wrought;
And flowers, and grass, and I, and all,
Will in one common ruin fall;
For Juliana comes, and she,
What I do to the grass, does to my thoughts and me.

And thus, ye meadows, which have been
Companions of my thoughts more green,
Shall now the heraldry become
With which I shall adorn my tomb;
For Juliana comes, and she,
What I do to the grass, does to my thoughts and me.

The Garden

How vainly men themselves amaze
To win the palm, the oak, or bays;
And their uncessant labors see
Crowned from some single herb or tree,
Whose short and narrow-vergèd shade
Does prudently their toils upbraid;
While all the flowers and trees do close
To weave the garlands of repose.

Fair Quiet, have I found thee here,
And Innocence, thy sister dear!
Mistaken long, I sought you then
In busy companies of men:
Your sacred plants, if here below,
Only among the plants will grow;
Society is all but rude,
To this delicious solitude.

No white nor red was ever seen
So amorous as this lovely green;
Fond lovers, cruel as their flame,

ought] ought to have done   thoughts more green] more hopeful thoughts   amaze]
drive stupid   prudently] by its wisdom   Society is all] All society is   To]
Compared to   amorous] lovesome

Cut in these trees their mistress' name.
Little, alas, they know or heed,
How far these beauties hers exceed!
Fair trees! wheresoe'er your barks I wound
No name shall but your own be found.

When we have run our passion's heat,
Love hither makes his best retreat:
The gods who mortal beauty chase,
Still in a tree did end their race.
Apollo hunted Daphne so,
Only that she might laurel grow,
And Pan did after Syrinx speed,
Not as a nymph, but for a reed.

What wondrous life is this I lead!
Ripe apples drop about my head;
The luscious clusters of the vine
Upon my mouth do crush their wine;
The nectarine and curious peach
Into my hands themselves do reach;
Stumbling on melons as I pass,
Insnared with flowers, I fall on grass.

Meanwhile the mind, from pleasure less,
Withdraws into its happiness:
The mind, that ocean where each kind
Does straight its own resemblance find;
Yet it creates, transcending these,
Far other worlds, and other seas;
Annihilating all that's made
To a green thought in a green shade.

Here at the fountain's sliding foot,
Or at some fruit-tree's mossy root,
Casting the body's vest aside,

curious] exquisite   pleasure less] lesser pleasure   body's vest] the vestment of
flesh

My soul into the boughs does glide:
There like a bird it sits and sings,
Then whets and combs its silver wings;
And, till prepared for longer flight,
Waves in its plumes the various light.

Such was that happy garden-state,
While man there walked without a mate:
After a place so pure and sweet,
What other help could yet be meet!
But 'twas beyond a mortal's share
To wander solitary there:
Two paradises 'twere in one
To live in Paradise alone.

How well the skillful gard'ner drew
Of flowers and herbs this dial new;
Where from above the milder sun
Does through a fragrant zodiac run;
And, as it works, th' industrious bee
Computes its time as well as we.
How could such sweet and wholesome hours
Be reckoned but with herbs and flowers!

KATHERINE PHILIPS (1631–1664)

To my Excellent Lucasia, on our Friendship

I did not live until this time
    Crowned my felicity,
When I could say without a crime,
    I am not thine, but thee.

This carcase breathed and walked and slept,
    So that the world believed
There was a soul the motions kept,
    But they were all deceived.

whets] preens

For as a watch by art is wound
  To motion, such was mine;
But never had Orinda found
  A soul till she found thine;

Which now inspires, cures, and supplies,
  And guides my darkened breast;
For thou art all that I can prize,
  My joy, my life, my rest.

No bridegroom's nor crown-conqueror's mirth
  To mine compared can be;
They have but pieces of this earth,
  I've all the world in thee.

Then let our flames still light and shine,
  And no false fear control,
As innocent as our design,
  Immortal as our soul.

Orinda] See p. 539.

VII

THE TRIBE OF BEN

Chiefly

1600–1650

THE TRIBE OF BEN

The present section, though it begins a decade later than the preceding one and presents a fashion of more permanent historical importance, covers essentially the same period, that is, the first half of the seventeenth century. Its purpose is to illustrate the practice and influence of Ben Jonson in the lyric. Some of the best and most characteristic of Jonson's lyrics will be found among the Lyrics in Plays (pp. 243–50). Many of his occasional pieces, such as the splendid tribute to Shakespeare prefaced to the First Folio (1623), lie outside our present province. We are here concerned with the briefer and more personal of his non-dramatic lyrics, and with the work of those poets who were 'sons of Ben' by reason of their personal allegiance to him and their literary indebtedness to the models—the Latin lyrists, Anacreon, the Greek anthology, and neo-Latin or humanist poetry—to which he showed the way.

With the notable exception of Herrick, the sons of Ben were also sons of Donne. Jonson himself was influenced by Donne, and their combined influence is over most seventeenth-century poets to the time of the Restoration, and in some cases even later. In particular, Carew, Godolphin, Cartwright and Cleveland might with equal justice appear as disciples of either Jonson or Donne, or, better still, be represented in both groups by different poems.[1] One might expect *a priori* that Jonson's imprint would be left upon the style and design, Donne's upon the content and mood, of the writing of their joint paternity. But this distinction will not hold. The chain of passionate reasoning which links the first and last lines of so many of Donne's lyrics is itself a striking exemplar of design, and his seeming indifference to rhythm found many imitators. As to mood, the attitude toward love, half passionate, half mocking, which Donne learned for himself in the days when he was 'a great

---

[1] Cleveland does appear in both, in this collection.

379

visitor of ladies' in London, Jonson learned, in suaver accents, from Horace. The truth is that they arrived by widely different avenues at a greater community of poetic practice than would at first seem possible in poets of such diverse qualities. Their combined example was naturally more potent than that of either alone could have been.

No less than Donne, though for different reasons, was Jonson out of patience with the Elizabethan lyrists, many of whom seemed to him to have 'no composition at all; but a kind of tuning and rhyming fall, in what they write.' 'It runs and slides,' he continues, 'and only makes a sound. Women's poets they are called, as you have women's tailors;

> They write a verse as smooth, as soft as cream,
> In which there is no torrent, nor scarce stream.'

One of the foremost classical scholars of his day, his instinctive recourse was to the solidity, the compactness, the balance and polish of the workmanship of classical writers. He even theorized about, and practised—not too successfully—the abolishment of rime, but eventually concluded that, as he told Drummond, 'couplets are the bravest sort of verses.' He is one of the bitterest critics of the sonnet and of all 'those that merely talk and never think.'

The shorter lyrics of Jonson fall into two groups: those about love and womankind, urbanely cynical in the classic manner; and occasional poems, which reveal the human side of the man, his tenderness and his genius for friendship. In both groups, as indeed in everything Jonson wrote, is apparent that sense of form which is his contribution to English poetry. To Jonson, form was not only a matter of perfection in detail, of smoothness of phrasing and transition, but even more a sense of the entire poem in its relation to its parts. He would have every lyric of a substance as carefully thought out and designed as the workmanship. Wandering ideas and loosely conceived figures must be repressed. Each poem must have that organic oneness which proceeds from a design in which every line and stanza is in clear, nicely calculated relationship to every other line and stanza, and to the whole thought and effect. Brevity and condensity of expression are naturally involved—a

wholesome antidote to the diffuseness of the Elizabethans. Since
the purpose is to reproduce the effect of Horace, Catullus, or
Anacreon under English conditions, classical allusion becomes less
a matter of external embellishment than of the thought and spirit.
Such poetry is classical in the best sense of the word. It aims at
beauty through constructive excellence rather than by rhapsody.
Choice in diction, selective in style, chaste, concentrated, finished,
it yet achieves at its best the spontaneity and naturalness of perfect
art.

Such was the theory—admirably exemplified by his own practice
of it, and enforced by his aggressive, yet genial and essentially
clubbable personality—which made Jonson the literary dictator of
his time, and the leader of the scholarly and courtly young poets
and dramatists who called themselves his sons. Delighting in his
society while he lived, they honored his memory when he died.
Six months after his death appeared a commemorative volume
unique in our literature, entitled *Jonsonus Virbius,* in which men
of all ranks and professions united to celebrate in verses English,
Latin, and Greek the greatness of the deceased laureate, and to
express the esteem and veneration in which they held him as a
man and as a literary figure.

The list of contributors to *Jonsonus Virbius* includes many of
the most characteristic of the sons of Ben, but there are several
notable omissions. Three of the most brilliant of the Mermaid
group were already dead: Beaumont, whose verse letter 'written
before he and Mr. Fletcher came to London' (p. 392) is one of
the most glowing tributes we have to those memorable sessions of
wine and wit, and to Jonson's power over the imagination and the
loyalty of younger men; Richard Corbet, the merry and jovial Dean
of Christ Church, Oxford, later a bishop, who was popular at the
Mermaid for his skill in extemporizing, a test frequently required by
Jonson of those who would be sealed of the tribe of Ben; and
clever young Thomas Randolph, known as his favorite son. His
ablest poetic disciples—Herrick, who though he eclipsed Jonson in
the lyric was avowedly the most loyal of his followers, and Carew,
whose occasional verses show close intimacy with Jonson—were for
some reason not represented in the volume. The same is true of

Sir Benjamin Rudyerd, whose candor and wit were praised by
Jonson in three epigrams, but who is of uncertain personal relationship with the tribe. The single specimen of Rudyerd's work here
quoted is a good example of the combined influence of Jonson
and Donne.

Among the contributors to *Jonsonus Virbius,* three are represented
in the present section—Cleveland, Godolphin, and Cartwright.
John Cleveland employed the satiric keenness he had learned from
Jonson in the Royalist cause, after being driven from Cambridge
by the Puritans. As we have seen in the previous section, he is
responsible for the worst excesses of the metaphysical conceit, producing 'a difficult plainness, difficult in the hearing, plain in the
considering thereof,' so that his position among the sons of Ben is
due rather to his admiration of Jonson's independence as a play-
wright and satirist than to imitation of his style. Sidney Godolphin
gave his life for the King in one of the early skirmishes of the
Civil War. His poetry was not published in his lifetime, and it is
probable that he did not take it with much seriousness, but he
was encouraged by competent judges as a young man of considerable promise, and his lyrics have the Jonsonian sense of design.
William Cartwright was a writer of plays in his youth, later a
priest, a reader in metaphysics at Oxford, and a remarkably successful teacher. In the preface to the posthumous edition of Cartwright's works, Jonson is reported as having once said, 'My son
Cartwright writes all like a man.' Despite the master's approval,
his poetry is uneven, but individual passages display unusual merit.
The name of one other contributor to *Jonsonus Virbius,* Edmund
Waller, reminds us, as do the fiery young Royalists, Cleveland and
Godolphin, of the close kinship in spirit of certain of the tribe of
Ben with those debonair cynics whom we call the Cavaliers, and
through them, with Restoration verse.

The sons of Ben inherited his love of form, his fondness for
learning well displayed, and at times his didacticism and heavy
satirical hand. They imitated the master in his versatility, many
of them attempting several or all of such divergent forms as drama,
the poetical epistle, epigram, lyric song and ode, commendatory
verse, and prologue and epilogue; yet few of them were literary

men in the sense which Jonson exemplified. Carew, Randolph, and Waller were courtiers; Herrick, Corbet, and Cartwright were clergymen. Nevertheless, they performed for the lyric the important service of absorbing and passing on Jonson's classicism, his assimilation of the temper and the formal constructiveness of classic art, which paved the way for the restrictive, and in some respects pseudo-classicism of the age of Anne, with its restraint of form, design, and expression against which the poets of the Romantic Revival were in revolt.

Chief of the sons of Ben are Robert Herrick and Thomas Carew. Herrick might, indeed, be called the most single-hearted of them all, since he alone has no trace of Donne and since, in his *Prayer to Ben Jonson* (p. 396) and *An Ode for Him* (p. 397), he expresses a devotion which Beaumont himself could scarcely match. Actually, in the judgment of most readers, Herrick surpasses Jonson as a lyric poet; and, despite his clear imitation of several poems of Jonson, it is probable that his debt to the master is chiefly for direction to Anacreon, Theocritus, Horace, and Catullus, whose lightness and grace he catches even more truly than does Jonson. During his nineteen years as a country parson at Dean Priory in Devonshire, he invented an exquisite pastoral vein of his own which is one of the permanent delights of seventeenth-century poetry. Owing to circumstances now irrecoverable, the publication of his volume *Hesperides* was delayed until too late for it to achieve the popularity it deserved, though individual pieces appear to have been remembered in the countryside where he lived, and others were set to music and sung. Herrick came into his own during the Romantic Revival, and such golden pieces as his *Corinna's Going A-maying* (p. 399) and *Gather ye rosebuds* (p. 401) are now firmly enshrined among the poems that everybody knows.

Carew's life was very different from Herrick's. After leaving Oxford he had a brief diplomatic career in Italy and at Paris, and was then recalled to England by Charles I, whose own artistic gifts had made him ambitious to see his court famous in art and letters. Thus Carew was from early manhood in daily attendance upon the King, and one of the accepted wits of a brilliant circle. He had but to open his lips to be appreciated and applauded. His poetry was produced not for the world but for the inner circle of the best society of England. Among his occasional poems are many to fair ones, whose anonymity is becomingly preserved in initials and pseudonyms, and we can well believe that he 'pleased the ladies with his courtly muse.'

A comparison of the work of these two men, so sharply contrasted in the circumstances of their lives, yet both true sons of Ben, is highly instructive in itself, as well as affording a picture of the Caroline lyric at its height. Both poets are consummate stylists in construction, ordering of thought, choice and placing of words, and nicety of versification. Both offer us miniatures in which every thought, every figure is carefully considered and finely wrought. Both are versatile without being either deep or passionate; in them is neither the didactic fiber of Jonson nor the spiritual depth of Donne. In Carew, indeed, are found many echoes of lines and phrases of Donne, but of Donne's 'wit' and intensity of feeling there is little. He is more prone to the use of metaphysical conceit than Herrick, in whom, as has been said, there is almost none, but his temperament and taste were such as to prevent the excessive use of intellectualized imagery. The classicism of both is that of men of the world. In neither is there the slightest use of allegory, or anything in the nature of mysticism. Theirs is the poetry of men who live upon the earth, content to enjoy its good things, regretful of the fleetness of time and the fragility of beauty, ready to seize the day and revel in its pleasures. But Herrick has more of the elasticity and freedom that come with the breath of the open air. His range of subject begins with 'brooks and blossoms, birds and bowers,' as charmingly set forth in *The Argument of his Book* (p. 397), and ends with heaven. Between lie many things—the seasons, country mirth, 'cleanly wantonness,' 'the court of Queen Mab and the Fairy King.' In Carew the view of life is narrower, more conventional. There is greater repression, more civility, more elegance and polish. There are occasional touches of truth in his observation of nature in such a poem as *The Spring* (p. 412), but he is more likely to introduce natural objects for decorative effect, and to use that kind of metaphor in which the work of man is applied to the illustration of nature.

Above all, they differ in personality. Herrick is genial, naive, playful at times. There is a spontaneousness about him, a sincerity that disarms criticism. One learns to love him as a man not wholly impeccable, nor seeking to have you believe that he is; a man of kindly heart, much beloved by his parishioners—though he found them rude and churlish at times—simple, unostentatious, loving mirth and playful gallantry, not a stranger to the cup or to full-blooded life, hating the unlovely, writing hard epigrams on what he detested, and haunted, like every true hedonist, with the thought of that inevitable time when

> All love, all liking, all delight,
> Lies drowned with us in endless night.

Carew, on the other hand, was evidently a man of much reserve and few friends, altogether sophisticated, never to be carried away into portrayal of self, of pointed and polished wit, and a gentleman in the use of it, a master in the art of the willfully perverse hyperbole of compliment. Beautiful and fanciful as much of his poetry is, there is always a suspicion of delicate raillery. If deeper feeling is present, it is skillfully masked, implied rather than expressed.

In a word, Carew is revealed in some of the most perfect of his verses as the first and one of the best of our writers of *vers de société*. This may be defined as writing which produces the effect of poetry from materials existing in the highly organized status of cultivated life. This kind of verse will be written whenever, in Athens, Rome, or London, this kind of society exists; and in England it came to perfection in the reigns of James and Charles. *Vers de société* can be written only by the man who knows from within the social life which he depicts; who knows the subtleties which relate good manners and social conventions to essential humanity; who is withheld from satire and cynicism by his genuine liking for the people of such a society and his understanding and respect for their feelings. Carew was such a man. *Vers de société* demands self-control, at times daring, ease, and elegance of manner, delicacy of touch, wit, an entire absence of pedantry, perfection of form and of finish. All this Carew had. He thus stands in the direct line of development from Jonson to Waller and the Cavaliers,

while Herrick is outside it—and above it. Their combined work
stands as the finest vindication of the theories and influence of
father Ben.

BEN JONSON (1572–1637)

On my First Son

Farewell, thou child of my right hand, and joy;
   My sin was too much hope of thee, loved boy.
Seven years thou wert lent to me, and I thee pay,
   Exacted by thy fate, on the just day.
O, could I lose all father now! For why
   Will man lament the state he should envỳ?
To have so soon 'scaped world's and flesh's rage,
   And if no other misery, yet age!
Rest in soft peace, and, asked, say 'Here doth lie
   Ben Jonson his best piece of poetry;
For whose sake henceforth all his vows be such
   As what he loves may never like too much.'

Inviting a Friend to Supper

Tonight, grave sir, both my poor house and I
   Do equally desire your company;
Not that we think us worthy such a guest,
   But that your worth will dignify our feast
With those that come, whose grace may make that seem
   Something, which else could hope for no esteem.
It is the fair acceptance, sir, creates
   The entertainment perfect, not the cates.
Yet shall you have, to rectify your palate,
   An olive, capers, or some better salad
Ush'ring the mutton; with a short-legged hen,
   If we can get her, full of eggs, and then

thou wert] one syllable. See p. 46.   father] fatherhood   Jonson his] Jonson's
As] That   may] he may   cates] delicacies

Lemons and wine for sauce; to these, a coney
    Is not to be despaired of, for our money;
And though fowl now be scarce, yet there are clerks,
    The sky not falling, think we may have larks.
I'll tell you of more, and lie, so you will come,
    Of partridge, pheasant, woodcock, of which some
May yet be there; and godwit, if we can,
    Knat, rail, and ruff too. Howsoe'er, my man
Shall read a piece of Vergil, Tacitus,
    Livy, or of some better book to us,
Of which we'll speak our minds amidst our meat;
    And I'll profess no verses to repeat;
To this, if aught appear which I not know of,
    That will the pastry, not my paper, show of.
Digestive cheese, and fruit there sure will be;
    But that which most doth take my muse, and me,
Is a pure cup of rich Canary wine,
    Which is the Mermaid's now, but shall be mine;
Of which had Horace or Anacreon tasted,
    Their lives, as do their lines, till now had lasted.
Tobacco, nectar, or the Thespian spring
    Are all but Luther's beer to this I sing.
Of this we will sup free, but moderately,
    And we will have no polly, or parrot by;
Nor shall our cups make any guilty men,
    But at our parting we will be as when
We innocently met. No simple word
    That shall be uttered at our mirthful board
Shall make us sad next morning, or affright
    The liberty that we'll enjoy tonight.

Epitaph on Salathiel Pavy, a Child of Queen Elizabeth's Chapel

      Weep with me, all you that read
        This little story;
      And know, for whom a tear you shed
        Death's self is sorry.

coney] rabbit   Knat] Sandpiper   profess] vow   to this I sing] compared to this which I sing of

'Twas a child that so did thrive
  In grace and feature,
As heaven and nature seemed to strive
  Which owned the creature.
Years he numbered scarce thirteen
  When fates turned cruel,
Yet three filled zodiacs had he been
  The stage's jewel;
And did act, what now we moan,
  Old men so duly,
As, sooth, the Parcæ thought him one,
  He played so truly.
So by error, to his fate
  They all consented;
But viewing him since, alas too late,
  They have repented,
And have sought, to give new birth,
  In baths to steep him;
But being so much too good for earth,
  Heaven vows to keep him.

Epitaph on Elizabeth, L. H.

Wouldst thou hear what man can say
In a little? Reader, stay.
Underneath this stone doth lie
As much beauty as could die;
Which in life did harbor give
To more virtue than doth live.
If at all she had a fault
Leave it buried in this vault.
One name was Elizabeth,
Th' other, let it sleep with death;
Fitter, where it died, to tell,
Than that it lived at all. Farewell.

filled zodiacs] full years   *Elizabeth, L. H.*] perhaps a compliment to Elizabeth, Lady Hatton, wife of Sir Edward Coke

Why I Write Not of Love

Some act of Love's bound to rehearse,
I thought to bind him in my verse:
Which when he felt, 'Away,' quoth he,
'Can poets hope to fetter me?
It is enough they once did get
Mars and my mother in their net:
I wear not these my wings in vain.'
With which he fled me, and again
Into my rimes could ne'er be got
By any art: then wonder not
That since, my numbers are so cold,
When Love is fled, and I grow old.

Song: To Celia

Kiss me, sweet; the wary lover
Can your favors keep, and cover,
When the common courting jay
All your bounties will betray.
Kiss again: no creature comes;
Kiss, and score up wealthy sums
On my lips thus hard-ly sundered
While you breathe. First give a hundred,
Then a thousand, then another
Hundred, then unto the tother
Add a thousand, and so more
Till you equal with the store
All the grass that Rumney yields,
Or the sands in Chelsea fields,
Or the drops in silver Thames,
Or the stars that gild his streams
In the silent summer nights
When youths ply their stol'n delights:
That the curious may not know

Rumney] Romney marsh

How to tell them as they flow;
And the envious, when they find
What their number is, be pined.

Song

That Women are but Men's Shadows

Follow a shadow, it still flies you,
    Seem to fly it, it will pursue;
So court a mistress, she denies you,
    Let her alone, she will court you.
Say, are not women truly then
Styled but the shadows of us men?

At morn and even, shades are longest;
    At noon, they are or short or none;
So men at weakest, they are strongest,
    But grant us perfect, they're not known.
Say, are not women truly then
Styled but the shadows of us men?

A Nymph's Passion

I love and he loves me again,
    Yet dare I not tell who;
For if the nymphs should know my swain,
    I fear they'd love him too;
        Yet if it be not known,
    The pleasure is as good as none,
For that's a narrow joy is but our own.

I'll tell, that if they be not glad,
    They may yet envy me;
But then if I grow jealous mad
    And of them pitied be,
        It were a plague 'bove scorn;
    And yet it cannot be forborne
Unless my heart would as my thought be torn.

pined] wasted with hunger   joy is] joy which is

He is, if they can find him, fair
And fresh and fragrant too,
As summer's sky or purgèd air,
And looks as lilies do
That are this morning blown:
Yet, yet I doubt he is not known,
And fear much more that more of him be shown.

But he hath eyes so round and bright,
As make away my doubt,
Where Love may all his torches light,
Though Hate had put them out;
But then t' increase my fears
What nymph soe'er his voice but hears
Will be my rival, though she have but ears.

I'll tell no more, and yet I love
And he loves me; yet no
One unbecoming thought doth move
From either heart, I know;
But so exempt from blame
As it would be to each a fame,
If love or fear would let me tell his name.

On a Lover's Dust, Made Sand for an Hour-glass

Do but consider this small dust,
Here running in the glass,
By atoms moved;
Could you believe that this
The body was
Of one that loved?
And in his mistress' flame playing like a fly
Turned to cinders by her eye?
Yes, and in death, as life unblest
To have 't expressed:
Even ashes of lovers find no rest.

The Dream

Or scorn or pity on me take,
I must the true relation make,
   I am undone tonight;
Love, in a subtile dream disguised,
  Hath both my heart and me surprised,
Whom never yet he durst attempt t' awake;
    Nor will he tell me for whose sake
      He did me the delight—
        Or spite;
     But leaves me to enquire
     In all my wild desire
Of Sleep again, who was his aid.
And Sleep ['s] so guilty and afraid
As since he dares not come within my sight.

FRANCIS BEAUMONT (1584–1616)

Master Francis Beaumont's Letter to Ben Jonson

The sun, which doth the greatest comfort bring
To absent friends, because the self-same thing
They know they see, however absent, is
Here our best hay-maker. (Forgive me this,
It is our country style.) In this warm shine
I lie, and dream of your full Mermaid wine.
O, we have water mixed with claret-lees,
Drink apt to bring in drier heresies
Than beer, good only for the sonnet strain,
With fustian metaphors to stuff the brain;
So mixed that given to the thirstiest one
'Twill not prove alms unless he have the stone.
'Tis sold by Puritans, mixed with intent
To make it serve for either sacrament.
I think with one draught man's invention fades:
Two cups had quite spoiled Homer's *Iliads;*

As] That   the stone] gall-stone, sufferers from which are forbidden wine

'Tis liquor that will find out Sutcliffe's wit,
Lie where he will, and make him write worse yet.
Filled with such moisture, in a grievous qualm,
Did Robert Wisdom write his singing psalm;
And so must I do this, and yet I think
It is a potion sent us down to drink
By special providence, keeps us from fights,
Makes us not laugh when we make legs to knights;
'Tis this that keeps our minds fit for our states,
A med'cine to obey our magistrates.
For we do live more free than you; no hate,
No envy at one another's happy state
Moves us, we are all equal, every whit;
Of land, that God gives men here, is their wit,
If we consider fully; for our best
And gravest man will, with his main house-jest,
Scarce please you; we want subtlety to do
The city tricks—lie, hate, and flatter too.
Here are none that can bear a painted show,
Strike when you wink, and then lament the blow,
Who, like mills set the right way for to grind,
Can make their gains alike with every wind.
Only some fellows with the subtlest pate
Amongst us, may perchance equivocate
At selling of a horse, and that's the most.
Methinks the little wit I had is lost
Since I saw you; for wit is like a rest
Held up at tennis, which men do the best
With the best gamesters.

     What things have we seen
Done at the Mermaid! heard words that have been
So nimble and so full of subtle flame,
As if that everyone from whom they came

Sutcliffe] a theological disputant of the time Wisdom] credited with the popular
version of a single psalm keeps us] which keeps us legs] bows land] earth
wink] have your eyes closed rest Held up] a rally kept going gamesters]
players

Had meant to put his whole wit in a jest,
And had resolved to live a fool the rest
Of his dull life; then when there hath been thrown
Wit able enough to justify the town
For three days past,—wit that might warrant be
For the whole city to talk foolishly
Till that were canceled—and when that was gone
We left an air behind us, which alone
Was able to make the two next companies
Right witty; though but downright fools, more wise.
When I remember this, and see that now
The country gentlemen begin to allow
My wit for dry-bobs, then I needs must cry,
I see my days of ballading grow nigh;
I can already riddle, and can sing
Catches, sell bargains, and I fear shall bring
Myself to speak the hardest words I find
Over as oft as any, with one wind,
That takes no medicines. But one thought of thee
Makes me remember all these things to be
The wit of our young men, fellows that show
No part of good, yet utter all they know;
Who like trees of the gard have growing souls
Only: strong destiny, which all controls,
I hope hath left a better fate in store
For me, thy friend, than to live ever poor,
Banished unto this home. Fate once again
Bring me to thee, who canst make smooth and plain
The way of knowledge for me, and then I
Who have no good but in thy company,
Protest it will my greatest comfort be
To acknowledge all I have to flow from thee.
Ben, when these scenes are perfect, we'll taste wine;
I'll drink thy muse's health, thou shalt quaff mine.

canceled] *I.e.,* the warrant. allow . . . dry-bobs] concede me wit enough for
jesting medicines] perhaps akin to the penny-worth of sugar-candy carried by
Falstaff to make him long-winded gard] (Dyce) garden growing] vegetable

The Indifferent

Never more will I protest
To love a woman but in jest;
For as they cannot be true
So to give each man his due,
      When the wooing fit is past,
      Their affection cannot last.

Therefore if I chance to meet
With a mistress fair and sweet,
She my service shall obtain,
Loving her for love again:
      Thus much liberty I crave
      Not to be a constant slave.

But when we have tried each other,
If she better like another,
Let her quickly change, for me;
Then to change am I as free.
      He or she that loves too long
      Sell their freedom for a song.

SIR BENJAMIN RUDYERD (1572–1658)

Why do we love

Why do we love these things which we call women,
   Which are like feathers blown with every wind,
Regarding least those which do most esteem them,
   And most deceitful when they seem most kind;
      And all the virtue that their beauty graces,
      It is but painted like unto their faces?

Their greatest glory is in rich attire,
   Which is extracted from some hopeful livers
Whose wits and wealth are bent to their desire,

So] So as   for me] so far as I am concerned   livers] beings

When they regard the gift more than the givers;
And to increase their hopes of future bliss,
They'll sometimes stretch their conscience for a kiss.

Some love the winds that bring in golden flowers,
And some are merely won with commendation;
Some love and hate, and all within two hours,
And that's a fault amongst them most in fashion;
But put them all within a scale together,
Their worth in weight will scarce pull down a feather.

And yet I would not discommend them all,
If I did know some worth to be in any;
'Tis strange, that since the time of Adam's fall,
That God did make none good, and made so many;
And if he did, for those I truly mourn,   .
Because they died before that I was born.

ROBERT HERRICK (1591–1674)

His Prayer to Ben Jonson

When I a verse shall make,
Know I have prayed thee,
For old religion's sake,
Saint Ben, to aid me.

Make the way smooth for me,
When I, thy Herrick,
Honoring thee, on my knee
Offer my lyric.

Candles I'll give to thee,
And a new altar;
And thou, Saint Ben, shalt be
Writ in my psalter.

An Ode for Ben Jonson

Ah Ben!
Say how, or when
Shall we thy guests
Meet at those lyric feasts
Made at the Sun,
The Dog, the Triple Tun,
Where we such clusters had
As made us nobly wild, not mad;
And yet each verse of thine
Outdid the meat, outdid the frolic wine.

My Ben!
Or come again,
Or send to us
Thy wit's great overplus;
But teach us yet
Wisely to husband it.
Lest we that talent spend,
And having once brought to an end
That precious stock, the store
Of such a wit the world should have no more.

The Argument of his Book

I sing of brooks, of blossoms, birds, and bowers,
Of April, May, of June, and Jùly flowers;
I sing of may-poles, hock-carts, wassails, wakes,
Of bridegrooms, brides, and of their bridal cakes;
I write of youth, of love, and have access
By these to sing of cleanly wantonness;
I sing of dews, of rains, and piece by piece
Of balm, of oil, of spice, and ambergris;
I sing of times trans-shifting, and I write

The Sun, etc.] taverns   clusters] bunches of grapes, wine   frolic] jolly   hock-
cart] the cart which carried home the last load of the harvest   wakes] festivals

How roses first came red, and lilies white;
I write of groves, of twilights, and I sing
The court of Mab, and of the Fairy King;
I write of hell; I sing, and ever shall,
Of heaven, and hope to have it after all.

To Perilla

Ah, my Perilla, dost thou grieve to see
Me, day by day, to steal away from thee?
Age calls me hence, and my gray hairs bid come
And haste away to mine eternal home;
'Twill not be long, Perilla, after this,
That I must give thee the supremest kiss.
Dead when I am, first cast in salt, and bring
Part of the cream from that religious spring,
With which, Perilla, wash my hands and feet;
That done, then wind me in that very sheet
Which wrapped thy smooth limbs when thou didst
    implore
The gods' protection but the night before;
Follow me weeping to my turf, and there
Let fall a primrose, and with it a tear:
Then lastly, let some weekly strewings be
Devoted to the memory of me;
Then shall my ghost not walk about, but keep
Still in the cool and silent shades of sleep.

Delight in Disorder

A sweet disorder in the dress
Kindles in clothes a wantonness;
A lawn about the shoulders thrown
Into a fine distractiòn,
An erring lace, which here and there
Enthralls the crimson stomacher,
A cuff neglectful, and thereby

distractiòn] confusion   erring] wandering

Ribands to flow confusèdly,
A winning wave, deserving note,
In the tempestuous petticoat,
A careless shoe-string, in whose tie
I see a wild civility,
Do more bewitch me than when art
Is too precise in every part.

To Laurels

A funeral stone
Or verse, I covet none;
But only crave
Of you that I may have
A sacred laurel springing from my grave;
Which being seen
Blest with perpetual green,
May grow to be
Not so much called a tree
As the eternal monument of me.

Corinna's Going A-maying

Get up, get up for shame, the blooming morn
Upon her wings presents the god unshorn.
See how Aurora throws her fair
Fresh-quilted colors through the air!
Get up, sweet slug-a-bed, and see
The dew bespangling herb and tree.
Each flower has wept, and bowed toward the east,
Above an hour since; yet you not dressed,
Nay not so much as out of bed?
When all the birds have matins said,
And sung their thankful hymns, 'tis sin,
Nay, profanation to keep in;
Whenas a thousand virgins on this day
Spring, sooner than the lark, to fetch in may.

civility] good breeding   the god unshorn] Apollo   slug-a-bed] one who lies late
may] hawthorn blossoms

Rise, and put on your foliage, and be seen
To come forth, like the spring-time, fresh and green
 And sweet as Flora. Take no care
 For jewels for your gown or hair;
 Fear not, the leaves will strew
 Gems in abundance upon you;
Besides, the childhood of the day has kept,
Against you come, some orient pearls unwept;
 Come, and receive them while the light
 Hangs on the dew-locks of the night,
 And Titan on the eastern hill
 Retires himself, or else stands still
Till you come forth. Wash, dress, be brief in praying:
Few beads are best, when once we go a-maying.

Come, my Corinna, come; and coming mark
How each field turns a street, each street a park
 Made green, and trimmed with trees; see how
 Devotion gives each house a bough
 Or branch; each porch, each door, ere this
 An ark, a tabernacle is,
Made up of white-thorn neatly interwove,
As if here were those cooler shades of love.
 Can such delights be in the street
 And open fields, and we not see 't?
 Come, we'll abroad, and let's obey
 The proclamation made for May,
And sin no more, as we have done, by staying;
But, my Corinna, come, let's go a-maying.

There's not a budding boy or girl this day
But is got up and gone to bring in may.
 A deal of youth, ere this, is come
 Back, and with white-thorn laden home.
 Some have dispatched their cakes and cream,
 Before that we have left to dream;
And some have wept, and wooed, and plighted troth,

orient] shining Titan] the sun beads] prayers left] ceased

And chose their priest, ere we can cast off sloth.
 Many a green-gown has been given;
 Many a kiss, both odd and even;
 Many a glance too has been sent
 From out the eye, love's firmament;   .
Many a jest told of the key's betraying
This night, and locks picked, yet w' are not a-maying.

Come, let us go, while we are in our prime,
And take the harmless folly of the time.
 We shall grow old apace and die
 Before we know our liberty.
 Our life is short, and our days run
 As fast away as does the sun,
And as a vapor, or a drop of rain,
Once lost can ne'er be found again,
 So when or you or I are made
 A fable, song, or fleeting shade,
 All love, all liking, all delight,
 Lies drowned with us in endless night.
Then while time serves, and we are but decaying,
Come, my Corinna, come, let's go a-maying.

To the Virgins, To Make Much of Time

 Gather ye rosebuds while ye may,
  Old Time is still a-flying;
 And this same flower that smiles today,
  Tomorrow will be dying.

 The glorious lamp of heaven, the sun,
  The higher he's a-getting,
 The sooner will his race be run,
  And nearer he's to setting.

 That age is best which is the first,
  When youth and blood are warmer;
 But being spent, the worse, and worst
  Times still succeed the former.

Then be not coy, but use your time,
And while ye may, go marry;
For having lost but once your prime,
You may forever tarry.

To Primroses Filled with Morning Dew

Why do ye weep, sweet babes?   Can tears
Speak grief in you,
Who were but born
Just as the modest morn
Teemed her refreshing dew?
Alas, you have not known that shower
That mars a flower,
Nor felt th' unkind
Breath of a blasting wind,
Nor are ye worn with years,
Or warped, as we,
Who think it strange to see
Such pretty flowers, like to orphans young,
To speak by tears before ye have a tongue.

Speak, whimpering younglings, and make known
The reason why
Ye droop and weep.
Is it for want of sleep,
Or childish lullaby?
Or that ye have not seen as yet
The violet?
Or brought a kiss
From that sweetheart to this?
No, no, this sorrow shown
By your tears shed
Would have this lecture read:
That things of greatest, so of meanest worth,
Conceived with grief are, and with tears brought forth.

Teemed] Poured out

To Anthea, Who May Command Him Anything

Bid me to live, and I will live
  Thy protestant to be;
Or bid me love, and I will give
  A loving heart to thee.

A heart as soft, a heart as kind,
  A heart as sound and free,
As in the whole world thou canst find,
  That heart I'll give to thee.

Bid that heart stay and it will stay,
  To honor thy decree;
Or bid it languish quite away,
  And 't shall do so for thee.

Bid me to weep, and I will weep,
  While I have eyes to see;
And having none, yet I will keep
  A heart to weep for thee.

Bid me despair, and I'll despair,
  Under that cypress tree;
Or bid me die, and I will dare
  E'en death, to die for thee.

Thou art my life, my love, my heart,
  The very eyes of me,
And hast command of every part
  To live and die for thee.

To Daffodils

Fair daffodils, we weep to see
  You haste away so soon;
As yet the early rising sun

protestant] suitor

Has not attained his noon.
Stay, stay,
Until the hasting day
Has run
But to the even-song;
And, having prayed together, we
Will go with you along.

We have short time to stay as you,
We have as short a spring;
As quick a growth to meet decay
As you, or anything.
We die
As your hours do, and dry
Away,
Like to the summer's rain,
Or as the pearls of morning's dew,
Ne'er to be found again.

Night Piece, To Julia

Her eyes the glow-worm lend thee,
The shooting stars attend thee,
And the elves also,
Whose little eyes glow
Like the sparks of fire, befriend thee.

No will-o'-th'-wisp mis-light thee;
Nor snake or slow-worm bite thee;
But on, on thy way,
Not making a stay,
Since ghost there's none to affright thee.

Let not the dark thee cumber;
What though the moon does slumber?
The stars of the night
Will lend thee their light,
Like tapers clear without number.

slow-worm] lizard   cumber] trouble

Then Julia, let me woo thee,
Thus, thus to come unto me:
    And when I shall meet
    Thy silv'ry feet,
My soul I'll pour into thee.

The Wake

Come, Anthea, let us two
Go to feast as others do;
Tarts and custards, creams and cakes,
Are the junkets still at wakes,
Unto which the tribes resort,
Where the business is the sport;
Morris-dancers thou shalt see,
Marian too in pageantry,
And a mimic to devise
Many grinning properties.
Players there will be, and those
Base in action as in clothes;
Yet with strutting they will please
The incurious villages.
Near the dying of the day
There will be a cudgel-play,
Where a coxcomb will be broke
Ere a good word can be spoke;
But the anger ends all here,
Drenched in ale, or drowned in beer.
Happy rustics best content
With the cheapest merriment,
And possess no other fear
Than to want the wake next year.

Upon Julia's Clothes

Whenas in silks my Julia goes,
Then, then, methinks, how sweetly flows
That liquefaction of her clothes.

junkets] sweetmeats   Marian] Maid Marian   incurious] uncritical   ends all]
all ends   content] are content

Next, when I cast mine eyes and see
That brave vibration each way free,
O, how that glittering taketh me!

Upon a Maid

Here she lies, in bed of spice,
Fair as Eve in Paradise;
For her beauty, it was such
Poets could not praise too much.
Virgins, come, and in a ring
Her supremest requiem sing;
Then depart, but see ye tread
Lightly, lightly o'er the dead.

His Prayer for Absolution

For those my unbaptizèd rhymes,
Writ in my wild unhallowed times;
For every sentence, clause, and word,
That's not inlaid with thee, my Lord,
Forgive me, God, and blot each line
Out of my book, that is not thine.
But if, 'mongst all, thou find'st here one
Worthy thy benedictiòn,
That one of all the rest shall be
The glory of my work, and me.

A Thanksgiving to God for his House

Lord, thou hast given me a cell
    Wherein to dwell,
A little house, whose humble roof
    Is weather-proof,
Under the spars of which I lie
    Both soft and dry;

brave] bright   such] such as   spars] rafters

Where thou my chamber for to ward
    Hast set a guard
Of harmless thoughts, to watch and keep
    Me while I sleep.
Low is my porch, as is my fate,
    Both void of state;
And yet the threshold of my door
    Is worn by th' poor,
Who thither come and freely get
    Good words or meat;
Like as my parlor, so my hall
    And kitchen's small;
A little buttery, and therein
    A little bin
Which keeps my little loaf of bread
    Unchipped, unflead.
Some brittle sticks of thorn or briar
    Make me a fire,
Close by whose living coal I sit,
    And glow like it.
Lord, I confess, too, when I dine,
    The pulse is thine,
And all those other bits that be
    There placed by thee:
The worts, the purslain, and the mess
    Of water-cress,
Which of thy kindness thou hast sent;
    And my content
Makes those, and my belovèd beet,
    To be more sweet.
'Tis thou that crown'st my glittering hearth
    With guiltless mirth;
And giv'st me wassail bowls to drink,
    Spiced to the brink.
Lord, 'tis thy plenty-dropping hand
    That soils my land,

ward] protect   unflead] not flayed   pulse] a dish of legumes or their seeds
worts] vegetables   purslain] a succulent herb   soils] fertilizes

And giv'st me for my bushel sown
    Twice ten for one.
Thou mak'st my teeming hen to lay
    Her egg each day;
Besides my healthful ewes to bear
    Me twins each year,
The while the conduits of my kine
    Run cream for wine.
All these, and better, thou dost send
    Me to this end:
That I should render, for my part,
    A thankful heart,
Which, fired with incense, I resign
    As wholly thine;
But the acceptance, that must be,
    My Christ, by thee.

His Creed

I do believe that die I must,
And be returned from out my dust;
I do believe that when I rise,
Christ I shall see with these same eyes;
I do believe that I must come
With others to the dreadful doom;
I do believe the bad must go
From thence to everlasting woe;
I do believe the good, and I,
Shall live with him eternally;
I do believe I shall inherit
Heaven, by Christ's mercies, not my merit;
I do believe the one in three,
And three in perfect unity;
Lastly, that Jesus is a deed
Of gift from God. And here's my creed.

Grace for a Child

Here a little child I stand,
Heaving up my either hand;
Cold as paddocks though they be,
Here I lift them up to thee,
For a benison to fall
On our meat, and on us all.

                              Amen.

RICHARD CORBET (1582–1635)

To his Son, Vincent Corbet

On his Third Birthday

What I shall leave thee none can tell,
But all shall say I wish thee well:
I wish thee, Vin, before all wealth,
Both bodily and ghostly health;
Nor too much wealth, nor wit, come to thee,
So much of either may undo thee.
I wish thee learning, not for show,
Enough for to instruct and know,
Not such as gentlemen require
To prate at table or at fire.
I wish thee all thy mother's graces,
Thy father's fortunes, and his places.
I wish thee friends, and one at court,
Not to build on, but support;
To keep thee, not in doing many
Oppressions, but from suffering any.
I wish thee peace in all thy ways,
Nor lazy nor contentious days;
And when thy soul and body part,
As innocent as now thou art.

paddocks] frogs   ghostly] spiritual   support] be loyal to

The Fairies' Farewell

Farewell, rewards and fairies,
  Good housewives now may say,
For now foul sluts in dairies
  Do fare as well as they;
And though they sweep their hearths no less
  Than maids were wont to do,
Yet who of late for cleanliness
  Finds sixpence in her shoe?

Lament, lament, old abbeys,
  The fairies' lost command,
They did but change priests' babies,
  But some have changed your land;
And all your children stol'n from thence
  Are now grown puritanes
Who live as changelings ever since
  For love of your demaines.

At morning and at evening both,
  You merry were and glad;
So little care of sleep and sloth
  These pretty ladies had;
When Tom came home from labor,
  Or Ciss to milking rose,
Then merrily went their tabor,
  And nimbly went their toes.

Witness those rings and roundelays
  Of theirs which yet remain,
Were footed in Queen Mary's days
  On many a grassy plain.
But since of late Elizabeth
  And later James came in,
They never danced on any heath
  As when the time hath been.

sixpence, changelings] allusions to fairy practices common in folk-lore, the leaving
of rewards and the 'changing' of new-born children   demaines] domains   rings,
roundelays] fairy dancing-places   Were] Which were

By which we note the fairies
    Were of the old profession,
Their songs were Ave Mary's,
    Their dances were procession;
But now alas, they all are dead
    Or gone beyond the seas,
Or farther for religion fled,
    Or else they take their ease.

A tell-tale in their company
    They never could endure,
And whoso kept not secretly
    Their mirth, was punished sure.
It was a just and Christian deed
    To pinch such black and blue;
O, how the commonwealth doth need
    Such justices as you!

Now they have left our quarters,
    A register they have,
Who looketh to their charters,—
    A man both wise and grave.
An hundred of their merry pranks,
    By one that I could name
Are kept in store; con twenty thanks
    To William for the same.

To William Churne of Staffordshire
    Give laud and praises due;
Who every meal can mend your cheer
    With tales both old and true.
To William all give audience,
    And pray ye for his noddle;
For all the fairies' evidence
    Were lost if it were addle.

register] registrar   con] offer   William Churne] servant to Corbet's father-in-law

THOMAS CAREW (1595?–1639?)

The Spring

Now that the winter's gone, the earth hath lost
Her snow-white robes, and now no more the frost
Candies the grass, or casts an icy cream
Upon the silver lake or crystal stream;
But the warm sun thaws the benumbèd earth,
And makes it tender; gives a second birth
To the dead swallow; wakes in hollow tree
The drowsy cuckoo and the humble-bee.
Now do a choir of chirping minstrels bring
In triumph to the world the youthful spring.
The valleys, hills, and woods in rich array
Welcome the coming of the longed-for May.
Now all things smile, only my love doth lour;
Nor hath the scalding noonday sun the power
To melt that marble ice, which still doth hold
Her heart congealed, and makes her pity cold.
The ox, which lately did for shelter fly
Into the stall, doth now securely lie
In open fields; and love no more is made
By the fireside, but in the cooler shade.
Amyntas now doth with his Chloris sleep
Under a sycamore, and all things keep
Time with the season; only she doth carry
June in her eyes, in her heart January.

A Cruel Mistress

We read of kings and gods that kindly took
A pitcher filled with water from the brook;
But I have daily tendered without thanks
Rivers of tears that overflow their banks.
A slaughtered bull appeasèd angry Jove,
A horse the sun, a lamb the god of love;
But she disdains the spotless sacrifice

Candies] Makes crystalline

Of a pure heart that at her altar lies.
Vesta is not displeased if her chaste urn
Do with repairèd fuel ever burn,
But my saint frowns, though to her honored name
I consecrate a never-dying flame.
Th' Assyrian king did none i' the furnace throw
But those that to his image did not bow;
With bended knees I daily worship her,
Yet she consumes her own idolater.
Of such a goddess no times leave record,
That burned the temple where she was adored.

Mediocrity in Love Rejected

Give me more love or more disdain!
   The torrid or the frozen zone
Bring equal ease unto my pain,
   The temperate affords me none;
Either extreme of love or hate
Is sweeter than a calm estate.

Give me a storm; if it be love,
   Like Danaë in that golden shower,
I swim in pleasure; if it prove
   Disdain, that torrent will devour
My vulture-hopes; and he's possessed
Of heaven, that's but from hell released.
   Then crown my joys or cure my pain:
   Give me more love or more disdain.

To My Inconstant Mistress

When thou, poor excommunicate
   From all the joys of love, shalt see
The full reward and glorious fate
   Which my strong faith shall purchase me,
   Then curse thine own inconstancy.

repairèd] renewed   Th' Assyrian king] Nebuchadnezzar

A fairer hand than thine shall cure
  That heart which thy false oaths did wound;
And to my soul, a soul more pure
  Than thine shall by love's hand be bound,
  And both with equal glory crowned.

Then shalt thou weep, entreat, complain
  To love, as I did once to thee;
When all thy tears shall be as vain
  As mine were then, for thou shalt be
  Damned for thy false apostasy.

Persuasions to Joy

If the quick spirits in your eye
Now languish, and anon must die;
If every sweet and every grace
Must fly from that forsaken face,
    Then, Celia, let us reap our joys
    Ere time such goodly fruit destroys.

Or, if that golden fleece must grow
Forever, free from agèd snow;
If those bright suns must know no shade,
Nor your fresh beauties ever fade,
Then fear not, Celia, to bestow
What, still being gathered, still must grow:
    Thus, either Time his sickle brings
    In vain, or else in vain his wings.

A Deposition from Love

I was foretold, your rebel sex
  Nor love nor pity knew,
And with what scorn you use to vex
  Poor hearts that humbly sue;
Yet I believed to crown our pain,
  Could we the fortress win,

quick] living   *A Deposition*] *On Being Deposed*

The happy lover sure should gain
  A paradise within.
I thought love's plagues like dragons sate,
Only to fright us at the gate.

But I did enter, and enjoy
  What happy lovers prove,
For I could kiss, and sport, and toy,
  And taste those sweets of love
Which, had they but a lasting state,
  Or if in Celia's breast
The force of love might not abate,
  Jove were too mean a guest.
But now her breach of faith far more
Afflicts than did her scorn before.

Hard fate! to have been once possessed,
  As victor, of a heart
Achieved with labor and unrest,
  And then forced to depart!
If the stout foe will not resign
  When I besiege a town,
I lose but what was never mine;
  But he that is cast down
From enjoyed beauty, feels a woe
Only deposèd kings can know.

Ingrateful Beauty Threatened

Know, Celia, since thou art so proud,
  'Twas I that gave thee thy renown;
Thou hadst in the forgotten crowd
  Of common beauties lived unknown,
Had not my verse exhaled thy name,
And with it imped the wings of fame.

That killing power is none of thine,
  I gave it to thy voice and eyes;

prove] experience   imped] mended, strengthened

Thy sweets, thy graces, all are mine;
   Thou art my star, shin'st in my skies;
Then dart not from thy borrowed sphere
Lightning on him that fixed thee there.

Tempt me with such affrights no more,
   Lest what I made I uncreate;
Let fools thy mystic forms adore,
   I'll know thee in thy mortal state;
Wise poets that wrapped truth in tales,
Knew her themselves through all her veils.

To a Lady Resembling his Mistress

Fair copy of my Celia's face,
Twin of my love, thy perfect grace
May claim with her an equal place.

Disdain not a divided heart,
Though all be hers, you shall have part;
Love is not tied to rules of art.

For as my soul first to her flew,
Yet stayed with me; so now 'tis true
It dwells with her, though fled to you.

Then entertain this wand'ring guest,
And if not love, allow it rest;
It left not, but mistook the nest.

Nor think my love, or your fair eyes
Cheaper 'cause from the sympathies
You hold with her, these flames arise.

To lead, or brass, or some such bad
Metal, a prince's stamp may add
That value which it never had.

But to the pure refinèd ore,
The stamp of kings imparts no more
Worth than the metal held before;

Only the image gives the rate:
To subjects of a foreign state
'Tis prized as much for its own weight.

So though all other hearts resign
To your pure worth, yet you have mine
Only because you are her coin.

Celia Singing

You that think love can convey
    No other way
But through the eyes, into the heart
    His fatal dart,
Close up those casements, and but hear
    This siren sing;
    And on the wing
Of her sweet voice it shall appear
That love can enter at the ear.

Then unveil your eyes, behold
    The curious mould
Where that voice dwells; and as we know
    When the cocks crow
    We freely may
    Gaze on the day;
So may you, when the music's done
Awake, and see the rising sun.

Red and White Roses

Read in these roses the sad story
Of my hard fate and your own glory:
In the white you may discover

curious] exquisite

The paleness of a fainting lover;
In the red, the flames still feeding
On my heart with fresh wounds bleeding.
The white will tell you how I languish,
And the red express my anguish:
The white my innocence displaying,
The red my martyrdom betraying.
The frowns that on your brow resided,
Have those roses thus divided;
O, let your smiles but clear the weather,
And then they both shall grow together.

A Song

Ask me no more where Jove bestows,
When June is past, the fading rose;
For in your beauty's orient deep
These flowers, as in their causes, sleep.

Ask me no more whither doth stray
The golden atoms of the day;
For in pure love heaven did prepare
Those powders to enrich your hair.

Ask me no more whither doth haste
The nightingale when May is past;
For in your sweet dividing throat
She winters, and keeps warm her note.

Ask me no more where those stars light
That downwards fall in dead of night;
For in your eyes they sit, and there
Fixèd become as in their sphere.

Ask me no more if east or west
The phoenix builds her spicy nest;
For unto you at last she flies,
And in your fragrant bosom dies.

orient] clear   dividing] descanting. See p. 243.

THOMAS RANDOLPH (1605–1635)

Upon his Picture

When age hath made me what I am not now,
And every wrinkle tells me where the plough
Of time hath furrowed; when an ice shall flow
Through every vein, and all my head wear snow;
When death displays his coldness in my cheek,
And I myself in my own picture seek,
Not finding what I am, but what I was,
In doubt which to believe, this, or my glass:
Yet though I alter, this remains the same
As it was drawn, retains the primitive frame
And first complexion; here will still be seen
Blood on the cheek, and down upon the chin;
Here the smooth brow will stay, the lively eye,
The ruddy lip, and hair of youthful dye.
Behold what frailty we in man may see,
Whose shadow is less given to change than he!

An Ode to Mr. Anthony Stafford to Hasten him into the Country

Come, spur away,
I have no patience for a longer stay,
But must go down
And leave the chargeable noise of this great town.
I will the country see,
Where old simplicity
Though hid in gray
Doth look more gay
Than foppery in plush and scarlet clad.
Farewell, you city wits that are
Almost at civil war;
'Tis time that I grow wise, when all the world grows mad.

chargeable] burdensome

More of my days
I will not spend to gain an idiot's praise,
Or to make sport
For some slight puny of the Inns of Court.
Then, worthy Stafford, say
How shall we spend the day,
With what delights
Shorten the nights,
When from this tumult we are got secure
Where mirth with all her freedom goes,
Yet shall no finger lose,
Where every word is thought, and every thought is pure?

There from the tree
We'll cherries pluck, and pick the strawberry.
And every day
Go see the wholesome country girls make hay,
Whose brown hath lovelier grace
Than any painted face
That I do know
Hyde Park can show;
Where I had rather gain a kiss than meet
(Though some of them in greater state
Might court my love with plate)
The beauties of the Cheap, and wives of Lombard street.

But think upon
Some other pleasures, these to me are none;
Why do I prate
Of women, that are things against my fate?
I never mean to wed
That torture to my bed;
My muse is she
My love shall be.
Let clowns get wealth and heirs; when I am gone,
And the great bugbear, grisly death,
Shall take this idle breath,
If I a poem leave, that poem is my son.

puny] freshman   finger lose] Randolph had lost one in a quarrel.   the Cheap]
Cheapside   Lombard street] wealthy mercantile district

Of this, no more;
We'll rather taste the bright Pomona's store:
No fruit shall 'scape
Our palates, from the damson to the grape.
Then full we'll seek a shade,
And hear what music's made;
How Philomel
Her tale doth tell,
And how the other birds do fill the choir;
The thrush and blackbird lend their throats,
Warbling melodious notes;
We will all sports enjoy, which others but desire.

Ours is the sky,
Where at what fowl we please our hawk shall fly;
Nor will we spare
To hunt the crafty fox or timorous hare,
But let our hounds run loose
In any ground they'll choose;
The buck shall fall,
The stag and all:
Our pleasures must from their own warrants be,
For to my muse, if not to me,
I'm sure all game is free;
Heaven, earth, are all but parts of her great royalty.

And when we mean
To taste of Bacchus' blessings now and then,
And drink by stealth
A cup or two to noble Berkeley's health,
I'll take my pipe and try
The Phrygian melody,
Which he that hears
Lets through his ears
A madness to distemper all the brain.
Then I another pipe will take
And Doric music make,
To civilize with graver notes our wits again.

Berkeley] George, eighth baron Berkeley (1601–1658)

JOHN CLEVELAND (1613–1658)

An Elegy on Ben Jonson

Who first reformed our stage with justest laws,
And was the first best judge in his own cause;
Who, when his actors trembled for applause,

Could with a noble confidence prefer
His own, by right, to a whole theater,
From principles which he knew could not err;

Who to his fable did his persons fit
With all the properties of art and wit,
And above all that could be acted, writ;

Who public follies did to covert drive,
Which he again could cunningly retrieve,
Leaving them no ground to rest on and thrive:

Here Jonson lies, whom had I named before,
In that one word alone I had paid more
Than can be now, when plenty makes me poor.

WILLIAM CARTWRIGHT (1611–1643)

A Valediction

Bid me not go where neither suns nor showers
    Do make or cherish flowers;
Where discontented things in sadness lie
    And nature grieves as I;
When I am parted from those eyes,
From which my better day doth rise,
        Though some propitious power
        Should plant me in a bower,
Where amongst happy lovers I might see
        How showers and sunbeams bring
        One everlasting spring,

Nor would those fall nor these shine forth to me:
  Nature herself to him is lost,
  Who loseth her he honors most.
Then, fairest, to my parting view display
  Your graces all in one full day,
Whose blessèd shapes I'll snatch and keep, till when
  I do return and view again:
So by this art fancy shall fortune cross,
And lovers live by thinking on their loss.

To Chloe, Who Wished herself Young Enough for Me

Chloe, why wish you that your years
  Would backwards run till they meet mine,
That perfect likeness, which endears
  Things unto things, might us combine?
Our ages so in date agree,
That twins do differ more than we.

There are two births, the one when light
  First strikes the new awakened sense;
The other when two souls unite;
  And we must count our life from thence:
When you loved me and I loved you,
Then both of us were born anew.

Love then to us did new souls give,
  And in those souls did plant new powers;
Since when another life we live,
  The breath we breathe is his, not ours;
Love makes those young whom age doth chill,
And whom he finds young, keeps young still.

Love, like that angel that shall call
  Our bodies from the silent grave,
Unto one age doth raise us all,
  None too much, none too little have;
Nay, that the difference may be none,
He makes two not alike, but one.

And now, since you and I are such,
　　Tell me what's yours, and what is mine?
Our eyes, our ears, our taste, smell, touch,
　　Do—like our souls—in one combine;
So, by this, I as well may be
Too old for you as you for me.

No Platonic Love

Tell me no more of minds embracing minds,
　　And hearts exchanged for hearts;
That spirits spirits meet, as winds do winds,
　　And mix their subtlest parts;
That two unbodied essences may kiss,
And then like angels, twist and feel one bliss.

I was that silly thing that once was wrought
　　To practise this thin love;
I climbed from sex to soul, from soul to thought;
　　But thinking there to move,
Headlong I rolled from thought to soul, and then
From soul I lighted at the sex again.

As some strict down-looked men pretend to fast
　　Who yet in closets eat,
So lovers who profess they spirits taste,
　　Feed yet on grosser meat;
I know they boast they souls to souls convey:
Howe'er they meet, the body is the way.

Come, I will undeceive thee: they that tread
　　Those vain aerial ways
Are like young heirs and alchemists, misled
　　To waste their wealth and days;
For searching thus to be forever rich,
They only find a med'cine for the itch.

SIDNEY GODOLPHIN (1610–1643)

Song

Or love me less or love me more,
   And play not with my liberty;
Either take all, or all restore,
   Bind me at least or set me free;
Let me some nobler torture find
Than of a doubtful, wavering mind;
Take all my peace,—but you betray
Mine honor, too, this cruel way.

'Tis true that I have nursed before
   That hope of which I now complain,
And having little, sought no more,
   Fearing to meet with your disdain;
The sparks of favor you did give
I gently blow to make them live,
And yet have gained by all this care
No rest in hope, nor in despair.

I see you wear that pitying smile
   Which you have still vouchsafed my smart,
Content thus cheaply to beguile
   And entertain an harmless heart:
But I no longer can give way
To hope, which doth so little pay;
And yet I dare no freedom owe
Whilst you are kind, though but in show.

Then give me more or give me less;
   Do not disdain a mutual sense,
Or your unpitying beauties dress
   In their own free indifference.
But show not a severer eye
Sooner to give me liberty,
For I shall love the very scorn
Which for my sake you do put on.

owe] own   a mutual sense] passion equal to mine

VIII

THE SPENSERIANS AND MILTON

Chiefly

1600–1630

THE SPENSERIANS AND MILTON

Among the instinctive responses of sensitive, poetic minds to an age of unrest and disillusion, we have already noted that of withdrawal into a dream world of beautiful unreality, usually laid in the past or inspired by the writers of a happier time. Such was the refuge sought by a group of poets who revived the cult of beauty, under the inspiration of Spenser, in the second and third decades of the seventeenth century. While Donne and Jonson were pointing the way toward a lyricism more intellectual in substance and with a stricter sense of form, which should express the new age, the Spenserians harked back to the manner of *The Shepherd's Calendar* and *The Faery Queen*. Briefly, they found in Spenser a sensuous love of beauty combined with an elaborate pictorial power, a strong tendency toward allegory, a use of classical imagery for decorative effect, a fondness for melody, a lingering sweetness, and a continuousness of diction which, coupled with a carelessness of design, results again and again in diffuseness. Like their master, these poets were worshipers of beauty rather than students of beauty's laws; they too were makers of 'linkèd sweetness long drawn out,' to whom the ornate detail of thought and image lovingly elaborated and prolonged, the joy of gentle onward motion, the elevation of the mood, the music of the verse outweighed considerations of subject and design.

Michael Drayton, as we have already seen,[1] was a vital link between Spenser and Spenser's later followers, to whom Drayton was a leader and a friend. But to some of them at least, Spenser's influence came direct. Completely Spenserian, for example, is the work of the brothers Phineas and Giles Fletcher, whose mutual admiration and affection is reflected in their artistic similarity. *Britain's Ida,* now known to be the work of Phineas Fletcher, was actually published as 'by that renowned poet, Edmund Spenser.'

[1] *Cf.* p. 56.

The best-known works of the brothers, *The Purple Island* and *Christ's Victory and Triumph,* are Spenserian both in their extended allegory and in their verse-form, a variation of the Spenserian stanza invented by Giles and adopted by his brother. It is clear that both poems were known to Milton. The account of Lucifer and the fallen angels in *Paradise Lost* owes something to *The Purple Island,* and *Paradise Regained* is said to owe more to *Christ's Victory and Triumph* than to any other English poem. But we are here concerned only with such lyrics as the Fletchers composed incidentally in the course of the longer works. The song from *Christ's Victory and Triumph* displays something of Spenserian richness of imagery and diffuseness, while those of Phineas, taken from his *Piscatory Eclogues* and a piscatory play, *Sicelides,* have a concentration learned of other models than Spenser. The serious bent of Phineas' mind is reflected in *Fond soul* (p. 437). Other minor members of the group were William Basse, Christopher Brooke, and John Davies of Hereford, of whom the latter two figure, along with Wither and Browne, in a collection of eclogues called *The Shepherd's Pipe* (1614).

Chief of the later Spenserians is William Browne of Tavistock. Educated at Oxford and the Inner Temple, he was in his youth intimate with Jonson and Drayton, and the influence of the latter upon his pastorals is strongly marked. Browne's poetry has a quiet serenity and grace which seem to have characterized his life. His best-known work, *Britannia's Pastorals,* sings of his beloved Devon with a fidelity reminiscent of Drayton's *Polyolbion.* The author sets out to tell the story of the loves of Marina, Celand, and Remond; but it soon appears that their shadowy amours are merely conventional, a leisurely pattern on which to embroider incidents and scenes from the countryside about him.

> Down in a valley, by a forest's side,
> Near where the crystal Thames rolls on her waves,
> I saw a mushroom stand in haughty pride,
> As if the lilies grew to be his slaves;

This sonnet (p. 446), though not from one of the pastorals, well typifies the qualities that make them readable: their nativeness to the English countryside and their charming simplicity of thought and diction. The woes of which Browne's shepherds complain are those of Devonshire peasants, and of all simple souls—the scolding wife, the tendance of infants, the crop uprooted by the hogs, the angry bull—quite as often as those pangs, more conventional in the eclogue, arising from the hard-heartedness of nymphs.

Though intimate with Donne through their mutual friend Christopher Brooke, Browne is never metaphysical. Since he wrote a belated sonnet-sequence, *Cælia,* we are not surprised to find him expressing loyalty to Sidney. But his avowed master was Spenser, to whom he penned a fine eulogy in *Britannia's Pastorals.* His relationship to Spenser is an excellent example of the way in which the influence of a great man works upon a lesser one. Spenser's great view of life—his cult of beauty—embraced the heights of human aspiration and idealism, as well as the commonplaces of everyday existence. Browne drew from the fountainhead the draught of which he was capable, and which he needed—a vision of the beauty and significance of the rural scenes amid which he lived, and the art of expressing that vision in pastoral and mythological guise.

Browne's verse has a musical limpidity which is altogether Spenserian, and a freshness of observation that is his own. Unfortunately, he shared Spenser's diffuseness and lack of constructive power, so that his reader soon abandons the attempt to follow his hazy narrative and seizes upon the charming lyrics with which it is interspersed. In these one feels not a little of the constructiveness of Jonson, and there are echoes of Jonson's ideas as well. *Shall I tell you whom I love?* (p. 441), for example, is reminiscent of Jonson's *If I freely may discover* (p. 244), though kindlier. As the author of the famous epitaph on the Countess of Pembroke, long attributed to Jonson, Browne succeeded for once in rivaling one of his masters at that master's best.

George Wither, the friend and associate of Browne, and scarcely less successful in the revival of the Spenserian pastoral, resembles Browne in workmanship and, up to a point, in the circumstances of his life. He was born in the country, spent two years at Oxford, and later came to London, where he made the acquaintance of Browne.

His satires *Abuses Stript and Whipt,* for a reason which is not quite clear, displeased the authorities and he was imprisoned. During his confinement he wrote the pastorals of *The Shepherd's Hunting,* which, with his *Fidelia* and *Fair Virtue,* contains the best of his work. His knowledge of the countryside lifts his pastorals above convention. When he portrays a hunting scene, for example, the hounds seem real, even when, like their counterparts in *The Faery Queen,* they bear the names of virtues and vices. In his lyrics there is a light-heartedness and spontaneity that made, and has kept him, popular. Few lyrics of the time are better known than his spirited *Shall I, wasting in despair,* or more expressive of an unaffected gaiety and goodwill toward men than his *Christmas Carol.* But after the three volumes named above, one could wish that, like Browne, he had ceased to write. His sympathies drew him to the Puritan cause and he became a captain of horse in Cromwell's army. His writing straggled off into innumerable devotional pamphlets and satires in verse and prose, in which there are depths to counterbalance the heights of his earlier work, despite, or because of, his amazing fecundity and fluency. Even the single lyric here selected to illustrate the great mass of his devotional verse (p. 456) is marred by a lapse of taste in the sequel, which is entitled *Hymn for a Widower or Widow Delivered from a Troublesome Yoke-fellow!* The simplicity and kindliness of his *Rocking Hymn* have won it occasional quotation in anthologies; but in most of his devotional verse he is didactic and, like a true Spenserian, interminable.

William Drummond was the 'laird' of Hawthornden, an estate near Edinburgh. After taking the degree of M. A. at the University of Edinburgh, he went, at his father's instigation, to study law in France. Upon the death of his father he renounced the law and retired to his country place to follow his bent toward reading and poetic composition. He was a bookish young man. A list of his reading for the year 1606 includes Sidney's *Arcadia,* the *Diana* of Montemayor, *Love's Labour's Lost, A Midsummer Night's Dream, Romeo and Juliet, Lucrece,* and *The Passionate Pilgrim.* Daniel, and Davison's *Poetical Rhapsody* are later mentioned and, significantly, a re-reading of the *Arcadia.*

Like Browne and Wither, Drummond was imitative of what was best in the poetry of his own, as well as of the preceding, generation. He was especially fortunate in that a number of his literary models were also his friends. Sir William Alexander, author of *Aurora,* one of the latest of the sonnet sequences, figures in Drummond's poems as the beloved 'Alexis.' With Drayton he corresponded for over a decade, although they never met. Jonson paid him an extended visit at Hawthornden and gave him the benefit of his judgment on writers and literature. Though his sensitive temperament must have found the robust Jonson disturbing rather than stimulating, Drummond has faithfully recorded the great man's opinions in his *Conversations with Ben Jonson.* He also indulges in critical praise of Donne, but there is little or none of the metaphysical in him. His conceits seem rather the hyperboles of Sidney.

Drummond's association with the Spenserians is artistic as well as personal. Like Spenser, he loved unusual words and sonorous proper names from classical mythology, a Spenserian trait which Milton, too, absorbed. His book of devotional poetry entitled *Flowers of Sion,* perhaps his finest achievement, is a remarkable blending of Spenser's conception of love and beauty with Christian thought. Drummond also played a part in molding the early poems of Milton, most distinguished of Spenser's poetic disciples, who seems especially to have known Drummond's sonnet beginning 'Dear quirister' (p. 457) and his song *Phœbus, arise* (p. 458). In sonnet and madrigal, however, Drummond was a belated Petrarchan, a devotee of Sidney and the sonneteers. His manner is that of the Elizabethans, Italianate, sentimental, romantic. He even emulated them in the translation of French and Italian originals. His verse is graceful and smooth and there are passages of unusual beauty; but in such lyrics as *This life which seems so fair* (p. 461) and *This world a hunting is* (p. 465), there is a meditative note, a melancholy which hints that perhaps his delicate imagination already apprehended something of the storm gathering over the Stuart court, where in his impressionable youth he had spent many happy hours—the storm which was to darken his later years and which, in destroying Charles I, hastened Drummond's own death.

The relationship already hinted at between Milton and the Spense-

rians was dominant at but one stage of a poetic career already dedicated to sublimer ends than theirs, and destined for greatness as
surely as theirs for obscurity. His reading of them was but one
interest of one period of his life—namely, his six years of retirement
at his father's country home at Horton, after his withdrawal from
the University. When we learn that his 'loving study' during these
years also embraced Shakespeare and Peele in English, as well as
literature in Greek, Latin, Hebrew, Spanish, French, and Italian, to
say nothing of mathematics, theology, science, and music, we realize
that only a natural affinity could account for his being drawn to the
Spenserians at all.

Yet it is quite certain that he was so drawn, both to Spenser himself and to his contemporaries and later followers. While still at
college Milton had practiced what he called the 'Petrarchian stanza,'
and his sonnet *To the Nightingale* (p. 468) is a single but unmis-
takable example of the love plaint. Poems which reveal his acquaintance with the work of Drummond and the Fletchers have
already been alluded to. He also had some association with Sir
Henry Wotton, a Spenserian of the earlier generation, who lived and
continued to write until Milton was in his thirties. Wotton was an
accomplished critic of painting and architecture, and had had ample
opportunity to develop his taste during his long residence abroad as
an ambassador at Venice. Evidently respecting his judgment,
Milton sent him a copy of *Comus*. Wotton's letter of thanks and
appraisal is a remarkable anticipation of the judgment of posterity
on the combination of tenderness and strength in Milton's art, and
on his supremacy in the lyric. 'I should much commend the tragical
part,' he writes, 'if the lyrical did not ravish me with a certain Doric
delicacy in your songs and odes, whereunto I must plainly confess
to have seen yet nothing parallel in our language.' It has been remarked that Wotton's little pastoral *And now all nature seemed in
love* (p. 156) anticipates Milton's *L'Allegro*.

But the clearest proof of Milton's Spenserianism is in the lyrics of
the Horton period quoted in the following pages. In them will be
found every trait mentioned above as characteristic of the school:
sweetness, melody, naturalness, continuousness in meter and in
sense, personification, classical allusion, pictorial vividness, and the

use of nature for decorative effect. It is quite evident that the young Milton had a sensuous delight in musical sound, and that he enjoyed the contrasting effect of sonorous classical names in an English setting, precisely as did Spenser himself.

To say that Milton was apprenticed to the art of the Renaissance is in no sense to minimize his profound artistic originality and his devotion to a lofty purpose. His first lyrical achievement, the *Ode on the Morning of Christ's Nativity,* written when he was twenty-one and an undergraduate at Cambridge, while it displays Spenserian sensuousness and touches of metaphysical conceit, is basically original to a striking degree. Its religious theme, its objectivity, its vigor and economy of phrase, and its range of thought and imagination are entirely his own. Spenser's odes have no such strength of measured cadence as *Lycidas.* Their music is that of the pipe and tabor compared to the organ. Milton adopted the sonnet, but with the Italian rather than the English rime scheme and, abandoning the theme of love, he poured into it nobility and dignity, immortal pathos and burning anger.

Yet it may be queried whether, even in the lofty artistic design and ethical nobility which lift him out of his time and make of him a world poet, Milton owed nothing to Spenser. Spenser was a Puritan, in the finest sense of the word. May not the younger man have first observed in him the union of beauty with a noble ideal? The infusion of resonant satire into the pastoral elegy, often described by admirers of *Lycidas* as an innovation, had been anticipated in the *Shepherd's Calendar.* The combination, in *Comus,* of gorgeous and fantastic scenic effects with a lesson in virtue might have been learned from the *Faery Queen* more readily than from the masques of Jonson and Fletcher. But speculations such as these raise questions which are endlessly debatable, if not unanswerable, and which are outside our present province. Of Milton as revealed in his lyrics, we can safely say that the greatest poet of the seventeenth century, and one of the greatest of the English race and of the world, was also, and to a somewhat greater extent than has always been recognized, a member of the school of Spenser; that he absorbed its influence during the formative stage of his poetic career; and that it must have contributed to the development in his poetry of those elements of sensuous beauty for which it will be remembered long after his theology is forgotten.

PHINEAS FLETCHER (1582–1650)

An Hymn

Drop, drop, slow tears,
    And bathe those beauteous feet,
Which brought from heaven
    The news and prince of peace:
Cease not, wet eyes,
    His mercies to entreat;
To cry for vengeance
    Sin doth never cease:
In your deep floods
    Drown all my faults and fears;
Nor let his eye
    See sin, but through my tears.

From *Sicelides*

[II. ii. Pas, a fisher in love with Cosma, sings.]

Who sows the seas, or ploughs the easy shore?
Yet I, fond I, more fond and senseless more:
Who strives in nets to prison in the wind?
Yet I in love a woman thought to bind:
    Fond, too fond thoughts, that thought in love to tie
    One more inconstant than inconstancy.

Look, as it is with some true April day,
The sun his glorious beams doth fair display,
And straight a cloud breaks into fluent showers,
Then shines, and rains, and clears, and straight it lours,
    And twenty changings in one hour do prove:
    So, and more changing, is a woman's love.

easy shore] unresisting sand

Fond then my thoughts, that thought a thing so vain;
Fond love, to love what could not love again;
Fond hopes, that anchor on so false a ground;
Fond thoughts that fired with love, in hope thus drowned:
  Fond thoughts, fond hope, fond heart, but fondest I
  To grasp the wind and love inconstancy.

From *A Father's Testament*

Fond soul

        Fond soul, is this
        The way to bliss?
Grasp both the Indies, let thy mighty hand
The iron North and golden South command;
        Transcend the moon,
        Fasten thy throne
Above the fixèd stars; above expressions,
Above thy thought enlarge thy vast possessions:
        Fond soul, all this
        Can not make up thy bliss.

        All these are vain,
        Full but with pain;
All creatures have their ends to serve, not bless thee;
As servants they may help, as lords oppress thee;
        They vex in getting
        Used, lost with fretting;
Can slaves advance? shades fill? can grief give rest?
That which was cursed for thee can't make thee blest:
        They all are vain
        And bring not bliss but pain.

        Fond soul, thy birth
        Is not of earth
Or heaven; thou earth and heaven itself survivest;
Though born in time, thou, dying, time out-livest.
        They fail, deceive thee,
        They age, die, leave thee;

Soar up, immortal spirit, and mounting fly
Into the arms of great Eternity:
  Not heaven or earth
  He, He thy end and birth.

GILES FLETCHER (1588?–1623)

From *Christ's Victory on Earth*

[The sorceress Panglory sings to Christ.]

Love is the blossom where there blows
Everything that lives or grows;
Love doth make the heavens to move,
And the sun doth burn in love;
Love the strong and weak doth yoke,
And makes the ivy climb the oak,
Under whose shadows lions wild,
Softened by love, grow tame and mild;
Love no med'cine can appease,
He burns the fishes in the seas,
Not all the skill his wounds can stench,
Not all the sea his fire can quench;
Love did make the bloody spear
Once a leafy coat to wear,
While in his leaves there shrouded lay
Sweet birds, for love that sing and play;
And of all love's joyful flame,
I the bud and blossom am.
  Only bend thy knee to me,
  Thy wooing shall thy winning be.

See, see the flowèrs that below
Now as fresh as morning blow,
And, of all, the virgin rose,
That as bright Aurora shows,
How they all unleavèd die,
Losing their virginity;

stench] staunch   That as] That like

Like unto a summer shade,
But now born, and now they fade.
Everything doth pass away,
There is danger in delay;
Come, come gather then the rose,
Gather it, or it you lose.
All the sand of Tagus' shore
Into my bosom casts his ore;
All the valley's swimming corn
To my house is yearly borne;
Every grape of every vine
Is gladly bruised to make me wine,
While ten thousand kings, as proud
To carry up my train, have bowed,
And a world of ladies send me,
In my chambers to attend me;
All the stars in heaven that shine,
And ten thousand more, are mine;
　　Only bend thy knee to me,
　　Thy wooing shall thy winning be.

WILLIAM BROWNE (1592–1643?)

In Obitum M.S., X Maii, 1614

May, be thou never graced with birds that sing,
　　Nor Flora's pride!
In thee all flowers and roses spring;
　　Mine only died.

From Britannia's Pastorals

A Shepherd's Moan

Glide soft, ye silver floods,
　　And every spring;
Within the shady woods,
　　Let no bird sing!

his] its

Nor from the grove a turtledove
Be seen to couple with her love,
But silence on each dale and mountain dwell,
Whilst Willy bids his friend and joy farewell.

But, of great Thetis' train
    Ye mermaids fair,
That on the shores do plain
    Your sea-green hair,
As ye in trammels knit your locks
Weep ye; and so enforce the rocks
In heavy murmurs through the broad shores tell
How Willy bade his friend and joy farewell.

Cease, cease, ye murd'ring winds
    To move a wave;
But if with troubled minds
    You seek his grave;
Know 'tis as various as yourselves,
Now in the deep, then on the shelves,
His coffin tossed by fish and surges fell,
Whilst Willy weeps and bids all joy farewell.

Had he, Arion-like,
    Been judged to drown,
He on his lute could strike
    So rare a soun,
A thousand dolphins would have come,
And jointly strive to bring him home.
But he on shipboard died, by sickness fell,
Since when his Willy bade all joy farewell.

Great Neptune, hear a swain!
    His coffin take,
And with a golden chain
    For pity make
It fast unto a rock near land,

plain] smooth   tell] to tell   judged] sentenced   soun] sound, music   strive]
striven

Where ev'ry calmy morn I'll stand,
And ere one sheep out of my fold I tell,
Sad Willy's pipe shall bid his friend farewell.

What Wight He Loved

Shall I tell you whom I love?
  Hearken then awhile to me;
And if such a woman move,
  As I now shall versify,
Be assured, 'tis she or none
That I love, and love alone.

Nature did her so much right
  As she scorns the help of art;
In as many virtues dight
  As e'er yet embraced a heart:
So much good so truly tried,
Some for less were deified.

Wit she hath without desire
  To make known how much she hath;
And her anger flames no higher
  Than may fitly sweeten wrath.
Full of pity as may be,
Though, perhaps, not so to me.

Reason masters every sense,
  And her virtues grace her birth,
Lovely as all excellence,
  Modest in her most of mirth:
Likelihood enough to prove
Only worth could kindle love.

Such she is: and, if you know
  Such a one as I have sung,
Be she brown, or fair, or so
  That she be but somewhile young,

tell] count   move] live   As she] That she

Be assured, 'tis she, or none
That I love, and love alone.

⌘

As careful merchants

As careful merchants do expecting stand,
  After long time and merry gales of wind,
Upon the place where their brave ship must land,
  So wait I for the vessel of my mind.

Upon a great adventure is it bound,
  Whose safe return will valued be at more
Than all the wealthy prizes which have crowned
  The golden wishes of an age before.

Out of the East jewels of worth she brings;
  Th' unvalued diamond of her sparkling eye
Wants in the treasures of all Europe's kings;
  And were it mine, they nor their crowns should buy.

The sapphires ringèd on her panting breast
  Run as rich veins of ore about the mould,
And are in sickness with a pale possessed,
  So true, for them I should disvalue gold.

The melting rubies on her cherry lip
  Are of such power to hold, that as one day
Cupid flew thirsty by, he stooped to sip,
  And, fastened there, could never get away.

The sweets of Candy are no sweets to me
  When hers I taste; nor the perfumes of price,
Robbed from the happy shrubs of Araby,
  As her sweet breath so powerful to entice.

O hasten then! and if thou be not gone
  Unto that wishèd traffic through the main,
My powerful sighs shall quickly drive thee on,
  And then begin to draw thee back again.

Wants] Is lacking   Candy] Crete

If, in the mean, rude waves have it oppressed,
It shall suffice I ventured at the best.

From *The Inner Temple Masque*

[Scene I.   A siren sings.]

Steer hither, steer your wingèd pines,
    All beaten mariners;
Here lie love's undiscovered mines,
    A prey to passengers;
Perfumes far sweeter than the best
Which make the Phoenix' urn and nest.
        Fear not your ships,
Nor any to oppose you save our lips,
        But come on shore,
Where no joy dies till love hath gotten more.

                .   .   .   .

For swelling waves, our panting breasts,
    Where never storms arise,
Exchange, and be awhile our guests;
    For stars, gaze on our eyes.
The compass Love shall hourly sing,
And, as he goes about the ring,
        We will not miss
To tell each point he nameth with a kiss:
        Then come on shore,
Where no joy dies till love hath gotten more.

[Circe utters a charm over the sleeping Ulysses.]

Son of Erebus and Night,
Hie away; and aim thy flight
Where consort none other fowl
Than the bat and sullen owl;
Where upon the limber grass
Poppy and mandragoras

---

mean] meantime   passengers] wayfarers   Fear] Be anxious about   compass]
the mariner's compass and also the range of the voice

With like simples not a few
Hang forever drops of dew.
Where flows Lethe without coil
Softly like a stream of oil.
Hie thee thither, gentle Sleep:
With this Greek no longer keep.
Thrice I charge thee by my wand,
Thrice with moly from my hand
Do I touch Ulysses' eyes,
And with the jaspis: then arise
Sagest Greek. . . .

❉

A Round

All.

Now that the spring hath filled our veins
   With kind and active fire,
And made green liveries for the plains,
   And every grove a choir;

Sing we a song of merry glee,
   And Bacchus fill the bowl:
1. Then here's to thee; *2.* And thou to me
   And every thirsty soul.

Nor care, nor sorrow e'er paid debt,
   Nor never shall do mine;
I have no cradle going yet,
   Not I, by this good wine.

No wife at home to send for me,
   No hogs are in my ground,
No suit in law to pay a fee,
   Then round, old Jocky, round.

simples] medicinal herbs   coil] noise, disturbance   moly] a fabulous magic herb
jaspis] jasper   Jocky] presumably the first singer

All.

Shear sheep that have them, cry we still,
    But see that no man 'scape
        To drink of the sherry,
        That makes us so merry,
    And plump as the lusty grape.

From *Cælia*

III

Fairest, when by the rules of palmistry
You took my hand to try if you could guess
By lines therein, if any wight there be
Ordained to make me know some happiness,
I wished that those charàcters could explain
Whom I will never wrong with hope to win;
Or that by them a copy might be ta'en,
By you alone what thoughts I have within.
But since the hand of nature did not set—
As providently loath to have it known—
The means to find that hidden alphabet,
Mine eyes shall be th' interpreters alone;
    By them conceive my thoughts, and tell me, fair,
    If now you see her that doth love me there?

✄

Sonnet

For her gait if she be walking,
    Be she sitting I desire her
    For her state's sake, and admire her
For her wit if she be talking:
    Gait and state and wit approve her;
    For which all and each I love her.

Whom] Who it is that   As] As if   fair] fair one   state] dignity   approve]
become

Be she sullen, I commend her
For a modest; be she merry
For a kind one her prefer I:
Briefly, everything doth lend her
So much grace and so approve her
That for everything I love her.

From *Visions*

VI

Down in a valley, by a forest's side,
Near where the crystal Thames rolls on her waves,
I saw a mushroom stand in haughty pride,
As if the lilies grew to be his slaves;
The gentle daisy, with her silver crown,
Worn in the breast of many a shepherd's lass,
The humble violet, that lowly down
Salutes the gay nymphs as they trimly pass:
These, with a many more, methought, complained
That nature should those needless things produce,
Which not alone the sun from others gained,
But turn it wholly to their proper use:
I could not choose but grieve, that nature made
So glorious flowers to live in such a shade.

On the Countess of Pembroke

Underneath this sable hearse
Lies the subject of all verse:
Sidney's sister, Pembroke's mother:
Death, ere thou hast slain another
Fair and learn'd and good as she,
Time shall throw a dart at thee.

Marble piles let no man raise
To her name, for after-days
Some kind woman born as she,

proper] own hearse] catafalque after-days] in after-time

Reading this, like Niobe,
Shall turn marble, and become
Both her mourner and her tomb.

GEORGE WITHER (1588–1667)

The Resolution

Shall I, wasting in despair,
Die because a woman's fair?
Or make pale my cheeks with care
'Cause another's rosy are?
Be she fairer than the day
Or the flowery meads in May—
  If she think not well of me
  What care I how fair she be?

Shall my seely heart be pined
'Cause I see a woman kind;
Or a well-disposèd nature
Joinèd with a lovely feature?
Be she meeker, kinder than
Turtledove or pelican,
  If she be not so to me
  What care I how kind she be?

Shall a woman's virtues move
Me to perish for her love?
Or her well-deservings known
Make me quite forget mine own?
Be she with that goodness blest
Which may merit name of Best,
  If she be not such to me,
  What care I how good she be?

'Cause her fortune seems too high,
Shall I play the fool and die?
She that bears a noble mind

tomb] monument   feature] form   pelican] believed to feed her young with her
own flesh

If not outward helps she find,
Thinks what with them he would do,
That without them dares her woo;
 And unless that mind I see,
 What care I how great she be?

Great, or good, or kind, or fair,
I will ne'er the more despair;
If she love me, this believe,
I will die ere she shall grieve;
If she slight me when I woo,
I can scorn and let her go;
 For if she be not for me,
 What care I for whom she be?

A Love Sonnet

I loved a lass, a fair one,
 As fair as e'er was seen;
She was indeed a rare one,
 Another Sheba Queen:
But, fool as then I was,
 I thought she loved me too:
But now, alas! she's left me,
 Falero, lero, loo!

Her hair like gold did glister,
 Each eye was like a star,
She did surpass her sister,
 Which passed all others far;
She would me 'honey' call,
 She'd—O, she'd kiss me too!
But now, alas! she's left me,
 Falero, lero, loo!

Many a merry meeting
 My love and I have had;

helps] wealth, position, etc. find] *I.e.,* in her suitor. *A Love Sonnet*] Seven
stanzas are omitted. Which] Who

She was my only sweeting,
    She made my heart full glad;
The tears stood in her eyes
    Like to the morning dew:
But now, alas! she's left me,
    Falero, lero, loo!

Her cheeks were like the cherry,
    Her skin as white as snow;
When she was blithe and merry
    She angel-like did show;
Her waist exceeding small,
    The fives did fit her shoe:
But now, alas! she's left me,
    Falero, lero, loo!

In summer time or winter
    She had her heart's desire;
I still did scorn to stint her
    From sugar, sack, or fire;
The world went round about,
    No cares we ever knew:
But now, alas! she's left me,
    Falero, lero, loo!

To maidens' vows and swearing
    Henceforth no credit give;
You may give them the hearing,
    But never them believe;
They are as false as fair,
    Unconstant, frail, untrue:
For mine, alas! has left me,
    Falero, lero, loo!

From *Fair Virtue*

Sonnet II

Hence away, you sirens, leave me,
    And unclasp your wanton arms;

show] appear   The fives] Size five

Sugared words shall ne'er deceive me
  Though you prove a thousand charms.
      Fie, fie, forbear;
      No common snare
  Could ever my affection chain;
        Your painted baits
        And poor deceits
  Are all bestowed on me in vain.

I'm no slave to such as you be;
  Neither shall a snowy breast,
Wanton eye, or lip of ruby
  Ever rob me of my rest;
        Go, go, display
        Your beauty's ray
  To some o'er-soon enamored swain:
        Those common wiles
        Of sighs and smiles
  Are all bestowed on me in vain.

I have elsewhere vowed a duty;
  Turn away your tempting eyes,
Show not me a naked beauty,
  Those impostures I despise;
        My spirit loathes
        Where gaudy clothes
  And feignèd oaths may love obtain:
        I love her so
        Whose look swears 'No,'
  That all your labors will be vain.

Can he prize the tainted posies
  Which on every breast are worn,
That may pluck the spotless roses
  From their never-touchèd thorn?
        I can go rest
        On her sweet breast

prove] try   ray] radiance

That is the pride of Cynthia's train;
  Then hold your tongues,
  Your mermaid songs
Are all bestowed on me in vain.

He's a fool that basely dallies
  Where each peasant mates with him;
Shall I haunt the throngèd valleys,
  Whilst there's noble hills to climb?
    No, no, though clowns
    Are scared with frowns,
  I know the best can but disdain;
    And those I'll prove,
    So shall your love
Be all bestowed on me in vain.

Yet I would not deign embraces
  With the greatest, fairest she,
If another shared those graces
  Which had been bestowed on me.
    I gave that one
    My love, where none
  Shall come to rob me of my gain.
    Your fickle hearts
    Makes tears, and arts
And all, bestowed on me in vain.

I do scorn to vow a duty
  Where each lustful lad may woo;
Give me her whose sun-like beauty
  Buzzards dare not soar unto:
    She, she it is
    Affords that bliss,
  For which I would refuse no pain;
    But such as you,
    Fond fools, adieu,
  You seek to captive me in vain.

mates] claims equality with

Proud she seemed in the beginning
And disdained my looking on,
But that coy one in the winning,
    Proves a true one, being won.
            Whate'er betide
            She'll ne'er divide
    The favor she to me shall deign;
            But your fond love
            Will fickle prove,
    And all that trust in you are vain.

Therefore know, .when I enjoy one,
And for love employ my breath,
She I court shall be a coy one
    Though I win her with my death.
            A favor there
            Few aim at dare;
    And if, perhaps, some lover plain,
            She is not won
            Nor I undone
    By placing of my love in vain.

Leave me, then, you sirens, leave me,
Seek no more to work my harms;
Crafty wiles cannot deceive me,
    Who am proof against your charms:
            You labor may
            To lead astray
    The heart that constant shall remain;
            And I the while
            Will sit and smile
    To see you spend your time in vain.

Sonnet V

I wandered out a while agone,
And went I know not whither;
But there do beauties many a one

that coy one] one who is coy   vain] foolish   plain] complain   agone] ago

Resort and meet together,
And Cupid's power will there be shown
If ever you come thither.

For like two suns, two beauties bright
I shining saw together,
And tempted by their double light
My eyes I fixed on either;
Till both at once so thralled my sight,
I loved, and knew not whether.

Such equal sweet Venus gave,
That I preferred not either;
And when for love I thought to crave,
I knew not well of whether,
For one while this I wished to have,
And then I that had liefer.

A lover of the curious 't eye
Might have been pleased in either;
And so, I must confess, might I,
Had they not been together.
Now both must love or both deny,
In one enjoy I neither.

But yet at last I 'scaped the smart
I feared at coming hither;
For seeing my divided heart—
I, choosing, knew not whether—
Love angry grew and did depart,
And now I care for neither.

⚜

A Christmas Carol

So now is come our joyful'st feast,
Let every man be jolly.
Each room with ivy leaves is dressed,

whether] which   curious 't] most fastidious   *A Christmas Carol*] Three stanzas
are omitted.

And every post with holly.
 Though some churls at our mirth repine,
 Round your foreheads garlands twine,
 Drown sorrow in a cup of wine,
And let us all be merry.

Now all our neighbors' chimneys smoke,
And Christmas blocks are burning;
Their ovens they with baked meats choke,
And all their spits are turning.
 Without the door let sorrow lie,
 And if for cold it hap to die,
 We'll bury 't in a Christmas pie,
And evermore be merry.

Rank misers now do sparing shun,
Their hall of music soundeth,
And dogs thence with whole shoulders run,
So all things there aboundeth.
 The country folk themselves advance,
 For crowdy-mutton's come out of France,
 And Jack shall pipe and Jill shall dance,
And all the town be merry.

Ned Swash hath fetched his bands from pawn,
And all his best apparel;
Brisk Nell hath bought a ruff of lawn
With droppings of the barrel;
 And those that hardly all the year
 Had bread to eat or rags to wear,
 Will have both clothes and dainty fare,
And all the day be merry.

Now poor men to the justices
With capons make their arrants,
And if they hap to fail of these

sparing] parsimony crowdy-mutton] a fiddler (Halliwell) bands] ruffs droppings of the barrel] tips for serving small beer make their arrants] find excuses
for going

They plague them with their warrants.
  But now they feed them with good cheer,
  And what they want they take in beer,
  For Christmas comes but once a year,
And then they shall be merry.

Hark how the wags abroad do call
Each other forth to rambling;
Anon you'll see them in the hall
For nuts and apples scrambling.
  Hark how the roofs with laughters sound!
  Anon they'll think the house goes round,
  For they the cellar's depth have found,
And there they will be merry.

The wenches with their wassail bowls
About the streets are singing,
The boys are come to catch the owls,
The wild mare in is bringing.
  Our kitchen boy hath broke his box,
  And to the dealing of the ox
  Our honest neighbors come by flocks,
And here they will be merry.

Now kings and queens poor sheep-cotes have,
And mate with everybody;
The honest now may play the knave,
And wise men play at noddy.
  Some youths will now a-mumming go,
  Some others play at rowland-hoe,
  And twenty other gameboys moe,
Because they will be merry.

Then wherefore in these merry days
Should we, I pray, be duller?
No, let us sing some roundelays

they feed them] the justices ply the poor men   catch the owls] a game   wild
mare] see-saw   broke his box] opened his Christmas collection-box   dealing]
dividing   mate] associate   noddy] a card-game resembling cribbage; also, a
simpleton   rowland-hoe] a game   gameboys] gambols   moe] more

To make our mirth the fuller.
And, whilèst thus inspired we sing,
Let all the streets with echoes ring,
Woods and hills and everything,
Bear witness we are merry.

Hymn for a Widower or a Widow
Deprived of a Loving Yoke-fellow

How near me came the hand of death,
When at my side he struck my dear,
And took away the precious breath
Which quickened my belovèd peer!
How helpless am I thereby made;
By day how grieved, by night how sad!
And now my life's delight is gone,
Alas, how am I left alone!

The voice which I did more esteem
Than music in her sweetest key;
Those eyes which unto me did seem
More comfortable than the day,—
Those now by me, as they have been,
Shall nevermore be heard or seen;
But what I once enjoyed in them
Shall seem hereafter as a dream.

Lord, keep me faithful to the trust
Which my dear spouse reposed in me;
To him now dead preserve me just
In all that should performèd be!
For though our being man and wife
Extendeth only to this life,
Yet neither life nor death should end
The being of a faithful friend.

Those helps which I through him enjoyed,
Let Thy continual aid supply,

Hymn, etc.] Two stanzas are omitted.   peer] mate

That though some hopes in him are void,
  I always may on Thee rely;
  And whether I shall wed again
    Or in a single state remain,
Unto Thine honor let it be,
And for a blessing unto me.

WILLIAM DRUMMOND (1585-1649)

Madrigal

Like the Idalian queen,
Her hair about her eyne,
With neck and breast's ripe apples to be seen,
At first glance of the morn
In Cyprus' gardens gathering those fair flowers
Which of her blood were born,
I saw, but fainting saw, my paramours.
The Graces naked danced about the place,
The winds and trees amazed
With silence on her gazed,
The flowers did smile, like those upon her face;
And as their aspen stalks those fingers band,
That she might read my case,
A hyacinth I wished me in her hand.

Sonnet

'Dear quirister, who from those shadows sends,
Ere that the blushing dawn dare show her light,
Such sad lamenting strains, that night attends,—
Become all ear—stars stay to hear thy plight:
If one whose grief even reach of thought transcends,
Who ne'er—not in a dream—did taste delight,
May thee impòrtune who like case pretends,
And seems to joy in woe, in woe's despite,
Tell me,—so may thou fortune milder try

eyne] eyes   paramours] paramour   aspen] tremulous   band] encircle   quiris-
ter] chorister

And long, long sing—for what thou thus complains,
Sith winter's gone and sun in dappled sky
Enamored smiles on woods and flow'ry plains?'
 The bird, as if my questions did her move,
 With trembling wings sobbed forth, 'I love, I love!'

Song

Phœbus, arise,
And paint the sable skies
With azure, white, and red;
Rouse Memnon's mother from her Tithon's bed
That she thy càreer may with roses spread;
The nightingales thy coming each-where sing;
Make an eternal spring;
Give life to this dark world which lieth dead.
Spread forth thy golden hair
In larger locks than thou wast wont before,
And emperor-like, decore
With diadem of pearl thy temples fair.
Chase hence the ugly night,
Which serves but to make dear thy glorious light.
This is that happy morn,
That day, long wishèd day
Of all my life so dark,—
If cruel stars have not my ruin sworn,
And fates my hopes betray—
Which, only white, deserves
An everlasting diamond should it mark;
This is the morn should bring unto this grove
My love, to hear and recompense my love.
Fair king, who all preserves,
But show thy blushing beams,
And thou two sweeter eyes
Shalt see than those which by Peneus' streams
Did once thy heart surprise;
Nay, suns, which shine as clear

complains] complain'st Sith] Since decore] adorn

As thou when two thou did to Rome appear.
Now Flora, deck thyself in fairest guise;
If that ye, winds, would hear
A voice surpassing far Amphion's lyre,
Your furious chiding stay;
Let Zephyr only breath
And with her tresses play,
Kissing sometimes those purple ports of death.
The winds all silent are,
And Phœbus in his chare,
Ensaffroning sea and air,
Makes vanish every star;
Night like a drunkard reels
Beyond the hills to shun his flaming wheels;
The fields with flowers are decked in every hue,
The clouds bespangle with bright gold their blue;
Here is the pleasant place,
And every thing save her, who all should grace.

Madrigal

Sweet rose, whence is this hue
    Which doth all hues excel?
    Whence this most fragrant smell?
And whence this form and gracing grace in you?
In fair Pæstana's fields perhaps you grew,
    Or Hybla's hills you bred,
Or odoriferous Enna's plains you fed,
Or Tmolus, or where boar young Adon slew;
Or hath the Queen of Love you dyed of new
In that dear blood, which makes you look so red?
    No, none of those, but cause more high you blissed:
    My lady's breast you bore, her lips you kissed.

Sonnet

Alexis, here she stayed among these pines,
Sweet hermitress, did all alone repair;

breath] breathe   chare] chariot   you blissed] made you blissful

Here did she spread the treasure of her hair,
More rich than that brought from the Colchian mines.
She set her by these muskèd eglantines,
The happy flowers seem yet the print to bear;
Her voice did sweeten here thy sugared lines,
To which winds, trees, beasts, birds did lend their ear.
Me here she first perceived, and here a morn
Of bright carnations did o'erspread her face;
Here did she sigh, here first my hopes were born,
And I first got a pledge of promised grace.
   But ah, what serves 't to have been made happy so,
   Sith passèd pleasures double but new woe?

Madrigal

   I fear not henceforth death,
Sith after this departure yet I breath;
      Let rocks and seas and wind
      Their highest treasons show;
      Let sky and earth combined
Strive, if they can, to end my life and woe;
Sith grief cannot, me nothing can o'erthrow:
   Or if that aught can cause my fatal lot,
   It will be when I hear I am forgot.

Sonnet

Thy head with flames, thy mantle bright with flowers,
Sweet Spring, thou 'turn'st with all thy goodly train;
The zephyrs curl the green locks of the plain,
The clouds for joy in pearls weep down their showers.
Turn thou, sweet youth? but ah! my pleasant hours
And happy days with thee come not again;
The sad memorials only of my pain
Do with thee, turn, which turn my sweets in sours.

muskèd] musky   Sith] Since   Thy head, etc.] The first two lines are transposed,
to preserve the rime scheme.   'turn'st] return'st   in sours] into sours

Thou art the same which still thou wert before,
Delicious, lusty, amiable, fair;
But she, whose breath embalmed thy wholesome air,
Is gone; nor gold nor gems can her restore.
  Neglected virtue, seasons go and come,
  While thine, forgot, lie closèd in a tomb.

Madrigal

The ivory, coral, gold,
Of breast, of lips, of hair,
So lively sleep doth show to inward sight,
That, 'wake, I think I hold
No shadow, but my fair:
Myself so to deceive,
With long-shut eyes I shun the irksome light.
Such pleasure thus I have,
Delighting in false gleams,
If death sleep's brother be,
And souls relieved of sense have so sweet dreams,
That I would wish me so to dream and die.

Madrigal

  This life, which seems so fair,
Is like a bubble blown up in the air
   By sporting children's breath,
   Who chase it everywhere
And strive who can most motion it bequeath:
And though it sometime seem of its own might,
Like to an eye of gold, to be fixed there,
And firm to hover in that empty height,
That only is because it is so light.
But in that pomp it doth not long appear;
For when it most admired is, in a thought,
Because it erst was naught, it turns to naught.

thine] thy virtues   a thought] an instant

Sonnet

My lute, be as thou wast when thou didst grow
With thy green mother in some shady grove,
When immelodious winds but made thee move,
And birds their ramage on thee did bestow.
Sith that dear voice which did thy sounds approve,
Which wont in such harmonious strains to flow,
Is reft from earth to tune those spheres above,
What art thou but a harbinger of woe?
Thy pleasing notes be pleasing notes no more,
But orphan-wailings to the fainting ear,
Each stroke a sigh, each sound draws forth a tear:
For which be silent as in woods before,
   Or if that any hand to touch thee deign,
   Like widowed turtle, still her loss complain.

Sonnet

What doth it serve to see sun's burning face,
And skies enameled with both the Indies' gold?
Or moon at night in jetty chariot rolled,
And all the glory of that starry place?
What doth it serve earth's beauty to behold,
The mountains' pride, the meadows' flowery grace,
The stately comeliness of forests old,
The sport of floods which would themselves embrace?
What doth it serve to hear the sylvans' songs,
The wanton merle, the nightingale's sad strains,
Which in dark shades seems to deplore my wrongs?
For what doth serve all that this world contains,
   Sith she for whom those once to me were dear,
   Can have no part of them now with me here?

ramage] song, note   For which] Wherefore   turtle] turtledove   jetty] jet-black
sylvans] wood-birds   merle] blackbird

Madrigal

The beauty and the life
Of life's and beauty's fairest paragon—
O tears! O grief!—hung at a feeble thread,
To which pale Atropos had set her knife;
The soul with many a groan
Had left each outward part,
And now did take his last leave of the heart;
Naught else did want, save Death, for to be dead,
When the afflicted band about her bed,
  Seeing so fair him come in lips, cheeks, eyes,
  Cried, 'Ah! and can Death enter Paradise?'

Madrigal

  My thoughts hold mortal strife;
  I do detest my life,
  And with lamenting cries,
  Peace to my soul to bring,
Oft call that prince which here doth monarchize.
  But he, grim grinning king,
Who caitiffs scorns, and doth the blest surprise,
Late having decked with beauty's rose his tomb,
Disdains to crop a weed, and will not come.

Thrice happy he

Thrice happy he who by some shady grove
Far from the clamorous world doth live his own;
Though solitaire, yet who is not alone,
But doth converse with that eternal love.
O, how more sweet is birds' harmonious moan,
Or the soft sobbings of the widowed dove,
Than those smooth whisperings near a prince's throne,
Which good make doubtful, do the evil approve!
O, how more sweet is Zephyr's wholesome breath,

And sighs perfumed, which do the flowers unfold,
Than that applause vain honor doth bequeath!
How sweet are streams to poison drunk in gold!
  The world is full of horrors, falsehoods, slights,
  Woods' silent shades have only true delights.

Phyllis

  In petticoat of green,
  Her hair about her eyne,
  Phyllis beneath an oak
  Sat milking her fair flock:
'Mong that sweet-strainèd moisture, rare delight,
Her hand seemed milk, in milk it was so white.

The Book of the World

Of this fair volume which we World do name
If we the sheets and leaves could turn with care,
Of him who it corrects, and did it frame,
We clear might read the art and wisdom rare,
Find out his power which wildest powers doth tame,
His providence extending everywhere,
His justice which proud rebels doth not spare,
In every page, no period of the same:
But silly we, like foolish children, rest
Well pleased with colored vellum, leaves of gold,
Fair dangling ribbands, leaving what is best,
On the great Writer's sense ne'er taking hold;
  Or if by chance we stay our minds on aught,
  It is some picture in the margin wrought.

For the Magdalene

'These eyes, dear Lord, once brandons of desire,
Frail scouts betraying what they had to keep,
Which their own heart, then others set on fire,

to] compared to   brandons] torches

Their traitorous black before thee here out-weep;
These locks, of blushing deeds the gilt attire,
Waves curling, wrackful shelves to shadow deep,
Rings wedding souls to sin's lethargic sleep,
To touch thy sacred feet do now aspire.
In seas of care behold a sinking bark,
By winds of sharp remorse unto thee driven;
O let me not be ruin's aimed-at mark!
My faults confessed, Lord, say they are forgiven.'
   Thus sighed to Jesus the Bethanian fair,
   His tear-wet feet still drying with her hair.

The World a Game

   This world a hunting is:
The prey poor man, the Nimrod fierce is Death;
   His speedy grayhounds are
   Lust, sickness, envy, care,
   Strife that ne'er falls amiss,
With all those ills which haunt us while we breath.
   Now, if by chance we fly
   Of these the eager chase,
   Old Age with stealing pace
Casts on his nets, and there we panting die.

Love Vagabonding

Sweet nymphs, if, as ye stray,
Ye find the froth-born goddess of the sea
All blubbered, pale, undone,
Who seeks her giddy son,
That little god of love,
Whose golden shafts your chastest bosoms prove,
Who, leaving all the heavens, hath run away,—
If aught to him that finds him she'll impart,
Tell her he nightly lodgeth in my heart.

wrackful] causing shipwreck   blubbered] tear-stained   prove] test   impart] give

WILLIAM BASSE (c. 1583–c. 1653)

Elegy on Shakespeare

Renownèd Spenser, lie a thought more nigh
To learnèd Chaucer; and rare Beaumont, lie
A little nearer Spenser, to make room
For Shakespeare in your threefold, fourfold tomb.
To lodge all four in one bed make a shift
Until doomsday, for hardly will a fift
Betwixt this day and that by fate be slain,
For whom your curtains may be drawn again.
If your precèdency in death doth bar
A fourth place in your sacred sepulcher,
Under this carvèd marble of thine own
Sleep, rare tragedian, Shakespeare, sleep alone;
Thy unmolested peace, unsharèd cave,
Possess as lord, not tenant, of thy grave,
   That unto us and others it may be
   Honor hereafter to be laid by thee.

The Angler's Song

As inward love breeds outward talk,
The hound some praise, and some the hawk;
Some better pleased with private sport
Use tennis, some a mistress court;
   But these delights I neither wish
   Nor envy, while I freely fish.

Who hunts doth oft in danger ride;
Who hawks lures oft both far and wide;
Who uses games may often prove
A loser, but who falls in love
   Is fettered in fond Cupid's snare;
   My angle breeds me no such care.

Of recreation there is none
So free as fishing is alone;
All other pastimes do no less

Than mind and body both possess;
My hand alone my work can do,
So I can fish and study too.

I care not, I, to fish in seas,
Fresh rivers best my mind do please,
Whose sweet calm course I contemplate
And seek in life to imitate;
In civil bounds I fain would keep,
And for my past offences weep.

And when the timorous trout I wait
To take, and he devours my bait,
How poor a thing, sometimes I find,
Will captivate a greedy mind;
And when none bite, I praise the wise
Whom vain allurements ne'er surprise.

But yet, though while I fish I fast,
I make good fortune my repast;
And thereunto my friend invite,
In whom I more than that delight,
Who is more welcome to my dish
Than to my angle was my fish.

As well content no prize to take,
As use of taken prize to make;
For so our Lord was pleasèd when
He fishers made fishers of men;
Where,—which is in no other game—
A man may fish and praise His name.

The first men that our Savior dear
Did choose to wait upon him here,
Blest fishers were, and fish the last
Food was that he on earth did taste;
I therefore strive to follow those
Whom he to follow him hath chose.

JOHN MILTON (1608–1674)

Song on May Morning

Now the bright morning star, day's harbinger,
Comes dancing from the east, and leads with her
The flowery May, who from her green lap throws
The yellow cowslip and the pale primrose.
  Hail, bounteous May, that dost inspire
  Mirth, and youth, and warm desire;
  Woods and grovès are of thy dressing,
  Hill and dale both boast thy blessing.
Thus we salute thee with our early song,
And welcome thee, and wish thee long.

To the Nightingale

O nightingale, that on yon bloomy spray
  Warbl'st at eve, when all the woods are still,
  Thou with fresh hope the lover's heart dost fill,
While the jolly Hours lead on propitious May.
Thy liquid notes that close the eye of day,
  First heard before the shallow cuckoo's bill,
  Portend success in love; O, if Jove's will
Have linked that amorous power to thy soft lay,
  Now timely sing, ere the rude bird of hate
  Foretell my hopeless doom in some grove nigh,
As thou from year to year hast sung too late
  For my relief, yet hadst no reason why.
Whether the Muse, or Love, call thee his mate,
  Both them I serve, and of their train am I.

An Epitaph on the Admirable Dramatic Poet, William Shakespeare

What needs my Shakespeare for his honored bones
The labor of an age in pilèd stones?
Or that his hallowed relics should be hid

jolly] joyous

Under a star-ypointing pyramid?
Dear son of memory, great heir of fame,
What need'st thou such weak witness of thy name?
Thou in our wonder and astonishment,
Hast built thyself a livelong monument.
For whilst to th' shame of slow-endeavoring art
Thy easy numbers flow, and that each heart
Hath from the leaves of thy unvalued book
Those Delphic lines with deep impression took;
Then thou, our fancy of itself bereaving,
Dost make us marble with too much conceiving;
And, so sepùlchered, in such pomp dost lie,
That kings for such a tomb would wish to die.

On his being Arrived to the Age of Twenty-three

How soon hath Time, the subtle thief of youth,
    Stol'n on his wing my three and twentieth year!
    My hasting days fly on with full career,
But my late spring no bud or blossom shew'th.
Perhaps my semblance might deceive the truth,
    That I to manhood am arrived so near,
    And inward ripeness doth much less appear,
That some more timely-happy spirits endu'th;
Yet be it less or more, or soon or slow,
    It shall be still in strictest measure even
To that same lot, however mean or high,
    Toward which Time leads me, and the will of
        heaven:
All is, if I have grace to use it so,
    As ever in my great Taskmaster's eye.

From *Arcades*

The Second Song

O'er the smooth enameled green,
Where no print of step hath been,

unvalued] invaluable   conceiving] imaginative thinking   endu'th] is inherent in
it] inward ripeness   even] proportionate, conformable   enameled] variegated
(*NED*); perhaps simply 'shining,' or (smoothly) 'covering' (the earth)

Follow me, as I sing
And touch the warbled string,
Under the shady roof
Of branching elm, star-proof,
Follow me:
I will bring you where she sits
Clad in splendor as befits
Her deity.
Such a rural queen
All Arcadia hath not seen.

The Third Song

Nymphs and shepherds, dance no more
By sandy Ladon's lilied banks;
On old Lycæus, or Cyllene hoar,
Trip no more in twilight ranks;
Though Erymanth your loss deplore,
A better soil shall give ye thanks.
From the stony Mænalus
Bring your flocks, and live with us;
Here ye shall have greater grace,
To serve the lady of this place.
Though Syrinx your Pan's mistress were,
Yet Syrinx well might wait on her.
Such a rural queen
All Arcadia hath not seen.

From *A Masque Presented at Ludlow Castle*

[*Lady.* Such noise as I can make to be heard farthest
I'll venture.   *She sings.*]

Sweet Echo, sweetest nymph, that liv'st unseen
Within thy airy shell,
By slow Meander's margent green,
And in the violet-embroidered vale
Where the love-lorn nightingale

warbled] melodious   grace] favor   *A Masque*] usually known as *Comus*

Nightly to thee her sad song mourneth well:
Canst thou not tell me of a gentle pair
   That likest thy Narcissus are?
    O, if thou have
   Hid them in some flow'ry cave,
    Tell me but where,
  Sweet queen of parley, daughter of the sphere!
So may'st thou be translated to the skies,
And give resounding grace to all heaven's harmonies.

[*Spirit.* If she be right invoked in warbled song,
         This will I try. *Sings.*]

Sabrina fair,
  Listen where thou art sitting
Under the glassy, cool, translucent wave,
  In twisted braids of lilies knitting
The loose train of thy amber-dropping hair;
  Listen, for dear honor's sake,
  Goddess of the silver lake,
    Listen, and save.

Listen, and appear to us,
In name of great Oceanus;
By the earth-shaking Neptune's mace,
And Tethys' grave majestic pace;
By hoary Nereus' wrinkled look,
And the Carpathian wizard's hook;
By scaly Triton's winding shell,
And old soothsaying Glaucus' spell;
By Leucothea's lovely hands,
And her son that rules the strands;
By Thetis' tinsel-slippered feet,
And the songs of Sirens sweet;
By dead Parthenope's dear tomb,
And fair Ligea's golden comb,
Wherewith she sits on diamond rocks,
Sleeking her soft alluring locks;

amber-dropping] coloring the drops by reflection   Carpathian wizard] Proteus
hook] crook   shell] conch

By all the nymphs that nightly dance
Upon thy streams with wily glance:
Rise, rise, and heave thy rosy head
From thy coral-paven bed,
And bridle in thy headlong wave,
Till thou our summons answered have.
      Listen and save.

Sabrina rises, attended by water-nymphs, and sings.

By the rushy-fringèd bank,
Where grows the willow and the osier dank,
   My sliding chariot stays,
Thick set with agate, and the azurn sheen
Of turkis blue, and emerald green,
   That in the channel strays;
Whilst from off the waters fleet
Thus I set my printless feet
O'er the cowslip's velvet head,
   That bends not as I tread.
Gentle swain, at thy request
   I am here!

Spirit.

Goddess dear,
We implore thy powerful hand
To undo the charmèd band
Of true virgin here distressed
Through the force, and through the wile
Of unblest enchanter vile.

Sabrina.

Shepherd, 'tis my office best
To help ensnarèd chastity.
Brightest lady, look on me:
Thus I sprinkle on thy breast

wily] beguiling   turkis] turquoise   printless] that leave no print

Drops that from my fountain pure
I have kept of precious cure;
Thrice upon thy finger's tip,
Thrice upon thy rubied lip:
Next this marble venomed seat,
Smeared with gums of glutinous heat,
I touch with chaste palms moist and cold.
Now the spell hath lost his hold;
And I must haste ere morning.hour
To wait in Amphitrite's bower.

Sabrina descends, and the Lady rises out of her seat.

Spirit.

Virgin, daughter of Locrine,
Sprung of old Anchises' line,
May thy brimmèd waves for this
Their full tribute never miss
From a thousand petty rills
That tumble down the snowy hills:
Summer drouth or singèd air
Never scorch thy tresses fair,
Nor wet October's torrent flood
Thy molten crystal fill with mud;
May thy billows roll ashore
The beryl and the golden ore;
May thy lofty head be crowned
With many a tower and terrace round,
And here and there thy banks upon
With groves of myrrh and cinnamon.

The dances ended, the Spirit epilogizes.

To the ocean now I fly,
And those happy climes that lie
Where day never shuts his eye,
Up in the broad fields of the sky;

brimmèd] brimming

There I suck the liquid air,
All amidst the gardens fair
Of Hesperus, and his daughters three,
That sing about the golden tree;
Along the crispèd shades and bowers
Revels the spruce and jocund spring;
The Graces and the rosy-bosomed hours,
Thither all their bounties bring
That there eternal summer dwells,
And west winds with musky wing
About the cedarn alleys fling
Nard and cassia's balmy smells.
Iris there with humid bow
Waters the odorous banks, that blow
Flowers of more mingled hue
Than her purfled scarf can shew,
And drenches with Elysian dew—
List, mortals, if your ears be true—
Beds of hyacinths and roses,
Where young Adonis oft reposes,
Waxing well of his deep wound
In slumbers soft, and on the ground
Sadly sits th' Assyrian queen;
But far above in spangled sheen
Celestial Cupid, her famed son, advanced,
Holds his dear Psyche sweet entranced
After her wand'ring labors long,
Till free consent the gods among
Make her his eternal bride,
And from her fair unspotted side
Two blissful twins are to be born,
Youth and Joy; so Jove hath sworn.
    But now my task is smoothly done,
I can fly or I can run,
Quickly to the green earth's end,
Where the bowed welkin slow doth bend
And from thence can soar as soon

crispèd] ruffled by the breeze   Nard, cassia] Spikenard, cinnamon   blow] make to
blossom   purfled] embroidered   advanced] elevated

To the corners of the moon.
  Mortals that would follow me,
Love Virtue, she alone is free;
She can teach ye how to climb
Higher than the sphery chime;
Or if Virtue feeble were,
Heaven itself would stoop to her.

⌘

On his Blindness

When I consider how my light is spent,   :
  Ere half my days in this dark world and wide,
  And that one talent which is death to hide
Lodged with me useless, though my soul more bent
To serve therewith my Maker, and present
  My true account, lest he returning chide,
  'Doth God exact day-labor, light denied?'
I fondly ask. But patience, to prevent
That murmur, soon replies, 'God doth not need
  Either man's work or his own gifts. Who best
Bear his mild yoke, they serve him best. His state
  Is kingly: thousands at his bidding speed,
And post o'er land and ocean without rest;
  They also serve who only stand and wait.'

fondly] foolishly

IX

THE DEVOTIONAL LYRISTS

Chiefly

1630–1680

THE DEVOTIONAL LYRISTS

It has been declared by various critics, and on various grounds, that the expression of religious emotion cannot be poetry. One must admit that all too frequently it is not. The believer, no matter how fine an artist, has a natural impulse toward spiritual exhortation, moral admonition, even doctrinal controversy, and by yielding to it may destroy that elusive quality called poetry. The term 'devotional' is intended to distinguish the lyrics of the present section from religious writing which is intended to convert or to teach. Even about devotional poetry, however, critical doubt has been expressed. 'The intercourse between God and the human soul,' says Dr. Johnson, 'cannot be poetical. . . . The ideas of Christian theology are too simple for eloquence, too sacred for fiction, and too majestic for ornament.' But he cannot have been thinking of the seventeenth century, for the lyrics which follow are a living refutation of his theory. Devotional poetry is not impossible. It *is* difficult and rare: it is achieved only when the most genuine ecstasy is united to the simplest of art. Historically, it emerges in its perfection when the souls of men are stirred to their depths by the conflict of religious doubt and faith, as they were in the Victorian Age and, even more profoundly, in the middle decades of the seventeenth century. Among the lyrics of the last-named period are many of an artistic beauty and a sincerity and intensity of feeling that any lover of poetry, believer or unbeliever, can appreciate.

Religious poetry in English is as old as our literature. Within our present period, a long line of poets had been inspired by that union of genuine devotion with the highest form of lyrical expression found in the Psalms of David, and had attempted to express these greatest of sacred songs in English paraphrase. There had likewise been a steady stream of popular religious poetry, original in substance though often expressed in Biblical style and phrase, here represented in the three lyrics of Robert Southwell (pp. 468–9). Southwell

479

was a Jesuit missionary whose activities during the religious agitation of the early 1590's caused him to be imprisoned, racked, and at last hanged as a traitor. His writing, like his life, was a means to the worship of God and to the uplift of the human soul, and his books, published after his death in 1595, sold widely among readers of both faiths. The popularity of his verse, obvious though much of it is in thought, and homely and old-fashioned in meter, is not difficult to understand, for he had a fervid and ingenious imagination, as is evident in so vivid and truly inspired a lyric as *The Burning Babe*. Interestingly enough in view of what was to come, Southwell, though deaf to other poetical fashions of his day, shows marked traces of the Sidneian conceit. *A Memento for Mortality* p. 493), long attributed to Beaumont, and the anonymous *Victorious time* (p. 489) show how readily the old pagan theme of *Sic transit gloria mundi* might take on, in the mind of a seventeenth-century Christian as in that of an ancient Hebrew psalmist, a religious coloring.

The prevalence of religious themes in the seventeenth-century lyric is illustrated in several sections of the book. *A stranger here* (p. 304), *Upon my lap my sovereign sits* (p. 308), *Yet if his majesty, our sovereign Lord* (p. 314), and *Come, honest sexton* (p. 316) are examples drawn not only from popular collections of hymns but also from secular song-books. Also among the metaphysical followers of Donne will be found devotional lyrics such as Habington's *When I survey the bright celestial sphere* (p. 357) and Marvell's *The Coronet* and *The Bermudas,* the latter especially fine in their employment of the same lovely imagery from nature which characterizes Marvell's secular work. Four pieces from Herrick's *Noble Numbers* —*His Prayer for Absolution, A Thanksgiving to God for his House, His Creed,* and *Grace for a Child*—are allowed to stand where he dutifully placed them, at the end of the 'unbaptizèd rhymes, Writ in my wild, unhallowed times' (pp. 406–9). If they lack the naturalness and abandon of the best of his *Hesperides,* they none the less exemplify the clarity and design he learned from Jonson; and *A Thanksgiving to God for his House* is one of the simplest, most human and moving poems in our language. Milton's sonnet *When I consider how my light is spent* (p. 475) is but one of many in

which the form of the Petrarchan love plaint was put by him to a
new and nobler purpose, and hackneyed Biblical phrases were somehow made to convey a new weight of thoughtful faith and passionate
self-dedication.

The great line of seventeenth-century devotional poets begins with
Donne, and the greatest of them, Herbert and Crashaw, exhibit his
influence to a marked degree. Donne's *Divine Poems* rank with
his *Songs and Sonets* as his highest poetic achievement. The *Holy
Sonnets,* of which three are quoted (pp. 489–91), were written
during the time when the shock of his wife's sudden death had
turned his deepest feelings heavenward; and the *Hymn to God, my
God, in my Sickness* could not be more vivid if it had actually been
written in the expectation of death. In his religious work, as has
been said, Donne is the same kind of poet as in the *Songs and
Sonets:* the theme is changed, the weight of passion is urging him to
a different goal, but the mind and art are the same. Here as of old
are impetuous, triumphant opening lines:

> At the round earth's imagined corners, blow
> Your trumpets, angels;

> Death, be not proud, though some have callèd thee
> Mighty and dreadful, for thou art not so.

Here are the same quaint, vivid conceits:

> Since I am coming to that holy room
> Where with thy choir of saints for evermore
> I shall be made thy music, as I come
> I tune the instrument here at the door.

Here in *A Hymn to God the Father* is the sinuous mind still playing with the facets of an idea. Here, above all, is the intense subjectivity, the 'naked, thinking heart,' that so fascinates the elect who
come to know it. It is not hard to understand why such a combination of qualities should prove irresistible to later religious poets, and
in particular to Donne's friend and protégé, George Herbert.

Herbert was a gentleman by birth and a rare scholar. He was
strongly drawn in early manhood to the life of a courtier and man
of the world. His poetry is a record of conflict, and of many re-

submissions to the divine love. His volume *The Temple,* published soon after his death in 1633, attained immediate popularity for its sincere faith, its metrical facility, variety, and appropriateness, but above all for its power to raise intimate personal emotion into the sphere of the universal and make of it a thing of new beauty and significance. Herbert's is not the ecstasy of the mystic, but rather the piety of one devoted to the spirit and ceremonies of the Church. His best poems have a logical groundwork learned from Donne, and like Donne he can unite strong feeling with clarity of thought; but his mind is far less complex, and his conceits are neither extended nor subtle. In such pieces as *The Pulley* and *The Collar,* the homely symbols of the power of God's love to lift or to restrain are used only in the titles, and the poems are quite intelligible without them. Even more naive is his use of acrostics, anagrams, and shaped verses. But such puerilities can be forgotten in, when they are not justified by, the depth and sincerity of his spiritual fervor.[1]

Richard Crashaw fell at Cambridge under the influence of the same Nicholas Ferrar in whose hands the dying Herbert had left the publication of *The Temple.* Ferrar, notable in science and a successful merchant, had forsaken the world and formed a small religious community at Little Giddings, where he sought to lead a spiritual life in accord with the principles of the Anglican Church, and the young poet came to share his ideals. After the outbreak of the Civil War, Crashaw fled abroad, and he died a priest of the Church of Rome. In token of his discipleship to Herbert, Crashaw named his volume of religious poems *Steps to the Temple,* but he is a poet of a very different sort. Naturally predisposed to that intense and sensuous visualization of religious scenes and personages which characterizes the Roman Church, he gave himself especially to mystical contemplation of the life of Saint Teresa. He early denounced those who would dissociate art from religion. He turns the passions of earth to worship and identifies the spiritual and the material in his devotion. In him are some of the excesses of the completely unworldly man; his writing is full of extravagances and

---

[1] A *tour de force* such as *Easter Wings* (p. 496), where the fall and rise of the song and of the soul of man are involved with the shortening and lengthening of the lines in a remarkable triple symbolism, has something more than ingenuity to recommend it.

of grave lapses in taste. But he is also capable of a sustained rhapsodic flight, of a splendor and warmth of color and light unknown to Herbert. His verse is full of conceit, but conceit based upon sensations rather than upon intellectualized abstractions. In the closing lines of *The Flaming Heart,* probably his most perfect achievement, he rises above conceit altogether. Of logical progress and design he has scarcely any.

Like all true rhapsodists, Crashaw does not lend himself to brief quotation, and cannot be fully appreciated in selections from his work. He requires to be read as he wrote, in great intoxicated draughts of dizzy emotion. His well-known *Wishes to his Supposed Mistress,* one of a small number of secular poems published with *Steps to the Temple,* is an exception to this rule. It begins with the oft-quoted invocation:

> Whoe'er she be,
> That not impossible she,
> That shall command my heart and me;

> Where'er she lie,
> Locked up from mortal eye,
> In shady leaves of destiny:

> Till that ripe birth,
> Of studied fate stand forth
> And teach her fair steps tread our earth;

> Till that divine
> Idea take a shrine
> Of crystal flesh, through which to shine:

> Meet you her, my wishes,
> Bespeak her to my blisses,
> And be ye called, my absent kisses.

Then follow his wishes—for beauty without artifice, in cheeks and eyes and tresses; for warmth and sensitiveness of heart without wantonness; for Sidneian showers of sweet discourse—in charming profusion, so that from them every reader who dreams of 'that not impossible she' may piece together a vision of his own. It is a charming and original bit of Platonism and deserves its fame.

To be named with Herbert and Crashaw among the greatest devotional poets of the century is Henry Vaughan, who signed himself 'Silurist,' or Welshman. He was a friend of Randolph, Cartwright, and Habington, and began to write in the style of Jonson and of Donne. The publication of a volume of secular verse was succeeded, however, by long years of religious study and contemplation, culminating in the production of two important volumes of religious poetry under the title of *Silex Scintillans* (1650, 1655). Though in many respects a disciple of Herbert, whose themes, phrases, metrical effects, and even titles, he borrowed, Vaughan struck out a new and original subject of religious contemplation— the relation of God and man as revealed in external nature. In his conception of the goodness of God as revealed to man in His works, his loving appreciation of nature's beauties, and his ethical insight and high seriousness, he is clearly the precursor of Wordsworth, who is known to have read Vaughan's works. Vaughan's realism in detail is based not only upon a close observation of nature but upon a sympathy and love extending to all living creatures. Like Crashaw he is a mystic, but his mysticism is normally more meditative, less emotional, than Crashaw's. At times, however, he is stirred to the inner deeps of his nature. The magnificent simplicity of his vision of eternity 'like a great ring of pure and endless light' carries conviction such as few mystical poems can command. Despite the narrowness of his theology, and the imperfect artistic sense and halting execution which make his writing unequal, Vaughan is at times a great poet.

As late as 1897, another devotional poet of the period, comparable in fervency to the great trio discussed above, though humbler in attainment, was discovered through the appearance on a London book-stall of two anonymous manuscripts of poetry and prose meditations. The author was identified as Thomas Traherne, son of a shoemaker in Hereford, who took the degree of B. A. at Oxford in 1656. Like Vaughan, Traherne retired to the country for a period of meditation. Determining upon a regimen of plain living and high thinking, he set himself to speculate upon the attainment of happiness, and arrived at the conclusion that its secret is something we are born with and lose, and that to achieve it we must return to the clearer vision of childhood. The theory is easily recognized as substantially that which has been given immortal form in Blake's *Songs of Innocence* and Wordsworth's *Intimations of Immortality*. There is a quality of cheerfulness about Traherne's devotion that makes him pleasant to read, though he lacked the ecstatic vision of Vaughan, the flaming imagination of Crashaw, and the breadth, as well as the metrical tact, of Herbert.

Francis Quarles was one of the first, and long remained by far the most popular, of what may be termed the devotional pamphlet-eers. His *Sion's Elegies* (1624) and *Sion's Sonnets* (1625) are sequences of 'divine sonnets' like those of Constable and Breton at the close of the previous century, but more immediately inspired by Wither's *Hymns and Songs of the Church*. But Quarles' most famous work is his *Emblems* (1635), probably the most popular book of verse published during the century. It is still reprinted for religious edification, with reproductions of the hideous allegorical woodcuts of the original edition. Quarles' verse is grotesquely figurative, allegorical, and enigmatic, overgrown with conceits and repetitious verbiage, and impaired by slovenly versification. At moments, however, the gauds and baubles of his ordinary poetic diction drop away and he writes with manly directness. If we may judge by the innumerable editions, he gave precisely the solace and moral support most welcome to thousands of his fellow countrymen in a troubled age.

The name of Edmund Waller, author of the noble lyric *Of the Last Verses in the Book*,[2] with its immortal tribute to the wisdom and prescience of old age,

> The soul's dark cottage, battered and decayed,
> Lets in new light through chinks that time has made;

figures also among the Cavalier poets to whom the last section of our anthology is devoted. The circumstance is suggestive. It is but one of many illustrations, and by no means the most extreme, of the contradictions and incongruities which make the seventeenth-century mind so fascinating and reveal the extent to which it was divided against itself. Devotion and cynicism, spirituality and license,

[2] Believed to have been written in his eightieth year.

mysticism and worldliness, morality and coarse wit, perfect taste and gross filth, are everywhere side by side in this amazing age, not only as between the writing of various groups, but within the work of the same man. Facile historians have found it convenient to divide all England into the hostile camps of Puritan and Cavalier, and to consider all the former as hypocrites, and all the latter as good loyal men, or—as is more usual in our country—to believe all supporters of the King utterly misguided and to assume that the virtues flourished in the Puritan party alone. Hence it is interesting to note that, among the devotional poets of the age, Habington and Crashaw were Romanists; Wither, Milton, and Marvell were Puritans; and all the others were members of the Established Church. The spirit of devotion in verse rose superior to the narrowness of dogma. With the return of Charles, the popularity of religious verse decreased, controversial prose coming more and more to take its place with devout readers. A few lesser poets of conservative taste continued to cultivate 'divine poetry' till the end of the century, and the Restoration Age was still to hear the loftiest poetical utterances which the English Muse has devoted to religion, the great epics of Milton. Meanwhile, the troubled decades spanned by the work of Herbert, Crashaw, Vaughan, and Traherne, including that which saw the publication of such gross miscellanies as *Wit and Drollery, Musarum Deliciæ,* and *Parnassus Biceps,* had given us a body of devotional poetry of a quantity and quality unequaled in any other half-century of our literature!

ROBERT SOUTHWELL (*c.* 1561–1595)

Times Go by Turns

The loppèd tree in time may grow again;
    Most naked plants renew both fruit and flower;
The sorriest wight may find release of pain,
    The driest soil suck in some moist'ning shower;
Times go by turns and chances change by course,
From foul to fair, from better hap to worse.

The sea of fortune doth not ever flow,
  She draws her favors to the lowest ebb;
Her tide hath equal times to come and go,
  Her loom doth weave the fine and coarsest web;
No joy so great but runneth to an end,
No hap so hard but may in fine amend.

Not always fall of leaf nor ever spring,
  No endless night, yet not eternal day;
The saddest birds a season find to sing,
  The roughest storm a calm may soon allay;
Thus with succeeding turns God tempereth all,
That man may hope to rise, yet fear to fall.

A chance may win that by mischance was lost;
  The net that holds no great, takes little fish;
In some things all, in all things none are crossed;
  Few all they need, but none have all they wish;
Unmeddled joys here to no man befall,
Who least hath some, who most hath never all.

Scorn Not the Least

Where wards are weak and foes encount'ring strong,
  Where mightier do assault than do defend,
The feebler part puts up enforcèd wrong,
  And silent sees that speech could not amend.
Yet higher powers must think, though they repine,
When sun is set, the little stars will shine.

While pike doth range, the seely tench doth fly,
  And crouch in privy creeks with smaller fish;
Yet pikes are caught when little fish go by,
  These fleet afloat while those do fill the dish.
There is a time even for the worm to creep,
And suck the dew while all her foes do sleep.

in fine] at last   win that] win that which   Unmeddled] Unmixed   wards]
guards   puts up] puts up with   that speech] what speech   seely] simple   go
by] get away

The merlin cannot ever soar on high,
  Nor greedy grayhound still pursue the chase;
The tender lark will find a time to fly,
  And fearful hare to run a quiet race:
He that high growth on cedars did bestow,
Gave also lowly mushrumps leave to grow.

In Aman's pomp poor Mardocheus wept,
  Yet God did turn his fate upon his foe;
The lazar pined while Dives' feast was kept,
  Yet he to heaven, to hell did Dives go.
We trample grass, and prize the flowers of May,
Yet grass is green when flowers do fade away.

The Burning Babe

As I in hoary winter's night
  Stood shivering in the snow,
Surprised I was with sudden heat
  Which made my heart to glow;
And lifting up a fearful eye
  To view what fire was near,
A pretty babe all burning bright
  Did in the air appear;
Who, scorchèd with excessive heat,
  Such floods of tears did shed
As though his floods should quench his flames
  Which with his tears were fed.
'Alas,' quoth he, 'but newly born,
  In fiery heats I fry,
Yet none approach to warm their hearts
  Or feel my fire but I!
My faultless breast the furnace is,
  The fuèl, wounding thorns,
Love is the fire, and sighs the smoke,

Aman, Mardocheus] Haman, Mordecai, in *Esther,* chapter IV.   lazar] leper   fry]
burn

The ashes, shame and scorns.
The fuel justice layeth on,
  And mercy blows the coals,
The metal in this furnace wrought
  Are men's defilèd souls,
For which, as now on fire I am
  To work them to their good,
So will I melt into a bath
  To wash them in my blood.'
With this he vanished out of sight
  And swiftly shrunk away;
And straight I callèd unto mind
  That it was Christmas day.

ANONYMOUS (Early Seventeenth Century)

Victorious Time

Victorious Time, whose wingèd feet do fly
More swift than· eagles in the azure sky,
Haste to thy prey, why art thou tardy now
When all things to thy powerful fate do bow?
O give an end to cares and killing fears,
Shake thy dull sand, unravel those few years
Are yet untold, since naught but discontents
Clouds all our earthly joy with sad laments,
That, when thy nimble hours shall cease to be,
We may be crowned with blest eternity.

JOHN DONNE (1572–1631)

From *Holy Sonnets*

VII

At the round earth's imagined corners, blow
Your trumpets, angels; and arise, arise

Are] Which are (l. 20)

From death, you numberless infinities
Of souls, and to your scattered bodies go;
All whom the flood did, and fire shall o'erthrow,
All whom war, dearth, age, agues, tyrannies,
Despair, law, chance hath slain, and you whose eyes
Shall behold God and never taste death's woe.
But let them sleep, Lord, and me mourn a space,
For if above all these my sins abound,
'Tis late to ask abundance of thy grace
When we are there; here on this lowly ground
    Teach me how to repent; for that's as good
    As if thou hadst sealed my pardon with thy blood.

X

Death, be not proud, though some have callèd thee
Mighty and dreadful, for thou art not so;
For those whom thou think'st thou dost overthrow
Die not, poor Death, nor yet canst thou kill me.
From rest and sleep, which but thy pictures be,
Much pleasure; then from thee much more must flow,
And soonest our best men with thee do go,
Rest of their bones, and soul's delivery.
Thou art slave to fate, chance, kings, and desperate men,
And dost with poison, war, and sickness dwell;
And poppy or charms can make us sleep as well
And better than thy stroke; why swell'st thou then?
    One short sleep past, we wake eternally,
    And death shall be no more; Death, thou shalt die.

XIII

What if this present were the world's last night?
Mark in my heart, O soul, where thou dost dwell,
The picture of Christ crucified, and tell
Whether that countenance can thee affright:
Tears in his eyes quench the amazing light,

Rest] Thou rest   swell'st thou] art thou puffed up?   amazing] terrifying

Blood fills his frowns, which from his pierced head fell.
And can that tongue adjudge thee unto hell,
Which prayed forgiveness for his foes' fierce spite?
No, no; but as in my idolatry
I said to all my profane mistresses,
Beauty, of pity, foulness only is
A sign of rigor; so I say to thee:
　　To wicked spirits are horrid shapes assigned;
　　This beauteous form assures a piteous mind.

✳

Hymn to God, my God, in my Sickness

Since I am coming to that holy room
　Where, with thy choir of saints for evermore,
I shall be made thy music, as I come
　I tune the instrument here at the door,
　And what I must do then, think here before.

Whilst my physicians by their love are grown
　Cosmographers, and I their map, who lie
Flat on this bed, that by them may be shown
　That this is my south-west discovery,
　Per fretum febris, by these straits to die,

I joy, that in these straits I see my west;
　For though their currents yield return to none,
What shall my west hurt me?　As west and east
　In all flat maps—and I am one—are one,
　So death doth touch the resurrection.

Is the Pacific sea my home? or are
　The eastern riches? is Jerusalem?
Anyan and Magellan and Gibraltar,

foulness] ugliness　rigor] severity　spirits] one syllable　*Per fretum febris*]
'Through the raging of fever', with a play on *fretum,* 'a strait'　riches] realms
Anyan] Bering

All straits, and none but straits, are ways to them,
Whether where Japhet dwelt, or Cham, or Shem.

We think that Paradise and Calvary,
    Christ's cross and Adam's tree, stood in one place;
Look, Lord, and find both Adams met in me:
    As the first Adam's sweat surrounds my face,
    May the last Adam's blood my soul embrace.

So, in his purple wrapped, receive me, Lord;
    By these, his thorns, give me his other crown;
And as to others' souls I preached thy word,
    Be this my text, my sermon to mine own:
    Therefore that he may raise, the Lord throws down.

A Hymn to God the Father

Wilt thou forgive that sin where I begun,
    Which was my sin, though it were done before?
Wilt thou forgive that sin, through which I run,
    And do run still, though still I do deplore?
        When thou hast done, thou hast not done,
            For I have more.

Wilt thou forgive that sin which I have won
    Others to sin, and made my sin their door?
Wilt thou forgive that sin which I did shun
    A year or two, but wallowed in, a score?
        When thou hast done, thou hast not done,
            For I have more.

I have a sin of fear, that when I have spun
    My last thread, I shall perish on the shore;
But swear by thyself, that at my death thy Son
    Shall shine, as he shines now and heretofore:
        And, having done that, thou hast done,
            I fear no more.

ANONYMOUS (Before 1619)

A Memento for Mortality

*Taken from the View of Sepulchers in the Abbey of
Westminster*

Mortality, behold and fear!
What a change of flesh is here!
Think how many royal bones
Sleep within this heap of stones,
Hence removed from beds of ease,
Dainty fare, and what might please,
Fretted roofs, and costly shows,
To a roof that flats the nose:
Which proclaims all flesh is grass,
How the world's fair glories pass;
That there is no trust in health,
In youth, in age, in greatness, wealth:
For if such could have reprived,
Those had been immortal-lived.
Know from this the world's a snare,
How that greatness is but care,
How all pleasures are but pain,
And how short they do remain:
For here they lie had realms and lands,
That now want strength to stir their hands;
Where from their pulpits sealed with dust
They preach, 'In greatness is no trust.'
Here's an acre sown indeed
With the richest royal seed
That the earth did e'er suck in
Since the first man died for sin;
Here the bones of birth have cried
'Though gods they were, as men have died.'
Here are sands, ignoble things,

A Memento for Mortality] Grierson in *Oxford Book of Seventeenth Century Verse,*
p. 240, suggests William Basse as the author.   Fretted] Carved   reprived] postponed death   had realms] who had realms   birth] high birth

Dropped from the ruined sides of kings;
With whom the poor man's earth being shown,
The difference is not easily known.
Here's a world of pomp and state
Forgotten, dead, disconsolate.
Think then this scythe that mows down kings,
Exempts no meaner mortal things.
Then bid the wanton lady tread
Amid these mazes of the dead;
And these, truly understood,
More shall cool and quench the blood
Than her many sports a-day,
And her nightly wanton play:
Bid her paint till day of doom,
To this favor she must come.
Bid the merchant gather wealth,
The usurer exact by stealth,
The proud man beat it from his thought—
Yet to this shape all must be brought.

GEORGE HERBERT (1593–1633)

To his Mother

As a New Year's Gift from Cambridge

My God, where is that ancient heat towards thee
Wherewith whole shoals of martyrs once did burn,
Besides their other flames? Doth poetry
Wear Venus' livery, only serve her turn?
Why are not sonnets made of thee, and lays
Upon thine altar burnt? Cannot thy love
Heighten a spirit to sound out thy praise
As well as any she? Cannot thy dove
Outstrip their Cupid easily in flight?
Or, since thy ways are deep, and still the same,
Will not a verse run smooth that bears thy name?

favor] appearance

Why doth that fire, which by thy power and might
Each breast does feel, no braver fuel choose
Than that which one day worms may chance refuse?

The Altar

A broken altar, Lord, thy servant rears,
Made of a heart and cèmented with tears;
Whose parts are as thy hand did frame;
No workman's tool hath touched the same.
A heart alone
Is such a stone
As nothing but
Thy power doth cut.
Wherefore each part
Of my hard heart
Meets in this frame
To praise thy name;
That if I chance to hold my peace,
These stones to praise thee may not cease.
O, let thy blessed sacrifice · be mine,
And sanctify this altar to be thine.

Redemption

Having been tenant long to a rich Lord,
Not thriving, I resolvèd to be bold,
And make a suit unto him to afford
A new small-rented lease and cancel th' old.
In heaven at his manor I him sought.
They told me there that he was lately gone
About some land which he had dearly bought
Long since on earth, to take possessiòn.
I straight returned, and knowing his great birth,
Sought him accordingly in great resorts,
In cities, theaters, gardens, parks, and courts.

At length I heard a ragged noise and mirth
Of thieves and murderers; there I him espied,
Who straight, 'Your suit is granted,' said, and died.

Easter Wings

Lord, who createdst man in wealth and store,
Though foolishly he lost the same,
Decaying more and more
Till he became
Most poor;
With thee
O, let me rise
As larks, harmoniously,
And sing this day thy victories;
Then shall the fall further the flight in me.

My tender age in sorrow did begin;
And still with sicknesses and shame
Thou didst so punish sin,
That I became
Most thin.
With thee
Let me combine,
And feel this day thy victory;
For if I imp my wing on thine,
Affliction shall advance the flight in me.

Jordan

Who says that fictions only and false hair
Become a verse? Is there in truth no beauty?
Is all good structure in a winding stair?

the fall] of man   further . . . me] lengthen my flight   imp . . . on] strengthen
by mending . . . with   Jordan] Perhaps the river symbolizes his turning from the
intricacies of amorous verse to the simplicity of religious feeling.

May no lines pass except they do their duty
   Not to a true, but painted chair?

Is it no verse except enchanted groves
And sudden arbors shadow coarse-spun lines?
Must purling streams refresh a lover's loves?
Must all be veiled, while he that reads, divines,
   Catching the sense at two removes?

Shepherds are honest people; let them sing.
Riddle who list for me, and pull for prime;
I envy no man's nightingale or spring;
Nor let them punish me with loss of rhyme,
   Who plainly say, 'My God, my King.'

Employment

   If as a flower doth spread and die,
      Thou wouldst extend me to some good,
   Before I were by frost's extremity
         Nipped in the bud,

   The sweetness and the praise were thine;
      But the extension and the room
   Which in thy garland I should fill, were mine
         At thy great doom.

   For as thou dost impart thy grace
      The greater shall our glory be.
   The measure of our joys is in this place,
         The stuff with thee.

   Let me not languish, then, and spend
      A life as barren to thy praise
   As is the dust, to which that life doth tend,
         But with delays.

---

painted] feigned   shadow] conceal   divines] conjectures   pull for prime] draw
cards for the winning hand   to thy praise] in praise of thee

All things are busy; only I
Neither bring honey with the bees,
Nor flowers to make that, nor the husbandry
    To water these.

I am no link of thy great chain,
But all my company is a weed.
Lord, place me in thy consort; give one strain
    To my poor reed.

The Windows

Lord, how can man preach thy eternal word?
    He is a brittle crazy glass,
Yet in thy temple thou dost him afford
    This glorious and transcendent place
    To be a window, through thy grace.

But when thou dost anneal in glass thy story,
    Making thy life to shine within
The holy preacher's, then the light and glory
    More rev'rend grows, and more doth win,
    Which else shows wat'rish, bleak, and thin.

Doctrine and life, colors and light in one,
    When they combine and mingle, bring
A strong regard and awe; but speech alone
    Doth vanish like a flaring thing,
    And in the ear, not conscience, ring.

Frailty

Lord, in my silence how do I despise
    What upon trust
Is stylèd honor, riches, or fair eyes,
    But is fair dust!
    I surname them gilded clay,

all . . . weed] I am as a weed among flowers   consort] company of musicians

Dear earth, fine grass or hay;
In all, I think my foot doth ever tread
        Upon their head.

But when I view abroad both regiments,
        The world's and thine,
Thine clad with simpleness and sad events,
        The other fine,
    Full of glory and gay weeds,
    Brave language, braver deeds,
That which was dust before doth quickly rise,
        And prick mine eyes.

O, brook not this, lest if what even now
        My foot did tread
Affront those joys wherewith thou didst endow
        And long since wed
    My poor soul, even sick of love,—
    It may a Babel prove,
Commodious to conquer heaven and thee,
        Planted in me.

Virtue

Sweet day, so cool, so calm, so bright,
The bridal of the earth and sky,
The dew shall weep thy fall tonight,
        For thou must die.

Sweet rose, whose hue angry and brave
Bids the rash gazer wipe his eye,
Thy root is ever in its grave,
        And thou must die.

Sweet spring, full of sweet days and roses,
A box where sweets compacted lie,
My music shows ye have your closes,
        And all must die.

regiments] governments   weeds] garments   Commodious] Sufficient   angry]
red   brave] striking   closes] in music, conclusions, resolutions

Only a sweet and virtuous soul,
Like seasoned timber, never gives,
But though the whole world turn to coal,
    Then chiefly lives.

The Quip

The merry World did on a day
With his train-bands and mates agree
To meet together where I lay,
And all in sport to jeer at me.

First, Beauty crept into a rose,
Which when I plucked not, 'Sir,' said she,
'Tell me, I pray, whose hands are those?'
But thou shalt answer, Lord, for me.

Then Money came, and chinking still,
'What tune is this, poor man?' said he;
'I heard in music you had skill:'
But thou shalt answer, Lord, for me.

Then came brave Glory, puffing by
In silks that whistled, who but he?
He scarce allowed me half an eye:
But thou shalt answer, Lord, for me.

Then came quick Wit and Conversation,
And he would needs a comfort be,
And, to be short, make an oration:
But thou shalt answer, Lord, for me.

Yet when the hour of thy design
To answer these fine things shall come,
Speak not at large, say, I am thine,
And then they have their answer home.

turn to coal] burn to embers   train-bands] citizen soldiers; here, 'comrades'

Life

I made a posy, while the day ran by:
'Here will I smell my remnant out, and tie
      My life within this band;'
But Time did beckon to the flowers, and they
By noon most cunningly did steal away,
      And withered in my hand.

My hand was next to them, and then my heart:
I took, without more thinking, in good part
      Time's gentle admonition,
Who did so sweetly death's sad taste convey,
Making my mind to smell my fatal day,
      Yet sug'ring the suspicion.

Farewell, dear flowers; sweetly your time ye spent,
Fit, while ye lived, for smell or ornament,
      And after death for cures.
I follow straight, without complaints or grief,
Since, if my scent be good, I care not if
      It be as short as yours.

The Collar

I struck the board and cried, 'No more!
      I will abroad.
What? Shall I ever sigh and pine?
My lines and life are free, free as the road,
    Loose as the wind, as large as store.
      Shall I be still in suit?
Have I no harvest but a thorn
To let me blood, and not restore
What I have lost with cordial fruit?
      Sure there was wine
Before my sighs did dry it; there was corn
Before my tears did drown it.

board] table   store] abundance   in suit] waiting for preferment or reward

Is the year only lost to me?
Have I no bays to crown it?
No flowers, no garlands gay? All blasted?
All wasted?
Not so, my heart! But there is fruit,
And thou hast hands.
Recover all thy sigh-blown age
On double pleasures. Leave thy cold dispute
Of what is fit and not. Forsake thy cage,
Thy rope of sands,
Which petty thoughts have made, and made to thee
Good cable, to enforce and draw,
And be thy law,
While thou didst wink and wouldst not see.
Away! Take heed!
I will abroad.
Call in thy death's head there. Tie up thy fears.
He that forbears
To suit and serve his need
Deserves his load.'
But as I raved and grew more fierce and wild
At every word,
Methought I heard one calling, 'Child!'
And I replied, 'My Lord.'

The Pulley

When God at first made man,
Having a glass of blessings standing by,
'Let us,' said he, 'pour on him all we can.
Let the world's riches, which dispersèd lie,
Contract into a span.'

So strength first made a way,
Then beauty flowed, then wisdom, honor, pleasure.
When almost all was out, God made a stay,
Perceiving that alone of all his treasure
Rest in the bottom lay.

'For if I should,' said he,
'Bestow this jewel also on my creature,
He would adore my gifts instead of me,
And rest in nature, not the God of nature;
    So both should losers be.

'Yet let him keep the rest,
But keep them with repining restlessness.
Let him be rich and weary, that at least
If goodness lead him not, yet weariness
    May toss him to my breast.'

Love

Love bade me welcome, yet my soul drew back,
    Guilty of dust and sin.
But quick-eyed Love, observing me grow slack
    From my first entrance in,
Drew nearer to me, sweetly questioning
    If I lacked anything.

'A guest,' I answered, 'worthy to be here.'
    Love said, 'You shall be he.'
'I, the unkind, ungrateful? ah, my dear,
    I cannot look on thee.'
Love took my hand and smiling did reply,
    'Who made the eyes but I?'

'Truth, Lord, but I have marred them; let my shame
    Go where it doth deserve.'
'And know you not,' says Love, 'who bore the blame?'
    'My dear, then I will serve.'
'You must sit down,' says Love, 'and taste my meat.'
    So I did sit and eat.

serve] wait at the table

RICHARD CRASHAW (1613?–1649)

In the Holy Nativity

A Hymn Sung as by the Shepherds

Chorus.

Come, we shepherds whose blest sight
Hath met love's noon in nature's night,
Come, lift we up our loftier song
And wake the sun that lies too long.

To all our world of well-stol'n joy
  He slept, and dreamt of no such thing,
While we found out heaven's fairer eye,
  And kissed the cradle of our King;
Tell him he rises now too late
To show us aught worth looking at.

Tell him we now can show him more
  Than he e'er showed to mortal sight,
Than he himself e'er saw before,
  Which to be seen needs not his light:
Tell him, Tityrus, where th' hast been,
Tell him, Thyrsis, what th' hast seen.

Tityrus.

Gloomy night embraced the place
  Where the noble infant lay:
The babe looked up, and showed his face:
  In spite of darkness it was day.
It was thy day, sweet, and did rise,
Not from the east but from thine eyes.

Chorus. It was thy day, sweet, &c.

Thyrsis.

Winter chid aloud, and sent
  The angry North to wage his wars:
The North forgot his fierce intent,

And left perfumes instead of scars.
By those sweet eyes' persuasive powers,
Where he meant frost he scattered flowers.

Chorus. By those sweet eyes, &c.

Both.

We saw thee in thy balmy nest,
   Young dawn of our eternal day;
We saw thine eyes break from the east,
   And chase the trembling shades away:
We saw thee, and we blessed the sight,
We saw thee by thine own sweet light.

Tityrus.

'Poor world,' said I, 'what wilt thou do
   To entertain this starry stranger?
Is this the best thou canst bestow—
   A cold and not too cleanly manger?
Contend, the powers of heav'n and earth,
To fit a bed for this huge birth.

Chorus. Contend, the powers, &c.

Thyrsis.

'Proud world,' said I, 'cease your contèst,
   And let the mighty babe alone,
The phœnix builds the phœnix' nest,
   Love's architecture is his own.
The babe whose birth embraves this morn
Made his own bed ere he was born.'

Chorus. The babe whose birth, &c.

Tityrus.

I saw the curled drops, soft and slow,
   Come hovering o'er the place's head,
Off'ring their whitest sheets of snow,
   To furnish the fair infant's bed.
'Forbear,' said I, 'be not too bold;
Your fleece is white, but 'tis too cold.'

embraves] beautifies   curled drops] rounded flakes

Chorus. Forbear, said I, &c.

Thyrsis.

I saw the obsequious seraphims
  Their rosy fleece of fire bestow,
For well they now can spare their wings,
  Since heaven itself lies here below.
'Well done,' said I; 'but are you sure
Your down, so warm, will pass for pure?'
  Chorus. Well done, said I, &c.

Both.

No, no, your King's not yet to seek
  Where to repose his royal head;
See, see how soon his new-bloomed cheek
  'Twixt's mother's breasts is gone to bed.
'Sweet choice,' said we, 'no way but so
Not to lie cold, yet sleep in snow!'
  Chorus. Sweet choice, said we, &c.

Full Chorus.

Welcome all wonders in one sight!
  Eternity shut in a span!
Summer in winter! day in night!
  Heaven in earth! and God in man!
Great little one, whose all-embracing birth
Lifts earth to heaven, stoops heaven to earth!

Welcome, though nor to gold nor silk,
  To more than Cæsar's birthright is:
Two sister seas of virgin-milk,
  With many a rarely-tempered kiss,
That breathes at once both maid and mother,
Warms in the one, cools in the other.

She sings thy tears asleep, and dips
  Her kisses in thy weeping eye;
She spreads the red leaves of thy lips,
  That in their buds yet blushing lie.

stoops] causes to stoop

She 'gainst those mother-diamonds tries
The points of her young eagle's eyes.

Welcome—though not to those gay flies,
   Gilded i' th' beams of earthly kings,
Slippery souls in smiling eyes—
   But to poor shepherds' homespun things,
Whose wealth's their flock, whose wit to be
Well read in their simplicity.

Yet when young April's husband showers
   Shall bless the fruitful Maia's bed,
We'll bring the first-born of her flowers,
   To kiss thy feet, and crown thy head.
To thee, dread Lamb! whose love must keep
The shepherds more than they the sheep,

To thee, meek Majesty, soft King
   Of simple graces and sweet loves,
Each of us his lamb will bring,
   Each his pair of silver doves;
Till burnt at last, in fire of thy fair eyes,
Ourselves become our own best sacrifice.

The Flaming Heart

*Upon the Book and Picture of the Seraphical Saint Teresa, as
She is usually expressed with a Seraphim Beside Her*

O heart, the equal poise of love's both parts,
Big alike with wounds and darts,
Live in these conquering leaves; live all the same,
And walk through all tongues, one triumphant flame;
Live here, great heart, and love and die and kill,
And bleed and wound, and yield and conquer still.
Let this immortal life, where'er it comes,

---

mother-diamonds] her own eyes   points] eyebeams   *The Flaming Heart*] the final
third of the poem.   The earlier portion is of different, and inferior, quality.

Walk in a crowd of loves and martyrdoms.
Let mystic deaths wait on 't, and wise souls be
The love-slain witnesses of this life of thee.

O sweet incendiary! show here thy art,
Upon this carcase of a hard cold heart,
Let all thy scattered shafts of light, that play
Among the leaves of thy large books of day,
Combined against this breast, at once break in
And take away from me my self and sin;
This gracious robbery shall thy bounty be,
And my best fortunes such fair spoils of me.
O thou undaunted daughter of desires!
By all thy dower of lights and fires,
By all the eagle in thee, all the dove,
By all thy lives and deaths of love,
By thy large draughts of intellectual day,
And by thy thirsts of love more large than they,
By all thy brim-filled bowls of fierce desire,
By thy last morning's draught of liquid fire,
By the full kingdom of that final kiss
That seized thy parting soul and sealed thee his,
By all the heav'ns thou hast in him,
Fair sister of the seraphim!
By all of him we have in thee,
Leave nothing of myself in me:
Let me so read thy life that I
Unto all life of mine may die.

A Song of Divine Love

Lord, when the sense of thy sweet grace
Sends up my soul to seek thy face,
Thy blessed eyes breed such desire
I die in love's delicious fire.
O love, I am thy sacrifice,
Be still triumphant, blessèd eyes;
Still shine on me, fair suns, that I
Still may behold though still I die.

Though still I die, I live again,
Still longing so to be still slain;
So gainful is such loss of breath,
I die even in desire of death.
Still live in me this loving strife
Of living death and dying life:
For while thou sweetly slayest me,
Dead to myself, I live in thee.

On the Assumption of the Virgin Mary

Hark! she is called, the parting hour is come;
Take thy farewell, poor world. Heaven must go home.
A piece of heavenly earth; purer and brighter
Than the chaste stars, whose choice lamps come to light
    her,
Whilst through the crystal orbs, clearer than they,
She climbs, and makes a far more milky way.
She's called; hark how the dear immortal dove
Sighs to his silver mate, 'Rise up, my love,
        Rise up, my fair, my spotless one,
        The winter's past, the rain is gone;
        The spring is come, the flowers appear,
        No sweets, save thou, are wanting here.
            Come away, my love,
            Come away, my dove,
                Cast off delay;
            The court of heaven is come
            To wait upon thee home;
                Come, come away!
                The flowers appear,
        Or quickly would, wert thou once here.
        The spring is come, or if it stay
        'Tis to keep time with thy delay.
The rain is gone, except so much as we
Detain in needful tears to weep the want of thee.
                The winter's past,
                Or if he make less haste,

His answer is, Why, she does so;
If summer come not, how can winter go?
Come away, come away!
The shrill winds chide, the waters weep thy stay,
The fountains murmur, and each loftiest tree
Bows lowest his leafy top to look for thee.
Come away, my love,
Come away, my dove,' &c.
She's called again. And will she go?
When heaven bids come, who can say no?
Heaven calls her, and she must away,
Heaven will not, and she cannot stay.
Go then; go, glorious on the golden wings
Of the bright youth of heaven, that sings
Under so sweet a burden. Go,
Since thy dread son will have it so.
And while thou goest, our song and we
Will, as we may, reach after thee.
Hail, holy queen of humble hearts!
We in thy praise will have our parts.
And though thy dearest looks must now give light
To none but the blest heavens, whose bright
Beholders, lost in sweet delight,
Feed for ever their fair sight
With those divinest eyes, which we
And our dark world no more shall see;
Though our poor joys are parted so,
Yet shall our lips never let go
Thy gracious name, but to the last
Our loving song shall hold it fast.
Thy precious name shall be
Thyself to us, and we
With holy care will keep it by us.
We to the last
Will hold it fast,
And no assumption shall deny us.
All the sweetest showers
Of our fairest flowers

Will we strow upon it.
    Though our sweets cannot make
    It sweeter, they can take
    Themselves new sweetness from it.
    'Maria,' men and angels sing,
    'Maria, mother of our king.
Live, rosy princess, live, and may the bright
Crown of a most incomparable light
Embrace thy radiant brows! O may the best
Of everlasting joys bathe thy white breast.
    Live, our chaste love, the holy mirth
    Of heaven, the humble pride of earth.
    Live, crown of women, queen of men;
    Live, mistress of our song; and when
    Our weak desires have done their best,
    Sweet angels come, and sing the rest.'

An Epitaph upon Husband and Wife,
which Died and were Buried Together

    To these, whom death again did wed,
    This grave's their second marriage-bed;
    For though the hand of fate could force
    'Twixt soul and body a divorce,
    It could not sunder man and wife,
    Because they both lived but one life.
    Peace, good Reader, do not weep.
    Peace, the lovers are asleep.
    They, sweet turtles, folded lie
    In the last knot love could tie.
    And though they lie as they were dead,
    Their pillow stone, their sheets of lead,
    (Pillow hard, and sheets not warm)
    Love made the bed; they'll take no harm.
    Let them sleep: let them sleep on,
    Till this stormy night be gone,
    Till the eternal morrow dawn;

Then the curtains will be drawn
And they wake into a light,
Whose day shall never die in night.

FRANCIS QUARLES (1592–1644)

On the Infancy of our Savior

Hail, blessèd Virgin, full of heavenly grace,
Blest above all that sprang from human race;
Whose heaven-saluted womb brought forth in one,
A blessèd Savior, and a blessèd son:
O, what a ravishment 't had been to see
Thy little Savior perking on thy knee!
To see him nuzzle in thy virgin breast,
His milk-white body all unclad, undressed!
To see thy busy fingers clothe and wrap
His spraddling limbs in thy indulgent lap!
To see his desperate eyes, with childish grace,
Smiling upon his smiling mother's face!
And, when his forward strength began to bloom,
To see him diddle up and down the room!
O, who would think so sweet a babe as this
Should e'er be slain by a false-hearted kiss!
Had I a rag, if sure thy body wore it,
Pardon, sweet Babe, I think I should adore it:
Till then, O grant this boon, a boon far dearer:
The weed not being, I may adore the wearer.

False world, thou ly'st

False world, thou ly'st: thou canst not lend
    The least delight;
Thy favors cannot gain a friend,
    They are so slight;

perking] sitting erect and lively   spraddling] sprawling   desperate] perhaps so
described because of his inevitable martyrdom   forward] growing   diddle] toddle
weed] garment

Thy morning pleasures make an end
    To please at night;
Poor are the wants that thou supply'st,
And yet thou vaunt'st, and yet thou vy'st
With heaven. Fond earth, thou boasts; false world, thou ly'st.

Thy babbling tongue tells golden tales
    Of endless treasure;
Thy bounty offers easy sales
    Of lasting pleasure;
Thou ask'st the conscience what she ails,
    And swear'st to ease her.
There's none can want where thou supply'st;
There's none can give where thou deny'st?
Alas, fond world, thou boasts; false world, thou ly'st.

What well-advisèd ear regards
    What earth can say?
Thy words are gold, but thy rewards
    Are painted clay;
Thy cunning can but pack the cards,
    Thou canst not play
Thy game at weakest, still thou vy'st;
If seen, and then re-vied, deny'st;
Thou art not what thou seem'st; false world, thou ly'st.

Thy tinsel bosom seems a mint
    Of new-coined treasure,
A paradise that has no stint,
    No change, no measure;
A painted cask, but nothing in 't,
    Nor wealth, nor pleasure;
Vain earth! that falsely thus comply'st
With man; vain man! that thus rely'st
On earth; vain man, thou dot'st, vain earth, thou ly'st.

make an end] cease   pack] stack   vy'st . . . seen . . . re-vied] card terms:
stakest . . . called . . . a counter-stake laid or raised   comply'st With] flatterest

What mean dull souls, in this high measure
    To haberdash
In earth's base wares, whose greatest treasure
    Is dross and trash?
The height of whose enchanting pleasure
    Is but a flash?
Are these the goods that thou supply'st
Us mortals with? are these the high'st?
Can these bring cordial peace?   False world, thou ly'st.

Even like two little bank-dividing brooks

Even like two little bank-dividing brooks
    That wash the pebbles with their wanton streams,
And having ranged and searched a thousand nooks,
    Meet both at length in silver-breasted Thames,
      Where in a greater current they conjoin,
So I my best belovèd's am; so he is mine.

Even so we met, and after long pursuit,
    Even so we joined; we both became entire.
No need for either to renew a suit,
    For I was flax, and he was flames of fire.
      Our firm-united souls did more than twine;
So I my best belovèd's am; so he is mine.

If all those glittering monarchs that command
    The servile quarters of this earthly ball
Should tender, in exchange, their shares of land,
    I would not change my fortunes for them all;
      Their wealth is but a counter to my coin;
The world's but theirs; but my belovèd's mine.

Nay more, if the fair Thespian ladies all
    Should heap together their diviner treasure,
That treasure should be deemed a price too small
    To buy a minute's lease of half my pleasure.
      'Tis not the sacred wealth of all the Nine
Can buy my heart from him, or his from being mine.

Nor time, nor place, nor chance, nor death can bow
  My least desires unto the least remove;
He's firmly mine by oath, I his by vow;
  He's mine by faith, and I am his by love;
    He's mine by water, I am his by wine;
Thus I my best belovèd's am; thus he is mine.

He is my altar; I, his holy place;
  I am his guest, and he my living food;
I'm his by penitence, he mine by grace;
  I'm his by purchase, he is mine by blood!
    He's my supporting elm, and I his vine;
Thus I my best belovèd's am; thus he is mine.

He gives me wealth, I give him all my vows;
  I give him songs, he gives me length of days;
With wreaths of grace he crowns my conquering brows,
  And I his temples with a crown of praise,
    Which he accepts as an everlasting sign
That I my best belovèd's am, that he is mine.

HENRY VAUGHAN (1622–1695)

The Search

  'Tis now clear day: I see a rose
  Bud in the bright east, and disclose
  The pilgrim sun. All night have I
  Spent in a roving ecstasy
  To find my Savior; I have been
  As far as Bethlem, and have seen
  His inn and cradle; being there
  I met the wise men, asked them where
  He might be found, or what star can
  Now point him out, grown up a man.
  To Egypt hence I fled, ran o'er
  All her parched bosom to Nile's shore,
  Her yearly nurse; came back, inquired

Amongst the doctors, and desired
To see the temple, but was shown
A little dust, and for the town
A heap of ashes, where some said
A small bright sparkle was a-bed
Which would one day, beneath the pole,
Awake, and then refine the whole.
    Tired here, I came to Sychar; thence
To Jacob's well, bequeathèd since
Unto his sons, where often they
In those calm golden evenings lay,
Wat'ring their flocks, and having spent
Those white days, drove home to the tent
Their well-fleeced train. And here, O fate,
I sit, where once my Savior sate;
The angry spring in bubbles swelled
Which broke in sighs still, as they filled
And whispered, Jesus had been there,
But Jacob's children would not hear.
Loath hence to part, at last I rise
But with the fountain in my eyes,
And here a fresh search is decreed,
He must be found where he did bleed;
I walk the garden, and there see
Ideas of his agony,
And moving anguishments that set
His blest face in a bloody sweat;
I climbed the hill, perused the cross
Hung with my gain and his great loss;
Never did tree bear fruit like this,
Balsam of souls, the body's bliss.
But O, his grave! where I saw lent,
For he had none, a monument,
An undefiled and new-hewed one,
But there was not the corner-stone;
'Sure,' then said I, 'my quest is vain,
He'll not be found where he was slain;

Ideas] Images

So mild a Lamb can never be
'Midst so much blood and cruelty.
I'll to the wilderness, and can
Find beasts more merciful than man;
He lived there safe, 'twas his retreat
From the fierce Jew, and Herod's heat,
And forty days withstood the fell
And high temptatiòns of hell;
With seraphins there talkèd he,
His father's flaming ministry;
He heaven'd their walks, and with his eyes
Made those wild shades a paradise;
Thus was the desert sanctified
To be the refuge of his bride;
I'll thither then; see, it is day,
The sun's broke through to guide my way.'
    But as I urged thus, and writ down
What pleasures should my journey crown,
What silent paths, what shades and cells,
Fair virgin flowers and hallowed wells
I should rove in, and rest my head
Where my dear Lord did often tread,
Sug'ring all dangers with success,
Methought I heard one singing thus:

        'Leave, leave thy gadding thoughts;
                Who pores
                And spies
            Still out of doors,
                Descries
            Within them naught.

        'The skin and shell of things,
                Though fair,
                Are not
            Thy wish nor prayer,
                But got
            By mere despair
                Of wings.

heat] rage

'To rack old elements,
 Or dust,
  And say
 Sure here he must
  Needs stay,
  Is not the way,
  Nor just.

Search well another world: who studies this,
Travels in clouds, seeks manna where none is.'

Peace

My soul, there is a country
 Far beyond the stars,
Where stands a wingèd sentry
 All skillful in the wars;
There above noise and danger
 Sweet peace sits crowned with smiles,
And one born in a manger
 Commands the beauteous files;
He is thy gracious friend,
 And—O my soul, awake!—
Did in pure love descend
 To die here for thy sake.
If thou canst get but thither,
 There grows the flower of peace,
The rose that cannot wither,
 Thy fortress and thy ease;
Leave then thy foolish ranges,
 For none can thee secure
But one who never changes,
 Thy God, thy life, thy cure.

Idle Verse

Go, go, quaint follies, sugared sin,
 Shadow no more my door;

rack] search ranges] wanderings

I will no longer cobwebs spin,
    I'm too much on the score.

For since amidst my youth and night
    My great preserver smiles,
We'll make a match, my only light,
    And join against their wiles;

Blind, desperate fits, that study how
    To dress and trim our shame,
That gild rank poison, and allow
    Vice in a fairer name;

The purls of youthful blood and bowels,
    Lust in the robes of love,
The idle talk·of feverish souls,
    Sick with a scarf or glove;

Let it suffice my warmer days
    Simpered and shined on you,
Twist not my cypress with your bays,
    Or roses with my yew;

Go, go, seek out some greener thing,
    It snows and freezeth here;
Let nightingales attend the spring,
    Winter is all my year.

The World

I saw eternity the other night
Like a great ring of pure and endless light,
    All calm as it was bright;
And round beneath it, time in hours, days, years,
    Driven by the spheres,
Like a vast shadow moved, in which the world
    And all her train were hurled:

on the score] in debt   purls] whirls

The doting lover in his quaintest strain
　　Did there complain;
Near him his lute, his fancy, and his flights,
　　Wit's sour delights,
With gloves and knots, the silly snares of pleasure,
　　Yet his dear treasure,
All scattered lay, while he his eyes did pore
　　Upon a flower.

The darksome statesman, hung with weights and woe,
Like a thick midnight fog moved there so slow
　　He did not stay, nor go;
Condemning thoughts, like sad eclipses, scowl
　　Upon his soul,
And clouds of crying witnesses without
　　Pursued him with one shout;
Yet digged the mole, and lest his ways be found
　　Worked underground,
Where he did clutch his prey, but One did see
　　That policy;
Churches and altars fed him; perjuries
　　Were gnats and flies;
It rained about him blood and tears, but he
　　Drank them as free.

The fearful miser on a heap of rust
Sat pining all his life there, did scarce trust
　　His own hands with the dust,
Yet would not place one piece above, but lives
　　In fear of thieves.
Thousands there were as frantic as himself,
　　And hugged each one his pelf:
The downright epicure placed heaven in sense,
　　And scorned pretense;
While others, slipped into a wide excess,
　　Said little less;

quaintest] most eloquent　　knots] true-love knots　　policy] stratagem　　free]freely

The weaker sort slight trivial wares enslave,
 Who think them brave;
And poor despisèd truth sat counting by
  Their victory.

Yet some, who all this while did weep and sing,
And sing and weep, soared up into the ring;
 But most would use no wing.
'O fools,' said I, 'thus to prefer dark night
  Before true light,
To live in grots and caves, and hate the day
 Because it shows the way,
The way which from this dead and dark abode
  Leads up to God,—
A way where you might tread the sun, and be
  More bright than he.'
But as I did their madness so discuss,
  One whispered thus:
'This ring the bridegroom did for none provide
  But for his bride.'

The Waterfall

With what deep murmurs through time's silent stealth
Doth thy transparent, cool, and wat'ry wealth
  Here flowing fall,
  And chide, and call,
As if his liquid, loose retinue stayed
Ling'ring, and were of this steep place afraid,
  The common pass
  Where, clear as glass,
  All must descend—
  Not to an end,
But quickened by this deep and rocky grave,
Rise to a longer course more bright and brave.

 Dear stream, dear bank, where often I
 Have sat and pleased my pensive eye,
 Why, since each drop of thy quick store

Runs thither whence it flowed before,
Should poor souls fear a shade or night,
Who came, sure, from a sea of light?
Or since those drops are all sent back
So sure to thee, that none doth lack,
Why should frail flesh doubt any more
That what God takes he'll not restore?

O useful element and clear!
My sacred wash and cleanser here,
My first consigner unto those
Fountains of life where the Lamb goes!
What sublime truths and wholesome themes
Lodge in thy mystical deep streams,
Such as dull man can never find
Unless that spirit lead his mind
Which first upon thy face did move,
And hatched all with his quick'ning love.
As this loud brook's incessant fall
In streaming rings restagnates all,
Which reach by course the bank, and then
Are no more seen, just so pass men.
O my invisible estate,
My glorious liberty, still late!
Thou art the channel my soul seeks,
Not this with cataracts and creeks.

They are all gone

They are all gone into the world of light,
   And I alone sit ling'ring here.
Their very memory is fair and bright,
   And my sad thoughts doth clear.

It glows and glitters in my cloudy breast
   Like stars upon some gloomy grove,
Or those faint beams in which this hill is dressed
   After the sun's remove.

restagnates all] becomes entirely stagnant   remove] departure

I see them walking in an air of glory,
    Whose light doth trample on my days,—
My days, which are at best but dull and hoary,
    Mere glimmering and decays.

O holy hope, and high humility,
    High as the heavens above!
These are your walks, and you have showed them me,
    To kindle my cold love.

Dear, beauteous death, the jewel of the just,
    Shining nowhere but in the dark;
What mysteries do lie beyond thy dust,
    Could man outlook that mark!

He that hath found some fledged bird's nest may know
    At first sight if the bird be flown;
But what fair well or grove he sings in now,
    That is to him unknown.

And yet, as angels in some brighter dreams
    Call to the soul when man doth sleep,
So some strange thoughts transcend our wonted themes,
    And into glory peep.

If a star were confined into a tomb,
    Her captive flames must needs burn there;
But when the hand that locked her up gives room,
    She'll shine through all the sphere.

O Father of eternal life, and all
    Created glories under thee!
Resume thy spirit from this world of thrall
    Into true liberty!

Either disperse these mists, which blot and fill
    My pèrspective still as they pass;

trample] make contemptible   well] spring   Resume] Take back   thy spirit]
I.e., my spirit, created by thee.   pèrspective] telescope

Or else remove me hence unto that hill,
  Where I shall need no glass.

THOMAS TRAHERNE (1637?–1674)

Poverty

As in the house I sate,
  Alone and desolate,
No creature but the fire and I,
The chimney and the stool, I lift mine eye
  Up to the wall,
  And in the silent hall
    Saw nothing mine
But some few cups and dishes shine,
  The table and the wooden stools
    Where people used to dine;
    A painted cloth there was,
Wherein some ancient story wrought
A little entertained my thought,
Which light discovered through the glass.

I wondered much to see
  That all my wealth should be
Confined in such a little room,
Yet hope for more I scarcely durst presume.
    It grieved me sore
    That such a scanty store
      Should be my all;
For I forgot my ease and health,
Nor did I think of hands or eyes,
    Nor soul nor body prize;
    I neither thought the sun,
Nor moon, nor stars, nor people, mine,
Though they did round about me shine;
And therefore was I quite undone.

lift] lifted

Some greater things, I thought,
Must needs for me be wrought,
Which till my craving mind could see
I ever should lament my poverty;
I fain would have
Whatever bounty gave,
Nor could there be
Without or love or deity;
For should not he be infinite
Whose hand created me?
Ten thousand absent things
Did vex my poor and wanting mind,
Which, till I be no longer blind,
Let me not see the King of Kings.

His love must surely be
Rich, infinite, and free;
Nor can he be thought a God
Of grace and power, that fills not his abode,
His holy court,
In kind and liberal sort;
Joys and pleasures,
Plenty of jewels, goods, and treasures,
To enrich the poor, cheer the forlorn,
His palace must adorn,
And given all to me;
For till his works my wealth became,
No love or peace did me inflame:
But now I have a Deity.

The Salutation

These little limbs,
These eyes and hands which here I find,
This panting heart wherewith my life begins,
Where have ye been?   Behind
What·curtain were ye from me hid so long?
Where was, in what abyss, my new-made tongue?

there be] live there

When silent I
So many thousand thousand years
Beneath the dust did in a chaos lie,
    How could I, smiles or tears,
Or lips or hands or eyes or ears, perceive?
Welcome, ye treasures which I now receive.

I that so long
Was nothing from eternity,
Did little think such joys as ear and tongue
    To celebrate or see:
Such sounds to hear, such hands to feel, such feet,
Such eyes and objects, on the ground to meet.

New-burnished joys
Which finest gold and pearl excel!
Such sacred treasures are the limbs of boys,
    In which a soul doth dwell;
Their organizèd joints and azure veins
More wealth include than the dead world contains.

From dust I rise,
And out of nothing now awake;
These brighter regions which salute mine eyes,
    A gift from God I take.
The earth, the seas, the light, the lofty skies,
The sun and stars are mine, if these I prize.

A stranger here
Strange things doth meet, strange glory see;
Strange treasures lodged in this fair world appear,
    Strange all and new to me;
But that they mine should be, who nothing was,
That strangest is of all, yet brought to pass.

organizèd] well-knit

Walking

To walk abroad is, not with eyes
But thoughts, the fields to see and prize;
  Else may the silent feet
    Like logs of wood
Move up and down, and see no good,
  Nor joy nor glory meet.

Even carts and wheels their place do change,
But cannot see, though very strange
    The glory that is by:
      Dead puppets may
Move in the bright and glorious day,
  Yet not behold the sky.

And are not men than they more blind,
Who having eyes yet never find
    The bliss in which they move?
      Like statues dead
They up and down are carrièd,
  Yet neither see nor love.

To walk is by a thought to go,
To move in spirit to and fro,
  To mind the good we see,
    To taste the sweet;
Observing all the things we meet,
  How choice and rich they be:

To note the beauty of the day,
And golden fields of corn survey,
  Admire each pretty flower
    With its sweet smell,
To praise their Maker, and to tell
  The marks of his great power;

mind] heed

To fly abroad, like active bees,
Among the hedges and the trees,
  To cull the dew that lies
    On ev'ry blade,
From ev'ry blossom, till we lade
  Our minds, as they their thighs;

Observe those rich and glorious things,
The rivers, meadows, woods, and springs,
  The fructifying sun;
    To note from far
The rising of each twinkling star
  For us his race to run.

A little child these well perceives,
Who, tumbling in green grass and leaves,
  May rich as kings be thought;
    But there's a sight
Which perfect manhood may delight,
  To which we shall be brought:

While in those pleasant paths we talk
'Tis that towards which at last we walk;
  For we may by degrees
    Wisely proceed
Pleasures of love and praise to heed,
  From viewing herbs and trees.

Insatiableness

This busy, vast, enquiring soul
  Brooks no control,
  No limits will endure,
  Nor any rest; it will all see,
Not time alone, but even eternity.
  What is it? Endless, sure.

'Tis mean ambition to desire
  A single world;
  To many I aspire,

Though one upon another hurled;
Nor will they all, if they be all confined,
　　Delight my mind.

This busy, vast, enquiring soul
　　Brooks no control;
'Tis very curious too:
Each one of all those worlds must be
Enriched with infinite variety
　　And worth, or 'twill not do.

'Tis nor delight nor perfect pleasure
　　To have a purse
That hath a bottom in its treasure,
Since I must thence endless expense disburse.
Sure there's a God, for else there's no delight,
　　One infinite.

EDMUND WALLER (1606–1687)

Of the Last Verses in the Book

When we for age could neither read nor write,
The subject made us able to indite;
The soul, with nobler resolutions decked,
The body stooping, does herself erect.
No mortal parts are requisite to raise
Her that, unbodied, can her Maker praise.

The seas are quiet when the winds give o'er;
So, calm are we when passions are no more!
For then we know how vain it was to boast
Of fleeting things, so certain to be lost.
Clouds of affection from our younger eyes
Conceal that emptiness which age descries.

curious] exacting   affection] passion

The soul's dark cottage, battered and decayed,
Lets in new light through chinks that time has made;
Stronger by weakness, wiser men become,
As they draw near to their eternal home.
Leaving the old, both worlds at once they view,
That stand upon the threshold of the new.

X

THE CAVALIERS AND DRYDEN

Chiefly

1640–1700

THE CAVALIERS AND DRYDEN

In the final section appear first the lyrics of those debonair gentle-men whose loyalty to Charles I gained them the name of Cavaliers, and of those who resemble them in their attitude toward love and life. A hallmark of the Cavalier spirit is a kind of devil-may-care gallantry, a little self-conscious sometimes, as though they were flinging it into the teeth of their Puritan enemies. At their best they voice a quixotic yet none the less stirring adherence to the ideals of a society which was on the verge of disaster. Most of them were men of the world, not literary figures. Poetry to them was a gesture. Though akin in spirit to the sons of Ben and, as has been said, related to the couplet tradition in the work of Waller, they were not interested in literary theory, classical or otherwise, and wrote well by happy accident, not by design.

The characteristic cynicism and flippancy of their love verse might be supposed to owe something to Donne. But the Cavaliers were neither intellectual nor 'conceited,' just as they were lacking in the unworldliness of the Spenserians and in any deep impulse toward devotion. Yet they became, through their Restoration successors, the most continuous element in the lyric tradition. Their preference for mere wit and their carelessness of art were factors in the drift toward a concentrated and uniform metrical pattern—the couplet. Similarly their worldliness of outlook resulted in that restriction of the subject of a lyric to the single theme of love which led to the sterility of Restoration *vers de société*.

A series of poets, of whom Wyatt is the earliest here included and Wither by no means the last, had already sounded that note of manly rebellion against a scornful mistress which is neither Hora-tian nor metaphysical in tone, but seems to have been the English reaction against Petrarchan humility. From manly rebellion to carefree mockery was but a step; the Cavaliers popularized the latter vein, but they did not invent it. It was beginning to be prevalent in popular verse—verse presumably independent of any special literary influence or fashion—as early as the turn of the century, as is evidenced by a number of anonymous pieces. Two of these, together with one by the facile and indefatigable Richard Brathwait, doubtless in imitation of Wither, preface the section. *Phyllida Flouts Me* (p. 540) might almost be said to strike the keynote of Cavalier song. Little is known of Thomas Bonham and Francis Andrewes, the authors, respectively, of the heartfelt lines *In Praise of Ale* (p. 549) and of *Phyllis Inamorata* (p. 550). Their verses, like the anonymous *Down in a garden* (p. 550), express Cavalier attitudes and have in common the Cavalier quality of being better in content than in workmanship. But, if his editors are correct in assigning his earliest compositions to the 1620's, the first poet to fulfill all of the qualifications, personal as well as literary, of a Cavalier, was Edmund Waller.

Waller's earliest known effort in verse refers to an adventure of Prince Charles in Spain which occurred in 1623, when the poet was seventeen. At this early age he seems not only to have entered Cambridge, but also to have begun his Parliamentary career. He was a man of wealth and position and a time-server in politics. He took the part of the popular leaders before the outbreak of the Civil War, yet incurred a fine and banishment for his participation in the Royalist conspiracy known as Waller's Plot. He returned from exile in France to serve as Commissioner of Trade under Cromwell, yet after the Restoration he sat in Parliament once more, until his death in 1687. Considering the length of his life and the estimation in which he was held as a poet both in his own time and later, he wrote surprisingly little. Three unauthorized editions of his poems were printed during his exile, including his gallant addresses to Sacharissa, the Lady Dorothy Sidney, who may or may not have been the inspiration of his best-known lyrics, such as *Go, lovely rose*. His later poetry is on more serious subjects, historical and religious.

Waller wrote for the most part in one of two meters—octosyllabics and the couplet. The former he used for much of his Cavalier love verse. In manner and thought, his indebtedness to Carew and in a lesser degree to Herrick is apparent, though he has neither Herrick's charm nor Carew's implication of deeper feeling beneath the play of polished wit. The best of Waller's 'amorous trifles' express in eloquent verse a vein of shallow but genuine feeling.

In longer works, such as *At Penshurst* and *The Battle of the Summer Islands,* we find him using the couplet with a smoothness and regularity of style which mark him as the true exponent of the new classicism. It has been previously remarked that a certain amateurishness of spirit characterized the Cavaliers, so that their content is usually better than their workmanship. To this rule Waller is an exception. He is a careful workman. There is, indeed, a balance between succeeding couplets, together with a habit of weighting the concluding pair of lines, that precisely anticipates the practice perfected by Dryden and Pope. A contemporary biographer describes Waller as 'one of the first refiners of our English language and poetry' and says that 'when he was a brisk young spark and first studied poetry, "Methought," said he, "I never saw a good copy of English verses; they want smoothness; then I began to essay."' In other words, Waller had a natural feeling for suavity of rhythm and simplicity of diction which fitted precisely the desire of the growing body of readers to whom careless workmanship and involved language were becoming distasteful. His couplets have neither the energy of Dryden's nor the balance, antithesis, and epigrammatic brilliancy of Pope's. In its deliberate avoidance of poetic 'rage'—of which, in truth, Waller was probably incapable—in the correctness of its sentiment and its tendency toward stereotyped diction, Waller's couplet poetry reveals for the first time how convention could stifle the lyric impulse. Its effect was to give wide popularity to a rimed couplet in which evenness, regularity, the avoidance of redundant syllables and elisions, strict observance of the caesura—all the qualities, in a word, that eighteenth-century taste demanded—were present.

The fame which Waller enjoyed throughout the Restoration and the age of Queen Anne is thus entirely deserved, not because he sat down and deliberately resolved on a new species of poetry, but because he chose just those qualities of thought, form, and diction which appealed to the people of his age, and wrote and re-wrote his verse in conformity therewith. He added to the *vers de société* of

Carew something of the sweetness of Herrick and the Spenserians, and by willingly bestowing upon it that minute attention to the niceties of style which Jonson had advised, he gave the whole a greater formality. The result is a kind of smooth antithetical diction and a construction of verse suited to the epigrammatic form of his thought, applied with consummate tact to unoriginal but cleverly chosen subject matter. Waller had the adaptability which makes for immediate acceptance and fame.

It is, of course, Sir John Suckling and Richard Lovelace who are the typical Cavalier lyrists. The work of both is similar to that of Carew, and reveals the continuing influence of Jonson and of Donne. But both are set apart from this influence by their Cavalier dilettantism of spirit. Their verse is the fruit of leisure hours precariously snatched from the heady excitement of court dissipation or the rigors of military adventure. Suckling inherited wealth and high social position when but eighteen years of age. He soon plunged into the gayest and wildest of lives and became no less famous for his verse and his wit than notorious for his lavish extravagance, inveterate gaming, and dissolute life. A Royalist by birth, he was accused of schemes to save Strafford, and fled the realm, to die a suicide in Paris when less than thirty-five years old. As a writer of *vers de société,* easy, delightful, daring, cynical, perfectly well-bred and at times of the highest artistic merit, Suckling at his best was unexcelled in his age. His quality is his own. He acclaimed Donne as the great lord of wit, but his debt to Donne is a matter of externals only: lacking both subtlety and intensity, he strives for neither. As for Jonsonian influence upon him, it has been urged that Suckling's *A Session of the Poets* was written to ridicule Ben's claim to the title of Poet Laureate—an attitude which no true son of Ben would have taken; and Suckling is said to have censured Carew for the trouble and pain expended on his verses, presumably as something beneath the dignity of a courtier. His own ideal, if he may be said to have had one, was to do precisely what Dryden remarked that he did better than any other poet—to express 'the conversation of a gentleman.' Cynical though he was, and licentious at times, he exhibits the inner contradictions so typical of the seventeenth-century mind, and is by no means devoid of the vein of seriousness and chivalrous idealism that characterizes Lovelace. The directness and light-hearted buoyancy which make his finest lyrics immortal are tempered with delicacy and tenderness in his narrative *Ballad of a Wedding.*

Richard Lovelace in his youth was described by Wood as 'being then accounted the most amiable and beautiful person that ever I beheld . . . of innate modesty, virtue, and courtly deportment.' He was educated at Oxford, and distinguished himself at court and in the field. He was twice thrown into prison, where indeed most of his poetry seems to have been written. Ultimately, he wasted his entire fortune 'in useless attempts to serve his sovereign,' and died in poverty. The usual unsatisfactory attempts have been made to identify the Lucasta and Althea of his verses with a certain Lucy Sacheverell. Whoever Althea may have been, the two songs addressed to her, *From Prison* and *Going to the Wars,* have an almost classic perfection. Their simplicity and chivalrous idealism mark the peak of Cavalier verse. *To Lucasta Going beyond the Seas* and *The Scrutiny* are less well known but share the rare quality of the two famous pieces, and *Gratiana Dancing and Singing* employs the excesses of courtly compliment with an absence of cynicism and an unusual and welcome warmth of feeling. Yet many of the minor lyrics fall into utter unintelligibility and into a slovenliness of style not to be accounted for by mere corruptness of the text. Lovelace has, in a word, the extreme unevenness of the gifted dilettante.

The group of lesser Cavaliers whose work belongs to the decades immediately preceding the Restoration includes some interesting transitional figures. Thomas Stanley and his friend Sir Edward Sherburne, both of the Middle Temple, were for the most part translators of classical and Italian verse; both, like Herrick's patron, the Earl of Westmorland, found moments amid the gaiety and gallantry for more serious expression of a time of troubled uncertainty. This serious undertone is not entirely lacking in Charles Cotton nor in Sir William Davenant, but they, with Henry Bold and the dashing Alexander Brome, prefer to troll out rollicking bacchanals and mocking love verse in the fashion of the moment. Cleveland, one of the latest of the avowed sons of Ben, was of this group. Brome translated Jonson's *Leges Conviviales.* Sir William

Davenant was Shakespeare's godson, and unofficial laureate after Jonson. Thus the echoes of great names were still to be heard. But poetry drooped with the death of King Charles I. The younger men who were shortly to evolve new ideals were as yet unknown. The two chief Caroline poets of repute whose popularity survived the Restoration were Cowley and Waller.

The conservative reaction which triumphed at the Restoration inevitably resulted in the deterioration of imaginative literature, and especially of the lyric. Specifically, the new classicism involved, along with restriction as to the form of poetry, a narrowing of its scope. Since each stage of the development—the early seventeenth century, the Restoration, and the age of Queen Anne—produced a literary figure of commanding importance, it is possible to describe this process of narrowing in concrete terms by comparing the artistic range of the three representative men—Ben Jonson, John Dryden, and Alexander Pope.

The plays of Jonson, despite his position as the father of restrictive classicism, exemplify nearly the whole spacious field of Elizabethan drama; his lyrics maintain the diversity, beauty, and originality that distinguished their kind in the great age of Elizabeth. In Dryden, at the height of his fame half a century after Jonson's death, though we still find a wide range of subject, limitations are discoverable in the character of his dramas and his lyrics. Aside from his operas and his adaptations of the work of Shakespeare and Milton, Dryden writes only two kinds of play, the heroic drama and the comedy of manners; while his lyrics, excepting the two odes for Saint Cecilia's Day and some perfunctory religious poems, are wholly amatory in the narrow and vitiated sense in which that term was employed in the time of Charles II. The noble conception and resonant music of *A Song for Saint Cecilia's Day* are worthy of the magnificent poet that Dryden never ceased to be; but the songs from his plays and masques, charming and musical as they are, are less diversified in feeling than one would expect from the diversity of the dramatic situations in which they are placed.

In Pope, whose precocious *Ode to Solitude*, 'written when I was not twelve years old,' falls in the very year of Dryden's death, 1700, we find no plays and very few lyrics, scarcely one which is not an applied poem. Occasional verse, satire, and criticism have usurped the field. There was no need that he should write his criticism in prose, as did Dryden, for verse had become in his hands essentially a medium for the expression of that kind of thought which we now associate with prose. The verse of Pope was a medium better fitted for the expression of the thought of Pope, where rhetorical brilliancy and telling antithesis rather than precision of thought were demanded, than any prose that could possibly have been devised.

As we approach the end of the seventeenth century, then, the lyrists become fewer. The Elizabethan lyric, whose province was the whole world; which dignified great and petty things alike with its fervor and sincerity, had given place to a product more and more restricted to a conventional treatment of subjects in an ever-narrowing range, a plaything for the idle hours of writers whose business was with occasional verse, social satire, heroic drama, or the comedy of 'a Utopia of gallantry.' Lines presaging the eighteenth-century conception of women as 'beauteous idiots,' equally compact of physical allure, witlessness, cunning, and perversity, are everywhere. To Dorset, Sedley, Etherege, Rochester, and Aphra Behn, to the whole dissolute, cynical, godless rout of Restoration court poets, even to Dryden himself, a lyric is a love-song, and nothing more. It may be languishing or disdainful, passionate or satirical; the animalism which inspires it may be frankly expressed or present by innuendo, but there its variety ends. Exceptions, Dryden aside, are the two little pieces (pp. 312, 376) of Katherine Philips, the 'matchless Orinda' of a coterie far removed from the court; *An Epitaph on his Grandfather* by Thomas Shipman, who, like the matchless Orinda, harks back to a more spacious time; Philip Ayres' *On a Fair Beggar,* though the phrase 'Made in Imitation of the Italians' on the title-page of Ayres' volume may be significant; the little song of George Granville, Lord Lansdowne, a disciple of Waller; and the sincere and dainty little lyrics that earned for Matthew Prior the name of 'the English Horatian.'

On the whole, however, it is not too much to say that the lyric had all but disappeared from English literature before the end of the century. A style the end of which is surprise, which demands the snap of a cracker of wit in every couplet, and yet maintains a rigid adherence to convention in meter, phrase, and manner, is precisely the style to destroy the lyric, the soul of which is simplicity, artistic freedom, and inevitability. To be moved by the simple and beautiful expression of an emotion which we are fain to repeat again and again because of the pleasure it gives us, is to be moved as poetry can move. To be amused once by the flash of Congreve's wit is enough. Thus at the end of the second century of our survey we find the lyric fallen into an insipidity of Chloes and Celias and Dorindas, more tolerable than the Fidessas and Zepherias of the sonneteers only when seasoned with cynical wit. And so the lyric, at least in its most familiar guise of the love-song, remained an object of condescension for half a century of prose and reason, until English poetry resumed its singing robes in the dawn of the Romantic Revival.

ANONYMOUS (Early Seventeenth Century)

Art thou that she

'Art thou that she than whom no fairer is?
Art thou that she desire so strives to kiss?'
　　'Say I am, how then?
　　Maids may not kiss
　Such wanton-humored men.'

'Art thou that she the world commends for wit?
Art thou so wise and mak'st no use of it?'
　　'Say I am, how then?
　　My wit doth teach me shun
　Such foolish, foolish men.'

Phyllida Flouts Me

O, what a plague is love,
　How shall I bear it?

Phyllida Flouts Me] This piece exists in several versions. The stanzas given are those in *Wit Restored* (1658); the text is that of the Shirburn Ballads MS. as given by Ault.

She will unconstant prove,
   I greatly fear it.
She so molests my mind
   That my wit faileth;
She wavers with the wind,
   As the ship saileth.
Please her the best I may,
She looks another way:
Alack and well-a-day!
    Phyllida flouts me.

At the fair yesterday,
   She would not see me,
But turned another way
   When she came nigh me.
Dick had her in to dine,
   He might intreat her.
Will had her to the wine,
   I could not get her.
With Daniel did she dance;
At me she looked askance.
O thrice unhappy chance!
    Phyllida flouts me.

I cannot work and sleep,
   Both, at all season:
Love wounds my heart so deep,
   Without all reason.
I do consume, alas,
   With care and sorrow,
E'en like a sort of beasts
   Pinde in a meadow.
I shall be dead, I fear,
Within this thousand year,
And all for very care:
    Phyllida flouts me.

intreat] persuade   Both] Either   all season] any time   consume] waste away
sort] herd   Pinde] Penned and pined

She hath a clout of mine,
  Wrought with good coventry,
Which she keeps for a sign
  Of my fidelity;
But, in faith, if she flinch,
  She shall not wear it:
To Tib, my tother wench,
  I mean to bear it.
Yet it will kill my heart
So quickly to depart.
Death, kill me with thy dart!
  Phyllida flouts me.

Fair maid, be not so coy,
  Never disdain me;
I am my mother's boy,
  Sweet, entertain me.
She'll give me, when she dies,
  All things befitting:
Her poultry and her bees,
  With her goose sitting;
A pair of mattress beds,
A barrel full of shreds,—
And yet, for all my goods,
  Phyllida flouts me.

Maiden, look what you do,
  And in time take me;
I can have other two,
  If you forsake me:
For Doll, the dairy-maid,
  Laughed on me lately,
And wanton Winifred
  Favors me greatly.
One threw milk on my clothes,
T'other plays with my nose;
What loving signs be those!
  Phyllida flouts me.

clout] kerchief   coventry] blue thread   flinch] draw back

Thou shalt eat curds and cream
  All the year lasting,
And drink the crystal stream,
  Pleasant in tasting;
Whig and whey whilst thou burst,
  And bramble-berries,
Pie-lids and pasty-crust,
  Pears, plums, and cherries;
Thy garments shall be thin,
Made of a wether's skin—
Yet all not worth a pin!
    Phyllida flouts me.

RICHARD BRATHWAIT (1588–1673)

From *A Strappado for the Devil*

The Wooer's Song

Foolish I, why should I grieve
  To sustain what others feel?
What! suppose frail women leave
  Those they loved, should I conceal
    Comfort's rest
    From my breast
For a fickle brittle woman?
    No, no, no!
    Let her go!
Such as these be true to no man.

Long retirèd hast thou been
  Sighing on these barren rocks,
Nor by sheep nor shepherd seen;
  Now return unto thy flocks;
    Shame, away,
    Do not stay

Whig] Buttermilk   whilst] until

With these moving-loving women!
    They remove
    From their love:
Such as these do oft undo men.

Tender-tinder of affection,
  If I harbor thee again,
I will do it by direction
  Of some grave experienced swain.
    Nor will I
    Love by th' eye,
But where judgment first hath tried;
    If I live
    E'er to love,
It is she shall be my bride.

EDMUND WALLER (1606–1687)

To Amoret

  Fair! that you may truly know,
What you unto Thyrsis owe;
I will tell you how I do
Sacharissa love, and you.
  Joy salutes me when I set
My blest eyes on Amoret;
But with wonder I am strook,
While I on the other look.
  If sweet Amoret complains,
I have sense of all her pains;
But for Sacharissa I
Do not only grieve, but die.
  All that of myself is mine
Lovely Amoret! is thine.
Sacharissa's captive fain
Would untie his iron chain;
And, those scorching beams to shun,

Thyrsis] the poet's name for himself

To thy gentle shadow run.
If the soul had free election
To dispose of her affection,
I would not thus long have borne
Haughty Sacharissa's scorn;
But 'tis sure some power above
Which controls our will in love!

If not love, a strong desire
To create and spread that fire
In my breast, solicits me,
Beauteous Amoret! for thee.

'Tis amazement, more than love,
Which her radiant eyes do move:
If less splendor wait on thine,
Yet they so benignly shine,
I would turn my dazzled sight
To behold their milder light.
But as hard 'tis to destroy
That high flame, as to enjoy:
Which how eas'ly I may do,
Heaven—as eas'ly scaled—does know!

Amoret! as sweet and good
As the most delicious food,
Which, but tasted, does impart
Life and gladness to the heart;

Sacharissa's beauty's wine,
Which to madness doth incline,
Such a liquor, as no brain
That is mortal can sustain.

Scarce can I to heaven excuse
The devotion which I use
Unto that adorèd dame:
For 'tis not unlike the same
Which I thither ought to send,
So that if it could take end,
'Twould to heaven itself be due,
To succeed her, and not you,

use] constantly pay

Who already have of me
All that's not idolatry;
Which, though not so fierce a flame,
Is longer like to be the same.
 Then smile on me, and I will prove
Wonder is shorter-lived than love.

To Phyllis

 Phyllis, why should we delay,
Pleasures shorter than the day?
Could we—which we never can—
Stretch our lives beyond their span,
Beauty like a shadow flies,
And our youth before us dies;
Or, would youth and beauty stay,
Love hath wings, and will away.
Love hath swifter wings than time:
Change in love to heaven does climb;
Gods, that never change their state,
Vary oft their love and hate.
 Phyllis, to this truth we owe
All the love betwixt us two.
Let not you and I enquire
What has been our past desire;
On what shepherds you have smiled,
Or what nymphs I have beguiled;
Leave it to the planets, too,
What we shall hereafter do:
For the joys we now may prove,
Take advice of present love.

On a Girdle

That which her slender waist confined
Shall now my joyful temples bind;
No monarch but would give his crown,
His arms might do what this has done.

It was my heaven's extremest sphere,
The pale which held that lovely deer;
My joy, my grief, my hope, my love,
Did all within this circle move.

A narrow compass, and yet there
Dwelt all that's good and all that's fair;
Give me but what this ribband bound,
Take all the rest the sun goes round!

Song

Stay, Phœbus, stay!
The world to which you fly so fast,
Conveying day
From us to them, can pay your haste
With no such object, nor salute your rise
With no such wonder as De Mornay's eyes.

Well does this prove
The error of those àntique books
Which made you move
About the world: her charming looks
Would fix your beams, and make it ever day,
Did not the rolling earth snatch her away.

To Flavia

'Tis not your beauty can engage
My wary heart:
The sun, in all his pride and rage,
Has not that art;
And yet he shines as bright as you,
If brightness could our souls subdue.

'Tis not the pretty things you say,
Nor those you write,

pale] fence   De Mornay] probably one of Queen Henrietta's French ladies-in-
waiting

Which can make Thyrsis' heart your prey;
  For that delight,
The graces of a well-taught mind,
In some of our own sex we find.

No, Flavia, 'tis your love I fear;
  Love's surest darts,
Those which so seldom fail him, are
  Headed with hearts;
Their very shadows make us yield:
Dissemble well, and win the field.

Go, lovely rose

  Go, lovely rose,
Tell her that wastes her time and me,
  That now she knows,
When I resemble her to thee,
How sweet and fair she seems to be.

  Tell her that 's young,
And shuns to have her graces spied,
  That had'st thou sprung
In deserts where no men abide,
Thou must have uncommended died.

  Small is the worth
Of beauty from the light retired;
  Bid her come forth,
Suffer herself to be desired,
And not blush so to be admired.

  Then die, that she
The common fate of all things rare
  May read in thee:
How small a part of time they share,
That are so wondrous sweet and fair.

resemble] liken

THOMAS BONHAM (d. 1629?)

In Praise of Ale

When that the chill sirocco blows
  And winter tells a heavy tale,
When pies and daws and rooks and crows
Do sit and curse in frost and snows,
    Then give me ale:

Ale in a Saxon rumkin then,
  Such as will make grimalkin prate,
Bids valor burgeon in tall men,
Quicken's the poet's wit and pen,
    Despises fate;

Ale, that the absent battle fights,
  And scorns the march of Swedish drum;
Disputes of princes, laws, and rights;
What's done and past tells mortal wights,
    And what's to come;

Ale, that the ploughman's heart up keeps
  And equals it to tyrants' thrones;
That wipes the eye that fain would weep,
And lulls in sweet and dainty sleep
    The o'erwearied bones.

Grandchild of Ceres, barley's daughter,
  Wine's emulous neighbor if but stale,
Ennobling all the nymphs of water
And filling each man's mouth with laughter—
    O, give me ale!

When that] When   sirocco] spelled by Bonham, Charocco; neither the spelling nor
the association with winter is known elsewhere.   rumkin] drinking-vessel   gri-
malkin] an old gossip   tall] bold   Swedish drum] of Gustavus Adolphus

FRANCIS ANDREWES (*c.* 1629)

Phyllis Inamorata

Come, be my valentine!
I'll gather eglantine,
Cowslips and sops-in-wine,
   With fragrant roses;
Down by thy Phyllis sit,
She will white lilies get,
And daffodillies fit
   To make thee posies.

I have a milk-white lamb,
New taken from the dam,
It comes where'er I am
   When I call 'Willie.'
I have a wanton kid,
Under mine apron hid,
A colt that ne'er was rid,
   A pretty filly.

I bear, in sign of love,
A sparrow in my glove,
And in my breast a dove,
   These shall be all thine;
Besides, of sheep a flock,
Which yieldeth many a lock,
And that shall be thy stock—
   Come, be my valentine!

ANONYMOUS (Before 1630)

Down in a garden

Down in a garden sat my dearest love,
Her skin more soft and white than down of swan,
More tender-hearted than the turtledove,

Phyllis Inamorata] text from *Seventeenth Century Lyrics* (1928) by Norman Ault,
and here reprinted with his kind permission   sops-in-wine] pinks

And far more kind than bleeding pelican.
I courted her; she rose, and blushing said,
'Why was I born to live and die a maid?'
With that I plucked a pretty marigold,
Whose dewy leaves shut up when day is done.
'Sweeting,' I said, 'arise, look and behold
A pretty riddle I'll to thee unfold:
These leaves shut in as close as cloistered nun,
Yet will they open when they see the sun.'
'What mean you by this riddle, sir?' she said,
'I pray expound it.' Then I thus began:
'Know maids are made for men, man for a maid.'
With that she changed her color and grew wan:
'Since that this riddle you so well unfold,
Be you the sun, I'll be the marigold.'

SIR JOHN SUCKLING (1609–1642)

Sonnet

Dost see how unregarded now
    That piece of beauty passes?
There was a time when I did vow
    To that alone;
  But mark the fate of faces:
The red and white works now no more on me,
Than if it could not charm, or I not see.

And yet the face continues good,
    And I have still desires,
Am still the self-same flesh and blood,
    As apt to melt,
  And suffer from those fires;
O, some kind power unriddle where it lies:
Whether my heart be faulty, or her eyes?

She every day her man doth kill,
    And I as often die;

I'll] which I'll

Neither her power, then, nor my will
Can questioned be.
What is the mystery?
Sure beauty's empires, like to greater states,
Have certain periods set, and hidden fates.

The Siege

'Tis now since I sat down before
That foolish fort, a heart,
(Time strangely spent) a year or more,
And still I did my part:

Made my approaches, from her hand
Unto her lip did rise,
And did already understand
The language of her eyes;

Proceeded on with no less art;
(My tongue was engineer)
I thought to undermine the heart
By whispering in the ear.

When this did nothing, I brought down
Great cannon-oaths, and shot
A thousand thousand to the town,
And still it yielded not.

I then resolved to starve the place
By cutting off all kisses,
Praising, and gazing on her face,
And all such little blisses.

To draw her out, and from her strength,
I drew all batteries in:
And brought myself to lie, at length,
As if no siege had been.

When I had done what man could do,
  And thought the place mine own,
The enemy lay quiet too,
  And smiled at all was done.

I sent to know from whence and where
  These hopes and this relief.
A spy informed, Honor was there,
  And did command in chief.

'March, march,' quoth I, 'the word straight give,
  Let's lose no time, but leave her;
That giant upon air will live,
  And hold it out for ever.

'To such a place our camp remove
  As will no siege abide;
I hate a fool that starves her love,
  Only to feed her pride.'

Song

Honest lover whosoever,
If in all thy love there ever
Was one wav'ring thought, if thy flame
Were not still even, still the same:
    Know this,
      Thou lov'st amiss,
      And, to prove true,
Thou must begin again, and love anew.

If when she appears i' th' room,
Thou dost not quake, and art struck dumb,
And in striving this to cover,
Dost not speak thy words twice over:
    Know this, &c.

all was] all that was   art struck, Persuad'st] 'not' is understood.

If fondly thou dost not mistake,
And all defects for graces take,
Persuad'st thyself that jests are broken
When she hath little or nothing spoken:
Know this, &c.

If when thou appear'st to be within,
Thou lett'st not men ask and ask again;
And when thou answerest, if it be
To what was asked thee, properly:
Know this, &c.

If when thy stomach calls to eat,
Thou cutt'st not fingers 'stead of meat,
And with much gazing on her face
Dost not rise hungry from the place:
Know this, &c.

If by this thou dost discover
That thou art no perfect lover,
And desiring to love true,
Thou dost begin to love anew:
Know this, &c.

Out upon it

Out upon it, I have loved
  Three whole days together;
And am like to love three more,
  If it prove fair weather.

Time shall moult away his wings,
  Ere he shall discover
In the whole wide world again
  Such a constant lover.

But the spite on 't is, no praise
  Is due at all to me:
Love with me had made no stays,
  Had it any been but she.

jests are broken] jokes are cracked

Had it any been but she,
And that very face,
There had been at least ere this
A dozen dozen in her place.

Song

I prithee send me back my heart,
Since I cannot have thine;
For if from yours you will not part,
Why then shouldst thou have mine?

Yet, now I think on 't, let it lie;
To find it were in vain,
For th' hast a thief in either eye
Would steal it back again.

Why should two hearts in one breast lie,
And yet not lodge together?
O love, where is thy sympathy,
If thus our breasts thou sever?

But love is such a mystery,
I cannot find it out:
For when I think I'm best resolved,
I then am in most doubt.

Then farewell care, and farewell woe!
I will no longer pine;
For I'll believe I have her heart
As much as she hath mine.

THOMAS STANLEY (1625–1678)

Expectation

Chide, chide no more away
The fleeting daughters of the day,

---

best resolved] closest to solving it

Nor with impatient thoughts outrun
    The lazy sun,
Or think the hours do move too slow;
    Delay is kind,
  And we too soon shall find
That which we seek, yet fear to know.

The mystic dark decrees
Unfold not of the Destinies,
Nor boldly seek to antedate
    The laws of fate;
Thy anxious search awhile forbear,
    Suppress thy haste,
  And know that time at last
Will crown thy hope, or fix thy fear.

Song

I prithee let my heart alone,
  Since now 'tis raised above thee;
Not all the beauty thou dost own
  Again can make me love thee.

He that was shipwrecked once before
  By such a siren's call,
And yet neglects to shun that shore,
  Deserves his second fall.

Each flatt'ring kiss, each tempting smile
  Thou dost in vain bestow,
Some other lovers might beguile,
  Who not thy falsehood know.

But I am proof against all art,
  No vows shall e'er persuade me
Twice to present a wounded heart
  To her that hath betrayed me.

Could I again be brought to love
Thy form, though more divine,
I might thy scorn as justly move
As now thou sufferest mine.

RICHARD LOVELACE (1618–1658)

To Lucasta
Going beyond the Seas

If to be absent were to be
Away from thee,
Or that when I am gone,
You or I were alone,
Then, my Lucasta, might I crave
Pity from blustering wind or swallowing wave.

But I'll not sigh one blast or gale
To swell my sail,
Or pay a tear to 'suage
The foaming blow-god's rage;
For whether he will let me pass
Or no, I'm still as happy as I was.

Though seas and land betwixt us both,
Our faith and troth,
Like separated souls,
All time and space controls;
Above the highest sphere we meet,
Unseen, unknown, and greet as angels greet.

So then we do anticipate
Our after-fate,
And are alive i' th' skies,
If thus our lips and eyes
Can speak like spirits unconfined
In heaven, their earthy bodies left behind.

blow-god] Æolus

To Lucasta
Going to the Wars

Tell me not, sweet, I am unkind,
    That from the nunnery
Of thy chaste breast and quiet mind
    To war and arms I fly.

True, a new mistress now I chase,
    The first foe in the field;
And with a stronger faith embrace
    A sword, a horse, a shield.

Yet this inconstancy is such
    As you too shall adore:
I could not love thee, dear, so much
    Loved I not honor more.

Gratiana Dancing and Singing

See with what constant motiòn,
Even and glorious as the sun,
    Gratiana steers that noble frame,
Soft as her breast, sweet as her voice,
That gave each winding law and poise,
    And swifter than the wings of fame.

She beat the happy•pavèment
By such a star-made firmament,
    Which now no more the roof envìes,
But swells up high with Atlas even,
Bearing the brighter, nobler heaven,
    And in her all the deities.

Each step trod out a lover's thought
And the ambitious hopes he brought,
    Chained to her brave feet with such arts,

Gratiana] trisyllabic   winding] convolution   firmament] the 'frame' of stanza 1
Which] The pavement   brave] handsome

Such sweet command, and gentle awe,
As when she ceased, we sighing saw
   The floor lay paved with broken hearts.

So did she move; so did she sing
Like the harmonious spheres that bring
   Unto their rounds their music's aid;
Which she performèd such a way
As all th' enamored world will say
   The Graces dancèd, and Apollo played.

The Scrutiny

Why should'st thou swear I am forsworn
   Since thine I vowed to be?
Lady, it is already morn,
   And 'twas last night I swore to thee
   That fond impossibility.

Have I not loved thee much and long,
   A tedious twelve hours' space?
I should all other beauties wrong,
   And rob thee of a new embrace,
   Should I still dote upon thy face.

Not but all joy in thy brown hair
   By others may be found;
But I must search the black and fair,
   Like skillful min'ralists that sound
   For treasure in un-plowed-up ground.

Then if, when I have loved my round,
   Thou prov'st the pleasant she,
With spoils of meaner beauties crowned,
   I laden will return to thee,
   Even sated with variety.

As] That   Since . . . vowed] After vowing . . .

To Althea from Prison

When Love with unconfinèd wings,
  Hovers within my gates,
And my divine Althea brings
  To whisper at the grates;
When I lie tangled in her hair
  And fettered to her eye,
The birds that wanton in the air
  Know no such liberty.

When flowing cups run swiftly round
  With no allaying Thames,
Our careless heads with roses bound,
  Our hearts with loyal flames;
When thirsty grief in wine we steep,
  When healths and draughts go free,
Fishes that tipple in the deep
  Know no such liberty.

When, like committed linnets, I
  With shriller throat shall sing
The sweetness, mercy, majesty,
  And glories of my king;
When I shall voice aloud how good
  He is, how great should be,
Enlargèd winds, that curl the flood,
  Know no such liberty.

Stone walls do not a prison make,
  Nor iron bars a cage;
Minds innocent and quiet take
  That for an hermitage:
If I have freedom in my love,
  And in my soul am free,
Angels alone, that soar above,
  Enjoy such liberty.

committed] caged

MILDMAY FANE, EARL OF WESTMORLAND
(c. 1602–1666)

In Praise of Fidelia

Get thee a ship well rigged and tight,
With ordnance-store, and manned for fight,
Snug in her timbers' mould for th' seas,
Yet large in hold for merchandise;
Spread forth her cloth, and anchors weigh,
And let her on the curled waves play,
Till, fortune-towed, she chance to meet
Th' Hesperian home-bound western fleet;
Then let her board 'em, and for price
Take gold ore, sugar canes, and spice:
Yet when all these sh' hath brought ashore,
In my Fidelia I'll find more.

SIR EDWARD SHERBURNE (1618–1702)

The Sweetmeat

Thou gav'st me late to eat
A sweet without, but within, bitter meat:
As if thou would'st have said 'Here, taste in this
What Celia is.'

But if there ought to be
A likeness, dearest, 'twixt thy gift and thee,
Why first what's sweet in thee should I not taste,
The bitter last?

Weeping and Kissing

A kiss I begged, but smiling she
Denied it me;
When straight, her cheeks with tears o'erflown—
Now kinder grown—

price] prize   straight] straightway

What smiling she'd not let me have
　　She weeping gave.
Then you whom scornful beauties awe,
　　Hope yet relief;
For love, who tears from smiles, can draw
　　Pleasure from grief.

The Fountain

Stranger, whoe'er thou art, that stoop'st to taste
These sweeter streams, let me arrest thy haste;
　　Nor of their fall
The murmurs (though the lyre
Less sweet be) stand t' admire.
　　But as you shall
See from this marble tun
The liquid crystal run,
　　And mark withal
How fixed the one abides,
How fast the other glides,
Instructed thus, the difference learn to see
'Twixt mortal life and immortality.

CHARLES COTTON (1630–1687)

Ode

The day is set did earth adorn,
　　To drink the brewing of the main;
And, hot with travel, will ere morn
　　Carouse it to an ebb again.
Then let us drink, time to improve,
　　Secure of Cromwell and his spies;
Night will conceal our healths and love,
　　For all her thousand thousand eyes.

who tears] who can draw tears　admire] wonder at　tun] vessel　set did]
seated which did　For] Despite

Chorus.

Then let us drink, secure of spies,
  To Phœbus and his second rise.

Without the evening dew and showers
  The earth would be a barren place,
Of trees and plants, of herbs and flowers,
  To crown her now enameled face;
Nor can wit spring, or fancies grow,
  Unless we dew our heads in wine,
Plump autumn's wealthy overflow
  And sprightly issue of the vine. *Chorus.*

Wine is the cure of cares and sloth,
  That rust the metal of the mind;
The juice that man to man does both
  In freedom and in friendship bind.
This clears the monarch's cloudy brows,
  And cheers the hearts of sullen swains,
To wearied souls repose allows,
  And makes slaves caper in their chains. *Chorus.*

Wine, that distributes to each part
  Its heat and motion, is the spring,
The poet's head, the subject's heart,
  'Twas wine made old Anacreon sing.
Then let us quaff it whilst the night
  Serves but to hide such guilty souls
As fly the beauty of the light
  Or dare not pledge our loyal bowls.

Chorus.

Then let us revel, quaff, and sing,
Health and his scepter to the king.

Les Amours

She that I pursue, still flies me;
  Her that follows me, I fly;

She that I still court, denies me;
　Her that courts me, I deny:
'Thus in one web we're subtly wove,
And yet we mutiny in love.

She that can save me, must not do it;
　She that cannot, fain would do;
Her love is bound, yet I still woo it;
　Hers by love is bound in woe:
Yet how can I of love complain,
Since I have love for love again?

This is thy work, imperious Child,
　Thine's this labyrinth of love,
That thus hast our desires beguiled,
　Nor seèst how thine arrows rove.
Then prithee, to compose this stir,
Make her love me, or me love her.

But, if irrevocable are
　Those keen shafts that wound us so,
Let me prevail with thee thus far,
　That thou once more take thy bow;
Wound her hard heart, and by my troth,
I'll be content to take them both.

Laura Sleeping

Winds, whisper gently whilst she sleeps,
　And fan her with your cooling wings,
Whilst she her drops of beauty weeps
　From pure and yet unrivaled springs.

Glide over beauty's field, her face,
　To kiss her lip and cheek be bold,
But with a calm and stealing pace,
　Neither too rude nor yet too cold.

rove] fly at random

Play in her beams and crisp her hair
   With such a gale as wings soft love,
And with so sweet, so rich an air
   As breathes from the Arabian grove,

A breath as hushed as lover's sigh,
   Or that unfolds the morning door;
Sweet as the winds that gently fly
   To sweep the spring's enameled floor.

Murmur soft music to her dreams,
   That pure and unpolluted run,
Like to the new-born crystal streams
   Under the bright enamored sun.

But when she waking shall display
   Her light, retire within your bar.
Her breath is life, her eyes are day,
   And all mankind her creatures are.

HENRY BOLD (1627–1683)

Chloris, forbear awhile

Chloris, forbear awhile,
   Do not o'erjoy me;
Urge not another smile,
   Lest it destroy me.
That beauty pleases most,
   And is best taking,
Which soon is won, soon lost,
   Kind, yet forsaking.
I love a coming lady, 'faith I do,
But now and then I'd have her scornful, too.

O'ercloud those eyes of thine,
   Bo-peep thy features;
Warm with an April shine,
   Scorch not thy creatures:

crisp] curl   that unfolds] that which opens   best] most   coming] forward

Still to display thy ware,
  Still to be fooling,
Argues how rude you are
  In Cupid's schooling.
Disdain begets a suit, scorn draws us nigh;
'Tis 'cause I would and cannot, makes me try.

Fairest, I'd have thee wise:
  When gallants view thee
And court, do thou despise;
  Fly, they'll pursue thee.
Fasts move an appetite,
  Make hunger greater;
Who's stinted of delight
  Falls to 't the better.
Be kind and coy by turns, be calm and rough,
And buckle now and then, and that's enough.

SIR WILLIAM DAVENANT (1606–1668)

Song

The lark now leaves his wat'ry nest,
  And, climbing, shakes his dewy wings,
He takes this window for the east,
  And to implore your light, he sings:
'Awake, awake, the morn will never rise
Till she can dress her beauty at your eyes.'

The merchant bows unto the seaman's star,
  The ploughman from the sun his season takes;
But still the lover wonders what they are
  Who look for day before his mistress wakes.
'Awake, awake, break through your veils of lawn,
Then draw your curtains, and begin the dawn.'

buckle] break down, give in

The Philosopher and the Lover

To a Mistress Dying

Lover.

Your beauty, ripe and calm and fresh
    As eastern summers are,
Must now, forsaking time and flesh,
    Add light to some small star.

Philosopher.

Whilst she yet lives, were stars decayed,
    Their light by hers relief might find;
But death will lead her to a shade
    Where love is cold, and beauty blind.

Lover.

Lovers, whose priests all poets are,
    Think every mistress when she dies
Is changed at least into a star;
    And who dares doubt the poets wise?

Philosopher.

But ask not bodies doomed to die
    To what abode they go;
Since knowledge is but sorrow's spy,
    It is not safe to know.

From *News from Plymouth*

[III. i. The house of Sir Solemn Trifle and his niece, Lady
    Loveright.
Topsail. I must now speak for myself, or rather sing. Begin.]

O thou that sleep'st like pig in straw,
    Thou lady dear, arise;

Open, to keep the sun in awe,
 Thy pretty pinking eyes.
And having stretched each leg and arm,
 Put on your clean white smock,
And then I pray, to keep you warm,
 A petticoat on dock.
Arise, arise! why should you sleep,
 When you have slept enough?
Long since French boys cried, 'Chimney-sweep!'
 And damsels, 'Kitchen-stuff!'
The shops were opened long before,
 And youngest prentice goes
To lay at 's mistress' chamber door
 His master's shining shoes.
Arise, arise! your breakfast stays:
 Good water-gruèl warm,
Or sugar-sops, which, Galen says,
 With mace, will do no harm.
Arise, arise! when you are up
 You'll find more to your cost,
For morning's draught in caudle cup,
 Good nutbrown ale and toast.

ALEXANDER BROME (1620–1666)

The Resolve

Tell me not of a face that 's fair,
 Nor lip and cheek that 's red,
Nor of the tresses of her hair,
 Nor curls in order laid;
Nor of a rare seraphic voice,
 That like an angel sings,—
Though, if I were to take my choice,
 I would have all these things.

---

pinking] blinking, narrow dock] rump sugar-sops] steeped slices of bread, sweetened mace] nutmeg cost] taste, habit caudle] a warm drink

But if that thou wilt have me love,
  And it must be a she,
The only argument can move
  Is, that she will love me.

The glories of your ladies be
  But metaphors of things,
And but resemble what we see
  Each common object brings.
Roses out-red their lips and cheeks,
  Lilies their whiteness stain:
What fool is he that shadows seeks,
  And may the substance gain!
Then if thou 'lt have me love a lass,
  Let it be one that 's kind,
Else I'm a servant to the glass
  That 's with canary lined.

The Mad Lover

I have been in love and in debt and in drink
  This many and many a year;
And those three are plagues enough, one would think,
  For one poor mortal to bear.
'Twas drink made me fall into love,
  And love made me run into debt,
And though I have struggled and struggled and strove,
  I cannot get out of them yet.
There's nothing but money can cure me,
  And rid me of all my pain;
    'Twill pay all my debts,
    And remove all my lets,
And my mistress, that cannot endure me,
  Will love me and love me again,—
Then I'll fall to loving and drinking amain.

if that] if   can] which can   stain] eclipse   lets] impediments

JOHN DRYDEN (1631–1700)

From *The Indian Emperor*

[IV. iii. A pleasant grotto in Mexico. An Indian woman
sings to a group of Spanish soldiers.]

Ah, fading joy, how quickly art thou past!
    Yet we thy ruin haste.
As if the cares of human life were few,
    We seek out new,
And follow fate that does too fast pursue.

See how on every bough the birds express
    In their sweet notes their happiness.
    They all enjoy and nothing spare,
But on their mother nature lay their care:
Why then should man, the lord of all below,
    Such troubles choose to know
As none of all his subjects undergo?

Hark, hark, the waters fall, fall, fall,
    And with a murmuring sound
    Dash, dash, upon the ground,
      To gentle slumbers call.

From *Tyrannic Love*

[IV. i. A cave near the Roman camp. Damilcar, a spirit,
stamps, and a bed arises with Saint Catharine in it.
The spirit sings.]

You pleasing dreams of love and sweet delight,
Appear before this slumbering virgin's sight;
    Soft visions set her free
    From mournful piety.
Let her sad thoughts from heaven retire,
And let the melancholy love
Of those remoter joys above
Give place to your more sprightly fire.

Let purling streams be in her fancy seen,
And flowery meads, and vales of cheerful green,
And in the midst of deathless groves
        Soft sighing wishes lie,
        And smiling hopes fast by,
And just beyond them ever-laughing loves.

From *An Evening's Love*

[II. i.   Madrid.   Wildblood, an Englishman, sings to Jacinta.]

You charmed me not with that fair face,
    Though it was all divine:
To be another's is the grace
    That makes me wish you mine.
The gods and fortune take their part
    Who, like young monarchs, fight,
And boldly dare invade that heart
    Which is another's right.
First, mad with hope, we undertake
    To pull up every bar;
But, once possessed, we faintly make
    A dull defensive war.
Now every friend is turned a foe
    In hope to get our store:
And passion makes us cowards grow,
    Which made us brave before.

From *Troilus and Cressida*

[III. ii.   Outside the lovers' chamber.
Pandarus.   Come, towze, rowze!   In the name of Love, strike
up, boys!]

        Can life be a blessing,
        Or worth the possessing,
Can life be a blessing, if love were away?
    Ah, no! though our love all night keep us waking,

And though he torment us with cares all the day,
    Yet he sweetens, he sweetens our pains in the taking;
There's an hour at the last, there's an hour to repay.

            In every possessing,
            The ravishing blessing,
In every possessing, the fruit of our pain,
    Poor lovers forget long ages of anguish,
Whate'er they have suffered and done to obtain;
    'Tis a pleasure, a pleasure to sigh and to languish,
    When we hope, when we hope to be happy again.

From *The Spanish Friar*

[V. i.   A bed-chamber.
Queen (*to Teresa, her waiting woman*).
Sing me the song which poor Olympia made
When false Bireno left her.]

            Farewell, ungrateful traitor!
                Farewell, my perjured swain!
            Let never injured creature
                Believe a man again.
            The pleasure of possessing
            Surpasses all expressing,
            But 'tis too short a blessing,
                And love too long a pain.

            'Tis easy to deceive us,
                In pity of your pain;
            But when we love, you leave us
                To rail at you in vain.
            Before we have descried it,
            There is no bliss beside it,
            But she, that once has tried it,
                Will never love again.

            The passion you pretended,
                Was only to obtain;

obtain] get your desire

But when the charm is ended,
  The charmer you disdain.
Your love by ours we measure,
Till we have lost our treasure;
But dying is a pleasure,
  When living is a pain.

✳

A Song for Saint Cecilia's Day

From harmony, from heavenly harmony,
  This universal frame began:
When nature underneath a heap
  Of jarring atoms lay,
And could not heave her head,
The tuneful voice was heard from high,
  'Arise, ye more than dead.'
Then cold and hot and moist and dry,
  In order to their stations leap,
  And Music's power obey.
From harmony, from heavenly harmony,
  This universal frame began:
  From harmony .to harmony
Through all the compass of the notes it ran,
  The diapason closing full in man.

What passion cannot music raise and quell?
  When Jubal struck the chorded shell,
  His listening brethren stood around,
  And, wondering, on their faces fell
  To worship that celestial sound.
Less than a god they thought there could not dwell
  Within the hollow of that shell
  That spoke so sweetly and so well.
What passion cannot music raise and quell?

  The trumpet's loud clangor
    Excites us to arms,

With shrill notes of anger
And mortal alarms.
The double, double, double beat
Of the thundering drum,
Cries, hark! the foes come:
Charge, charge! 'tis too late to retreat.

The soft complaining flute
In dying notes discovers
The woes of hopeless lovers,
Whose dirge is whispered by the warbling lute.

Sharp violins proclaim
Their jealous pangs and desperation,
Fury, frantic indignation,
Depth of pains and height of passion
For the fair, disdainful dame.

But, O! what art can teach,
What human voice can reach
The sacred organ's praise?
Notes inspiring holy love,
Notes that wing their heavenly ways
To mend the choirs above.

Orpheus could lead the savage race,
And trees, unrooted, left their place
Sequacious of the lyre:
But bright Cecilia raised the wonder higher;
When to her organ vocal breath was given,
An angel heard, and straight appeared
Mistaking earth for heaven.

Grand Chorus.

As from the power of sacred lays
The spheres began to move,
And sung the great Creator's praise
To all the blest above;

discovers] reveals   Sequacious of] Following

So when the last and dreadful hour
This crumbling pageant shall devour,
The trumpet shall be heard on high,
The dead shall live, the living die,
And Music shall untune the sky.

From *King Arthur*

[IV. i. A wood. Nymphs and sylvans sing the following
song to a minuet.]

How happy the lover,
    How easy his chain,
    How pleasing his pain!
How sweet to discover
    He sighs not in vain!
For love, every creature
Is formed by his nature;
    No joys are above
    The pleasures of love.

In vain are our graces,
    In vain are your eyes,
    If love you despise;
When age furrows faces,
    'Tis time to be wise.
Then use the short blessing
That flies in possessing:
    No joys are above
    The pleasures of love.

✽

Rondelay

Chloe found Amyntas lying
    All in tears, upon the plain,
Sighing to himself, and crying,
    'Wretched I, to love in vain!
Kiss me, dear, before my dying,
    Kiss me once, and ease my pain!'

untune] destroy (as it had created)   sylvans] spirits of the woods

Sighing to himself, and crying,
  'Wretched I, to love in vain!
Ever scorning and denying
  To reward your faithful swain:
Kiss me, dear, before my dying;
  Kiss me once, and ease my pain!

'Ever scorning and denying
  To reward your faithful swain!'
Chloe, laughing at his crying,
  Told him that he loved in vain.
'Kiss me, dear, before my dying;
  Kiss me once, and ease my pain!'

Chloe, laughing at his crying,
  Told him that he loved in vain;
But repenting and complying,
  When he kissed, she kissed again:
Kissed him up, before his dying,
  Kissed him up, and eased his pain.

To a Fair Young Lady Going out of Town in the Spring

Ask not the cause why sullen spring
  So long delays her flowers to bear;
Why warbling birds forget to sing,
  And winter storms invert the year:
Chloris is gone, and fate provides
To make it spring where she resides.

Chloris is gone, the cruel fair;
  She cast not back a pitying eye,
But left her lover in despair,
  To sigh, to languish, and to die.
Ah, how can those fair eyes endure,
To give the wounds they will not cure?

up] effectually

Great god of love, why hast thou made
   A face that can all hearts command,
That all religions can invade,
   And change the laws of every land?
Where thou hadst placed such power before,
Thou shouldst have made her mercy more.

When Chloris to the temple comes,
   Adoring crowds before her fall;
She can restore the dead from tombs,
   And every life but mine recall.
I only am by love designed
To be the victim for mankind.

From *The Secular Masque*

[Janus, Chronos, and Momus enter first; then:
Horns within.   Enter Diana.]

Diana.

With horns and with hounds I waken the day,
And hie to my woodland walks away;
I tuck up my robe, and am buskined soon,
And tie to my forehead a wexing moon;
I course the fleet stag, unkennel the fox,
And chase the wild goats o'er summits of rocks;
With shouting and hooting we pierce through the sky,
And Echo turns hunter and doubles the cry.

Chorus.

With shouting and hooting we pierce through the sky,
And Echo turns hunter and doubles the cry.

wexing] waxing   course] hunt

SIR CHARLES SEDLEY (1639?–1701)

Song

Not, Celia, that I juster am
 Or better than the rest;
For I would change each hour like them,
 Were not my heart at rest.

But I am tied to very thee
 By every thought I have;
Thy face I only care to see,
 Thy heart I only crave.

All that in woman is adored
 In thy dear self I find;
For the whole sex can but afford
 The handsome and the kind.

Why then should I seek farther store,
 And still make love anew?
When change itself can give no more
 'Tis easy to be true.

Love still has something of the sea

Love still has something of the sea,
 From whence his mother rose;
No time his slaves from doubt can free,
 Nor give their thoughts repose.

They are becalmed in clearest days,
 And in rough weather tossed;
They wither under cold delays,
 Or are in tempests lost.

One while they seem to touch the port,
 Then straight into the main
Some angry wind in cruel sport
 The vessel drives again.

Thy face I only] Thy face alone, I

At first Disdain and Pride they fear,
    Which, if they chance to 'scape,
Rivals and Falsehood soon appear
    In a more dreadful shape.

By such degrees to joy they come,
    And are so long withstood,
So slowly they receive the sum,
    It hardly does them good.

'Tis cruel to prolong a pain;
    And to defer a joy,
Believe me, gentle Celemene,
    Offends the wingèd boy.

An hundred thousand oaths your fears
    Perhaps would not remove,
And if I gazed a thousand years
    I could no deeper love.

Hears not my Phyllis

'Hears not my Phyllis how the birds
    Their feathered friends salute?
They tell their passion in their words:
    Must I alone be mute?'
        Phyllis, without frown or smile,
        Sat and knotted all the while.

'The god of love in thy bright eyes
    Does like a tyrant reign;
But in thy heart a child he lies
    Without his dart or flame.'
        Phyllis, without frown or smile,
        Sat and knotted all the while.

'So many months in silence passed,
    And yet in raging love,

knotted] knotting was a kind of fancy work.

Might well deserve one word at last
My passion should approve.'
Phyllis, without frown or smile,
Sat and knotted all the while.

'Must then your faithful swain expire
And not one look obtain,
Which he to soothe his fond desire
Might pleasingly explain?'
Phyllis, without frown or smile,
Sat and knotted all the while!

Phyllis is my only joy

Phyllis is my only joy,
   Faithless as the winds or seas,
Sometimes coming, sometimes coy,
   Yet she never fails to please;
      If with a frown
      I am cast down,
      Phyllis smiling
      And beguiling
Makes me happier than before.

Though alas! too late I find
   Nothing can her fancy fix,
Yet the moment she is kind
      Which though I see,
I forgive her all her tricks;
      I can't get free.
      She .deceiving,
      I believing,—
What need lovers wish for more?

SIR GEORGE ETHEREGE (1635?–1691)

A Song

Ye happy swains whose hearts are free
From love's imperial chain,

My . . . approve] Which should approve my passion   coming] forward

Take warning and be taught by me
    T' avoid th' enchanting pain;
Fatal the wolves to trembling flocks,
    Fierce winds to blossoms, prove,
To careless seamen, hidden rocks,
    To human quiet, love.

Fly the fair sex, if bliss you prize;
    The snake's beneath the flower:
Whoever gazed on beauteous eyes,
    That tasted quiet more?
How faithless is the lovers' joy!
    How constant is their care
The kind with falsehood to destroy,
    The cruel, with despair!

To a Lady Asking Him How Long He Would Love Her

It is not, Celia, in our power
    To say how long our love will last;
It may be we within this hour
    May lose those joys we now do taste:
The blessèd that immortal be,
From change in love are only free.

Then since we mortal lovers are,
    Ask not how long our love will last;
But while it does, let us take care
    Each minute be with pleasure passed:
Were it not madness to deny
To live because we're sure to die?

APHRA BEHN (1640–1689)

Love Armed

Love in fantastic triumph sate,
    Whilst bleeding hearts around him flowed,

The blessed . . . only] Only the blessed . . .

For whom fresh pains he did create,
    And strange tyrannic power he showed;
From thy bright eyes he took his fire,
    Which round about in sport he hurled;
But 'twas from mine he took desire
    Enough t' undo the amorous world.

From me he took his sighs and tears,
    From thee his pride and cruelty;
From me his languishments and fears,
    And every killing dart from thee:
Thus thou and I the god have armed,
    And set him up a deity,
But my poor heart alone is harmed,
    Whilst thine the victor is, and free.

CHARLES SACKVILLE, EARL OF DORSET
(1638–1706)

Song

Phyllis, for shame! let us improve
    A thousand several ways
These few short minutes snatched by love
    From many tedious days.

Whilst you want courage to despise
    The censures of the grave,
For all the tyrants in your eyes
    Your heart is but a slave.

My love is full of noble pride,
    And never shall submit
To let that fop, Discretion, ride
    In triumph over wit.

False friends I have, as well as you,
    Who daily counsel me
Fame and ambition to pursue,
    And leave off loving thee.

When I the least belief bestow
  On what such fools advise,
May I be dull enough to grow
  Most miserably wise!

On a Lady Who Fancied Herself a Beauty

Dorinda's sparkling wit and eyes
  United cast too fierce a light,
Which blazes high, but quickly dies,
  Pains not the heart, but hurts the sight.

Love is a calmer, gentler joy,
  Smooth are his looks, and soft his pace:
Her Cupid is a blackguard boy,
  That runs his link full in your face.

JOHN WILMOT, EARL OF ROCHESTER
(1648–1680)

Love and Life

All my past life is mine no more,
  The flying hours are gone,
Like transitory dreams given o'er,
Whose images are kept in store
  By memory alone.

The time that is to come is not:
  How can it then be mine?
The present moment's all my lot,
And that, as fast as it is got,
  Phyllis, is only thine.

Then talk not of inconstancy,
  False hearts, and broken vows;
If I, by miracle, can be
This live-long minute true to thee,
  'Tis all that heaven allows.

blackguard boy] street urchin   link] torch

THOMAS SHIPMAN (1632–1680)

An Epitaph upon my Grandfather

Here lies an agèd corpse, which late
Incaged a soul, whom neither fate
Nor times could change from its first state.

Oppressèd more with age than cares;
Respected more for silver hairs
Than gold; for wisdom more than years.

Happy in every child he had;
Happy in self; and only sad
Being born in good days, but deceased in bad.

PHILIP AYRES (1638–1712)

On a Fair Beggar

Barefoot and ragged, with neglected hair,
She whom the heavens at once made poor and fair,
  With humble voice and moving words did stay,
  To beg an alms of all who passed that way.

But thousands viewing her became her prize,
Willingly yielding to her conquering eyes
  And caught by her bright hairs, whilst careless she
  Makes them pay homage to her poverty.

'So mean a boon,' said I, 'what can extort
From that fair mouth, where wanton Love to sport
  Amidst the pearls and rubies we behold?
Nature on thee has all her treasures spread;
Do but incline thy rich and precious head,
  And those fair locks shall pour down showers of gold.'

boon] entreaty

GEORGE GRANVILLE, LORD LANSDOWNE
(1667–1735)

Song

The happiest mortals once were we,
I loved Myra, Myra me;
Each desirous of the blessing,
Nothing wanting but possessing;
I loved Myra, Myra me:
The happiest mortals once were we.

But since cruel fates dissever,
Torn from love, and torn forever,
Tortures end me,
Death befriend me!
Of all pains, the greatest pain
Is to love, and love in vain.

ANONYMOUS (1692)

Corinna is divinely fair

Corinna is divinely fair,
Easy her shape and soft her air;
Of hearts she had the absolute sway
Before she threw her own away:
The power now languishes by which she charmed,
Her beauty sullied, and her eyes disarmed.

Like nature, she is apt to waste
Her treasure where 'tis valued least:
So peasants surfeit—where it grows—
On fruit the eastern sun bestows;
But all the delicacy fades before
It can, through oceans, reach our distant shore.

MATTHEW PRIOR (1664–1721)

An Ode

The merchant, to secure his treasure,
  Conveys it in a borrowed name:
Euphelia serves to grace my measure,
  But Chloe is my real flame.

My softest verse, my darling lyre
  Upon Euphelia's toilet lay,
When Chloe noted her desire
  That I should sing, that I should play.

My lyre I tune, my voice I raise,
  But with my numbers mix my sighs;
And whilst I sing Euphelia's praise,
  I fix my soul on Chloe's eyes.

Fair Chloe blushed, Euphelia frowned,
  I sung and gazed, I played and trembled:
And Venus to the Loves around
  Remarked how ill we all dissembled.

Answer to Chloe Jealous

Dear Chloe, how blubbered is that pretty face!
  Thy cheek all on fire, and thy hair all uncurled:
Prithee quit this caprice; and, as old Falstaff says,
  Let us e'en talk a little like folks of this world.

How canst thou presume thou hast leave to destroy
  The beauties which Venus but lent to thy keeping?
Those looks were designed to inspire love and joy:
  More ord'nary eyes may serve people for weeping.

To be vexed at a trifle or two that I writ,
  Your judgment at once, and my passion, you wrong;
You take that for fact, which will scarce be found wit:
  Od's life! must one swear to the truth of a song?

blubbered] tear-stained

What I speak, my fair Chloe, and what I write, shows
   The difference there is betwixt nature and art:
I court others in verse, but I love thee in prose;
   And they have my whimsies, but thou hast my heart.

The god of us verse-men—you know, child, the Sun,
   How after his journeys he sets up his rest:
If at morning o'er earth 'tis his fancy to run,
   At night he reclines on his Thetis's breast.

So when I am wearied with wandering all day,
   To thee, my delight, in the evening I come;
No matter what beauties I saw in my way:
   They were but my visits, but thou art my home.

Then finish, dear Chloe, this pastoral war,
   And let us like Horace and Lydia agree,
For thou art a girl as much brighter than her,
   As he was a poet sublimer than me.

WILLIAM CONGREVE (1670–1729)

Amoret

Fair Amoret is gone astray:
   Pursue and seek her, every lover!
I'll tell the signs by which you may
   The wandering shepherdess discover.

Coquet and coy at once her air,
   Both studied, though both seem neglected;
Careless she is, with artful care,
   Affecting to seem unaffected.

With skill her eyes dart every glance,
   Yet change so soon you'd ne'er suspect them;
For she'd persuade they wound by chance,
   Though certain aim and art direct them.

She likes herself, yet others hates
For that which in herself she prizes;
And while she laughs at them, forgets
She is the thing that she despises.

INDEXES

INDEX I

[of topics in the introductory matter]

A New Courtly Sonnet of the Lady Greensleeves, 272
A Proper Song, 39
Æneid, 52
air, 269
Alexander, Sir William, 'Alexis,' 433
Alexandrine, 44
Allison, Richard, 271
alliteration, 39
Anacreon, 271, 379, 381, 383
Andrewes, Francis, 534
Anglo-Saxon poetry, 38–9
  metrical influence of, 50
Arbor of Amorous Devices, 113–4
Areopagus, 46, 108, 110
Ariosto, 49, 54, 323
Arnold, Matthew, 28, 31–2
Art of English Poesy, 49
Ascham, Roger, 51
Ayres, Philip, 19, 539

Back and side go bare, 219
Bacon, Francis, 55
ballad meter, 38–9
ballads (*See* Broadsides.)
barginet (*See* Bergeret.)
Barnes, Barnabe, 42, 163, 164
Barnfield, Richard, 43, 107, 111–2, 113, 163, 268
Basse, William, 430
Bateson, Thomas, 271
Beaumont and Fletcher, 217, 219, 381
Beaumont, Francis, 381, 383, 480
beauty, as an element of poetry, 4, 7–8
Behn, Aphra, 539
Belvedere, or The Garden of the Muses, 113
Bennett, Joan, 324
bergeret, 42
Best, Charles, 164

Blake, William, 485
blank verse, 45, 46
Blow, John, 271
Bodenham, John, 107, 113
Bold, Henry, 537
Boleyn, Anne, 25, 51
Bolton, Edmund, 19, 111
Bonham, Thomas, 534
Boyle, Elizabeth, 165
branle (*See* Brawl.)
Brathwait, Richard, 434
brawl, 43
Breton, Nicholas, 43, 107, 111, 112, 113–4, 164, 485
Britton's Bower of Delights, 113
broadsides, 273
Brome, Alexander, 537
Brooke, Christopher, 430, 431
Brooke, Rupert, 19
Browne, William, 43, 56, 165, 430–1, 432, 433
Browning, Robert, 17, 18–9
Bryan, Sir Francis, 53
Burns, Robert, 14
Byrd, William, 268, 270
Byron, 3

C., E., 164
C., H., [Henry Cheke?] 54
caesura, 37
Campion, Thomas, 39, 44, 46, 114, 269–70, 273, 274
Canand, J., 53
canzon, 42
canzonet, 42
Carew, Thomas, 28, 46, 267, 379, 381, 383–6, 534, 535–6
Cartwright, William, 379, 382, 383, 484
catharsis, 8

591

Catullus, 218, 271, 381, 383
Cavaliers, 28, 273, 329, 382, 385–6, 485, 486, 533–8
qualities of, 217, 533–6
Chapman, George, 113, 163–4, 167, 218
Chappell, W., 267–8
Charles I, 383, 385, 433, 533, 538
Charles II, 331, 486, 538
Chaucer, 109
Chester, Robert, 113
Churchyard, Thomas, 53
classical meter, 39
influence of, 39, 45, 50
classicism, 381, 383–4, 535, 538
Cleveland, John, 329, 330–1, 379, 382, 537
commonplace books, 53
complaint, 43
composers, 268, 270–2
conceit, 50, 167, 323–5, 330–1, 433, 481, 483
Congreve, William, 540
Conrad, Joseph, 8–9
Constable, Henry, 40, 107, 111, 112, 163, 485
contention, 43
Corbet, Richard, 381, 383
Cotton, Charles, 537
couplet, 46, 380, 533–5
Courtly Makers, 49–56
Cowley, Abraham, 328, 329, 330–1, 538
Crashaw, Richard, 329, 481, 482–3, 484, 485, 486
Crowne, John, 46

Daniel, Samuel, 46, 163, 165, 213, 271, 432
Dante, 49
Davenant, Sir William, 46, 537–8
Davies, Sir John, 114, 164, 167
Davies, John, of Hereford, 167, 430
Davison, Francis, 113, 114, 164, 432
Dekker, Thomas, 112, 214, 216, 218–9
De La Mare, Walter, 10
Desportes, Philippe, 167

Devereux, Lady Penelope, 'Stella,' 25, 162
Devotional Lyrists, 479–86
devotional poetry, 273, 329, 432, 479, 480–1, 486
Dickinson, Emily, 4
ditty, 42
Donne, John, 18, 20, 45–6, 51, 111, 112, 114, 161, 322–7, 328, 331, 380, 384, 431, 433
influence of, 273, 326, 327–31, 379, 382, 383, 384, 429, 480, 481, 482, 484, 533, 536
Dorset, Earl of, 539
Dowden, Edward, 113
Dowland, John, 268, 270
Down in a garden, 534
Dowson, Ernest, 20n.
Drayton, Michael, 31, 42, 49–50, 55, 56, 107, 111, 112, 163, 165, 429, 430, 433
Drummond, William, 56, 327, 380, 432–4
Dryden, John, 46, 216, 217, 327–8, 535, 536, 538–9
Du Bellay, Joachim, 161
Dyer, Sir Edward, 50, 55, 110, 164

eclogue, 42, 108
Edwards, Richard, 53, 54
eighteenth century, qualities of, 535, 538–9, 540
Eliot, T. S., 322, 324
Elizabeth, 54, 55, 109, 110, 214, 268, 321
emotion, as an element of poetry, 4, 7–10
England's Helicon, 42, 107, 111, 113, 114
England's Parnassus, 113
enjambement, 38, 44
epigram, 273
Erskine, John, 14
Essex, Earl of, 111
Este, Michael, 271
Etherege, Sir George, 539

Farnaby, Giles, 271
feminine ending, 38
feminine rime, 37
Ferrar, Nicholas, 482
figures of speech, 16
Fletcher, Giles, the Elder, 163, 164
Fletcher, Giles, the Younger, 429–30, 434
Fletcher, John, 43, 46, 108, 214, 217, 218, 381, 435
Fletcher, Phineas, 429–30, 434
foot, metrical, 37
Ford, John, 216
Ford, Thomas, 271
'fourteener,' 38–9
French poetry, influence of, 39–40, 433, 434
Frost, Robert, 3, 24
Fyleman, Rose, 20

Galsworthy, John, 5
Gascoigne, George, 54, 107, 111, 161
Gifford, Humphrey, 55
Godolphin, Sidney, 379, 382
Goodere, Sir Henry, 56
Gorgeous Gallery of Gallant Inventions, 53
Greek Anthology, 379
Greek literature, influence of, 39, 434
Greene, Robert, 30, 43, 44, 107, 111, 112, 162–3
Greensleeves (See A New Courtly Sonnet of the Lady Greensleeves.)
Greville, Fulke, 109–10, 161–2
Grierson, H. J. C., 325, 330
Griffin, Bartholomew, 113, 164
Grimald, Nicholas, 53

Habington, William, 161, 217, 330, 480, 484, 486
Hamlet, 112
Handful of Pleasant Delights, 53
Hans Beerpot, his Invisible Comedy, 112
Hardy, Thomas, 5, 19, 25
Harvey, Gabriel, 46, 55, 108, 110
Hawes, Stephen, 50

Hebrew literature, influence of, 434
Helton, Roy, 33
Henry VIII, 49, 51
Herbert, George, 329, 330, 481–2, 483, 484, 485, 486
Herbert of Cherbury, Edward, Lord, 330
Herrick, Robert, 11, 30, 46, 112, 218, 271, 274, 331, 379, 381, 383–6, 480, 534, 536, 537
Heywood, John, 51, 53
Heywood, Thomas, 216, 218
Horace, 381, 383, 533
Hoskins, John, 330
Housman, A. E., 4, 12, 31
Howell, Thomas, 55
humanist poetry, 379
Hume, Tobias, 271
hymns, collections of, 480

I saw fair Chloris, 273
idyl, 42
imagery, 16
imagination, as an element of poetry, 4, 13
Italian poetry, influence of, 39–40, 45, 433, 434, 435

James I, 50, 385
jig, 43
Johnson, Samuel, 3–4, 328, 479
Jones, Robert, 271
Jonson, Ben, 28, 39, 43, 44, 45, 46, 113, 167, 213, 216, 218, 219, 271, 323, 326, 330, 379–81, 382, 383, 385, 429, 430, 433, 435, 537, 538
    influence of, 273, 329, 381–6, 480, 484, 536
Jonsonus Virbius, 381, 382

Kalendrier des Bergers, 109
Keats, John, 7, 28
Kendall, Timothy, 53
King, Henry, 330
Kipling, Rudyard, 13
Knight of the Burning Pestle, 112

Lamb, Charles, 331
lament, 43

Lansdowne, Lord, 539
Latin poetry, influence of, 39, 434
Lawes, Henry, 271
Lawes, William, 271
line, metrical, 37
Lodge, Thomas, 44, 107, 108, 111, 112, 113, 163, 164, 167
Lovelace, Richard, 30, 536, 537
Lowell, James Russell, 218
Lowes, John Livingston, 14
Lyly, John, 108, 216, 217, 218, 219
Lynche, Richard, 164
lyric
    Caroline, 384
    decline of, 539–40
    definition of, 5
    Elizabethan, qualities of, 10, 43–5, 321, 539
    in prose, 5–6
    mediums of, 15–23, 31
    meters of, 22–3, 37–46
    mood, 9–10
    qualities of best, 24–7
    reading of, 11–2
    Restoration, qualities of, 273, 538–9
    secondary values in, 27–9
    theme, 10–3
Lyrics in Plays, 213–74
Lyrics in Song-books, 267–74

Mabbe, Thomas, 218
madrigal, 41, 42, 269, 270
Mantuan, 108, 109
Marlowe, Christopher, 21, 45, 107, 111, 112, 113, 219
Marot, Clément, 108, 109
Marston, John, 113, 214, 218, 219
Marvell, Andrew, 331, 480, 486
masculine rime, 37
Masefield, John, 16, 19, 21
Massinger, Philip, 46, 217
Meredith, George, 8
Meres, Francis, 56, 164
Mermaid Tavern group, 381
metaphor, 16
metaphysical conceit, 328–9, 382, 435
metaphysical poetry, 327–9, 330, 331, 480, 533

Metaphysical Poets, 321–31
meter, 37
    Elizabethan variety in, 43–4
    freedom of, 37
    types of, 39
Middleton, Thomas, 216–7, 219
Millay, Edna St. Vincent, 12, 19
Milton, John, 3, 46n., 168, 217, 331, 430, 433–6, 480–1, 486, 538
miscellanies
    Elizabethan, 53–4, 113–4, 164
    Cavalier, 486
Montemayor, Jorge de, 432
Moore, George, 18
More, Anne, 325
Morley, Thomas, 41, 268, 270
Munday, Anthony, 107, 111, 112, 113, 218
music, 45, 267–70, 274
musicians, 268

Nashe, Thomas, 8, 26, 44, 214, 217
neo-Latin poetry, 379
Noyes, Alfred, 12, 19, 22

octosyllabics, 44, 534
Ovid, 323
Oxford, Earl of, 50, 55, 163

Paradise of Dainty Devices, 53
passion, 43
Passionate Pilgrim, 113, 213, 432
pastoral, 42, 107, 273
Pastoral Lyrists, 107–14
Peele, George, 108, 112, 214, 216, 434
Peerson, Martin, 271
Pembroke, Countess of, 111, 165
Percy, William, 163
personal, as applied to lyric, 13
Petrarch, 42, 49, 51, 162
    influence of, 49, 50, 161, 162, 164–5, 167, 273, 321, 323, 324, 325, 433, 434, 481, 533
Phelps, William Lyon, 4
Philips, Katherine, 331, 539
Phoenix Nest, 113, 114
Phyllida Flouts Me, 534

Pilkington, Francis, 271
plagiarism, 167
Plautus, 214
Playford, Henry, 271
Plays, Lyrics in, 213–9
Poe, Edgar Allan, 22
Poetical Rhapsody, 113, 114, 164, 432
poetry
    definitions of, 3–4
    language of, 16–7
    prejudices against, 6–7
    themes of, 12–3
    types of, 4–5
Pope, Alexander, 46, 535, 538, 539
Porter, Walter, 267
'Poulter's measure,' 44, 51
Prior, Matthew, 539
Procter, Thomas, 54
Psalms, paraphrases of, 479
Puritans, 382, 486
Puttenham, George, 49, 50, 52

Quarles, Francis, 485
quatorzain (*See* Sonnet.)

Raleigh, Sir Walter, 8, 21, 43, 50,
    55–6, 111, 112, 113, 163
Ralph Roister Doister, 214
Randolph, Thomas, 381, 383, 484
Ravenscroft, Thomas, 271
refrain, 22, 45
religious poetry (*See* Devotional
    poetry.)
resolution, metrical, 38
rhythm, 37–8
rime, 37
Robinson, Clement, 53, 272
Robinson, Edwin Arlington, 3, 20
Rochester, Earl of, 539
rondeau, 51
Ronsard, Peter, 167
Rosseter, Philip, 271
Rossetti, Dante Gabriel, 168
roundelay, 43
Rudyerd, Sir Benjamin, 382
run-on line (*See Enjambement.*)

S., R., of the Inner Temple, 113
Sacheverell, Lucy, 'Lucasta,' 'Althea,'
    537
St. Leger, Anthony, 53
Sandburg, Carl, 3, 8
Schelling, F. E., 7n.
Sedley, Sir Charles, 539
septenary, 44
sestine, 43
seventeenth century, qualities of, 321–
    2, 485, 536–40
Shakespeare, William, 22–3, 27, 28,
    40, 43, 44, 45, 46, 53, 56, 107,
    111–2, 113, 164, 165, 166, 167,
    213, 214, 217–8, 219, 268, 379,
    434, 538
shaped verses, 482
Shelley, Percy Bysshe, 10, 21
Sherburne, Sir Edward, 537
Shipman, Thomas, 539
Shirley, James, 214, 216, 219
Sidney, Lady Dorothy, 'Sacharissa,'
    534
Sidney, Sir Philip, 23, 25, 39, 44, 45,
    55, 107, 108, 109–10, 113, 161,
    162, 163, 165, 167, 324
    imitation of, 34
    influence of, 110, 112, 161–2, 165,
    431, 433, 480
simile, 16
sincerity, as a test of poetry, 25
Skelton, John, 50
Smith, William, 164
song, the, 42
    function of, in drama, 214–7
song-books, 267, 270, 271–2, 274, 480
Song-books, Lyrics in, 267–74
Songs and Sonnets, 52, 53, 107, 113,
    161
songs in plays, 379
sonnet, 40, 44, 161, 267, 380, 435
Sonneteers, 161–8, 273, 433
sonnet-series, 162, 330
Sons of Ben, 329, 379–86, 533, 536,
    537
Southwell, Robert, 479–80
Spanish literature, influence of, 434

Spenser, Edmund, 8, 39, 40-1, 45, 46, 54, 55, 107, 108-9, 113, 161, 163, 164, 165, 323
influence of, 112, 429-36
Spenserian stanza, 40-1, 430
Spenserians, 112, 161, 217, 273, 327, 429-36, 533, 536
Stanley, Thomas, 537
stanza, 37
style, 27
Suckling, Sir John, 217, 536-7
Surrey, Earl of, 28, 40, 49, 52, 53, 54, 55, 107, 161
Swinburne, Algernon Charles, 10
imitation of, 34
Sylvester, Joshua, 164

Tennyson, Alfred, Lord, 21, 22, 26, 28, 32
terzine, 43
Theocritus, 107, 383
three-men's songs, 214, 216
Tichborne, Chidiock, 55
Tinker, C. B., 10n.
Tofte, Robert, 164
Tom Tyler, 219
Tottel, Richard, 52-3, 54, 113, 161
Tottel's Miscellany (See Songs and Sonnets.)
tragedy, enjoyment of, 8
Traherne, Thomas, 484-5, 486
Tribe of Ben, 379-86 (See also 'Sons of Ben.')
truth, as an element of poetry, 4, 7-8
Turberville, George, 53, 55

Udall, Nicholas, 214

Vaughan, Henry, 329, 484, 485, 486
Vaux, Lord, 44, 53
Vergil, 108
vers de société, 385, 533, 535-6
verse, 37
Victorious time, 480

W., A., 114
Waller, Edmund, 46, 382, 383, 385, 485, 533, 534-6, 538
influence of, 539
Walton, Isaac, 111, 330
Watson, Thomas, 113, 162, 163, 164, 167, 270
Webster, John, 32, 217, 219
Weelkes, Thomas, 21, 271
Westmorland, Earl of, 537
Whetstone, George, 55
Wilbye, John, 268, 271
Wilson, John, 271
Wither, George, 43, 56, 430, 431, 433, 485, 486, 533, 534
word-music, as an element of poetry, 21
Wordsworth, William, 3, 26, 166, 168, 484, 485
Wotton, Sir Henry, 55, 111, 114, 330, 434
Wyatt, Sir Thomas, 25, 28, 49, 51-2, 53, 54, 107, 161, 533

Yeats, William Butler, 14
Yonge, Nicholas, 270
Young, Bartholomew, 111

Zepheria, 163

INDEX II

[of authors (in capitals), first lines (in roman), and titles (in italics)]

	Page
A broken altar, Lord, thy servant rears	495
A Christmas Carol	453
A Complaint by Night of the Lover Not Beloved	70
A Contemplation upon Flowers	354
A Coronet for his Mistress Philosophy	194
A Cruel Mistress	412
A Delectable Dream	87
A Deposition from Love	414
A Description of Love	151
A Description of Such a One as he would Love	65
A Description of the Spring	156
A Ditty	168
A face that should content me wondrous well	65
A Father's Testament	437
A funeral stone	399
A Gentlewoman Forsweareth Hereafter to be Won with Flattering Promises	85
A Hymn to God the Father	492
A kiss I begged, but smiling she	561
A Lecture upon the Shadow	346
A Love-Song	317
A Love Sonnet	448
A Madrigal 'My love in her attire'	293
A Masque Presented at Ludlow Castle	470–5
A Memento for Mortality. Taken from the View of Sepulchers in the Abbey of Westminster	493
A Nymph's Passion	390
A Palinode	154
A Passion	147
A Praise of his Lady	59
A Proper Song	274
A Renouncing of Love	63
A Round	444
A Shepherd's Moan	439
A Song 'Ask me no more'	418
A Song 'Ye happy swains'	580

Page

A Song for Saint Cecilia's Day 573
A Song of Divine Love 508
A Sonnet made on Isabella Markham 74
A Sonnet of the Moon 204
A Strange Passion of a Lover 82
A stranger here 304
A Strappado for the Devil 543–4
A sweet disorder in the dress 398
A Thanksgiving to God for his House 406
A Valediction 422
A Valediction Forbidding Mourning 340
A Vision upon this Conceit of the Faery Queen 184
A woman's face is full of wiles 87
Absence, hear thou my protestation 347
Accurst be Love 192
Adieu, farewell earth's bliss 228
Against Them who Lay Unchastity to the Sex of Women . . 356
Aglaura 261–2
Ah Ben! 397
Ah, fading joy, how quickly art thou past 570
Ah, my Perilla, dost thou grieve to see 398
Ah, Robin 59
Ah, sweet Content, where is thy mild abode 193
Ah, were she pitiful as she is fair 180
Ah, what is love? It is a pretty thing 140
Alas, my heart 143
Alas, so all things now do hold their peace 70
ALDRICH, HENRY 312–3
Alexander and Campaspe 222–3
Alexis, here she stayed among these pines 459
All kings, and all their favorites 337
All my past life is mine no more 583
Amid my bale I bathe in bliss 82
Amoret 587
Amoretti 188–90
An Elegy 'O faithless world' 348
An Elegy on Ben Jonson 422
An Epitaph on the Admirable Dramatic Poet, William Shakespeare 468
An Epitaph upon Husband and Wife, which Died and were Buried Together 511
An Epitaph upon my Grandfather 584
An Evening's Love 571

Page

An evil spirit, your beauty, haunts me still 205
An Hymn 436
An Ode 'As it fell' 146
An Ode 'Now each creature' 187
An Ode 'The merchant' 586
An Ode for Ben Jonson 397
An Ode to Mr. Anthony Stafford to Hasten him into the Country . 419
And now all nature seemed in love 156
And wilt thou leave me thus 67
ANDREWES, FRANCIS 550
ANONYMOUS 56, 57,
  74, 77, 78, 274–8, 291–308, 313–7, 365, 489, 493–4, 540–3, 550, 585
Answer to Chloe Jealous 586
Arcades 469–70
Are they shadows that we see 258
Arraignment of Paris 224–5
Art thou poor, yet hast thou golden slumbers 241
Art thou that she 540
As careful merchants 442
As I in hoary winter's night 488
As in the house I sate 524
As inward love breeds outward talk 466
As it fell upon a day 146
As virtuous men pass mildly away 340
As withereth the primrose by the river 154
As you came from the holy land 149
As You Like It 232–4
Ask me no more where Jove bestows 418
Ask not the cause why sullen spring 576
Astrophel and Stella 168–76
At liberty I sit and see 77
At the round earth's imagined corners, blow 489
Away with these self-loving lads 132
AYRES, PHILIP 584

Back and side go bare, go bare 219
BACON, FRANCIS 95–6
Barefoot and ragged, with neglected hair 584
BARNES, BARNABE 193
BARNFIELD, RICHARD 144–7, 203
BASSE, WILLIAM . . . . 466–7, 493n.
BEAUMONT, FRANCIS 254–5, 392–5
BEAUMONT, THOMAS 366

Page

Beauty sat bathing by a spring 131
Beauty, sweet love, is like the morning dew 186
Because I breathe not love to everyone 172
BEHN, APHRA 581–2
Bermudas 367
BEST, CHARLES 204
Bid me not go where neither suns nor showers 422
Bid me to live, and I will live 403
Black beauty, which above that common light 350
Blame not my lute 68
Bloody Brother 256–7
Blow, blow, thou winter wind 233
Blurt, Master Constable 250–1
BOLD, HENRY 565–6
BOLEYN, GEORGE, VISCOUNT ROCHFORD 61–2
BOLTON, EDMUND 154–5
BONHAM, THOMAS 549
BRATHWAIT, RICHARD 543–4
Brave flowers, that I could gallant it like you 354
BRETON, NICHOLAS 133–7
Bright shines the sun, play, beggars, play 288
Bright star of beauty, on whose eye-lids sit 205
Britannia's Pastorals 439–42
Brittle beauty that nature made so frail 72
Broken Heart 260
BROME, ALEXANDER 568–9
BROOKE, FULKE GREVILLE, LORD 132–3, 177–80
Brown is my love 277
BROWNE, WILLIAM 439–47
By the rushy-fringèd bank 472

C., E. 193–4
Cælia 445
Cælica 178–80
Call for the robin redbreast and the wren 259
Calm was the day, and through the trembling air 120
Camella fair 304
CAMPION, THOMAS 280–8
Can life be a blessing 571
Canzonet, To his Coy Love 207
Care-charmer Sleep, son of the sable Night 186
CAREW, THOMAS 412–8
CARTWRIGHT, WILLIAM 422–4

Page

Celestina 260
Celia Singing 417
CHAPMAN, GEORGE 194
Charm me asleep, and melt me so 310
CHETTLE, HENRY . . . . 144, 240, 241n.
Chide, chide no more away 555
Chloe found Amyntas lying 575
Chloe, why wish you that your years 423
Chloris, forbear awhile 565
Christ's Victory on Earth 438
CLEVELAND, JOHN 364–5, 422
Cold's the wind, and wet's the rain 241
Come, Anthea, let us two 405
Come away, come away, death 234
Come, be my valentine 550
Come, cheerful day 284
Come, honest sexton, take thy spade 316
Come live with me, and be my love 148
Come, my Celia, let us prove 246
Come, my dainty doxies 251
Come sleep! O sleep, the certain knot of peace . . . 171
Come, spur away 419
Come, we shepherds whose blest sight 504
Come, you pretty false-eyed wanton 284
Complaint of a Lover Rebuked 71
Complaint of the Absence of Her Lover Being upon the Sea . 72
Comus . . . . 470n.
CONGREVE, WILLIAM 587–8
CONSTABLE, HENRY . . . . 144n.
Contention of Ajax and Ulysses 263
CORBET, RICHARD 409–11
Corinna is divinely fair 585
Corinna's Going A-maying 399
CORNISH, WILLIAM 59
Corydon's Supplication to Phyllis 135
COTTON, CHARLES 562–5
COWLEY, ABRAHAM 359–64
Crabbed age and youth 152
CRASHAW, RICHARD 504–11
Crownèd with flowers 303
Cupid abroad was 'lated in the night 183
Cupid and my Campaspe played 222
Cupid, in a bed of roses 304

		Page
Cymbeline		237–8
Cynthia, because your horns look divers ways		179
Cynthia, whose glories are at full forever		178
Cynthia's Revels		243–4
Damætas' Jig		155
Damelus' Song to His Diaphenia		144
DANIEL, SAMUEL		185–8, 258–9
DAVENANT, SIR WILLIAM		566–8
David and Bethsabe		226
DAVIES, JOHN, OF HEREFORD		208–9
DAVIES, SIR JOHN		208
DAVISON, FRANCIS		278–9
Dear Chloe, how blubbered is that pretty face		586
Dear, do not your fair beauty wrong		259
Dear, if you change		277
Dear love, for nothing less than thee		338
Dear quirister, who from those shadows sends		457
Dear, when I did from you remove		349
Death, be not proud, though some have called thee		490
Death of Robert, Earl of Huntingdon		240
DEKKER, THOMAS		241–3
Delia		185–8
Delight in Disorder		398
Description of Spring, Wherein Each Thing Renews Save Only the Lover		70
Description of the Contrarious Passions in a Lover		63
DE VERE, EDWARD, EARL OF OXFORD		88, 183–4
DEVEREUX, ROBERT, EARL OF ESSEX		147
Diaphenia, like the daffadowndilly		144
Diella		195
Do but consider this small dust		391
Do not fear to put thy feet		255
DONNE, JOHN		332–47, 489–92
Dorinda's sparkling wit and eyes		583
Doron's Description of Samela		138
Doron's Jig		139
DORSET, CHARLES SACKVILLE, EARL OF		582–3
Dost see how unregarded now		551
Doubt you to whom my muse these notes intendeth		172
Down in a garden		550
Down in a valley, by a forest's side		446
Downe-a-downe, downe-a-downe		129

Page

DRAYTON, MICHAEL 96–102, 152–4, 205–7
Drink to me only with thine eyes 290
Drink today, and drown all sorrow 256
Drinking 363
Drop, drop, slow tears 436
DRUMMOND, WILLIAM 457–65
DRYDEN, JOHN 570–7
Dutch Courtesan 252–3
DYER, SIR EDWARD 89–90, 143–4, 204

Easter Wings 496
Elegy 88
Elegy on Shakespeare 466
ELIZABETH 79
Emaricdulfe 193–4
Emperor of the East 261
Employment 497
England, be glad 56
Epitaph on Elizabeth, L. H. 388
Epitaph on Salathiel Pavy, a Child of Queen Elizabeth's Chapel 387
ESSEX, ROBERT DEVEREUX, EARL OF 147
ETHEREGE, SIR GEORGE 580–1
Even like two little bank-dividing brooks 514
Even such is time, which takes in trust 95
Expectation 555

Fain would I change that note 295
Fain would I have a pretty thing 274
Fain would I wed 288
Faint amorist, what! dost thou think 176
Fair Amoret is gone astray 587
Fair and fair, and twice so fair 224
Fair copy of my Celia's face 416
Fair daffodils, we weep to see 403
Fair is my love for April in her face 181
Fair is my love, when her fair golden hairs 190
Fair is the rose 303
Fair Julia sitting by the fire 309
Fair Maid of the Exchange 253–4
Fair stood the wind for France 98
Fair! that you may truly know 544
Fair Virtue 449–53
Fairest, when by the rules of palmistry 445

Page

Faithful Shepherdess 255–6
False world, thou ly'st 512
FANE, MILDMAY, EARL OF WESTMORLAND 561
Farewell, adieu, that courtly life 221
Farewell, love, and all thy laws forever 63
Farewell, rewards and fairies 410
Farewell, thou child of my right hand, and joy 386
Farewell, ungrateful traitor 572
Faustina hath the fairer face 278
Fear no more the heat o' the sun 237
Fedele's Song 131
Ferdinando Ieronimi's Sonnet 85
Fidessa 194–5
Fine knacks for ladies 291
Fine young folly, though you were 262
First Song 'Doubt you' 172
FLETCHER, GILES 438–9
FLETCHER, JOHN 239, 255–8
FLETCHER, PHINEAS 436–8
Follow a shadow, it still flies you 390
Follow your saint 282
Fond soul 437
Foolish I, why should I grieve 543
For her gait if she be walking 445
For pity, pretty eyes, surcease 192
For Soldiers 86
For the first twenty years,—since yesterday 346
For the Magdalene 464
For those my unbaptizèd rhymes 406
FORD, JOHN 242, 260
FORD, THOMAS . . . . 297n.
Forget not yet 68
Frailty 498
Fresh spring, the herald of love's mighty king 189
From harmony, from heavenly harmony 573
Full fathom five thy father lies 239
Full many a glorious morning have I seen 198

Gammer Gurton's Needle 219–20
GASCOIGNE, GEORGE 82–5
Gather ye rosebuds, while ye may 401
Get thee a ship well rigged and tight 561
Get up, get up for shame, the blooming morn 399

Page

GIFFORD, HUMPHREY 86–8
Give me more love or more disdain 413
Give me my scallop-shell of quiet 93
Give me my work, that I may sit and sew 85
Give place, you ladies, and be gone 59
Glide soft, ye silver floods 439
Glories, pleasures, pomps, delights, and ease 260
Go and catch a falling star 332
Go, go, quaint follies, sugared sin 518
Go, happy book, and let my Candia see 366
Go, lovely rose 548
Go, soul, the body's guest 90
God Lyæus, ever young 258
GODOLPHIN, SIDNEY 425
Good folk, for gold or hire 206
Gorbo, as thou cam'st this way 152
Grace for a Child 409
GRANVILLE, GEORGE, LORD LANSDOWNE 585
Gratiana Dancing and Singing 558
Green groweth the holly 58
GREENE, ROBERT 137–43, 180–3
GREVILLE, FULKE, LORD BROOKE 132–3, 177–80
GRIFFIN, BARTHOLOMEW 194–5
Gulling Sonnets 208

HABINGTON, WILLIAM 262–3, 355–9
Had we but world enough and time 368
Hail, blessèd Virgin, full of heavenly grace 512
Hamlet . . . . 75n.
Happy were he could finish forth his fate 147
HARINGTON, JOHN, THE ELDER 74–5
Hark, hark! the lark at heaven's gate sings 237
Hark! she is called, the parting hour is come 509
HARRINGTON, HENRY 312
HAUGHTON, WILLIAM . . . . 241n.
Having been tenant long to a rich Lord 495
Having this day my horse, my hand, my lance 171
Haymakers, rakers, reapers, and mowers 242
He is stark mad, whoever says 339
Hears not my Phyllis 579
Hecatompathia 176–8
Hence, all you vain delights 256
Hence away, you sirens, leave me 449

Page

HENRY THE EIGHTH 57–8
Her eyes the glow-worm lend thee 404
Her hair the net 305
HERBERT, GEORGE 494–503
HERBERT OF CHERBURY, EDWARD, LORD 349–51
Here a little child I stand 409
Here lies an agèd corpse, which late 584
Here she lies, in bed of spice 406
Here she was wont to go, and here, and here 249
HERRICK, ROBERT 310–1, 396–409
Hey nonny no 307
HEYWOOD, JOHN 59–61
HEYWOOD, THOMAS 252
His Ballad of Agincourt 98
His Creed 408
His golden locks time hath to silver turned 225
His Prayer for Absolution 406
His Prayer to Ben Jonson 396
Hobbinol's Lay of Fair Elisa, Queen of Shepherds 114
Hold back thy hours, dark Night, till we have done 255
Holy Sonnets 489–91
Honest lover whosoever 553
Horestes 221–2
HOSKINS, JOHN 347–8
Hot sun, cool fire, tempered with sweet air 226
How happy is he born or taught 102
How happy the lover 575
How many new years have grown old 302
How near me came the hand of death 456
How soon hath Time, the subtle thief of youth 469
How vainly men themselves amaze 373
HOWARD, HENRY, EARL OF SURREY 70–4
HOWELL, THOMAS 81–2
*Hymn for a Widower or a Widow Deprived of a Loving Yoke-
    fellow* 456
Hymn to God, my God, in my Sickness 491

I am two fools, I know 334
I can love both fair and brown 333
I did not live until this time 375
I do believe that die I must 408
I fear not henceforth death 460
I find no peace, and all my war is done 63

Page

I have been in love and in debt and in drink 569
I have not spent the April of my time 194
I heard a noise 305
I live, and yet methinks I do not breathe 299
I loathe that I did love 75
I long to talk with some old lover's ghost 341
I love and he loves me again 390
I loved a lass, a fair one 448
I made a posy, while the day ran by 501
I pray thee leave, love me no more 207
I prithee let my heart alone 556
I prithee send me back my heart 555
I saw eternity the other night 519
I saw fair Chloris walk alone 309
I saw my lady weep 291
I serve a mistress whiter than the snow 131
I sing of brooks, of blossoms, birds, and bowers 397
I sing the praise of honored wars 295
I struck the board and cried, No more 501
I sundry see, for beauty's gloss 80
I wandered out a while agone 452
I was foretold, your rebel sex 414
I, with whose colors Myra dressed her head 178
I wot full well that beauty cannot last 81
Idea 205–7
Idle Verse 518
If all be true that I do think 312
If all the world and love were young 148
If as a flower doth spread and die 497
If ever I marry 78
If fathers knew 292
If I could shut the gate against my thoughts 296
If I freely may discover 244
If Jove himself be subject unto love 176
If music and sweet poetry agree 203
If the quick spirits in your eye 414
If there were, O! an Hellespont of cream 208
If to be absent were to be 557
If women could be fair 183
If yet I have not all thy love 335
If you do love as well as I 350
In crystal towers 291
In love his kingdom great two fools there be 196

Page

In Obitum M. S., X Maii, 1614 439
In petticoat of green 464
In Praise of a Beggar's Life 288
In Praise of Ale 549
In Praise of Fidelia 561
In Praise of Music and Poetry 203
In the Holy Nativity. A Hymn Sung as by the Shepherds . . . 504
In the merry month of May 134
In time of yore when shepherds dwelt 133
In truth, O Love, with what a boyish kind 170
Ingrateful Beauty Threatened 415
Insatiableness 528
Inviting a Friend to Supper 386
It fell upon a holy eve 118
It is not, Celia, in our power 581
It was a lover and his lass 233

Jolly shepherd, shepherd on a hill 155
JONSON, BEN 243–50, 290, 386–92
Jordan 496

King Arthur 575
KING, HENRY 352–4
Kiss me, sweet; the wary lover 389
Knight of the Burning Pestle 254
Know, Celia, since thou art so proud 415

Lady, when I behold 278
LANSDOWNE, GEORGE GRANVILLE, LORD 585
Laura 195–6
Laura Sleeping 564
Lawn as white as driven snow 238
Lay a garland on my hearse 255
Leave me, O love 175
Les Amours 563
Let me not to the marriage of true minds 201
Let others sing of knights and paladins 186
Life 501
Like as the waves make towards the pebbled shore 198
Like the Idalian queen 457
Like to Diana in her summer weed 138
Like to the clear in highest sphere 128
Like to the falling of a star 353

Page

Little think'st thou, poor flower 343
Locrine 226–7
LODGE, THOMAS 126–30, 190–2
Look, Delia, how we esteem the half-blown rose 185
Look how the pale queen of the silent night 204
Lord, how can man preach thy eternal word 498
Lord, in my silence how do I despise 498
Lord, thou hast given me a cell 406
Lord, when the sense of thy sweet grace 508
Lord, who createdst man in wealth and store 496
Lost is my quiet 317
Love 503
Love and Life 583
Love Armed 581
Love bade me welcome, yet my soul drew back 503
Love for such a cherry lip 250
Love guards the roses of thy lips 190
Love, if a god thou art 278
Love in fantastic triumph sate 581
Love in my bosom like a bee 127
Love in thy youth 314
Love is the blossom where there blows 438
Love me or not 287
Love not me for comely grace 299
Love still has something of the sea 578
Love that liveth and reigneth in my thought 71
Love Vagabonding 465
LOVELACE, RICHARD 557–60
Lovers' Infiniteness 335
Love's Deity 341
Love's Labour's Lost 230–2
Loving in truth and fain in verse my love to show 168
LYLY, JOHN 222–4
LYNCHE, RICHARD 195

MABBE, JAMES 260
Macbeth 235–7
Madrigal 'Dear, when I did' 349
Madrigal 'Faustina hath' 278
Madrigal 'I fear not' 460
Madrigal 'Like the Idalian queen' 457
Madrigal 'My thoughts' 463
Madrigal 'Sweet rose' 459

                                                        Page
Madrigal 'The beauty' 463
Madrigal 'The ivory' 461
Madrigal 'This life' 461
Madrigal I: To Cupid 278
Maesia's Song 141
Maids to bed and cover coal 303
Maid's Tragedy 255
Mark Antony 364
MARLOWE, CHRISTOPHER 148
MARSTON, JOHN 252–4
MARVELL, ANDREW 366–75
Masque of the Inner Temple 254–5
MASSINGER, PHILIP 261
Master Francis Beaumont's Letter to Ben Jonson 392
May, be thou never graced with birds that sing 439
MAY, THOMAS 259
Measure for Measure 235
Mediocrity in Love Rejected 413
Menaphon's Song 182
Merchant of Venice 232
Methought I saw the grave where Laura lay 184
Midas 223–4
MIDDLETON, THOMAS 250–1
MILTON, JOHN 468–75
More Dissemblers Besides Women 251
Mortality, behold and fear 493
MUNDAY, ANTHONY 131–2, 240
Muses that sing love's sensual empery 194
My flocks feed not, my ewes breed not 144
My friend, the things that do attain 73
My galley chargèd with forgetfulness 64
My God, where is that ancient heat towards thee 494
My heart is like a ship on Neptune's back 193
My love bound me 280
My love in her attire doth show her wit 293
My love is of a birth as rare 370
My Love is Past 177
My lute, awake, perform the last 66
My lute, be as thou wast when thou didst grow 462
My mind to me a kingdom is 89
My mind was once the true survey 372
My mistress' eyes are nothing like the sun 202
My once dear love, hapless that I no more 352

Page

My Phyllis hath the morning sun 191
My prime of youth is but a frost of cares 88
My shag-hair Cyclops, come, let's ply 223
My soul, there is a country 518
My sweetest Lesbia 281
My thoughts hold mortal strife 463
My true love hath my heart and I have his 168

NASHE, THOMAS 227–9
Never love unless you can 286
Never more will I protest 395
News from Plymouth 567–8
Nice Valour 256
Night Piece, To Julia 404
No longer mourn for me when I am dead 199
No more, my dear, no more these counsels try 173
No Platonic Love 424
Not at first sight, nor yet with a dribbed shot 169
Not, Celia, that I juster am 578
Now each creature joys the other 187
Now that the spring hath filled our veins 444
Now that the winter's gone, the earth hath lost 412
Now the bright morning star, day's harbinger 468
Now the lusty spring is seen 257
Now thou hast loved me one whole day 332
Now what is love? I pray thee tell 151
Now winter nights enlarge 285
Nox Nocti Indicat Scientiam 357
Nymphs and shepherds, dance no more 470

O death, rock me asleep 61
O faithless world, and thy most faithless part 348
O happy dames, that may embrace 72
O heart, the equal poise of love's both parts 507
O love, how strangely sweet 252
O, mistress mine, where are you roaming 234
O nightingale, that on yon bloomy spray . . . . . 468n.
O, the fickle state of lovers 310
O thou that sleep'st like pig in straw 567
O, what a plague is love 540
O words, which fall like summer dew on me 125
Ode 'Absence, hear thou' 347
Ode 'The day is set' 562

Page

O'er the smooth enameled green 469
Of Black Beauty 350
Of his Cynthia 132
Of his Love Called Anna 64
Of Myself 359
Of Pan we sing, the best of singers, Pan 247
Of the Last Verses in the Book 529
Of this fair volume which we World do name 464
Old Couple 259
Old Wives' Tale 225–6
Olden Love-Making 133
On a day—alack the day 230
On a Fair Beggar 584
On a Girdle 546
On a Lady Who Fancied Herself a Beauty 583
On a Lover's Dust, Made Sand for an Hour-glass 391
On a Spark of Fire Fixing on a Gentlewoman's Breast . . . 309
On a time 307
On Chloris Walking in the Snow 309
On his being Arrived to the Age of Twenty-three 469
On his Blindness 475
On his Mistress, Elizabeth of Bohemia 349
On my First Son 386
On the Assumption of the Virgin Mary 509
On the Countess of Pembroke 446
On the Infancy of our Savior 512
On the Life of Man 95
Once did my thoughts 300
Once I thought 298
One day I wrote her name upon the strand 189
Open the door 307
Or love me less or love me more 425
Or scorn or pity on me take 392
Others as Fair, but not so Faithful 80
Our Blessed Lady's Lullaby 308
Our passions are most like to floods and streams . . . 92
Out upon it 554
OXFORD, EDWARD DE VERE, EARL OF 88, 183–4

Pack, clouds, away! and welcome, day 252
Pan's Anniversary 247–8
Parthenophil and Parthenophe 193

Page

Particular Entertainment of the Queen and Prince at Althrope
  1603 245–6
Passion XXXVII 'If Jove' 176
Passion C. My Love Is Past 177
Pastime with good company 57
Pasoral III 'Who can live' 136
Patient Grissill 241–2
Peace 518
PEELE, GEORGE 224–7
PEERSON, MARTIN . . . . 308n.
Perigot and Willie's Roundelay 118
Persuasions to Joy 414
PHILIPOTT, THOMAS 309–10
PHILIPS, KATHERINE 312, 375–6
Philomela's Ode that she Sung in her Arbor 142
Phœbe's Sonnet 129
Phœbus, arise 458
Phyllida and Corydon 134
Phyllida Flouts Me 540
Phyllis 190–2
Phyllis 'In petticoat of green' 464
Phyllis, for shame! let us improve 582
Phyllis Inamorata 550
Phyllis is my only joy 580
Phyllis, why should we delay 546
PICKERING, JOHN 221–2
Poetaster 244–5
Polyhymnia 225
Poverty 524
PRIOR, MATTHEW 586–7
Private Music . . . . 308n.
Prothalamion 120

QUARLES, FRANCIS 310, 512–5
Queen and Huntress, chaste and fair 244
Queen of Arragon 262–3

RALEIGH, SIR WALTER 90–5, 148–51, 184
RANDOLPH, THOMAS 419–21
Rape of Lucrece 252
Read in these roses the sad story 417
Red and White Roses 417
Redemption 495

Page

Renownèd Spenser, lie a thought more nigh 466
Resolved to dust entombed here lieth Love 177
Restore thy tresses to the golden ore 185
REYNOLDS, HENRY 311–2
Ring out your bells 174
Risposta 300
Robin is a lovely lad 306
ROCHESTER, JOHN WILMOT, EARL OF 583
ROCHFORD, GEORGE BOLEYN, VISCOUNT . . . 61–2
Rondeau 62
Rondelay 575
Rosalind's Description 128
Rosalind's Madrigal 127
Roses, their sharp spines being gone 239
ROWLANDS, RICHARD 308–9
RUDYERD, SIR BENJAMIN 395–6
Rural Poesy 125

Sabina has a thousand charms 317
Sabrina fair 471
SACKVILLE, CHARLES, EARL OF DORSET 582–3
Sad Shepherd 249–50
Sapho and Phao 223
Scorn Not the Least 487
SEDLEY, SIR CHARLES 578–80
See the chariot at hand here of love 248
See with what constant motìon 558
Sephestia's Song to Her Child 137
Set me whereas the sun doth parch the green 71
Shake off your heavy trance 254
SHAKESPEARE, WILLIAM 152, 196–202, 229–40
Shall I compare thee to a summer's day 197
Shall I tell you whom I love 441
Shall I, wasting in despair 447
She that I pursue, still flies me 563
Shepherd, who can pass such wrong 130
SHERBURNE, SIR EDWARD 561–2
SHIPMAN, THOMAS 584
SHIRLEY, JAMES 263
Shoemakers' Holiday 241
Sic Vita 353
Sicelides 436
SIDNEY, SIR PHILIP 125–6, 168–76

Page

Silent Woman 247
Since I am coming to that holy room 491
Since there's no help, come, let us kiss and part 206
Sing lullaby, as women do 83
Sing to Apollo, god of day 223
Sing we and chant it 276
Sister, awake 294
Sitting by a river's side 142
Slow, slow, fresh fount, keep time with my salt tears . . . 243
So now is come our joyful'st feast 453
So oft as I her beauty do behold 188
So, so, break off this last lamenting kiss 345
Some act of Love's bound to rehearse 389
Some say Love 182
Son of Erebus and Night 443
Song 'Go and catch' 332
Song 'Honest lover' 553
Song 'I prithee let' 556
Song 'I prithee send' 555
Song 'Not, Celia' 578
Song 'Or love me less' 425
Song 'Phœbus, arise' 458
Song 'Phyllis, for shame' 582
Song 'Stay, Phœbus' 547
Song 'Still to be neat' 247
Song 'Sweetest love' 336
Song 'The happiest mortals' 585
Song 'The lark now leaves' 566
Song ' 'Tis true our life' 312
Song: To Celia 389
Song on May Morning 468
Song. That Women are but Men's Shadows 390
Sonnet 'Alexis, here she stayed' 459
Sonnet 'Dear quirister' 457
Sonnet 'Dost see' 551
Sonnet 'For her gait' 445
Sonnet 'My lute' 462
Sonnet 'Tell me no more' 352
Sonnet 'Thy head with flames' 460
Sonnet 'Were I as base' 203
Sonnet 'What doth it serve' 462
Sonnet II 'Hence away' 449
Sonnet V 'I wandered out' 452

Page

Sonnets 196–202
SOUTHWELL, ROBERT 486–9
Spanish Friar 572–3
SPENSER, EDMUND 114–25, 188–90
Spring, the sweet spring, is the year's pleasant king 227
Stand still, and I will read to thee 346
STANLEY, THOMAS 555–7
Stay, Phœbus, stay 547
Steer hither, steer your wingèd pines 443
Stella, think not that I by verse seek fame 174
STEVENSON, WILLIAM 219–20
Still to be neat, still to be dressed 247
Stranger, whoe'er thou art, that stoop'st to taste 562
STRODE, WILLIAM 309
SUCKLING, SIR JOHN 261–2, 551–5
Summer's Last Will and Testament 227–9
Sun's Darling 242–3
SURREY, HENRY HOWARD, EARL OF 70–4
Sweet are the thoughts that savor of content 141
Sweet day, so cool, so calm, so bright 499
Sweet Echo, sweetest nymph, that liv'st unseen 470
Sweet, if you like 279
Sweet, let me go 300
Sweet love, mine only treasure 289
Sweet nymphs, if, as ye stray 465
Sweet Phyllis, if a silly swain 135
Sweet rose, whence is this hue 459
Sweet Suffolk owl 306
Sweetest love, I do not go 336
SYLVESTER, JOSHUA 203

Take, O, take those lips away 235
Tell me, dearest, what is love 254
Tell me no more how fair she is 352
Tell me no more of minds embracing minds 424
Tell me not of a face that's fair 568
Tell me not, sweet, I am unkind 558
Tell me, where is fancy bred 232
Tempest 239
Tethys' Festival 258–9
That time of year thou may'st in me behold 200
That which her slender waist confined 546
The Aged Lover Renounceth Love 75

Page

The Altar 495
The Angler's Song 466
The Anniversary 337
The Apparition 339
The Argument of his Book 397
The Author, loving these homely meats 208
The Author's Epitaph, made by Himself 95
The beauty and the life 463
The Bellman's Song 303
The Blossom 343
The Book of the World 464
The Broken Heart 339
The Burning Babe 488
The Character of a Happy Life 102
The Collar 501
The Computation 346
The Coronet 366
The Crier 206
The Dance 306
The day is set did earth adorn 562
The Definition of Love 370
The Devil is an Ass 248–9
The Dream 'Dear love' 338
The Dream 'Or scorn or pity' 392
The earth, late choked with showers 126
The earth, with thunder torn, with fire blasted 180
The expense of spirit in a waste of shame 202
The Expiration 345
The Fair Singer 370
The Fairies' Farewell 410
The Flaming Heart 507
The Fountain 562
The Frailty and Hurtfulness of Beauty 72
The Funeral 342
The Garden 373
The glories of our blood and state 263
The happiest mortals once were we 585
The hardness of her heart and truth of mine 208
The Indian Emperor 570
The Indifferent 'I can love' 333
The Indifferent 'Never more' 395
The Inner Temple Masque 443–4
The ivory, coral, gold 461

Page

The lark now leaves his wat'ry nest 566
The Lie 90
The loppèd tree in time may grow again 486
The Lover Compareth his State to a Ship in Perilous Storm Tossed
   on the Sea 64
The Lover Complaineth the Unkindness of his Love 66
The Lover in Liberty Smileth at Them in Thraldom, that Some-
   time Scorned his Bondage 77
The Lover Showeth how he is Forsaken of Such as he Sometime
   Enjoyed 65
The Lover to the Thames 80
The lowest trees have tops . . . . ˙204
The Lullaby of a Lover 83
The Mad Lover 569
The merchant, to secure his treasure 586
The merry World did on a day 500
The Mower to the Glow-Worms 371
The Mower's Song 372
The Nymph Selvagia her Song 130
The Nymph's Reply 148
The Passing-Bell 316
The Passionate Man's Pilgrimage 93
The Passionate Shepherd 136
The Passionate Shepherd to His Love 148
The Philosopher and the Lover. To a Mistress Dying . . . 567
The proverb reporteth, no man can deny 220
The Pulley 502
The Quip 500
The Red Rose 81
The Relic 344
The Resolution 447
The Resolve 568
The Roundelay 152
The Salutation 525
The Scrutiny 559
The sea hath many thousand sands 301
The Search 515
The Second Song 'O'er the smooth' 469
The Secular Masque 577
The Shepherd's Garland 152
The Shepherd's Wife's Song 140
The Siege 552
The silver swan 303

Page

The Soldier's Song 295
The soote season that bud and bloom forth brings 70
The Spring 'Now that the winter's gone' 412
The Spring 'Though you be absent' 360
The stately dames of Rome their pearls did wear 85
The sun, which doth the greatest comfort bring 392
The Surrender 352
The Sweetmeat 561
The Thief 362
The Things that Cause a Quiet Life 73
The Third Song 'Nymphs and shepherds' 470
The thirsty earth soaks up the rain 363
The Thought 350
The Triple Fool 334
The Triumph of Charis 248–9
The Unknown Shepherd's Complaint 144
The Wake 405
The Waterfall 521
The Windows 498
The Wish 361
The Wooer's Song 543
The World 519
The World a Game 465
The world's a bubble, and the life of man 95
There is a garden in her face 287
There is a jewel which no Indian mines 300
There is a lady 297
These eyes, dear Lord, once brandons of desire 464
These little limbs 525
They are all gone 522
They flee from me, that sometime did me seek 65
They meet but with unwholesome springs 356
Think'st thou, Kate 297
This busy, vast, enquiring soul 528
This is Mab, the mistress-fairy 245
This life, which seems so fair 461
This only grant me, that my means may lie 359
This world a hunting is 465
Thou art not fair 283
Thou gav'st me late to eat 561
Thou robb'st my days of business and delights 362
Thou sleepest fast 74
Thou stately stream that with the swelling tide 80

Page

Though I am young and cannot tell 249
Though my carriage be but careless 298
Though you be absent here, I needs must say 360
Thrice blessèd be the giver 278
Thrice happy he 463
Thrice the brinded cat hath mewed 235
Thrice toss these oaken ashes 286
Through the shrubs as I can crack 139
Thy head with flames, thy mantle bright with flowers . . . 460
TICHBORNE, CHIDIOCK 88–9
TILNEY, CHARLES . . . . 226n.
Times Go by Turns 486
'Tis not your beauty can engage 547
'Tis now clear day: I see a rose 515
'Tis now since I sat down before 552
'Tis true our life is but a long disease 312
To a Fair Young Lady Going out of Town in the Spring . . . 576
To a Lady Asking Him How Long He Would Love Her . . . 581
To a Lady Resembling his Mistress 416
To Althea from Prison 560
To Amoret 544
To Anthea, Who May Command Him Anything 403
To Celia 290
To Chloe, Who Wished herself Young Enough for Me . . . 423
To Colin Clout 131
To Daffodils 403
To Flavia 547
To his Coy Mistress 368
To his Friend 81
To his Mistress. Sending her the Arcadia 366
To his Mother. As a New Year's Gift from Cambridge . . . 494
To his Son, Vincent Corbet. On his Third Birthday . . . 409
To Laurels 399
To Lucasta. Going beyond the Seas 557
To Lucasta. Going to the Wars 558
To make a final conquest of all me 370
To me, fair friend, you never can be old 200
To Music, to Becalm his Fever 310
To my Excellent Lucasia, on our Friendship 375
To my Inconstant Mistress 413
To Perilla 398
To Phyllis 546
To Primroses Filled with Morning Dew 402

Page

To Roses in the Bosom of Castara 355
To the Nightingale 468
To the ocean now I fly 473
To the Queen 92
To the Virginian Voyage 96
To the Virgins, To Make Much of Time 401
To the World. The Perfection of Love 355
To these whom death again did wed 511
To walk abroad is, not with eyes 527
TOFTE, ROBERT 195–6
Tom Tyler and his Wife 220–1
Tonight, grave sir, both my poor house and I 386
TRAHERNE, THOMAS 524–9
Troilus and Cressida 571–2
Trust the form of airy things 312
TURBERVILLE, GEORGE 80–1
Twelfth Night 234–5
Two Gentlemen of Verona 229–30
Two Noble Kinsmen 239–40
Tyrannic Love 570–1

Under the greenwood tree 232
Underneath this sable hearse 446
Upon a Maid 406
Upon his Picture 419
Upon Julia's Clothes 405
Upon my lap my sovereign sits 308
*Upon the Book and Picture of the Seraphical Saint Teresa, as She
is usually expressed with a Seraphim Beside Her* . . . 507

Valentinian 257–8
VAUGHAN, HENRY 515–24
VAUX, THOMAS, LORD 75–7
VERSTEGAN, RICHARD . . . . 308n.
Victorious Time 489
Virgin, daughter of Locrine 473
Virtue 499
Visions 446
Volpone 246
Vow to Love Faithfully, Howsoever He Be Rewarded . . . 71

W., A. 288–90
Walking 527

Page

WALLER, EDMUND 529–30, 544–8
Was it a form 311
WATSON, THOMAS 176–8
We be three poor mariners 299
We cobblers lead a merry life 226
We must not part as others do 365
We read of kings and gods that kindly took 412
WEBSTER, JOHN 259
Weep not, my wanton, smile upon my knee 137
Weep, weep, ye woodmen, wail 240
Weep with me, all you that read 387
Weep you no more, sad fountains 294
Weeping and Kissing 561
Well then; I now do plainly see 361
Were I a king 88
Were I as base as is the lowly plain 203
Western wind 57
WESTMORLAND, MILDMAY FANE, EARL OF . . . 561
What doth it serve to see sun's burning face 462
What guile is this, that those her golden tresses 188
What I shall leave thee none can tell 409
What if a day 280
What if this present were the world's last night 491
What needs my Shakespeare for his honored bones 468
What? No, perdie! Ye may be sure 62
What sugared terms, what all-persuading art 195
What Wight He Loved 441
What word is that, that changeth not 64
When age hath made me what I am not now 419
When by thy scorn, O murderess, I am dead 339
When, Celia, I intend 315
When daisies pied and violets blue 231
When for the thorns with which I long, too long 366
When God at first made man 502
When I a verse shall make 396
When I behold 313
When I consider how my light is spent 475
When I do count the clock that tells the time 196
When I have seen by time's fell hand defaced 199
When I survey the bright 357
When I was fair and young 79
When icicles hang by the wall 231
When in disgrace with fortune and men's eyes 197

Page

When in the chronicle of wasted time 201
When Love with unconfinèd wings 560
When my grave is broke up again 344
When nature made her chief work, Stella's eyes 169
When on mine eyes 313
When she was born she came with smiling eye 195
When that the chill sirocco blows 549
When thou must home 283
When thou, poor excommunicate 413
When to her lute 282
When to the sessions of sweet silent thought 198
When we for age could neither read nor write 529
Whenas in silks my Julia goes 405
Whenas man's life, the light of human lust 180
Whenas the mildest month 81
Whenas the nightingale chanted her vespers 364
Whenas the rye reach to the chin 226
Whence comes my love? O heart, disclose 74
Where the remote Bermudas ride 367
Where wards are weak and foes encount'ring strong . . . 487
Whether men do laugh or weep 293
WHETSTONE, GEORGE 85–6
While that the sun 275
White Devil 259
WHITNEY, GEFFREY 291
Who can live in heart so glad 136
Who first reformed our stage with justest laws 422
Who is Sylvia? what is she 229
Who says that fictions only and false hair 496
Who sows the seas, or ploughs the easy shore 436
Whoever comes to shroud me, do not harm 342
Whoso list to hunt 63
Why art thou slow, thou rest of trouble, Death 261
Why canst thou not 297
Why do we love 395
Why do ye weep, sweet babes? Can tears 402
Why I Write Not of Love 389
Why should'st thou swear I am forsworn 559
Why so pale and wan, fond lover 261
WILMOT, JOHN, EARL OF ROCHESTER 583
Wilt thou forgive that sin where I begun 492
Winds, whisper gently whilst she sleeps 564
Winter's Tale 238

Page

Wit Restored . . . . 540n.
With horns and with hounds I waken the day 577
With how sad steps, O moon, thou climb'st the skies 170
With what deep murmurs through time's silent stealth 521
WITHER, GEORGE 447–57
Woman's Constancy 332
Wooing Stuff 176
WOTTON, SIR HENRY 102–3, 156–7, 348–9
WOTTON, SIR JOHN 155–6
Wouldst thou hear what man can say 388
WYATT, SIR THOMAS 62–70

Ye blushing virgins happy are 355
Ye buds of Brutus' land, courageous youths, now play your parts . 86
Ye dainty nymphs, that in this blessèd brook 114
Ye Gods, you gave to me a wife 317
Ye happy swains whose hearts are free 580
Ye little birds that sit and sing 253
Ye living lamps, by whose dear light 371
Yet if his majesty our sovereign lord 314
You birds whose warblings prove 260
You brave heroic minds 96
You charmed me not with that fair face 571
You meaner beauties of the night 349
You pleasing dreams of love and sweet delight 570
You that think love can convey 417
You who are earth and cannot rise 355
YOUNG, BARTHOLOMEW 130–1
Your beauty, ripe and calm and fresh 567
Your shining eyes 295